Bench Strength

More Praise for Bench Strength

"In all the years Kerry worked with me, he never researched anything halfway–it was always in-depth, to the point that brought out insights that occasionally you didn't want to know because it contradicted where you wanted to conclude. But his work was always value added to the process."

—Len Farber, retired General Director of the Tax Policy Branch, Department of Finance and formerly with the global law firm Norton Rose Fulbright

"The historical context in Bench Strength with respect to the Supreme Court's decisions–pre-*Charter* and post-*Charter*–is fascinating and illuminating. I learned a lot by reading Kerry's well-researched book and no doubt it will impact my continuing taxation career. This book should be mandatory reading for taxation students and senior practitioners alike."

—Kim G C Moody, FCPA, TEP, Founder of Moodys Tax / Moodys Private Client, Speaker, Author, Coach

"Bench Strength is truly a whodunnit about the history of tax avoidance in Canada and a must-read for anyone bent on studying, litigating, or deciding tax avoidance disputes."

—Michael O'Connor, CPA, CA, former Senior Corporate Tax Executive

"Bench Strength gives a comprehensive history of SCC tax avoidance jurisprudence that tosses the tables of the tax establishment, dares them to ignore their heritage, and invites students to question how this story was largely forgotten."

—Edward Short, CPA, CMA, retired Chief (Director) of the Personal, Business and Property Income Group of the Department of Finance's Tax Legislation Division (Tax Policy Branch)

Bench Strength

JUDGING A CENTURY OF TAX AVOIDANCE IN CANADA

KERRY HARNISH

Sutherland House Experts
TORONTO, 2025

Sutherland House Experts Corporation
260 Heath Street West
Suite 605
Toronto, Ontario
M5P 3L6

First edition, January 2025

Manufactured in Turkey
Cover designed by Jordan Lunn and Simon Cooper
Photography by Colwyn Griffith

Library and Archives Canada Cataloguing in Publication
Title: Bench strength : judging a century of tax avoidance in Canada / Kerry Harnish ; foreword by Professor Brian J. Arnold.
Names: Harnish, Kerry, author. | Arnold, Brian J., writer of foreword
Description: Includes bibliographical references and index.
Identifiers: Canadiana (print) 20240464699 | Canadiana (ebook) 20240466470 | ISBN 9781738396443 (softcover) | ISBN 9781738396450 (EPUB)
Subjects: LCSH: Income tax—Law and legislation—Canada. | LCSH: Tax avoidance—Canada. | LCSH: Tax evasion—Law and legislation—Canada. | LCSH: Taxation—Law and legislation—Canada.
Classification: LCC KE5759 .H37 2024 | DDC 343.7105/2—dc23

ISBN 978-1-7383964-5-0
eBook 978-1-998365-45-6

For Dorothy

Contents

	Foreword	xi
	Preface	xiv
Part I	**Introduction**	**1**
Part II	**The Pre-Charter-Era Judges**	**11**
	Patrick Kerwin: Purportedly "No Grand Vision" in His Opinions	**17**
	Pioneer Laundry (1938)	*20*
	Emily Merritt (1942)	*23*
	Wrights' Canadian Ropes (1946)	*37*
	Fraser D.R. & Co. (1947)	*42*
	Atlantic Sugar Refineries (1947)	*44*
	Ronald McIntosh (1958)	*46*
	William Bannerman (1959)	*48*
	Robert B. Curran (1959)	*50*
	Douglas Abbott: From Cabinet to the Supreme Court	**58**
	British Columbia Electric Railway Co. (1958)	*60*
	Hollinger North Shore Exploration (1963)	*70*
	Joseph Irwin (1964)	*82*

Vina-Rug (Canada) Limited (1968) 84
Furness, Withy & Company (1968) 88
Tara Exploration and Development (1972) 88
J. Harold Wood (1969) 89

Ronald Martland: A Legal Purist **93**
Minerals Limited (1958) 95
Irrigation Industries (1962) 98
Samuel Ciglen (1970) 101
James A. Cameron (1972) 106
The Deltona Corporation (1973) 109
John Christopher Doyle (1977, 1978) 111
Alberta & Southern Gas Company Limited (1978) 119
Frank M. Covert et al. (1980) 128

Wilfred Judson: Terse, Very Terse **137**
Conn Smythe (1969) 138
Ronald Fraser (1964) 148
Oakfield Developments (1971) 149
Consolidated Holding Company Limited (1971) 153
Ernest Stickel (1974) 156
Jack Appleby (1974) 158

John Cartwright: Born to the Law **164**
Dominion Taxicab Association (1954) 164
Highway Sawmills (1966) 166
Foreign Power Securities (1967) 169

Part III The Chief Justice **179**

Brian Dickson: A Judge's Journey **180**
Ethel Annabelle Angle (1974) 181
William Moldowan (1977) 189
Gene A. Nowegijick (1983) 193
Elizabeth Savage (1983) 196
Bronfman Trust (1987) 199
McClurg (1990) 201

Part IV The Charter-Era Judges **205**

Bertha Wilson: Being a Trailblazer Isn't Easy **209**

Stubart Investments (1984) 212
James Richardson & Sons (1984) 229
Imperial General Properties Ltd. (1985); George Golden et al. (1986) 234
Parliament enacts the GAAR (1988) 237
Mattabi Mines Ltd. (1988) 238
McKinlay Transport (1990) 245

Frank Iacobucci: The Key Messenger **252**

Sie-Mac Pipeline Contractors (1993) 256
Slattery (1993) 259
Symes (1993) 260
Antosko (1994) 263
John M. Tennant (1996) 266
Duha Printers (Western) Limited (1998) 270
Melville Neuman (1998) 276
Ludco Enterprises (2001) 278
Brian J. Stewart (2002); Jack Walls (2002) 289

John Major: A Litigator to the Core **298**

Jake Friesen (1995) 299
Will-Kare Paving (2000) 301
John R. Singleton (2001) 305
Warren Jarvis (2002); Dr. Chee Ling (2002) 308
Canada Trustco (2005); Mathew (2005) 319

Marshall Rothstein: An Affinity for Income Tax Cases **336**

Allan McLarty (2008) 337
Earl Lipson (2009) 342
Bastien Estate (2011); Dubé (2011) 347
Copthorne Holdings (2011) 351
John H. Craig (2012) 353

GlaxoSmithKline (2012) *356*
Envision Credit Union (2013) *360*

Beverley McLachlin: The Rule of Law and "Conscious Objectivity" **363**
Hickman Motors (1997) *364*
Shell Canada (1999) *367*

Part V Statistical Results: The Judges and the Supreme Court **372**

Results of Each Selected Judge's Approach to Income Tax **374**

Comparing the Results in Income Tax Disputes (Pre-Charter v. Charter Eras) **381**

Part VI Concluding Reflections **384**

Epilogue *416*
Annex (List of Tax Avoidance Cases) *444*
Acknowledgments *449*
Bibliography *451*
Index *454*

Foreword

THIS BOOK IS A unique contribution to tax literature. Anyone who works in tax—as a tax adviser, tax official or academic—knows that this literature is vast. Books and journals on technical aspects of taxation, government reports, tax and fiscal policy studies, tax planning guides, analyses from a broad range of perspectives (historical, sociological, economic, philosophical, gender—and I've probably missed some new ones) abound.

As a result, creating something new and different in the overstuffed world of tax publications is extremely difficult, but the author has succeeded in making *Bench Strength* new and different. It deals with an aspect of tax that has been largely ignored: the influence of Supreme Court income tax decisions and the judges who wrote them over the entire span of our federal income tax system.

Bench Strength examines the tax decisions of nine of the most influential Supreme Court judges from 1938 to the end of 2019. This approach shows how the attitudes of these Supreme Court judges to income taxation and tax avoidance changed over time. As well as providing brief biographical details about each judge, the author identifies the historical, political and economic factors that may have influenced their decisions. Along the way, he relates several fascinating anecdotes, usually about unsavoury taxpayers.

The Supreme Court judges whose tax decisions are the central focus of the book were selected on the basis of the importance of their decisions in income tax cases. Although some may quibble about who was selected (I would have had trouble choosing), there is little doubt that those who were selected decided many important tax cases that merit discussion. Four of the judges served on the Supreme Court before the adoption of the *Charter of Rights and Freedoms* in 1982 (Justices Patrick Kerwin, Douglas Abbott, Wilfred Judson, and Ronald Martland, with John Cartwright as alternate), and four after that time (Justices Bertha Wilson, Frank Iacobucci, John Major, and Marshall Rothstein, with Beverley McLachlin as alternate). The chief justice of this hypothetical supreme tax court is Brian Dickson, whose tenure bridges the two eras.

The broad time frame covered by the book allows the author to identify several surprising shifts in the tax decisions of the Supreme Court. The major shifts include the following:

- from an original emphasis on commercial substance to strict adherence to legal form;
- from a consideration of the context and purpose of the tax legislation (as well as the words) in tax avoidance cases in an era of literal interpretation, to a plain-meaning interpretive approach in an era of a supposedly textual, contextual and purposive approach to interpretation; and
- from ignoring the *Duke of Westminster* principle (taxpayers are entitled to arrange their affairs to minimize tax) to relying on that principle as foundational.

The author attributes these major shifts to the influence of the *Charter*, which he backs up with a very convincing statistical analysis (Part V) of the tax decisions of the selected judges and the tax decisions of the Supreme Court. This came as a real surprise to me, since I would have thought the *Charter* would make judges more sensitive to tax policy considerations and more judicially active; instead, they have used their judicial activism to carve out a different approach for income tax cases based on literal interpretation, respect for legal form and taxpayers' entitlement to certainty.

Kerry Harnish is a lawyer by training and was for many years a tax policy officer in the Tax Legislation Division of the Tax Policy Branch of the Department of Finance, where his primary responsibility was to develop income tax policy and draft the necessary legislation. Not surprisingly, his views of the tax system and tax avoidance are the product of his experience in trying to curb tax avoidance, and these views are on full display in *Bench Strength.* However, it would be a mistake for potential readers to think that this book is just a diatribe against tax avoidance and the Supreme Court judges who facilitate it. The book is much more. In fact, I think the author has done a good job of confining his personal comments about tax avoidance largely to the final chapter dealing with the future, instead, letting the decisions of the judges speak for themselves.

From my many conversations with Kerry Harnish over the years, I know that he has a deep academic interest in and also a burning passion for tax law and a long-standing commitment to improving the tax system. He has poured his heart and soul into *Bench Strength*, as well as his wisdom and experience. The research for the book, which is evident from the bibliography and the footnotes, is impressive.

Bench Strength is a book for tax people, for people who work in tax and for people who care about tax (beyond just what they have to pay each year). It is full of information about the development of Canadian jurisprudence on tax avoidance and the Supreme Court judges who were primarily responsible, adding interesting stories about the cases and the characters. It is a serious book but an entertaining read and, like all good books, it will make you think.

Brian J. Arnold
Senior Adviser
Canadian Tax Foundation

Preface

THE SUPREME COURT OF Canada decided the *Canada Trustco* dispute on October 19, 2005, which was the Court's first decision under the general anti-avoidance rule (GAAR) enacted by Parliament in 1988. I read a hard copy of the decision in my office on the 17th floor of the Department of Finance's former home on O'Connor Street in Ottawa and was astonished by what I was reading.

After gathering my thoughts, I walked up the hall and spoke to my manager at the Department of Finance, Davine Roach, in her office and then to my colleague Daryl Boychuk in his office. I mentioned how the decision was a continuation of the Supreme Court's income tax precedent since 1994 that is inconsistent with the precedent that I studied in law school in the years 1979–82. I left their offices with two takeaways. Davine emphasized that the *Canada Trustco* decision like many significant income tax decisions should be considered in light of the life experiences of the judges and the culture of the times in which it was decided. Daryl's point was more practical and elusive: if you agree with Davine (I did), prove it.

To even attempt to do so, I had to stop playing hockey three to five times a week, winter and summer. I had to read not only almost four hundred cases (and the related lower-court decisions) but also numerous historical books and bibliographies that captured the essence of the evolving times and the judges themselves. In a sense, this reading took me back to St. Andrews Junior High and Halifax West High School and my favourite non-hockey subject: Canadian, British and American history. My research project ate up significant portions of my spare time, and I never knew for many years how to tell the story that needed to be told. Over time, I ran out of steam, which lasted years, not months.

Sadly, Davine Roach—who headed up the Domestic Corporations, Corporate Reorganizations and Resource Taxation section in the Tax Legislation Division—died in May 2019 six months after she retired. I had worked for Davine for 18 years, and her death came as a shock. I left Finance's intense long-workday culture a few months later, intent on completing some version of my project.

My initial plan was to concentrate on completing two academic papers: one was focused on the Supreme Court's approach to the sham doctrine—when the justices look beyond the legal appearance of a transaction or document, to prevent abuse or injustice; the other paper sought to detail and explain the quantitative results of a database I created in respect of the Court's decisions. In late 2019, Professor Thaddeus Hwong of York University agreed to help me with my database by applying software to the data to quantify several variables. I approached Thaddeus not only because he is a leading academic in the application of quantitative methods to income tax decisions but also because he wrote his PhD dissertation on his own findings from analyzing a database he'd created on Supreme Court income tax decisions.

I completed the sham paper first and sought external feedback before submitting it to a scholarly journal. The feedback was good, and I expanded the paper to analyze a matter suggested by the reviewer. Despite this positive feedback, I was unable to get the paper published in the journal. My own reviewer expressed surprise and told me no one else had ever approached the sham doctrine in the way I did.

Meanwhile, I realized that something was missing while writing a draft of the second paper about my database. It did not give a sense of the whole as told through the opinions of the most influential

Supreme Court judges in income tax over one hundred years—between 1920 and 2019 inclusive. To remedy this, I decided to choose whom I perceive to be the nine most influential Supreme Court judges in income tax over that period and to write at length about their opinions. When doing so, I decided to weave into the narrative key aspects of my unpublished paper on the sham doctrine, thereby bypassing academia and its gatekeepers.

The selected bench of nine would form my Supreme Court all-star team in income tax law. I also decided to describe in brief who these nine individuals were, based on their backgrounds and life experiences before they became judges. This has been done to add context to their opinions as they unfold judge by judge and opinion by opinion over the 1920–2019 period. Once I determined this format, I decided to rarely refer to the views of tax practitioners and tax academics about the cases. Repeatedly citing their views would have turned this project into a mini–tax treatise, and that was not my intention. I envisioned a relatively easy, interesting and at times lively read for those attracted to the subject matter, that focuses on the opinions of the judges and is not bogged down by too much technical detail, which I describe in brief in most cases profiled to explain the issue and opinion. An exception is made to provide more detail for some cases, including *Canada Trustco*.

The views of others about the cases are available in the tax literature and may differ from my view. The main exception to my rule is that I do refer to certain case comments of Gwyneth McGregor, the then editor of the journal of the Canadian Tax Foundation made in the 1950s and 1960s, and to the views of Professor Brian J. Arnold on more recent matters.

I also, on occasion, weave into the narrative historical people and events that relate to certain cases. Their profile has an added touch for no other reason but my sensing that the dispute concerns a matter possessing relevance that transcends the confines of the income tax system. I therefore place the dispute in its broader historical or legal context. The first two cases profiled are such disputes: *Pioneer Laundry* and *Emily Merritt* from 1938 and 1942, respectively. The Supreme Court's decisions in these two cases flow through the life of the Court's income tax decisions until the 1982–84 period.

After completing a draft, I approached Edward Short, an accountant and former colleague, to read it and provide feedback. He readily agreed to do so despite it interrupting his sailing down home off the coasts of the Maritimes. Ed's feedback was critical in moving this project forward, and he provided several useful insights, including a variation of the title.

Next, I approached Canada's premier income tax law academic, Brian J. Arnold, to determine his views. Brian also liked the draft and agreed to write the book's foreword should the work be published. I think Brian liked the relaxed nature of the read, which is relative in the sense that income tax is an exhausting, dry, and detailed-oriented subject matter for almost everyone. For Brian, I am sure the draft took him back in time to the University of Western Ontario Law School when he began teaching income tax in 1969.

Thaddeus, Ed and Brian, thank you. Any errors in *Bench Strength* are mine, not yours.

Technological disruption struck during the period *Bench Strength* was researched and written, which changed everything about the way in which the important policy issues central to achieving a better functioning democracy and economy are (or are not) communicated to, and considered by, citizens. Political journalist Paul Wells captured the essence of this disruption and its risks in his Substack series.

Wells wrote:

> Even institutions that wouldn't mind journalistic attention are having increasing trouble getting any. The Supreme Court of Canada is close to being a news desert. Press

> galleries sit empty in the Senate. Complex departments and policy files get only drive-by visits from reporters who have no inkling of a story's background and evolution. It's not their fault, their industry is collapsing. But when they do show up at random intervals, it's all just a bit weird [Every Phone a Printing Press: The End of the Media, Chapter Two: Everything Everywhere, Substack.com, July 3, 2023].

I mention this because my intent is to place the information and the issues raised about the Supreme Court's approach to income tax in their historical and legal contexts for potential readers who want to engage in a substantive policy debate about the Court's approach to tax avoidance.

It may help readers to know as background information that, in 1997, the *Alberta Law Review* published a paper I wrote on statutory interpretation that opens with the following paragraph:

> A pivotal debate is occurring within the tax profession, both in the academic press and the courts. Arguments are being marshalled as to what rule of interpretation should be paramount when interpreting the *Income Tax Act* [footnote omitted]. Should the primary rule be grounded in the *legislated purpose (object) approach* or the *modern judicial plan meaning approach*? [Interpreting the *Income Tax Act*: Purpose v. Plain Meaning and the Effect of Uncertainty in the Tax Law, 1997, 35-3 *Alberta Law Review* 687, https://canlii.ca/t/skwh, retrieved on 2024-09-01.]

I mention the above article for five reasons. First, I was contacted recently about the article by a person who knows about this book and who told me that he had just read the article, and it was "very good," which came as a surprise because the article was panned in a 1997 review, and it has garnered four citations only in the intervening 27 years. Second, I argued in it that the use of the judicial plain-meaning approach contributes to "the tangled web of uncertainty weaved by all of us [drafters, advisors and judges]" in tax law, and that the legislated purposive approach held out the possibility of better balancing rights and responsibilities under tax law while helping lead us all, including taxpayers, out of that tangled web.

Third, my thinking on the subject matter has evolved since I wrote the article, and *Bench Strength* reflects that evolution. In 1996–97, I failed to grasp the extent to which non-tax academics on the left had, by then, exerted in their writings significant pressure on the Supreme Court of Canada to infuse into the legislated purposive approach their subjective social values and *Charter* values, while carving out from their agenda a plain-meaning safe harbour for commercial / tax law.

Fourth, while that article still resides in academia, *Bench Strength* by-passes academia and tax publishers and maybe, just maybe, it can reach a broader readership interested in learning more about the Canadian income tax system and the approach the Supreme Court takes when deciding income tax avoidance disputes. For that reason, it is softcover under $40 a copy, rather than a sky-high priced $80 to $200 tax book sold to tax professionals and law libraries, which few taxpayers would have any hope of affording or staying awake long enough to read. The fifth and final reason is that, like in that article, I have written *Bench Strength* from a working-class perspective.

Bench Strength tells the story of Canada's statutory income tax law through the decisions of the Supreme Court of Canada and its most influential judges in income tax over the 1920–2019 period. This story needs to be told and is followed by a brief review of the related statistical results.

What you are about to read raises significant questions about the approach the Supreme Court and its judges have taken in deciding tax avoidance cases before and after the enactment of the *Charter of Rights and Freedoms* on April 17, 1982. The judges through their decisions speak for themselves, and the most important part of the narrative is their opinions—the approach each judge used to reach the particular result and the reasons, if any, he or she gave for taking the chosen approach.*

Kerry Harnish

---

*When possible, *Bench Strength's* citations and excerpts of decisions of the Supreme Court of Canada and the former Exchequer Court of Canada are (1) in the case of the Supreme Court, from the hard copy or online version of the decision in *Supreme Court Reports* (SCR) and at Navigation by Date: 2024 – SCC Cases (scc-csc.ca); and (2) in the case of the Exchequer Court, from the hard copy or online version of the decision in *Exchequer Court Reports* (Ex. CR) and at https://lexum.com/en/blog/the-reports-of-the-exchequer-court-of-canada-now-available-online/. When no officially published decision is available, commercial services that published the decision are cited. Commercial reporting services cited include *Canada Tax Cases* (CTC), *Dominion Tax Cases* (DTC), *Tax Appeal Board Cases* (Tax ABC) and *Dominion Law Reports* (DLR). In a few cases, the excerpt comes from the Supreme Court's case file. In the case of British citations, references are to *Appeal Cases* (AC), *United Kingdom House of Lords Reports* (UKHL), *British Tax Cases* (BTC) and *All England Reports* (All ER) and, in the case of the United States, include references to *United States Supreme Court Reports* (US) and *Federal Court* decisions (e.g., F. 3rd). (The Tax Court of Canada (TCC), the Federal Court (FC) and the Federal Court of Appeal (FCA) each has a website at which they publish their decisions but only so far back in time.)

Note: Page citations in respect of older Supreme Court decisions at the Court's website do not necessarily align to the page(s) in the hard copy of the decision, which is accessible within the link as a PDF file. This discrepancy has been noted in two citations, but there may be others.

Please note that online resources are subject to change. While every effort has been made to ensure the accuracy of cited links at the time of publication, their long-term accessibility cannot be guaranteed due to potential website reorganizations or content migrations. This includes links to government news releases, budget materials and legislation.

PART I

Introduction

THE INTERPRETATIVE APPROACH THE Supreme Court of Canada took in income tax avoidance cases during the 1990s and early 2000s concerned and motivated me. I was concerned about the ramifications the Court's formalistic approach had on the integrity of the income tax system, which was largely out of step with the approach it cultivated and applied before 1984. This concern motivated me to undertake a research project focused on the Court's income tax decisions over the 1920–2019 period, which resulted in my authoring this book. What started as a detailed analysis of the Court's interpretative approach in income tax cases led to an examination of the judges who influenced and defined their respective approaches.

In this book, I endeavour to chart the development of the Supreme Court's interpretative approach to income tax law over the period by reference to the Court's nine judges who, in my view, exercised the greatest influence on its development. To better understand the contribution these judges made and the outcomes of the decisions in which they participated, I have also endeavoured to provide some insight into the cultural, economic, personal and political influences that likely informed each judge's approach to interpreting and applying income tax law.

Individual court decisions are typically parsed word by word by readers with varying and often contrary interpretations. But what, if anything, would be revealed if one read all of the Supreme Court's income tax decisions in sequence as they unfolded in their historical and income tax contexts? Could the reader gain a better understanding by discerning general themes that are not evident when looking at snapshots in time? What follows is an attempt to answer those two questions.

The Supreme Court's approach to the interpretation of income tax law evolved during the period, with the Court, through its judges, shifting from requiring that transactions be consistent with commercial substance and reality to emphasizing the legal form of a taxpayer's legal relations. The existence of such a shift in judicial preference does not explain when and why it occurred and its effect on the results. To begin, it is necessary to identify the most influential decisions and judges and broaden the analysis from that starting point.

Prior to the enactment of the *Charter of Rights and Freedoms* (*Charter*) on April 17, 1982,[1] the Supreme Court's judges invariably lived during a cultural period that emphasized individual duties over rights. These judges were willing to look through the legal form of a taxpayer's transactions to consider their commercial substance, provided it was clear that the object and spirit of the statutory income tax law would be avoided if they applied the strict or literal interpretive approach to determine the meaning of the text in issue. The pre-*Charter* results of this period review speak for themselves: The Court decided for the Crown in 72 percent of all income tax disputes and in 83 percent of all income tax avoidance disputes.

[1] *The Charter of Rights and Freedoms* is Part I of the *Constitution Act*, 1982 (ss. 1–34), which was added to Canada's Constitution on the proclamation of the *Canada Act*, 1982 (U.K.), c. 11, Schedule B (proclaimed into law on April 17, 1982). The equality provision (s. 15) did not come into force until three years later on April 17, 1985 (see subs. 32(2) of the *Charter*). The Constitution Acts, 1867 to 1982 (Justice.gc.ca).

The pre-*Charter* income tax statistics thus support the thesis that the Supreme Court's judges during the period chose to place more emphasis on a taxpayer's obligations than on a taxpayer's rights. The phrase "commercial reality" and the words "context," "object," "purpose," "spirit" and "substance" are a judicial tell when interpreting a provision's text; if a judge uses any one of them favourably in his or her opinion, normally (but not always) they signal a decision favourable to the Crown's position in a tax avoidance case and against a taxpayer.

A reader of the Supreme Court's income tax decisions can discern a definite shift after 1983 toward judges' emphasizing the legal form of a taxpayer's transactions regardless of their commercial substance. The results flip with the Court deciding for the taxpayer in 56 percent of all income tax disputes and in 73 percent of all income tax avoidance disputes. By doing so, taxpayers went to succeeding in more than 70 percent of all income tax avoidance disputes from less than 20 percent before the *Charter*.

The *Charter*-era statistics thus support the thesis that the Supreme Court's judges during the era have placed more emphasis on the taxpayer's rights than on the taxpayer's obligations. The phrases "legal form" and "plain meaning" and the words "strict" and "literal" are a judicial tell in relation to interpreting a provision's text; if a judge uses anyone of them favourably in his or her opinion, normally (but not always) they signal a decision favourable to the taxpayer's position in a tax avoidance case and against the Crown.

We should not, however, jump to the conclusion that the enactment of the *Charter* in 1982 caused a judicial shift that champions or enables tax avoidance. Its enactment is the culmination in Canada of a broader cultural and legal shift toward emphasizing the rights of individuals over their obligations.

The bottom line is that the *Charter*-era judges and their opinions have broadened a taxpayer's right to effect transactions that result in the successful avoidance of income tax. Their emphasis on the importance of legal form is premised on the need to provide taxpayers, usually high-income taxpayers, with certainty and predictability in planning commercial and personal affairs for tax purposes. Identifiable judges led this shift, and, as it intensified, allowed tax avoidance results to succeed despite the use of transactions having little or no commercial substance or reality.

Behind the emphasis of legal form or commercial substance is something else—the elusive *why* a judge emphasized legal form or commercial substance when reaching a decision. Often on display in a decision is the known *how* the judge reached the decision, using interpretive tools and related reasons.

This judicial emphasis on legal form versus commercial substance (or *vice versa*) traces to the dual nature of income taxation under the statutory law, which is both legal and commercial. That law imposes tax on concepts such as "income" and "profit" and in doing so uses terms such as "business," "gross revenue," "outlay," "expense," "cost" and "capital cost" to name but a few of the many legal-commercial concepts found in the statutory income tax law. These concepts are of fundamental importance to achieve the *Income Tax Act*'s overriding purpose, which is to impose an income tax on an accurate measurement of each taxpayer's worldwide net income for every taxation year the taxpayer has net income. But the devil is in the details my investigation reveals, and one of the most important details is what judges emphasize and the way in which they interpret the statutory law.

Whether the legal form or commercial substance of transactions is emphasized in tax avoidance cases derives for the most part from a choice that has to be made when a taxpayer's legal transactions make no commercial sense—their purpose is tax avoidance. Which of these competing approaches should be emphasized? Once made, the choice narrows down to applying interpretative rules that emphasize either the text of the statutory law or its context, object and spirit.

Bench Strength offers a lens on this interpretive influence. I've discovered that the life experiences and the culture of the times in which the judges lived most influenced the interpretive approach they adopted in the tax cases profiled. Where they lived is also relevant, especially in the sense that judges tend to embody the regional cultural, economic and legal influences that predominate in those places. Together, these influences affect their judicial choices far more than the rules of statutory interpretation or legal precedent, which are, like the tools in my carpenter-cousin's pouch, selected and deployed based on experience to achieve the desired result.

Bench Strength's most startling finding is the Supreme Court's negation during the pre-*Charter* era of the British *Duke of Westminster* principle—taxpayers are entitled to arrange their affairs to minimize tax—which emphasizes the legal form of a taxpayer's transactions and interprets the statutory income tax law based on the strict rule,[2] and the Court's adherence to the *Duke of Westminster* principle during the *Charter* era. This finding is conspicuous in terms of its timing and the role that precedent is supposed to play in deciding cases. The *Duke of Westminster* decision dates to May 7, 1935 (*Appeal Cases* published it in 1936), and the Supreme Court's adherence to the principle and strict rule of interpretation in income tax cases should have occurred, if it were to occur, in the years after 1935 when the Court was subject to oversight by the Judicial Committee of the Privy Council in London—not after 1982.

This counter-intuitive timeline suggests that Canadian sentiment about taxation during the pre-*Charter* era differed significantly from that at the judicial level in the United Kingdom despite the fact that the Supreme Court was, for much of that era, subject to British oversight. This should not come as a surprise because Canada was changing during the period in a North American context where what was happening in the United States had intensifying influence on those changes.

[2] *Commissioners of Inland Revenue v. Duke of Westminster (Hugh Richard Arthur)*, (1935), [1936] AC 1 (HL), p. 19 (Lord Tomlin enunciated the principle). The strict approach tends to mean that the statutory text will be read strictly against the Crown in a taxing provision but against the taxpayer in a provision that provides a tax preference.

But as Professor Emeritus Brian J. Arnold noted in 2001, adherence to the *Duke of Westminster* principle became in the *Charter* era "a matter of blind belief, an article of faith."[3] He also described the strict interpretive rule as follows: "unless a taxpayer's situation is literally within the words of the charging provision of the statute, the tax is not exigible."[4] As a clarification, Arnold also showed by example in 2001 that Supreme Court judges were not referring in a consistent manner to their interpretive approach and concluded that "the court's approach is confused and inconsistent."[5]

Confusion and inconsistency should be expected if the Supreme Court and its judges had lost touch in the *Charter* era with the fundamental nature of its past precedent before establishing a new base of precedent to work with and apply. When establishing that new base, the Court often reads down its older precedent, confines it to its facts or overturns it.

The selection of the most influential judges has been augmented in my investigation by a statistical analysis of their decisions. The information gleaned has been balanced with contexts that are not disclosed in the decisions and primarily found in historical books and biographies as well as in academic studies that discuss the judges' careers or decisions.

In my research, I found a dearth of information in legal academia about the approach individual Supreme Court judges take to income tax and its avoidance. Biographies of judges have little, if any, meaningful comments on their approach to income taxation despite the importance of income tax as the federal government's primary source of revenue. Two notable exceptions are the following works: *Chief Justice W.R. Jackett: By the Law of the Land* by

[3] Brian J. Arnold, "Reflections on the Relationship Between Statutory Interpretation and Tax Avoidance," (2001), 49:1 *Canadian Tax Journal* 1, p. 15.
[4] *Ibid.*, p. 6.
[5] *Ibid.*, p. 32.

Richard Pound and *Judging Bertha Wilson: Law as Large as Life* by Ellen Anderson.

Early in my writing adventure, it became obvious that the Supreme Court decided a disproportionately larger number of income tax cases before 1983. The best explanation for the skewing of decisions (and related data) to the pre-1983 period is the implementation of the leave requirement as of late January 1975. Under it, the Court does not hear tax cases entering the judicial process after the change unless it first grants the appellant leave to appeal. The Court normally declines to review a lower court tax decision unless it considers the issue to be of national importance. Over time, this has dramatically reduced the number of income tax cases the Court decides.

It also became clear that the Supreme Court's approach to income tax and its avoidance changed *circa* 1982–84. This raised a curiosity because I graduated from Dalhousie Law School in the spring of 1982, and mine was the last class to graduate in the pre-*Charter* era.

Her Majesty Queen Elizabeth II signed into law the *Charter of Rights and Freedoms* on April 17, 1982, marking a shift for Canadians and their institutions in not only their legal relationships but also in cultural terms. In short, an era no longer existed in which societal obligations were emphisized over individual rights in the highest law of the land and in Canadian culture; henceforth, for most, individual rights became the more important cultural touchstone.

Those of an older generation may view matters differently, although it's my view that questioning the emphasis on rights without meaningful regard to societal obligations is scarcely encouraged by elites in the Canadian media or academia. A similar division in opinion about a cultural and economic direction can occur based on class. This, too, is discouraged by Canadian elites to the extent it does not align with their own belief system and values.

More importantly, these differences play out in varying degrees within the institutions that develop and draft Canadian income tax law, its administrators, the homes and businesses that comply (or do not comply) and the courts that interpret and apply the law, because those within these institutions are products of different socio-economic classes. No one should be surprised that the judiciary by and large is representative of a class that differs from not only the average taxpayer but also from the average on-the-ground income tax auditor. This is normally not discussed to any extent in an income tax context and certainly was not at Dalhousie Law School *circa* 1979–82.

My process for selecting nine judges to examine avoids skewing to the quantitative results; the selections are balanced by the pre-*Charter* and *Charter* eras.

Unquantified qualitative weight is given to the relative importance of certain judicial opinions over the 1920–2019 period; some opinions, as I contend, are more important than others in terms of their effect on the subsequent approach to income tax and its avoidance. While there is an element of subjectivity when giving more weight to some judicial opinions rather than others, readers can evaluate the results for themselves.

What follows is divided into five parts. The narrative in Part II (The Pre-*Charter*-Era Judges), Part III (The Chief Justice) and Part IV (The *Charter*-Era Judges) compresses a timeline of decades, and a big-picture pattern evolves. As the narrative advances, commentary is provided that seeks to place Canada's national income tax law and the Supreme Court's role in deciding income tax disputes in their historical context. Much of this commentary is provided in the introductions to Parts II and IV, and in the concluding Part VI.

Part II opens with context to the pre-*Charter* era and identifies the four judges from that era included in the selected nine. It explains why one leading judge from the era was not selected. A section is dedicated to each judge and considers several of their most important decisions. Practically all the decisions shed light on the approach each respective judge took to income tax. In more contentious decisions, some have differing opinions,[6] which are considered as the narrative advances over time, judge by judge, decision by decision. The discussion of the judges and their opinions is supplemented on occasion by delving into the facts in, and on the periphery of, the tax dispute under examination. This is done with a view to shedding light on aspects of Canada's history as it relates to the decision and its wider historical or legal significance.

Part III (The Chief Justice) identifies the judge selected as the hypothetical chief justice on the illustrative group of nine. It explains this selection and analyzes some of that judge's most important decisions.

Part IV (The *Charter*-Era Judges) follows the pattern in Part II by providing context to the *Charter* era. Part IV then selects four judges from the era and explains why one leading candidate was not selected. It also focuses on the significant shift that occurred in the approach the judges took to the statutory income tax law during the era. As this shift evolves, Part IV takes a more critical-analysis approach when considering the selected judges' most important income tax decisions. The analysis also critiques the Supreme Court's approach to the general anti-avoidance rule (GAAR) enacted in 1988 and, on occasion, compares the *Charter*-era approach to that taken by the pre-*Charter* judges.

Part V (Statistical Results) provides statistical information about the judges' income tax decisions as well as the macro results for the

[6] Supreme Court of Canada judgements can include a number of separate opinions. A judge's opinion may differ from that of a colleague as to the result but even judges who agree on the result may disagree on the reasons for the result. Decisions can be unanimous (with all judges agreeing with one opinion) or non-unanimous. In non-unanimous decisions, a breakdown can include a majority opinion for a litigant (with which some other judges on the panel concur), with one or more minority opinions for the same litigant as the majority but with differing reasons, and with one or more dissenting opinions that disagree with the result for differing reasons. Although rare, it is possible that no majority occurs for either litigant, with the immediate lower court's decision standing on that issue.

Supreme Court over the hundred-year period in my investigation. This information and related commentary supplement the discussion of the judges and their opinions, with one table focused on the judges' approach to income tax and a second table focused on the outcome of the Supreme Court's decisions with a division in the data on April 17, 1982, when the *Charter* became law.

Bench Strength concludes in Part VI with general observations about income tax, the Supreme Court and its judges.

PART II

The Pre-Charter-Era Judges

THE JUDGES OF THE Supreme Court of Canada before 1982 formed a narrow group of men by the standards of the 21st century. The Canada of the first three quarters of the 20th century was populated by individuals who were overwhelmingly white, spoke English or French as their mother tongue and practised either the Roman Catholic or a Protestant Christian faith.

Canada was just beginning to change by the early 1980s. Despite significant growth in immigration levels from non-European countries in the 1970s, Canada's visible minority population was less than five percent as recently as 1981, the year before the enactment of the *Charter*.[7]

As well, regardless of the reason, few women managed during this period to scale the heights of the law profession, commerce, academia, politics or government bureaucracy. Those who did were trailblazers who encountered the type of resistance that is

[7] Éric Caron Malenfant, Anne Milan, Mathieu Charron and Alain Bélanger, "Demographic Changes in Canada from 1971 to 2001 Across an Urban-to-Rural Gradient," Statistics Canada, 2007, pp. 20–21 at The Daily, Thursday, April 26, 2007. Study: Demographic changes across an urban-to-rural gradient (statcan.gc.ca) (accessed February 1, 2021).

common when an outsider seeks acceptance into a group. In a team sport such as hockey, that outsider competes to make a team with established hierarchy, rhythms, friendships and disagreements. Making the team means displacement of another player's friend, a new competitor and the challenge for the team to move forward in a cohesive manner. Anyone who has ever replaced a player in such a situation knows that the reaction of the team is never predictable and that acceptance does not come easily. This seeking by outsiders of initial entry to a group plays out daily in corporations large and small, bureaucracies, politics, media and in academia. I was curious whether this phenomenon of social acceptance of group dynamics played out in the judiciary, too.

The men appointed to the Supreme Court in the pre-*Charter* era invariably came from privileged backgrounds. The dominant cultural theme during the era was duty to God, family and country.

Many of the Supreme Court's judges in the pre-*Charter* era served overseas during the First or Second World Wars. They returned from that darkness forever changed, whether physically or mentally. Those who served overseas include Charles Locke, John Cartwright, Douglas Abbott, Henry Nolan, Roland Ritchie, Brian Dickson, William McIntyre and Willard Estey, the son of a Supreme Court Justice. (Peter Cory, a *Charter*-era judge, also served overseas.) They were guardians of the Canada they had served and defended in war and peace.

The enactment in 1917 of a national income tax is the most significant fiscal development in the history of post-confederation Canada.[8] Over time, the tax became the dominant source of revenue for the federal government, but this was not initially the case. Until the outbreak of the Second World War, federal income tax was imposed on a narrow group of high-income Canadians, corporations and trusts. The Supreme Court heard relatively few federal

[8] Robert B. Bryce, *Maturing in Hard Times: Canada's Department of Finance through the Great Depression* (Montreal-Kingston: McGill-Queen's University Press for The Institute of Public Administration of Canada, 1986), p. 19.

income tax disputes prior to 1940. But with war, the fundamental nature of Canada's income tax system changed in mere months.

Canada seized the provincial power to tax income.[9] Under Liberal Finance Minister J.L. Ilsley's leadership and vision, Parliament extended income tax to pay for the war by having it reach down to tax the income of the lower middle and working classes in addition to high-income and wealthy Canadians. The top marginal tax rate was about 90 percent of taxable income, and, by 1943, income tax was the dominant source of federal revenues (60 percent), well outpacing sales taxes (11 percent), excise taxes (6.5 percent) and tariffs imposed on imported goods (5.6 percent).[10]

---

[9] Income tax in what is now Canada began in the early 1830s as a municipal tax on property in the City of Saint John in the pre-confederation colony of New Brunswick. A person's property included the person's income. The tax rate was low, and the tax spread to other cities in the Maritime colonies, including Halifax, and to Upper Canada (what is now Ontario). After Confederation in 1867, over time the provinces that were not taxing personal income began to do so. The provinces also began imposing corporate tax, and by the late 1930s, all of the provinces imposed personal and corporate income tax. The tax rates imposed were relativity low, and there was no federal-provincial coordination of the imposition of income tax. This became a significant policy issue during the Great Depression when Canada and the provinces sought in an uncoordinated way to impose higher taxes on high-income individuals and corporations. After the Second World War, the provinces recovered their ability to impose income tax, and Canada and the provinces began negotiations on the way in which they would coordinate the imposition of income tax on a go-forward basis. All provinces except Quebec agreed over time to allow Canada to administer and collect their personal income tax. Canada also administers and collects corporate income tax for all provinces except Alberta and Quebec.

[10] Both the *Income War Tax Act*, 1927, and the *Excess Profits Tax Act*, 1940, imposed income tax during the Second World War. The percentages were computed using tables in J. Harvey Perry, *Taxes, Tariffs, and Subsidies: A History of Canadian Fiscal Development*, Volume II (Toronto: University of Toronto Press, 1955), pp. 624–27. Income taxes were about 25 percent of federal revenue by 1935 and about 29 percent by 1939. For this purpose, income taxes include excess profits tax and non-resident (NR) withholding taxes. NR taxes are imposed on amounts such as interest, rent, royalties and dividends paid from Canada to NR persons, with excess profits taxes being a significant source of revenue during and initially following the Second World War. In 1943, income taxes represented 60 percent of federal revenue. With the end of the war and decline in tax from excess profits, income tax revenue comprised about 54 percent of revenue by 1949.

Following the end of the Second World War in September 1945, two new developments coincided that would change forever Canada's legal and income tax systems. Parliament modernized the *Income War Tax Act*, breaking from its combined American and British approach, resulting in the *Income Tax Act*, 1948, effective for 1949 and subsequent taxation years.

The *Income War Tax Act* took an American approach in several tax policy areas, most noticeably, by imposing tax on a taxpayer's total income from all sources. In contrast, the British imposed income tax under separate schedules, each applicable to a specific source(s), without a combined total to which the regular income tax rate applied. But the *Income War Tax Act* also followed the British approach in certain important ways, including the statutory language used to determine the deductibility of expenditures when calculating income from a business or property source.

Canada's modern income tax statute charted a new way forward for taxing income. Ministerial discretion was no longer the main way in which tax avoidance would be constrained. Up to 90 rules granting discretion were repealed.[11] The rules repealed included the discretion to limit the deduction of interest, depreciation, depletion, unreasonable amounts and artificial amounts. The new direction also granted taxpayers the right to calculate their business income using best commercial principles as modified by the statutory law.

With these new rights came the right to appeal both the facts as well as the law in dispute to a new tribunal established to handle the appeals. Taxpayers and the Crown could further appeal to the Exchequer Court as a matter of right, with a further appeal to the Supreme Court as a matter of right if the tax in dispute met a modest $500 threshold.

Two other events coalesced at the same time, which placed the Supreme Court and its judges at the centre of navigating this new

[11] Robert McMechan and Gordon Bourgard, "The Origins of the Tax Court," *Tax Court Practice* (Toronto: Carswell, 1993), p. 6.

direction in Canadian income tax law. The first event occurred just as the modern *Income Tax Act* took effect. In 1949, Parliament ended a litigant's right to appeal a decision to the Judicial Committee of the Privy Council in London, England. The Supreme Court was finally supreme.

The second related event is that Parliament expanded the Supreme Court to nine judges from seven in late 1949. Liberal Prime Minister Louis St. Laurent appointed a new justice from Ontario and a new justice from Quebec, with both provinces having three members on a court of nine.[12] The expanded Court convened in early 1950, which coincided with the first filings of income tax returns for the 1949 tax year under the modernized *Income Tax Act*, 1948 (the 1948 ITA).

The 1949–50 timing of these events could not have been better from the perspective of having the Supreme Court interpret the new legislation. On February 27, 1950, the Supreme Court began hearing oral arguments over three days in *Reference re Bowater's Pulp & Paper Mills Ltd.*,[13] which concerned income taxation and the terms of union of the Dominions of Canada and Newfoundland and Labrador. Newfoundland and Labrador had for many years exempted Bowater from customs duties and other taxes, including income tax. After Parliament enacted *An Act to approve the Terms of Union of Newfoundland with Canada*, 1949, it amended the 1948 ITA to clarify that Bowater's exemption from income tax did not apply federally. Canada then referred the matter to the Court to decide the dispute; Bowater maintained that the exemption applied until the legislature of Newfoundland and Labrador ended it.

---

[12] On a go-forward basis, the influence of the three Maritime and four Western provinces would be a normative three of nine Supreme Court judges despite the fact Canada expanded effective March 31, 1949, to include its newest and most Eastern province, Newfoundland and Labrador. It is unclear whether those in Ottawa, Quebec City and Toronto noticed or cared that a permanent imbalance may have resulted.

[13] *Reference re Bowater's Pulp & Paper Mills Ltd.*, [1950] SCR 608. *Reference re Bowater's Pulp & Paper Mills Ltd.* – SCC Cases (scc-csc.ca).

On June 9, 1950, the Court held that Bowater's income tax exemption did not apply for federal purposes in a 6–1 split.

More generally, income tax disputes flowed freely to the Supreme Court over the next three decades as an unprecedented post-war economic boom accompanied the changes; they quickly represented an expanding proportion of the Court's docket until the late 1970s. In many of the years, income tax disputes consumed 10 percent or more of all cases the Court heard. In Canada's centennial year, 1967, the Court decided 20 income tax cases involving 26 different issues and 24 taxpayers.

Five Supreme Court judges were identified in my research as the strongest candidates for selection as the most influential during the pre-*Charter* era, other than as the chief justice: Chief Justices Patrick Kerwin and John Cartwright, as well as Justices Douglas Abbott, Wilfred Judson and Ronald Martland. The selections are presented in the order of their appointment to the Supreme Court; Part II concludes with reasons for the omission of one in my final selection.

PATRICK KERWIN: PURPORTEDLY "NO GRAND VISION" IN HIS OPINIONS

Conservative Prime Minister Richard B. Bennett elevated Patrick Kerwin to the Supreme Court from the High Court of Ontario in 1935, replacing Justice Frank Hughes.

Patrick Kerwin was born and raised in Sarnia, Ontario, across from Port Huron, Michigan. His father's family worked in shipping on the Great Lakes; his father, also named Patrick, was a captain who owned two ships until one sank, along with a valuable cargo. In ill health, he opened a liquor store in Sarnia above which the family lived; he passed when his son was eight years old. Mrs. Kerwin closed the store and with her children moved in with her parents who were also merchants in Sarnia. At 14, Kerwin quit secondary school to help his mother make ends meet, and his first job was delivering meat for a Sarnia grocery by horse and wagon. He would eventually return to school.[14]

Kerwin, who adhered to his Roman Catholic faith, married a protestant who converted, and he was involved throughout his career in inter-faith groups. He was also a low-key family man who avoided the public spotlight.

After leading his class at Osgoode Hall Law School in Toronto, Kerwin returned to southwestern Ontario to practise law in 1911. He practised in Guelph, Ontario until late 1932, where he ran a law partnership with Hugh Guthrie while Guthrie was a Liberal member of Parliament. Guthrie was a Unionist in Prime Minister Sir Robert Borden's Union government during the First World War, and then a Conservative cabinet minister during the 1930s. The firm's main client was the local municipal government, and Kerwin acted in civil matters, including municipal tax disputes. He was also a special prosecutor in criminal matters for Ontario.

Hugh Guthrie was the federal Minister of Justice when Kerwin was appointed to the High Court of Ontario in 1932. Initial

[14] Stephen G. McKenna, *Grace and Wisdom: Patrick G. Kerwin 1889–1963* (Ottawa: Petra Books, 2017). This section relies on McKenna for Kerwin C.J.'s family and professional background (McKenna is his grandson).

skepticism about the appointment soon ended, and Kerwin has been described as one of the best trial court judges in Ontario's history. Both Canadian and American reporters who covered his trials described his demeanour and fairness in glowing terms.[15] Kerwin had a breadth of legal experience that few lawyers have, ranging from civil litigation to municipal law, from criminal prosecutions to representing a Jesuit Institution before a Royal Commission.

When Kerwin was relatively new to the Supreme Court, Liberal Prime Minister Mackenzie King asked him to undertake a special assignment during one all too muggy summer in Ottawa. He laboured throughout that suffocating summer in the pre–air conditioner age, in the former Supreme Court building, only for King to tell him on completion that the government dropped the matter.

Kerwin became sick working in that decrepit former horse stable during the summer, and Georgina Kerwin, Patrick's wife, was not impressed with King's failure to advise Kerwin sooner that his input was no longer needed. She felt King's actions were appalling and that the incident shortened Kerwin's life. The mere mention of King's name was off limits in her presence.[16]

Appointed the chief justice in 1954, Kerwin is said, by legal scholars, to have been "neither a legal technician in the narrowest sense nor a philosophical jurist in the broadest scope."[17] There is an economy to Kerwin's decisions, which, they note, is combined with a sensitivity to precedent and ensuring that decisions do not wander into creative general statements that enunciate broad

---

[15] *Ibid.*, pp. 67–70 and 82–4. Also, see Balcome, McBride and Russell, *Supreme Court of Canada Decision-Making, infra* note 17, Chapter 11.

[16] *Ibid.*, pp. 129–130. McKenna expanded on Georgina Kerwin's recollection of the incident involving Justice Kerwin and Prime Minister King in an article published in September 2024. In it, McKenna wrote that his grandmother not only never forgave King but also that King "told Justice Kerwin, 'Oh, we're not doing that anymore' and walked away." Stephen McKenna, "A Caring Grandfather," *Fifty-Five Plus*, September–Ottawa Edition, 2024, pp. 86–89.

[17] Randall P.H. Balcome, Edward J. McBride, and Dawn A. Russell, *Supreme Court of Canada Decision-Making: The Benchmarks of Rand, Kerwin, and Martland* (Toronto: Carswell, 1990), p. 184.

judicial principles.[18] He is said to have "allowed no grand vision nor passionate conviction to obtrude in his reasons for judgment."[19] There appears to be an important exception to this suggestion, which is described later.

It can be said that Patrick Kerwin was strongly pro-Crown in income tax disputes, especially if the matter concerned tax avoidance. He heard 77 income tax cases, of which 25 involved tax avoidance issues, during his 28 years as a Supreme Court judge.

Irish by descent, Chief Justice Kerwin's selection is not because of the number of income tax cases he decided. Rather, it is because he was at the centre of disputes before he became chief justice, in which the Supreme Court did not follow the British *Duke of Westminster* principle when applying the *Income War Tax Act.* The disputes include *Pioneer Laundry* (1938),[20] *Emily Merritt* (1942),[21] and *Fraser D.R. & Co* (1947).[22] The first and third decisions concerned the Minister's exercise of discretion to limit taxpayer deductions in a tax avoidance context.

---

[18] *Ibid.*, pp. 151–58. In an address on November 13, 1952, Kerwin J. advised attendees at the Toronto Lawyers' Club that his view of broad judicial principles is that "while it is not true to say that principles of wide application should never be enunciated, the necessary coincidence of time and event will arise only in infrequent and impelling circumstances." See McKenna, *Grace and Wisdom, supra* note 14, p. 259.

[19] *Ibid.*, p. 169.

[20] *Pioneer Laundry & Dry Cleaners Ltd. v. MNR,* (1938), [1939] SCR 1; the Privy Council reversed the Supreme Court at (1939), [1920–1940] DTC 499, [1938–39] CTC 411, [1940] AC 127 (JCPC). *Pioneer Laundry & Dry Cleaners Ltd. v. The Minister of National Revenue* – SCC Cases (scc-csc.ca).

[21] *Emily L. Merritt v. MNR,* [1942] SCR 269; allowing the Crown's appeal from [1941] Ex. CR 175, [1941–1946] 2 DTC 513, [1940–41] CTC 226. *Minister of National Revenue v. Merritt* – SCC Cases (scc-csc.ca). The Exchequer Court's decision is at *Emily L. Merritt v. Minister of National Revenue* – Office of the Commissioner for Federal Judicial Affairs Canada (fja-cmf.gc.ca).

[22] *Fraser D.R. & Company Limited v. MNR,* [1947] SCR 157; the Privy Council affirmed the Supreme Court's decision at (1948) [1949–1950] 4 DTC 521, [1948] CTC 297, [1949] AC 24 (JCPC). *Fraser D.R. & Co. v. Minister of National Revenue* – SCC Cases (scc-csc.ca).

Pioneer Laundry (1938)

The then Justice Kerwin wrote the 1938 swing opinion in *Pioneer Laundry* that denied, 3–2, a blatant tax avoidance gambit. The taxpayer emerged from a complex corporate reorganization having acquired a related company's almost fully depreciated capital assets at a substantially increased cost, which it used to renew depreciation deductions on the same old assets. The Minister indicated that there had been no change in the beneficial ownership of the depreciable property and exercised his discretion to deny almost all of the taxpayer's claim.

Arguing before the Supreme Court, the taxpayer contended that the Minister had acted on an unsound legal principle when exercising discretion: clearly, the argument went, the taxpayer had acquired beneficial ownership of the depreciable property from the related company, and the Exchequer Court's decision should be reversed.

Justice Albert Hudson of the Supreme Court found for the Minister because the taxpayer was mostly relying on British authorities decided under "statutes, somewhat differently worded from ours … [and the *Income War Tax Act*] does not define or limit the field for operation of such discretion." (Justice Oswald Crocket concurred.[23]) While they conceded the taxpayer was technically a different corporation, they found that the Minister had not acted unreasonably because the taxpayer was the "alter ego" of the original corporation with the same shareholders, no new capital and almost identical assets.

Justice Henry Davis dissented, finding that the taxpayer as a separate legal entity acquired the depreciable property and the Minister had not established fraud or improper conduct, which would allow him to ignore its separate personality. (Chief Justice Sir Lyman Duff concurred.[24]) But in so deciding, they admitted

---

[23] *Pioneer Laundry*, *supra* note 20, SCC pp. 9–10.

[24] *Ibid.*, pp. 5–6.

being "influenced in this case by the insistence of many great [British] judges upon the full recognition of the separate legal entity of a joint stock company."[25] After being so influenced, they applied the 1935 British *Duke of Westminster* decision to counter

[25] *Ibid.*, p. 6. The reference in the dissent to being "so influenced" by the British judges is a particular interest because, in a unanimous decision issued two years before the *Duke of Westminster* decision, Duff C.J. expressed support for and applied a substance over legal form approach in *M.D. Donald Ltd. v. Brown (Assessor of Tax for B.C.)*, [1933] SCR 411. In the case, three related individuals purchased land with rental buildings, which they transferred to a corporation of which they were shareholders. Their corporation did not pay for the property, but it did file tax returns reporting rental income from rentals managed by one of the three individuals who deposited the receipts into a non-corporate bank account. In 1928, the corporation conveyed the land and buildings back to the three individuals for "$1 and other good and valuable consideration"; the land was sold for $210,000 in 1929. The B.C. *Income Tax Act* had a broad definition of "income" and it included "all … profits arising … from real and personal property, or from money … invested, … or from any venture, business, … of any kind whatsoever." The assessor imposed income tax on the corporation for the resulting gain of $77,000, which assessment was upheld by the Court of Revision and the Court of Appeal (Note: the income definition appears to apply to capital gains, which may come as a surprise to some people who assume capital gains were not within the meaning of the federal and provincial definitions of income at the time.) The decisions of the lower courts were brief, but Duff C.J. indicated they appeared to be premised on the individuals entering into a scheme that sought to "evade" income tax. [At the time, the words "evade" and "avoid" were in the process of being distinguished in American tax literature, and Duff appears to have used the word "evade" in a tax avoidance sense (not criminal evasion).] Duff held that, based on the detailed facts, the corporation was intended to be the "depository" of title to the property while the individuals continued to have all responsibilities for, and enjoy all of, the benefits related to the property. In other words, they owned the property and the gain was not the corporation's gain to be taxed. Toward the end of his decision, Duff discusses the way in which intent to enter a transaction relates to substance and form (p. 422): "the word 'evade' is … a rather ambiguous one. It may mean that the intention was to engage in a transaction not touched by the *Taxation Act*; if so, nobody has any ground of complaint. *It may be, on the other hand, that you are imputing an intention to put a transaction, which is in substance within the taxing provisions, into a form which, on the face of it, takes it out of the taxing provisions; and such a scheme as that must fail*" [emphasis added]. *M.D. Donald Ltd. v. Brown* – SCC Cases (scc-csc.ca).

"the familiar argument that we ought always look 'at the substance' of the thing."[26]

Kerwin decided the split by focusing on the wording of the relevant provisions of the *Income War Tax Act* and held for the Minister on the basis he exercised his discretion without disregarding any statutory provision in the Act and there was no ground to impeach his doing so. As for that British precedent, Kerwin stated, "[t]he English cases referred to by counsel for the appellant do not appear to me to assist in the determination of the matter."[27] These cases included the *Duke of Westminster* precedent and administrative law decisions in which the British judiciary fettered the discretion Parliament vested in Ministers. The Judicial Committee of the Privy Council at London agreed with the two dissenting judges and in October 1939 reversed the Supreme Court's decision in *Pioneer Laundry*, but that was the prelude to something more significant.

In response, Finance Minister Colonel J.L. Ralston worked on measures that would reverse the Privy Council's position. Mackenzie King had brought Ralston into cabinet to protect his political flank on the right from non-Liberal supporters and veterans with the outbreak of the Second World War. Ralston was the battle-hardened front-line commander of the Nova Scotia Highlanders during the First World War and the former Liberal Minister of National Defence in the 1920s. A leading lawyer who practised in Montreal in the late 1930s, Ralston had resigned his seat in the Nova Scotia Legislative Assembly to enlist during the First World War and was revered by veterans.

In his 1940 Budget, Minister Ralston recommended that Parliament broaden the Revenue Minister's discretion in the *Income War Tax Act* to disallow tax avoidance schemes, thus reversing the Privy Council's

---

[26] *Ibid.*, p. 7.

[27] *Ibid.*, SCC p. 11. Kerwin J. also stated (p. 11): "It appears that the discretion conferred upon him by section 5 has been exercised without disregarding any statutory provision and I can find no ground upon which his determination may be challenged."

decision in *Pioneer Laundry*.[28] The Council's decision was not only ill timed; the Council revealed itself incapable of understanding the sentiment existing about income taxation in Canada. Once the war ended, its days for overseeing the Supreme Court were numbered.

After the amendments, Ralston became the Minister of National Defence. His replacement at Finance was J.L. Ilsley, the Minister of National Revenue, who, as a lawyer, practised in rural Nova Scotia and was a veteran Liberal member of Parliament.

With the wind in his sails from Parliament backing his approach, Patrick Kerwin crossed the St. Clair River into Michigan and gave an address at Lansing on September 4, 1940. Kerwin focused on the Canadian constitution and soon turned to the power to tax. He compared the Supreme Court's approach to the power to tax to that of the United States Supreme Court. Kerwin stated, "Our court … felt that [U. S.] Chief Justice Marshall's famous declaration, 'the power to tax involves the power to destroy', could not be justified so far as our constitution was concerned."[29]

Emily Merritt (1942)

What follows takes the reader through obscure aspects of Canada's fiscal history to place *Emily Merritt* in its historical context. This journey is not a short excursion. No full appreciation of Justice Kerwin's

[28] SC, 1940, c. 34, s. 10 (depletion), s. 16 (deprecation) and s. 17 (unreasonable expenses). The s. 17 changes expanded the Minister's discretion under a special anti-avoidance rule dating to 1933, which the Bennett government enacted, to disallow the deduction of an expense incurred in respect of any transactions which, in the Minister's opinion, unduly or artificially reduced income. This rule was revised over time and remained in force until the enactment of the general anti-avoidance rule in 1988. In 1940, Minister Ralston advised the House of Commons that his tax proposals included certain changes "designed to remove anomalies and facilitate administration." *House of Commons Debates*, July 3, 1940, p. 1028. Resolution 12 at p. 1032 confirms Ralston had the Privy Council's *Pioneer Laundry* decision in mind when he advanced the amendments; its wording describes the key facts in that case.

[29] McKenna, *Grace and Wisdom, supra* note 14, p. 242. McKenna includes several of his grandfather's speeches in a special section to the biography.

1942 majority decision in *Emily Merritt,*[30] can be understood without tracing to amendments made to an obscure but important anti-avoidance rule in 1930, 1934 and 1936.

The anti-avoidance rule Kerwin considered in 1942 and its later versions are intended to prevent individual and non-resident shareholders from avoiding tax on dividends in respect of the accumulated surpluses inside Canadian corporations. Similarly, it is worth knowing that the two key judges who decided the *Emily Merritt* dispute at trial and on appeal came to the dispute with distinct political and overlapping contexts and connections.

Mackenzie King's minority government made a so-called *technical* amendment to the *Income War Tax Act* just before calling the 1930 election. The disturbing part of the amendment was buried within the government's 1930 Budget. It was a gift-wrapped present sent from Canada's treasury to wealthy owners of Canadian corporations, which included successful breweries and distilleries. The intended primary destination of this gift appears to have been the affluent enclave of Westmount, Quebec.

This present extended an exemption from taxable dividend treatment for corporate pre-1930 undistributed earnings. The King government changed the anti-avoidance rule to apply only to "the extent that the company has on hand undistributed income earned in the taxation period 1930 and subsequent periods."[31] Rather than pointing that out in his Budget speech, Finance Minister Charles Dunning portrayed the proposal as tightening only, meant to apply corporate tax to "undistributed income when such undistributed income is received by a corporation on the sale or winding up of another corporation."[32] What was left unsaid and its significance is troubling.

---

[30] *Emily Merritt, supra* note 21. *Minister of National Revenue v. Merritt* – SCC Cases (scc-csc.ca).

[31] SC, 1930, c. 24 (amending the *Income War Tax Act*, 1927), s. 4 replacing s. 19 with ss. 19(1) and (2). See ss. 19(1). Amended ss. 19(1) is like current ss. 84(2) of the *Income Tax Act*, 1985.

[32] *House of Commons Debates,* May 1, 1930, p. 1624. See Resolutions 1 and 6 at p. 1677.

The change to exempt pre-1930 surpluses from the anti-avoidance rule was both deceptive and significant in economic and tax policy terms. The deceptive aspect of the change is that the press and average citizens experiencing the first grips of the Great Depression would have noticed if King had announced a "tax holiday" on dividend taxation for some of Canada's wealthiest citizens just before the fall election of 1930. The economic and tax policy significance of the change is that it encouraged the winding-up and liquidation of successful Canadian corporations early in the Great Depression—just as it was starting to devastate the economic and social circumstances of millions of Canadians.

Yet, economists and historians appear to have struggled to understand why Canada's Great Depression was so severe in terms of a retraction in business investment despite the retreat in consumer spending being less intense. Historians Robert Bothwell, Ian Drummond and John English stated, "[the] behaviour of business investment is even more curious and mysterious," noting the decline in business investment was 79 percent between 1929 and 1933. They added that, as late as 1938, "new business investment spending was only 61 percent of what it had been in 1929."[33]

In comparison, they stated, personal consumption held up relatively well "both in the early 1930s and thereafter ... [and advanced after 1933] farther and faster than investment spending. . . . [It fell] only 18 percent between 1929 and 1933."[34] This spending appears to have been propped up by high-income individuals spending some of their tax-free distributions from their liquidated Canadian corporations. Consumer spending began to increase after 1933, and, by 1937, equalled 1929 levels.[35] This suggests consumer spending is insufficient to jump-start an economy in severe contraction; business reinvestment is the key ingredient for the recovery of an

[33] Robert Bothwell, Ian Drummond, and John English, *Canada 1900–1945* (Toronto: University of Toronto Press, 1987), pp. 250–52.

[34] *Ibid.*

[35] *Ibid.*

economy, and tax rates are but one factor in a complex number of variables that influence investment.

Strangely, it does not appear that King's exemption from tax for certain corporate distributions was subjected to significant public scrutiny. This may be explained by the deceptive aspects to the change. Nevertheless, if an economist or historian wanted an explanation for why the intensity of Canada's Great Depression may have been so severe in terms of reduced business investment, a good place to start is that 1930 change.

It is clear the change represented a significant windfall for some of Canada's wealthiest families. The Molson family of Montreal was one of the first beneficiaries of the change. Campbell Leach discussed the 1930 change in his 1976 book *Coopers & Lybrand in Canada*. Leach wrote about the tax-free distributions that could occur if a company was liquidated and stripped of its surplus.[36] Under the plan Leach discussed, a new company called Molson's Brewery Limited was incorporated. At the time, the accounting firm was called McDonald, Currie, and Hartland deM. Molson joined the firm as an accountant soon after the announcement of the change. He would go on to chair the firm, and Liberal Prime Minister Louis St. Laurent appointed Molson to the Senate in 1949.

Another group of businessmen who benefited from the change were the owners of distilleries who reaped large pre-1930 profits from shipping liquor during prohibition to the United States. Before the 1930 windfall change, the King government had upset those owners in March 1930 (effective July 1, 1930) by ending customs' clearances of liquor outbound from Canadian ports.[37]

---

[36] Campbell W. Leach, *Coopers & Lybrand in Canada: A Chronicle of the McDonald, Currie Years 1910–1973* (Coopers & Lybrand, 1976), pp. 25–26.

[37] Peter Newman, *Bronfman Dynasty* (Toronto: McClelland & Stewart, 1978), p. 111; and see pp. 108–09. In general terms, a shipper gave Customs a bond for twice the value of the cargo, which could not be recovered unless the shipper provided Customs a certificate of receipt of the cargo from a foreign Customs (the purpose of the Canadian bond was to ensure the liquor was not returned to Canada).

Without such clearance, the liquor could not be shipped legally from a Canadian port. The Americans had sought this change for years. It does not appear that the timing of the two changes—a tightening for customs clearances accompanied by an income tax windfall—was coincidental. *Quid pro quo* appears to have occurred.

The nature and timing of King's 1930 change is thus fascinating from several perspectives. It also followed the Customs scandal of 1926, which involved some members of the alcohol industry bribing officials within the Customs department with the knowledge, or tacit support, of members of the King government.

One might suspect that the Bronfman family of Montreal, which had made a fortune from the alcoholic distilled beverage business amid the U.S. years of prohibition, took advantage of the change. Why wouldn't it have done so, given the extent to which it could benefit? At the time, family members and their companies had been implicated in the Customs scandal.[38] Interestingly, the Molson

---

For U.S.-bound liquor, where no landing could be made legally, the certificates came from officials in various other countries, making it appear that is where the cargo was received. The officials were bribed for the certificates. The Canadian shipper used such certificates to get the bonds back from Canadian Customs once the liquor was turned over to Americans off the coast of the United States.

[38] Several Bronfman-controlled companies are discussed in the 1927 Royal Commission's investigation of distilleries and breweries. See the Commission's Interim Reports (No. 1 to 10) at PCO593(PAGES)-ENG (lac-bac.gc.ca). The non-compliance was so significant that the Royal Commission summarized it at pp. 51–52 and listed the various companies investigated with the findings elsewhere in the report. The non-compliance included failure to file tax returns under the *Business Profits War Tax Act*, 1916, and unreported income for income tax purposes from 1917 to 1920 with Henry Bronfman striking a special deal under which an arbitrary assessment on eight members of the family was made at a total amount of $200,000 (including interest on back taxes). The deal covered the 1921 year in advance without statutory authority. Also see Dave McIntosh, *The Collectors: A History of Canadian Customs and Excise* (Ottawa: NC Press Limited in association with Revenue Canada, Customs and Excise and the Canadian Government Publishing Centre, Supply and Services Canada, 1984), p. 277 (Chapter 5: The Customs Scandal of 1926, pp. 253–88). For the 1927 Royal Commission's general findings, see: PCO593(PAGES)-ENG (lac-bac.gc.ca).

family and its companies were not implicated in the scandal, and the brewery overpaid $26,410 in tax, which was refunded.[39]

The Customs scandal is appalling in every respect. Ex-Customs Minister Jacques Bureau was accused of destroying the contents of nine filing cabinets that contained documents of an incriminating nature. Opposition Conservative member Harry Stevens charged that, "the Prime Minister, the Minister of Justice, the Minister of Marine, the ex-Minister of Customs—this government … [knew] with abundance of proof, that the grossest violations of the customs laws were being perpetrated in this country."[40]

At the centre of the scandal was the extent to which distillers were involved in greasing the wheels, so to speak, when exporting their product during prohibition to the United States. Large profits were involved, and money talks—especially in politics.

A few additional historical facts are needed with respect to the Customs scandal before considering the Supreme Court's decision in *Emily Merritt.* First, historian Peter Waite described opposition Conservative member Richard B. Bennett as a "vital" member of the Parliamentary committee that investigated the Customs scandal in 1926, which gave him direct knowledge of several details.[41] Second, the subsequent Royal Commission exposed further details about the involvement of leading distillers of alcohol.[42]

Third, the Custom department was dismantled and moved inside the new Department of National Revenue. That included the Department of Finance's taxation division, which moved to Customs in 1924 (Finance had administered Canada's income tax system since

[39] *Ibid.* The Royal Commission did identify non-compliant excess deductions for income tax purposes, which were referred to National Revenue. The result of the investigation of Molson's is at p. 92.

[40] *House of Commons Debates*, February 2, 1926, p. 681.

[41] P.B. Waite, *In Search of R.B. Bennett* (Montreal-Kingston: McGill-Queen's University Press, 2012), pp. 27–28; and John Boyko, *Bennett: The Rebel Who Challenged and Changed a Nation* (Toronto: Key Porter Books, 2010), pp. 137–45.

[42] The Bronfman brothers co-opted officials at Custom's Regina office—for example, see McIntosh, *The Collectors, supra* note 38, p. 273.

late 1917). Robert Breadner, who had been a leading tax official at Finance (the former Commissioner of Taxation, Finance), became the Commissioner of Customs at the new Department of National Revenue.[43] Non-customs' officials led the new department forward.

Fourth, Kerwin had been, as mentioned, the law partner of Hugh Guthrie. In 1927, R.B. Bennett defeated Guthrie in the pursuit of the leadership of the national Conservative Party. When forming his incoming 1930 majority government, Bennett appointed Guthrie the Minister of Justice and the Attorney General of Canada.

Finally, as prime minister, Bennett at some point learned about King's 1930 pre-election gift. His 1934 Budget ended the relief for distributions received out of pre-1930 corporate surpluses.[44] Bennett made few friends for doing so, including those who were contributing significant funds to political parties.

It is time to consider *Emily Merritt* with the above context in mind, but there will be one more diversion into historical facts after establishing the first issue considered at trial.

Emily Merritt of Ontario owned 259 shares of the capital stock of The Security Loan and Savings Company. In 1937, Security Loan agreed to sell its business assets to The Premier Trust Company. The wrinkle was that Security Loan directed Premier Trust to pay the purchase price to the shareholders of Security Loan who received cash as well as Premier Trust shares in their proportionate Security Loan share interest.

On the disposition of her 259 shares of Security Loan, Merritt received $25,690 in cash plus 130 shares of Premier Trust, on which she (and presumably the other shareholders) did not pay a deemed-dividend tax. But the deemed dividend anti-avoidance rule applied to a distribution of Security Loan's undistributed after-tax earnings *in any form* on a winding-up, discontinuance or reorganization of a corporate business. Security Loan had undistributed

[43] Bryce, *Maturing in Hard Times, supra* note 8; see Bryce's note 45 (p. 241) for Breadner becoming Commissioner.

[44] SC, 1934, c. 55 (amending the *Income War Tax Act*, 1927), s. 10.

after-tax earnings that arose before 1935, which in the case of Merritt represented a $10,192 share interest.

President Maclean of the Exchequer Court applied a commercial substance approach when interpreting the words in the deemed-dividend rule.[45] He gave the rule a broad application and found that a commercial rather than legal meaning applied to each word in the phrase "winding-up, discontinuance or reorganization." MacLean held that what occurred was within the "meaning and spirit" of the terminology. A discontinuation of Security Loan's business resulted in "a real and commercial sense." It was immaterial whether this occurred by sale, amalgamation, or another manner.

The anti-avoidance rule was also applied despite the fact Premier Trust made the distribution for Security Loan. This result was the same tax-wise as it would have been if Security Loan received the sale proceeds from Premier Loan and had distributed the net-after-tax amount as a dividend to its shareholders such as Merritt. But this did not end the dispute.

At this point, a diversion to another obscure relevant aspect of Canada's fiscal history may assist. Alexander Kenneth (A.K.) Maclean had been a leading Liberal member of the House of Commons throughout most of the first two decades of the 20th century. He and Conservative PM Sir Robert Borden were the elected members for Halifax.

Until late 1917, Maclean was the Liberal opposition's finance critic. A progressive Liberal, he had been pounding away on the floor of the House of Commons for years about Finance Minister Sir Thomas White's failure to table a bill legislating a federal income tax as the slaughter of the First World War continued without any sign of an end in the trenches of western Europe. Borden, desperate for fresh troops, struck a deal in mid-1917 in which his fellow lawyer and Haligonian (via Cape Breton) participated.

---

[45] *Merritt*, *supra* note 21, Ex. CR p. 182. The Exchequer Court decision is at *Emily L. Merritt v. Minister of National Revenue* – Office of the Commissioner for Federal Judicial Affairs Canada (fja-cmf.gc.ca).

Borden agreed in the late spring of 1917 that his Conservative members would pass an income tax bill on the condition that one hundred thousand men be conscripted into service for duty at the front. That would bring the total members of Canada's armed forces up to five hundred thousand out of a total male population of about four million. It is almost unfathomable more than a century later.

Once the *Income War Tax Act* was proclaimed into law in the early fall of 1917, Maclean and several other leading Liberals, including Hugh Guthrie, crossed the floor of the House of Commons and joined Borden's Union government for the fall election in support of conscription. That election divided English and French Canada like no disagreement had before. The Unionists won a massive majority government (153–82 seats), which included 113 Conservative-Unionists and 39 Liberal-Unionists.[46] The Liberals won only 20 seats outside Quebec. The nation was divided; necessity can cause wounds, which are still playing out in one way or another more than a century later.

Maclean was the incoming Union government's acting Minister of Finance. Minister (without portfolio) A.K. Maclean tabled the Union government's 1918 Budget—not Finance Minister Sir Thomas White.[47] Maclean's 1918 Budget advanced a progressive agenda.

[46] Bob Plamondon, *Blue Thunder: The Truth about Conservatives from MacDonald to Harper* (Toronto: Key Porter Books, 2009), p. 126. Note: An Independent Unionist was elected in Manitoba.

[47] The historical record indicates that Sir Thomas White's health had deteriorated from the sustained workload he confronted day after day during the War as Minister of Finance and as acting prime minister when Borden travelled to London to attend meetings of the Imperial War Cabinet. He went to California to recover. See Sir Thomas White, *The Story of Canada's War Finance* (Montreal: Bank of Commerce, 1921), p. 67. Nevertheless, Maclean's acting as Minister of Finance was politically convenient for Conservative-Unionists and Liberal-Unionists, as it was MacLean's 1918 Budget that enhanced the progressivity of the income tax system in ways (see next note) that had been rejected by White and Borden in 1917. It is not unreasonable to suggest that the move to progressivity was part of the bargain that brought several Liberals into PM Borden's

It led to the enactment of measures that had been advanced by the Liberal opposition, including Maclean, as the debate on the parameters of the income tax bill raged in the House of Commons and Senate throughout the summer of 1917.[48]

Unlike some Liberals who joined the Union government, Maclean returned to the Liberal fold after the war ended. Haligonians returned him to Ottawa as a Liberal in the 1921 election. Mackenzie King's Liberals won minority government status when propped up by Thomas Crerar's Progressives, whose seat count stormed past Arthur Meighen's Conservatives.

In 1923, Mackenzie King appointed Maclean the President of the Exchequer Court. The appointment may relate to King's failure to include MacLean in his cabinet. While Maclean had returned to the Liberal fold in 1920, he had also left it in 1917. Worse, the Liberal-Unionist Maclean and his supporters in Nova Scotia backed

---

Union Government. If so, it makes political sense that it would be Maclean, not White, who tabled the 1918 Budget. Also, around the time the Budget was being finalized and delivered, White left California for Washington where he met with U.S. Treasury officials to discuss double tax issues arising because Canada and the U.S. were in some cases taxing the same corporate income. At the time, Canada did not have the constitutional authority to enter an international income tax treaty. Instead, Canada and the U.S. reached a side arrangement to address the concern.

[48] *House of Commons Debates*, April 30, 1918, pp. 1253–65 (The 1918 Budget Speech of the Acting Minister of Finance, A.K. Maclean). The changes to the personal income tax system included the following: (1) the personal exemption for a single person without dependents was reduced to $1,000 from $1,500, and for a married person and a person with dependents to $2,000 from $3,000; and (2) enhanced the supertax schedule to 12 rates from 6, applicable to income above $6,000. The top supertax rate shot up to 50 percent of income from 25 percent. The previous top marginal rate of 25 percent applied to income above $100,000. The 6 new supertax rates applied to income above $200,000, with a 30 percent supertax applying to income exceeding $200,000 but not exceeding $400,000 and ending with a top supertax rate of 50 percent on annual income in excess of $1 million. Supertaxes applied in addition to the normal tax rate of 4 percent subject to a lower 2 percent normal tax on the amount of income made taxable because of the reduction of the personal exemption. On Maclean's recommendation, Parliament also increased the corporate tax rate to 6 percent from 4 percent.

King's main rival, William Fielding, in the 1919 Liberal leadership race to replace former Prime Minister Sir Wilfrid Laurier. Maclean had been Fielding's Attorney General in an earlier provincial government, and, as the former Liberal Premier of Nova Scotia and King's Minister of Finance, Fielding may have felt he owed his colleague Maclean for his past support and may have advocated that King make the appointment.

President Maclean presided over the Exchequer Court until his death in late July 1942, three months after the Supreme Court issued its decision in *Emily Merritt*. Over those 20 years, "MacLean sat sixty-seven times as an ad hoc judge of the Supreme Court"; Professor Ian Bushnell wrote of Maclean that his "abilities as a judge would make him one of the greatest ever to sit on a Canadian bench."[49]

Maclean had also been Guthrie's Liberal colleague until they crossed the floor of the House of Commons; Guthrie never returned to the Liberals. These underlying interconnections in *Emily Merritt* are subtly woven into the context surrounding the case.

The difficulty for Maclean in *Emily Merritt* was that the newly elected King government caused Parliament in 1936 to again amend the anti-avoidance rule. The revised rule continued to apply "to the extent that the company has on hand undistributed income." Other changes were made; to do so, the rule was repealed and then re-enacted in its revised form. The application clause (coming into force) of the re-enacted rule appeared to provide that it no longer applied to corporate income earned before 1935. The clause states:

> [By *Statutes of Canada*, 1936, c. 38, s. 22, it was enacted that:] Sections . . . eleven . . . *shall be applicable to the income of the year 1935 and fiscal periods ending therein and of all subsequent periods* [emphasis added].

[49] Ian Bushnell, *The Federal Court of Canada: A History, 1875–1992* (Toronto: Published for the Osgoode Society for Canadian Legal History by the University of Toronto Press, 1997), pp. 105 (greatest judge) and 109 (Supreme Court cases).

This wording opened a Pandora's Box. It suggested the 1935 King government reinstated (up to the end of 1934) the 1930 relieving amendment, which the Bennett government had repealed in 1934.

The legislative drafting of the 1936 amendment is deceptive in the extreme. Unlike in 1930, it failed to provide any exemption for pre-1935 surplus directly in the anti-avoidance rule. If that were done, it would be obvious to anyone paying attention. Rather, the apparent on-going relief was stuffed into an application clause, which few people would notice unless looking for it or by magically stumbling onto it.

What was the Mackenzie King government up to in the middle of the Great Depression, re-enacting, by a hidden laneway, a back-door tax exemption that encouraged corporate winding-ups, dissolutions and reorganizations of businesses? Was it rewarding its election donors, like it had for pre-1930 corporate surpluses in the lead-up to the 1930 election? That certainly appears to be the case. One can only marvel in disbelief.

The interpretive issue was apparent. Did the clause's reference to "the income of the year 1935 and fiscal periods ending therein and of all subsequent periods" refer to *corporate income* being earned (if so, corporate income earned before 1935 was not subject to the anti-avoidance rule)? Alternatively, was the income being referred to *shareholder income* received in 1935 or subsequent periods (and if so, surely the deemed-dividend rule applied to Merritt's receipt)?

Maclean held that the income referred to in the application clause was pre-1935 corporate income and *not* shareholder income. That is a reasonable interpretation of the text in issue. He allowed Merritt's appeal. The Crown appealed.

In his majority decision, Justice Kerwin affirmed Maclean's broad interpretation of the anti-avoidance rule. It is a commercial substance over legal form rule that applies to distributions in any form whatever to shareholders on a winding-up, discontinuance, or reorganization of a business.

Kerwin then focused on the application clause. He noted that Maclean had reached his decision based on reading the legislative history of the provision in issue. Kerwin did the same but without the detailed analysis Maclean undertook. Instead, Kerwin simply disagreed with the suggestion that the reference to income in the application clause was a reference to corporate undistributed income. While his approach might imply that the application clause referred to a shareholder receiving a corporate distribution of pre-1935 surplus after 1934, he did not say that was the case. Rather, after noting early in his opinion that the rule applied in general terms to the type of distribution under consideration, Kerwin stated only that "no question could really be raised as to the liability of the respondent [Merritt] to be taxed on such amount."

The legislative text as amended unfolded over less than three pages of the decision. Kerwin did not mention if the King or Bennett government enacted the amendments. He cited the legislative history as if he were leaving it to hang in the air for all to see and smell.

Kerwin concluded his decision by doing two things. First, he noted the obvious about the dry arcane prose: "The 1934 amendment removed from subsection 1 of section 19 the words at the end thereof that had been included for the first and only time in 1930, 'earned in the taxation period 1930 and subsequent period.' Then, in 1936, came sections 11 and 22 of chapter 38, which have already been transcribed."

Second, Kerwin suggested that this legislative history established that "the proper conclusion to be drawn from the fact that the words 'earned in the taxation period 1930 and subsequent periods' were dropped in 1934 is that Parliament intended to alter the law as it existed under the 1930 legislation. . . . . It appears to me to be not only in accord with the letter but also the spirit of that Act." The Crown's appeal was allowed.

Justice Kerwin had just applied the spirit of the 1934 law as enacted by the Bennett government and read down the text of the

King government's 1936 application clause. The income referred to was post-1934 shareholder income and not the corporation's pre-1935 income. The result was the 1936 changes did not exempt corporate earnings earned before 1935 from deemed-dividend treatment.[50] When doing so, Kerwin did not cite nor discuss the *Duke of Westminster* principle, which does not give weight to the law's spirit. (Justices Thibaudeau Rinfret, Albert Hudson and Robert Taschereau concurred; Justice Cornelius A. Masten *(ad hoc)* dissented.)

There is something else that is significant about Kerwin's majority decision in *Emily Merritt.* His (and Maclean's) commercial substance approach is similar to that of the United States Supreme Court in its seminal 1935 business substance over form decision in *Gregory*.[51] It took the opposite approach to that taken by the House Lords in its seminal 1935 *Duke of Westminster* decision, which emphasizes the legal form of a transaction and applied the strict approach to interpreting statutory tax law.[52] *Merritt* equates to *Gregory* and not to the *Duke* on the commercial substance versus legal form issue.

The *Gregory* decision was decided a few months before the *Duke of Westminster* decision. The U.S. Supreme Court found that the transaction had "no business or corporate purpose—[it was] a mere device which put on the form of a corporate reorganization as a disguise for concealing its real character, and the sole object and accomplishment of which was the consummation of a preconceived plan, not to reorganize a business or any part of a business, but to transfer a parcel of corporate shares to the petitioner."[53]

---

[50] *Merritt, supra* note 21, SCC pp. 278–79.

[51] *Evelyn F. Gregory v. Helvering (Commissioner of Inland Revenue)*, 293 US 465 (1935). For an article that contextualizes the decisions in *Gregory* and the *Duke of Westminster*, see Assaf Likhovski, "The Duke and the Lady: Helvering v Gregory and the History of Tax Avoidance Adjudication," (2004), 25:3 *Cardoza Law Review* 953–1018.

[52] *Duke of Westminster, supra* note 2.

[53] *Gregory, supra* note 51, p. 469.

There is also an important factual distinction between *Gregory* and *Merritt* that is revealing of Kerwin's approach. Gregory, a Brooklyn socialite, controlled both the corporation that transferred the shares and the corporation that acquired the shares, which were distributed to her under a U.S. tax-deferred corporate reorganization rule. In comparison, there is no suggestion that Merritt controlled the two corporations.

While the U.S. Supreme Court had discerned a broad business purpose over form rule, Kerwin was more restrained. Like Maclean, he took a commercial substance over legal form approach when interpreting an anti-avoidance rule as compared to a general rule.

Kerwin dissented in the next decision, which overturned the Minister's exercise of discretion to deny a deduction. The Crown appealed, and the Privy Council's decision would be precedent-setting in terms of the parameters of when the judiciary can intervene where a Minister exercises discretion under the statutory law of the United Kingdom and its then-Dominions.

Wrights' Canadian Ropes (1946)

In 1946, Kerwin was the only justice to dissent in the Supreme Court's reversal for the taxpayer in *Wrights' Canadian Ropes.*[54] It was a transfer pricing dispute in which the taxpayer, Wrights' Canadian Ropes, made payments in 1940, 1941 and 1942 to the English company Wrights' Ropes, which reduced the taxpayer's taxable income.

If a person or a group of persons controlled a Canadian company, subs. 6(1) of the *Income War Tax Act* (and s. 8 of the *Excess Profits Tax Act*) allowed the deduction of a payment made to a person outside Canada for management fees, services or the use of

[54] *MNR v. Wrights' Canadian Ropes Limited*, [1946] SCR 139, allowing the taxpayer's appeal; the Privy Council dismissed the Crown's appeal (and varied the Order) at (1946), [1941–1946] 2 DTC 927, [1947] CTC 1, [1947] AC 109. *Wrights' Canadian Ropes Limited v. The Minister of National Revenue* – SCC Cases (scc-csc.ca). Note: in Canada, the decision has been overtaken in the *Charter* era by Supreme Court precedent on the judicial review of the exercise of Ministerial discretion.

intellectual property only to the extent the Minister was satisfied the payments were "reasonable for services actually rendered." Subsection 6(2) also granted the Minister the discretion to disallow a taxpayer's deduction of an "expense" that was in excess of what was "reasonable and normal for the business." Subsection 6(3) made the Minister's exercise of discretion "final and conclusive."

Nevertheless, it was unclear whether subs. 6(1) and (2) were independent provisions or whether the Minister could exercise his discretion under subs. 6(2) only if subs. 6(1) applied. In other words, if the discretion in subs. 6(2) was independent of the discretion in subs. 6(1), it did not matter who controlled the Canadian company when applying subs. 6(2). This distinction was important because the foreign Wrights' Ropes did not appear to control Wrights' Canadian Ropes; Wrights' Ropes owned 478 shares of 1,500 shares (49.86 percent), another English company owned 479 shares (49.93 percent) and three individuals in Canada owned one share each. The evidentiary record did not establish on what basis the three individuals owned their shares, although one was the taxpayer's lawyer.

The Minister initially proposed to apply subs. 6(1) on the assumption Wrights' Ropes controlled Wrights' Canadian Ropes, thereby limiting the deduction of the cross-border payments to $7,500 a year. But the taxpayer advised that it was not controlled by Wrights' Ropes; the Minister then exercised his discretion under subs. 6(2) to limit the deduction to $7,500 a year as an amount that was "reasonable and normal for the business." No reasons were provided for exercising this discretion. The taxpayer appealed.

The Minister was successful at trial, with the Exchequer Court holding that, based on the facts, the Minister duly exercised his discretion under subs. 6(2). The taxpayer appealed on the basis subs. 6(2) did not apply unless subs. 6(1) applied, which it argued was not the case.

Chief Justice Thibaudeau Rinfret held that subs. 6(2) did not apply unless subs. 6(1) applied, and this was not the case because the record failed to establish that Wrights' Ropes controlled Wrights' Canadian Ropes. Rinfret could not understand why there was doubt about the control issue, since the Minister agreed Wrights' Ropes owned 49.86 percent of the taxpayer's shares. He also found that subs. 6(2) did not apply because the amounts deducted were not "expenses" described in subs. 6(2).

Justice Kerwin, in dissent, held that the record did not establish that Wrights' Canadian Ropes was not controlled by Wrights' Ropes and that subs. 6(1) could apply to limit the deductions. Kerwin's use of the double negative is important because its nuance suggests that the taxpayer had failed to prove it was not controlled by Wrights' Ropes or a group of persons that included Wrights' Ropes. Further, he held that, while the Minister's exercise of discretion under subs. 6(2) may have been a quasi-judicial decision, the Minister had given the taxpayer every opportunity to explain its position, and nothing in the record indicated the Minister exercised his discretion improperly.

Kerwin also described the steps the Minister took to provide the taxpayer with opportunities to respond with written representations to the proposed reassessments, which it failed to do other than to provide the agreement to pay the commissions and to advise that it was not controlled by Wrights' Ropes. This left open the possibility that the taxpayer was controlled by a group of persons that included Wrights' Ropes. For Kerwin, the onus was on the taxpayer to respond to the proposed reassessments with reasons why they were incorrect, and, in the absence of doing so, the Minister did not have to provide further reasons. Subsection 6(3) provided the exercise of Ministerial discretion was "final and conclusive."

The three remaining justices split from the reasoning of the Chief Justice and Kerwin. They agreed subs. 6(1) did not apply but found that subs. 6(2) could apply despite subs. 6(1) not applying. In three separate opinions, Justices Hudson, Kellock and Estey found that the Minister could exercise his discretion in subs. 6(2) to limit the deductions, but only if done based on sound legal principles, as required under the Privy Council's 1939 decision in *Pioneer Laundry*. The Minister had failed to explain why the deductions exceeded an amount "reasonable and normal for the business" in each year.

This did not reflect sound legal principles, and the majority allowed the taxpayer's appeal and sent the matter back to the Minister to be "dealt with by him in accordance with the reasons of the majority." The Minister appealed.

Although the Privy Council agreed that the Minister could exercise his discretion to deny the deductions under subs. 6(2) despite subs. 6(1) not applying, it took issue with the lack of facts to support the exercise of discretion and the statutory rule that the Supreme Court had relied on to refer the matter back to the Minister. For the Council, it was conclusive to the issue of whether Wrights' Ropes controlled the taxpayer, as contemplated by subs. 6(1), that the Minister agreed Wrights' Ropes owned only 49.86 percent of the taxpayer's shares. The Council did not comment on the lack of evidence on the status of the three shares held by individuals who might have, along with Wrights' Ropes, formed a group of persons in control of Wrights' Canadian Ropes. It also found that subs. 6(2) could be applied to the payments made because they were expenses, in general terms.

The Privy Council devoted considerable time to analyzing the parameters of the meaning of "in his discretion," and it would be this analysis that made its decision precedent-setting in terms of the legal boundaries of the exercise of ministerial discretion. The terminology made the Minister the "judge" of what is "reasonable" in the circumstances. The Council held that Parliament must have intended that a taxpayer had a right of appeal despite subs. 6(3) providing that the ministerial exercise of discretion was "final and conclusive." While the judiciary is not bound to accept this exercise of discretion, its judicial discretion is "strictly circumscribed."

The onus was on the taxpayer to establish the ground for interfering with the Minister's exercise of discretion, which is not subject to judicial interference unless the Minister had contravened a sound principle of law. The Minister remained the sole judge of what is reasonable and, if it is reasonable under sound legal principles, it was not for the judiciary to substitute its own decision on what is reasonable. But the Minister could not act in an arbitrary manner.

Citing Justice Davis' dissent in the Supreme Court's 1938 decision in *Pioneer Laundry*, the Council held that the judiciary could intervene only if the Minister's exercise of discretion was "manifestly against sound and fundamental principles."

But unlike in *Pioneer Laundry*, the taxpayer's attack against the reassessments was that the Minister failed to provide reasons. On this, the Council held that there was nothing in subs. 6(2) that required the Minister to provide reasons but that this did not mean the Minister could remain silent. The taxpayer should have been provided the facts before the Minister when he made his decision. If the facts are insufficient in law to make the decision, it cannot be upheld. But if they are sufficient in law to support the decision, the judiciary cannot intervene to reverse or change the decision.

In the case, the Council held that the facts in the record, which consisted of the documents, were insufficient in law to support the Minister's decision. The commission contract was *bona fide*, and it should not be presumed the commissions were other than reasonable. While there may have been facts in the Vancouver Inspector's Report that supported the reassessments that had not been provided to the taxpayer, that report was not before the judiciary and could not be relied on.

The Privy Council also found that the Supreme Court should not have ordered the matter be returned to the Minister as that meant he could re-exercise his discretion. Instead, it should have exercised its inherent judicial discretion to end the dispute. The Minister had failed in a dispute duly litigated successfully by the taxpayer, and the deductions should therefore be allowed. Otherwise, the Minister would have a second opportunity to determine the matter in an unfavourable manner against the taxpayer under subs. 6(2) thus denying the "fruits of their victory." Canada's loss of tax revenues was the United Kingdom's gain.

Despite the Privy Council's decision in *Wrights' Canadian Ropes*, Justice Kerwin and his decision in *Pioneer Laundry* not to apply British tax avoidance precedent would be vindicated in an important way on October 13, 1948. On that day, the Council affirmed the Supreme Court's 1947 decision in *Fraser D.R. & Co.* When doing so, it distinguished its 1939 decision to reverse the Court's decision in *Pioneer Laundry*. The Privy Council's days overseeing the Supreme Court were ending, and Kerwin was about to be free of British oversight in tax avoidance cases.

Fraser D.R. & Co. (1947)

Fraser D.R. & Co. Limited of Alberta claimed allowances in respect of timber limits in its fiscal 1941–42 taxation year, despite the fact that it had been allowed to deduct the amount it paid to acquire the limits. It maintained that, since it had a licence to cut the timber, it could deplete the value of the timber resource on Crown land at a rate of $1.40 per 1,000 board feet cut. This took a lot of nerve. The Minister exercised his discretion to allow only such amount as he deemed "just and fair," which was nothing. Fraser had no undeducted costs in respect of the limits.

Justice Kerwin noted in *Fraser D.R. & Co.* that Parliament legislated in 1940 against the Privy Council's 1939 decision in *Pioneer Laundry* putting in question the Council's earlier decision. Kerwin also distinguished the Council's decision in *Wrights' Canadian Ropes* on the basis there was nothing in its reasons that "is of assistance in determining the present appeal."[55] This language harkened back to his decision in *Pioneer Laundry* when he distinguished the British precedent on the basis the decisions "do not appear to assist in the determination of the matter."

Kerwin found that the depletion rule rather than the depreciation rule was in issue and that it too had been amended in 1940.[56]

[55] *Fraser D.R. & Co., supra* note 22, SCC p. 160. *Fraser D.R. & Co. v. Minister of National Revenue* – SCC Cases (scc-csc.ca).

[56] In general terms, under the *Income War Tax Act*, depletion referred to capital allowances calculated based on the proportion of a finite natural resource such as the amount of timber a taxpayer harvested from a timber tenure, while depreciation referred to the physical wear on capital assets such as a taxpayer's buildings, machinery and equipment. The Minister of National Revenue had the discretion to limit taxpayer claims for depletion and depreciation.

Why Kerwin noted this is unclear, but it could have been to emphasize that Parliament responded to the Privy Council's 1939 decision in *Pioneer Laundry* by amending *both* rules to broaden the Minister's discretion. He dismissed the taxpayer's appeal on the basis that the Minister had the discretion to limit the amount claimed and could decide that no amount was allowable. (Justice Taschereau concurred.)

Justice James Estey noted that Parliament's amendments in 1940 ensured that the Minister "now has discretion to make or refuse an allowance."[57] The Minister's amended pleadings indicated that the allowance was denied because the taxpayer had already deducted its entire costs for the timber limits. Estey dismissed the taxpayer's appeal on the basis the Minister had not violated any fundamental principles in exercising his discretion.

Justice Ivan Rand side stepped the controversy by ignoring that there had been an amendment. He dismissed the taxpayer's appeal on the basis the Minister had the discretion to limit the claim. (Four judges decided the case.)

On appeal, the Privy Council took the high road. It noted that Parliament had amended the statutory law in dispute immediately after the Council's 1939 decision: "When an amending Act alters the language of the principal Statute, the alteration must be taken to have been made deliberately." The Council also found that Parliament has the power "to obviate judicial decisions which the Department considers to be attended with undesirable results."[58] It held that the Minister had the discretion under Canada's then–statutory income tax law to disallow the allowance. This is what Kerwin held 10 years earlier in his swing opinion in *Pioneer Laundry*.

The next decision concerns the tax treatment of gains realized from disposing of derivative contracts.

---

[57] *Ibid.*, SCC p. 169.

[58] *Ibid.*, JCPC at [1949–1950] DTC p. 524.

Atlantic Sugar Refineries (1947)
With the British declaration of war against Nazi Germany on September 3, 1939, Canadian sugar refineries experienced a significant surge in public demand for sugar, surpassing normal levels. The Canadian government asked sugar refineries to purchase more sugar as the government was about to implement wide-ranging controls in respect of the economy. Atlantic Sugar Refineries of Saint John purchased 15,515 tons of sugar in total on September 7, 8 and 9, 1939. The price was well in excess of the price in prewar conditions.[59] Canada declared war the next day, on September 10, 1939.

Atlantic Sugar Refineries decided to speculate in sugar on the New York Coffee and Sugar Exchange. It sold 3,500 tons of sugar short between September 11, 1939, and October 9, 1939. Atlantic Sugar Refineries closed its short sales, realizing gains; additional transactions were not possible due to government controls. The tax issue was whether the gains were taxable business income or tax-exempt capital gains.

Justice Kerwin, for the majority, found that the taxpayer's intent when executing the short sales was to "offset losses, either actual or feared … [and the president and therefore the company's] intention … [was] to secure a profit."[60] He thus connected the short sales to the intent of the company's president and its business income source. After doing so, Kerwin held that the gains were business profits, based on applying Canadian and British decisions after acknowledging the short sales were isolated transactions. (Chief Justice Rinfret and Justice Taschereau concurred.)

Justice Charles Locke reached the same result with similar reasons. He provided additional facts and context. Locke discussed hedging operations, which he indicated the taxpayer engaged in

---

[59] *Atlantic Sugar Refineries Limited v. MNR*, [1949] SCR 706. *Atlantic Sugar Refineries v. Minister of National Revenue* – SCC Cases (scc-csc.ca).
[60] *Ibid.*, p. 707.

(it owned sugar) despite its president's testimony that the short sales were not intended as hedges. He also indicated that any resulting loss for a sugar refinery from shorting sugar would have been business losses. As such, the resulting gains were business income without the need to cite precedent. (Justice Roy Kellock concurred.)

Although Chief Justice Kerwin had an economy to his opinions, he spoke on occasion in public about the law in general and the Supreme Court's approach to income tax. In September 1955, Kerwin spoke at Harvard University. He returned to the subject matter of his speech at Lansing 15 years earlier. The occasion was Harvard's celebration of the 200th anniversary of the birth of its graduate John Marshall, Chief Justice of the United States Supreme Court.

Kerwin stated that Marshall's "famous dictum [that the 'power to tax involves the power to destroy'] … was capped by Mr. Justice Holmes' epogram [*sic*] … 'not … so long as this Court sits.'"[61] He thus confirmed his rejection of Marshall's aversion to tax and aligned himself with Oliver Wendell Holmes.

Chief Justice Kerwin also indicated at Harvard that the Supreme Court of Canada (1) held in 1908 that the provincial power to tax income delegated to the City of Saint John extended to taxing the salaries of local federal officials, (2) held in 1922 that the federal power to tax income applied to taxing the remunerations paid to provincial cabinet ministers, and (3) held in 1936 that the provincial power to tax income applied to the pay of the active militia and federal civil servants. He added that the federal and provincial powers to tax income apply to amounts paid to judges. Kerwin stated, "Neither the independence, nor any other attribute of the

[61] McKenna, *Grace and Wisdom, supra* note 14, pp. 299–301. The 1927 case is *Pan Handle Oil Company v. Mississippi*, 277 US 218 (1927). The U.S. Supreme Court split 5–4, with the majority holding that Mississippi's sales tax on dealer sales of gasoline was *void* with respect to sales to the United States. Mississippi could not collect the taxes from dealers whose right to sell to a constitutionally independent federal government would be breached. Holmes J. led those in dissent.

judiciary could be affected by a general income tax which charged their official income on the same footing as any other citizens."[62]

By the late 1950s, Kerwin was not well. Three of his final decisions are considered here. They are precedent-setting decisions under Canada's modernized *Income Tax Act* (ITA), 1948, and the consolidated 1952 ITA. The first decision dates to January 1958 before Kerwin took a six-month leave to recover from his illness.

Ronald McIntosh (1958)

Ronald McIntosh sold his grocery store in 1948 and decided with an associate to buy vacant land in Sarnia and to subdivide it into lots on which to build houses for sale. He and his associate had a falling out; McIntosh sold some of his lots at a profit.

The Minister taxed the gains on the basis they were business income from an adventure in the nature of trade. So-called *adventure* income tax disputes date in the United Kingdom to the early 19th century and the enactment of a national income tax to pay for the Napoleonic wars. In Canada, adventure activity is expressly included in the meaning of a business in the ITA.

McIntosh argued his gains were not from an adventure in the nature of trade, that his differences with the associate meant the land was an investment, and the gains were tax-exempt capital gains. This argument found no traction in the lower courts and no sympathy in the Supreme Court.

---

[62] *Ibid.* At Harvard, Kerwin C.J. cited the following cases: (1) United States Supreme Court, *McCulloch v. Maryland*, (1819) 4 Wheaton 316, p. 431; *Pan Handle Oil, ibid.*, p. 233; (2) Supreme Court of Canada, *Abbott v. Saint John*, (1908) 40 SCR 597; *Caron v. The King*, (1922), 64 SCR 255 (affirmed by the Privy Council at [1917–1927] CTC 117, [1924] AC 999); and *Worthington et al. v. A. G. of Manitoba*, [1936] SCR 40 (affirmed by the Privy Council at [1935–37] CTC 237 and [1937] AC 260). Kerwin also cited the Privy Council's decision in *Judges v. A.G. of Saskatchewan*, (1937), [1935–37] CTC 277 (which appeal bypassed the Supreme Court). *Abbott v. City of Saint John* – SCC Cases (scc-csc.ca); *Caron v. The King* – SCC Cases (scc-csc.ca); *Forbes v. The Attorney General of Manitoba / Worthington v. The Attorney General of Manitoba* – SCC Cases (scc-csc.ca).

In less than two pages, Chief Justice Kerwin managed to set down two important principles in the context of deciding Canadian adventure disputes. First, while an individual cannot be presumed to carry on a business, as is the case with a corporation, an individual can carry on a business, in which case the profits are taxable. The issue in an adventure dispute involving an individual fixes upon whether the individual invests money and only occasionally sells an investment or does more. An isolated sale can result in taxable profits, relying on British precedent.

Second, it is "impossible to lay down a test that will meet the multifarious circumstances that may arise in all fields of human endeavour" when deciding adventure disputes.[63] It all depends on the facts. Kerwin referred readers to three decisions of the Supreme Court, only two of which are published decisions. They are the Court's 1952 decision in *Thomas Campbell,*[64] and its 1953 decision in *Edith Noak.*[65] The surprise citation is the Court's decision in *Byron B. Kennedy.*[66] It comes at a reader out of the blue. Who knew an unreported decision of the Supreme Court would be cited and relied on?

Byron Kennedy was described as a "speculative builder of high-class residences" for a period of about 22 years. In the posh Forest Hill district in Toronto, he built numerous grand homes. In 2017, one mansion in Forest Hill sold for $15 million.

Kennedy's tax case concerned the Ontario government's expropriation of 16 of his lots to build a highway north of Forest Hills.

---

[63] *Ronald Gordon McIntosh v. MNR*, [1958] SCR 119, p. 121. *McIntosh v. Minister of National Revenue* – SCC Cases (scc-csc.ca).

[64] *Thomas Campbell v. MNR*, (1952), [1953] 1 SCR. 3. *Campbell v. Minister of National Revenue* – SCC Cases (scc-csc.ca).

[65] *Judith Noak v. MNR*, [1953] 2 SCR 136. *Noak v. Minister of National Revenue* – SCC Cases (scc-csc.ca).

[66] *Byron B. Kennedy v. MNR*, [1953] SCR viii; [1952] Ex. CR 258. The judges who dismissed the appeal are identified in the Supreme Court's file 7881. The Exchequer Court decision is at *Kennedy v. Minister of National Revenue* – Office of the Commissioner for Federal Judicial Affairs Canada (fja-cmf.gc.ca).

Kennedy failed to report the $12,117 received as income in 1948. While Kennedy's accounting records were in disarray, the Minister's auditors located the receipts and reassessed Kennedy. He appealed unsuccessfully all the way to the Supreme Court. *Byron B. Kennedy* is an oral decision from the bench by Justices Kerwin, Kellock, Locke, Cartwright and Fauteux, dismissing Kennedy's appeal from the Exchequer Court's 1952 decision.

The Supreme Court began by the late 1950s to exercise its judicial discretion to distinguish between individual owner-level personal expenses and commercial outlays incurred when carrying on a business. Kerwin articulated in the next decision from 1959 the existence of a judicial discretion in such cases when applying the "for the purpose of gaining or producing income" deductibility test.

William Bannerman (1959)

The dispute in *Bannerman* concerns the deductibility of certain legal, travel and telephone expenses that William Bannerman of Toronto incurred in the context of a nasty dispute with another shareholder over the winding-up of a company.[67] Bannerman and his nominees owned 50 percent of the capital stock of Concrete Column Clamps Limited. He also rented assets to Concrete Clamps, which stopped paying the rent once the dispute erupted.

Dominico of Vocisano of Montreal managed Concrete Clamps and was the other 50 percent shareholder. As president, Vocisano held the casting vote in the case of a tie in shareholder votes.[68] Concrete Clamps supplied the Montreal construction market with patented concrete clamps, which it rented to contractors, and it earned over $1.5 million in annual revenue by 1951.

---

[67] *William Bannerman v. MNR*, [1959] SCR 562, dismissing the taxpayer's appeal from [1957] Ex. CR 367. *Bannerman v. Minister of National Revenue* – SCC Cases (scc-csc.ca). The Exchequer Court decision is at https://reports.fja-cmf.gc.ca/fja-cmf/j/en/item/397582/index.do?q=Bannerman.

[68] *Re Concrete Column Clamps Ltd. and Bannerman et al.*, [1953] 4 DLR 60 (Que. Sup. Ct), p. 61.

The *Bannerman* case arose in the aftermath of a fraud Vocisano had perpetrated on Bannerman and Canada. It came out during the dispute that Bannerman had participated in a more modest tax fraud beginning in the early 1940s in which he and Vocisano agreed to pad corporate expenses, which their company deducted while they split the related cash.

Vocisano turned greedier and eventually diverted significant amounts owed to Concrete Clamps to a non-corporate bank account, kept some cash receipts and failed to report these amounts in the company's books. The Minister's auditors identified the fraud, which suppressed Concrete Clamps gross revenues by $543,000.

Bannerman maintained he was "amazed and astounded" and conducted his own review.[69] He then successfully sued to wind up Concrete Clamps in a precedent-setting case in which the Quebec Superior Court stripped Vocisano of the casting vote and ordered the appointment of a liquidator and the winding-up of Concrete Clamps because it would be "just and equitable" as allowed under s. 10 of the then Dominion *Winding-up Act*.[70] (The winding-up does not appear to have occurred, with the parties entering arbitration.) The liquidator also sued Vocisano for $2 million.

From an income tax perspective, Bannerman had rented property to Concrete Clamps, and he had a taxable rental profit during the shareholder dispute, even though Concrete Clamps had failed to pay $15,000 of the earned rent. He sought to deduct his expenses to obtain the winding-up order on the basis that it allowed him to collect the unpaid rent. The tax issue was whether the expenses were deductible in calculating Bannerman's income from a source of income.

Chief Justice Kerwin approached the matter by considering the income-producing purpose test underlying deductibility and noted that many of the decisions under the previous statutes were inapplicable. The essential aspect of his decision is that there exists

[69] *Ibid.*, p. 66.

[70] *Winding-up Act*, RSC, 1927, c. 213.

a judicial discretion in difficult cases when determining whether an outlay was made for the purpose of producing income. Kerwin stated, "since in one sense it might be said that almost every outlay or expense was made or incurred for that purpose, a line must be drawn in the individual case depending upon the circumstances bearing in mind" that capital outlays are not deducible unless expressly allowed.[71]

In applying this judicial discretion, Chief Justice Kerwin (1) found that Bannerman was not engaged in a business personally; (2) rejected Bannerman's claim that the expenses protected his Concrete Clamps' shares as a source producing dividends if the company were wound up, holding this was "unlikely"; (3) rejected Bannerman's argument that the expenses resulted in collecting the rents Concrete Clamps owed him, which as receivables had to be included in income—this was rejected on the basis Bannerman never sued to collect the rent and it did not matter if suing to wind up the company resulted in his being paid; and (4) held that, in any event, the expenses were incurred on account of capital for which no deduction existed. (Justices Taschereau, Fauteux, Abbott and Judson concurred.)

The last of Chief Justice Kerwin's opinions profiled is one of those rare decisions that has a life of its own. It is not cited often, but when it is, its meaning is disputed in the context of being central to the decision. It will doubtless be cited and considered decades into the future if, and when, that unusual income tax issue arises.

Robert B. Curran (1959)

In the late 1940s, Robert Curran was the manager of Imperial Oil Limited's production department (western division). Curran earned what would then have been considered a handsome salary of $25,000 annually and was a member of Imperial Oil's pension plan. At a minimum, Curran was expected to receive a pension of

[71] *Bannerman, supra* note 67, SCC p. 564.

$12,500 a year at age 65. He could expect more because his pension was based on 50 percent of his salary during the last five years of work at Imperial Oil.[72]

At that time, Robert (Bobby) Brown Jr. controlled a majority interest in Federated Petroleums Limited and owned a substantial interest in Home Oil Limited. The late journalist and author, Peter C. Newman, described Brown as one of a handful of men, including Frank McMahon, who were the original "adventurous high-rollers" that gave colour to the Alberta oil patch. Bobby Brown died by the time Newman wrote *The Canadian Establishment* in 1973.[73]

Back in 1951, Brown (and his brother and sister) sought to acquire a majority interest in Home Oil through their shareholdings in Federated Petroleums and two other companies within the Brown group. This was frustrated by the resistance of Major Lowery, president and managing director of Home Oil, who wanted a "suitable" replacement.

For that replacement, Brown wanted to hire Curran to initially work for one of the Brown companies, with a planned eventual acquisition of Home Oil. Curran demanded a lump sum of $250,000. Brown accepted, and the ensuing two contracts were well structured from a tax avoidance perspective.

Under the first contract of August 15, 1951, Brown agreed to pay Curran $250,000 for his lost pension benefits, future expected salary increases and future significant prospects in the industry. Under the second contract on that same day, Federated Petroleums agreed to hire Curran as its general manager at a salary of $25,000 a year. This employment contract stipulated that the directors of

---

[72] *Robert B. Curran v. MNR*, [1959] SCR 850, dismissing the taxpayer's appeal from [1957] Ex. CR 377, which dismissed the taxpayer's appeal from (*sub nom* No. 337) 56 DTC 224, (1956) 15 Tax ABC 73 (ITAB). *Curran v. Minister of National Revenue* – SCC Cases (scc-csc.ca). The Exchequer Court decision is at *Curran v. Minister of National Revenue* – Office of the Commissioner for Federal Judicial Affairs Canada (fja-cmf.gc.ca).

[73] Peter Newman, *The Canadian Establishment* (Toronto: McClelland and Stewart, 1973), p. 225.

Federated Petroleums could require Curran to serve as the manager of any other company, which would be Home Oil if plans worked out.

Clouding the issue of whether Curran had a source of income in respect of the $250,000 lump sum was the fact that he never started employment with Federated Petroleums, which assigned the employment contract to Home Oil. Curran started employment as president and general manager of Home Oil on October 1, 1951.

Brown thought that he had found a replacement for Major Lowery. Curran thought he was home free in avoiding tax on the $250,000 because he did not *technically* receive the $250,000 from his employer, did not carry on a business and he did not engage in an adventure in the nature of trade. The evidence at trial revealed that Brown did not personally pay $250,000 to Curran; instead, a company within the original Brown group paid the amount. Neither that company nor Federated Petroleums employed Curran; nor did Brown.

The Minister's auditors balked at the apparent non-taxability of the $250,000 lump sum and sought to tax it as ordinary income under s. 3 of the 1948 ITA. Three alternative arguments were made: (1) the receipt was employment income (relying on a deeming rule in s. 24A that required an employer make the payment), (2) it was for services Curran rendered to an oil company, or (3) the amount was a taxable benefit under a specific anti-avoidance rule (which did not apply to a *bona fide* arm's length transaction). Curran was reassessed and taxed on the $250,000 as ordinary income. He appealed.

Assistant Chairman Cecil Snyder of the Income Tax Appeal Board dismissed Curran's appeal on the basis that "regardless of what it may be called,"[74] Curran received the amount as remuneration.[75] Justice Jacques Dumoulin of the Exchequer Court found that the receipt was not employment income. But he relied on an

---

[74] *Curran, supra* note 72, ITAB at 56 DTC p. 230.

[75] *Ibid.* In *Curran*, the Income Tax Appeal Board applied the Supreme Court's 1953 decision in *Henry Goldman v. MNR*, [1953] 1 SCR 211. *Goldman v. Minister of National Revenue* – SCC Cases (scc-csc.ca).

obscure 1927 decision of the Exchequer Court in *Morrison*,[76] to sweep the $250,000 receipt into Curran's income under s. 3 of the 1948 ITA: "In very wide terms, section 3 renders taxable 'income for the year from *all sources* and without restricting the generality of the foregoing [emphasis in original].'"[77] Curran appealed.

The main question posed to the Supreme Court was whether the amount Curran received was a tax-exempt capital receipt or taxable as ordinary income under the 1948 ITA. A related question was whether the $250,000 receipt was divisible between tax-free capital and taxable income. Heward Stikeman and W.R. Jackett were lead counsel for the taxpayer and the Crown, respectively.

Chief Justice Kerwin noted that the 1948 ITA, unlike the *Income War Tax Act*, did not have an extensive description of what constituted income. This appeared to bode well for Curran, as the *Morrison* decision could have been distinguished on the basis that it interpreted and applied s. 3 of the *Income War Tax Act*. But s. 3 of the 1948 Act did refer to income from all sources, and such income includes—without restricting the meaning of income from all sources—income from each business, property, office and employment of a taxpayer. Well, what does "without restricting the meaning" suggest? It suggests that amounts having the character of income are income from an unlisted source.

When considering the issue, Kerwin acknowledged the *Duke of Westminster* principle, without citing the decision, and then turned the principle inside out. He started by finding that, despite the principle, the answer to the primary question of whether the receipt was income turned on the *fair* meaning of the word [income] in s. 3. Kerwin stated:

> The word [income] must receive its ordinary meaning bearing in mind the distinction between capital and income and

[76] *Allan Morrison v. MNR*, (1927), [1928] Ex. CR 75. *Morrison v. Minister of Customs and Excise* – Office of the Commissioner for Federal Judicial Affairs Canada (fja-cmf.gc.ca).

[77] *Curran*, *supra* note 72, Ex. CR p. 391.

> the ordinary concepts and usages of mankind. Under the authorities it is undoubted that clear words are necessary in order to tax the subject and that the taxpayer is entitled to arrange his affairs so as to minimize the tax. However, he does not succeed in the attempt if the transaction falls within the *fair* meaning of the words of the taxing enactment [emphasis added].[78]

Next, he turned the principle inside out by finding that the *substance* of the matter was that Curran worked for the compensation and that it was his income. This was determined based on the "true character" of the amount, as found in the two agreements and the surrounding circumstances.

> In the present case the *substance* of the matter was the engagement by the appellant to work for Mr. Brown or one of the companies in which the latter was interested and the agreement by the appellant with Federated Petroleums. It is true that in order to fulfill his obligations under the contracts the appellant was obliged to resign his position with Imperial Oil Limited and thereby gave up not only the annual salary, a like amount which he was to receive, but also his pension rights and further prospects. However, the payment of $250,000 was made *for personal service only* and that conclusion really disposes of the matter as it is impossible to divide the consideration. The mere fact that *the first agreement* of August 15, 1951, states that Brown agreed to pay the appellant $250,000 in consideration of the loss of pension rights, chances for advancement and opportunities for re-employment in the oil industry *cannot change the true character of the payment. Its true nature must be found in the terms of the two agreements and the surrounding circumstances* including the fact that the $250,000 did not come from Imperial Oil Limited [emphasis added].[79]

[78] *Ibid.*, SCC pp. 854–55.
[79] *Ibid.*, p. 856.

The above language is the closest Kerwin came to expressly saying the British *Duke of Westminster* principle does not apply when interpreting the ITA, and he did it 20 years after the Privy Council overturned that finding in *Pioneer Laundry* when interpreting the *Income War Tax Act.* When read more than 60 years later, Kerwin's 1959 decision in *Curran* echoes a passionate conviction he sustained throughout the intervening two decades in his income tax opinions.

Chief Justice Kerwin held that Curran's $250,000 was an indivisible amount having been received by him solely for providing *personal service* to Brown or one of his companies and not for a loss of rights. The Chief Justice had just looked through the payment's form and found the substance of the receipt to be income. (Justices Locke and Judson concurred.)

Justice Ronald Martland found that Brown never sought to acquire capital rights that Curran held in Imperial Oil. This meant that "the essence of the matter was the acquisition of services and the consideration was paid so that those services would be made available."[80] For Martland, Curran received the $250,000 for "services"; however, for Kerwin, it was received for "service." It is interesting to observe that a self-employed person works under contracts for "*services*" and that an employee works under a contract for "*service.*"

Martland considered in detail Curran's position that the receipt could not be taxed as ordinary income on the basis that there was no employer-employee relationship, which must exist to engage the rule deeming certain receipts to be employment income (then s. 24A, now subs. 6(3)). The particular provision ensures that certain amounts received before, during, and after an employer-employee relationship is taxable as employment income if there is or was an employer-employee relationship.

Justice Martland found that just because the provision did not apply due to the lack of an employer-employee relationship, this did not mean the amount was not income: "I do not think that it follows

[80] *Ibid.*, SCC p. 861.

that payments which would fall within s. 24A, except for the fact they were made by someone other than the employer, of necessity cannot be income within the provisions of s. 3."[81] He included the $250,000 in Curran's income because it was income. (Justices Locke and Judson concurred.)

Interestingly, Justices Locke and Judson concurred with the judgments of both Kerwin and Martland, rendering the decisions co-majority judgments. This appears to mean that there is a majority opinion that applies on the basis that Curran received the $250,000 either for (Kerwin) "service only" or for (Martland) "services." In other words, the legal form of the contracts did not matter; the relevant point was that the true character of the receipt was income.

Justice Robert Taschereau, in partial dissent, found that a portion of the receipt was a non-taxable capital receipt for a loss of Curran's employment benefits at Imperial Oil. The other portion was for "services" Curran rendered to his new "employer" despite it not being paid by his employer.[82] Taschereau would have sent the matter back to the Exchequer Court to apportion the amount between taxable and non-taxable portions.

Shortly after the decision, Gwyneth McGregor of the Canadian Tax Foundation noted in a case comment published in the *Canadian Tax Journal*—reflecting on Curran's $250,000 receipt—that the Supreme Court's "finding that it was taxable income could be made only in the broadest grounds, taking 'income' in its ordinarily understood sense as anything that is not capital."[83] Another view is that the *Curran* decision merely required that the statutory text be given a fair reading in light of the commercial substance of the contracts and not a strict meaning, despite the *Duke of Westminster* principle, when determining the *character* of income.

[81] *Ibid.*, SCC p. 862.

[82] *Ibid.*, SCC p. 857.

[83] Gwyneth McGregor, "About the Courts: The Case of the Quarter Million," (1960) 8:1 *Canadian Tax Journal* 22, p. 23.

Curran and Brown clashed over operational strategies within an oil company. Curran was released from his contracts about 14 months after he agreed to join the Brown group. He retained the $250,000 under the release, less income tax.

With respect to Chief Justice Kerwin's influence in income tax matters, the Supreme Court did not apply the British *Duke of Westminster* decision in a majority income tax opinion before 1984. The Court could have done so in *Curran.* But the Court's resistance to the British principle in tax avoidance cases traces to Kerwin's swing opinion in *Pioneer Laundry* to form a majority with Justices Hudson and Crocket and the fact Kerwin was the Court's most influential judge during his long tenure.[84] With respect to the Court's not applying the *Duke of Westminster* principle in income tax avoidance cases, it held up for almost 50 years despite the Privy Council's overturning *Pioneer Laundry.*

It is also noteworthy that after being reversed in *Pioneer Laundry*, the Supreme Court never again expressly held that it was not following the *Duke of Westminster* principle on the basis that it is inapplicable in a Canadian income tax context. Yet Kerwin's conviction against the *Duke of Westminster* decision is evident in his opinion in *Curran* and in the cumulative sense of his failure to cite the decision in an income tax avoidance context, and, further, that it was not applied in a majority Supreme Court income tax avoidance decision until long after he departed the Court.

For these reasons, Chief Justice Patrick Kerwin is selected in this book as one of the nine most influential Supreme Court justices in income tax over one hundred years. Patrick Kerwin died as the Chief Justice of the Supreme Court of Canada in 1963. He was replaced as a member of the Court by Justice Wishart Flett Spence.

---

[84] Peter McCormick, *Supreme at Last: The Evolution of the Supreme Court of Canada* (Toronto: James Lorimer and Company Ltd., 2000), p. 44. McCormick suggests that his statistical analysis shows that "Kerwin was the leader both of the Rinfret Court and his own." See Chapter 4 (The Kerwin Court: July 1954 to February 1963 "The Technician"). Kerwin C.J. was found statistically to have formed a relatively consistent majority with the three jurists from Quebec (Taschereau, Rinfret (subsequently Abbott) and Fauteux).

DOUGLAS ABBOTT: FROM CABINET TO THE SUPREME COURT

Liberal Prime Minister Louis St. Laurent appointed his cabinet colleague Douglas Abbott to the Supreme Court on Dominion Day, July 1, 1954, replacing Chief Justice Thibaudeau Rinfret. Immediately after being sworn in by the Governor General as the Chief Justice, Kerwin administered the oath of office to Abbott. A political storm ensued from the appointment. Abbott was not only a leading Liberal politician but also a protestant member of the English elite in his native Roman Catholic and francophone Quebec. Even the *Montreal Gazette* questioned such a politically charged appointment.[85]

Why is Justice Abbott included in the chosen nine, since academics perceive him as not wielding significant influence in the Supreme Court's written record?[86] He was the Liberal Minister of Finance, who oversaw the tax policy choices made in the 1948 ITA. It was thanks to Abbott, dubbed "The Wizard of Ottawa" by leading U.S. government officials, that parliamentarians in hearings reviewing the bill clause by clause during the summer of 1948, learned about his tax policy choices.[87]

On June 15, 1948, Finance Minister Douglas Abbott advised the House of Commons' Standing Committee on Banking and Commerce that, "The purpose of this act [the modern ITA] ... is that if a man is really in receipt of income and it is above the exemption

---

[85] James G. Snell and Frederick Vaughan, *The Supreme Court of Canada: History of the Institution* (Toronto: University of Toronto Press published for The Osgoode Society for Canadian Legal History 1985), pp. 199–200.

[86] McCormick, *supra* note 84. McCormick ranked Abbott J. 10th out of 12 Supreme Court judges cited or named in other decisions of the 1963–99 period. See Table 5.4, p. 79.

[87] For "The Wizard of Ottawa," see "Douglas Abbott, 87 Judge and Politician," *Toronto Star*, March 18, 1987, A20; for parliamentary hearings on the modernized income tax statute, see *Standing Committee on Banking and Commerce*, Session 1947–48, Senate Debates, *Minutes of Proceedings and Evidence*, Tuesday, June 15 to Thursday June 18, 1948.

limits he should pay taxes on it, and he should not be entitled to avoid the payment of taxes by cloaking the transaction in some other guise."[88] Abbott knew the politics behind and the tax policy choices underlying the modern income tax law, and, following his appointment in July 1954, he applied that knowledge in the Supreme Court, presiding over a remarkably high volume of income tax disputes.

Abbott came to his political and judicial appointments as a former commercial law / tax law practitioner in Montreal and a veteran of the First World War. His political and judicial career spanned the course of the rise of income tax revenues as the primary source of revenues for the federal government—and the concurrent tax planning to avoid that tax.

It can be said that Abbott was strongly pro-Crown in income tax disputes. He heard 112 income tax cases, of which 45 concerned tax avoidance, during his 19 years as a Supreme Court judge.

Justice Abbott would have heard even more income tax cases except that it appears he recused himself from hearing some disputes in the initial years after his appointment in 1954. Owing to having been lobbied extensively when he was the Minister of Finance, Abbott heard only five income tax cases before 1958, after which he began to hear the bulk of such cases.

Two disputes stand out in which Abbott appears to have recused himself. The first case is *Home Oil.* As the Minister of Finance, Abbott would have been knowledgeable of the issue concerning the calculation of depletion allowance in respect of oil wells. For a five-member panel, Justice Ivan Rand delivered the Court's unanimous reversal for *Home Oil* in late 1955.[89]

The *Home Oil* issue concerned significant amounts of income tax for affected taxpayers—and for Canada. It would have been Finance Minister Douglas Abbott who ensured a regulation was passed in 1951 that clarified the computation of depletion

[88] *Ibid.*, *Standing Committee*, p. 565.

[89] *Home Oil Co. Ltd. v. MNR*, [1955] SCR 733. *Home Oil Co. Ltd. v. Minister of National Revenue* – SCC Cases (scc-csc.ca).

allowances in respect of oil wells effective that year. After Home Oil's success, Imperial Oil challenged the regulation partly on the basis it was *ultra vires*—beyond the authority of the executive to pass. Like in *Home Oil*, Abbott was not on the seven-member panel that decided *Imperial Oil* in 1960. The Crown was successful.[90]

This book maintains that recognizing Abbott's approach to income tax and its avoidance is important in the context of better understanding the Supreme Court's decisions from the mid-1950s to the mid-1970s. A generally conservative justice who supported civil rights, Abbott was well-liked and affable. Yet, Richard Pound, a leading tax practitioner in Montreal, criticized Abbot's self-confidence in respect of the intent underlying the modern ITA.

Pound wrote: "Douglas Abbott ... [was] completely certain that he knew exactly what was intended by every tax provision which happened to come before him."[91] If so, he would have done it behind the scenes in conferences held by judges hearing disputes. This would have been bad news for taxpayers and their advisors trying to benefit from tax avoidance.

Justice Abbott's most significant contribution to the Supreme Court's approach to income tax is that the Court adopted his methodology (with one change) for applying the "for the purpose of gaining or producing income" test to determine the deductibility of expenses and capital outlays under the modern ITA.

British Columbia Electric Railway Co. (1958)

The Supreme Court's methodology for deducting outlays when computing business income traces to Abbott's 1958 majority

---

[90] *MNR v. Imperial Oil Ltd.*, [1960] SCR 735. While all seven judges in *Imperial Oil* found the regulation was within the authority of the executive to enact, the panel split in the outcome, in part. Justices Cartwright, Martland and Ritchie dissented in part from Justice Judson's majority decision (Justices Taschereau and Locke concurred) with Chief Justice Kerwin agreeing with Judson but clarifying certain matters. *Minister of National Revenue v. Imperial Oil Co.* – SCC Cases (scc-csc.ca).

[91] Richard W. Pound, *Chief Justice W.R. Jackett: By the Law of the Land* (Montreal-Kingston: McGill-Queen's University Press, 1999), p. 68.

opinion in *British Columbia Electric Railway Co.*,[92] which is largely forgotten. Perhaps this is because tax professionals apply his methodology without much additional thought or credit. But by 1993, the Supreme Court appears to have lost touch with the methodology; in its 1993 *Symes* decision, judges speculated about why and when the test is more liberal than its predecessor, a case relating to whether nanny expenses are deductible when computing business income.[93]

But way back in the late 1950s, the initial dispute about the parameters of the methodology concerned a franchise that the predecessor of the British Columbia Electric Railway Co. (BCER)—Vancouver Power Company—obtained in 1907. It acquired the franchise from various municipalities along the lower Fraser Valley on the B.C. mainland, including Surrey, Langley, Matsqui and Chilliwack.[94] Vancouver Power was granted the right to construct and operate a railway to transport freight on a right-of-way between New Westminster and Chilliwack. In return, it agreed to run one passenger train daily each way.

All went well until the BCER's passenger revenue began to decline with the advent of the automobile. By 1950, the company's passenger service was seriously undermining its freight service profits, and it decided to close the passenger service.[95] But, under

---

[92] *British Columbia Electric Railway Company Limited v. MNR*, [1958] SCR 133, dismissing the taxpayer's appeal for different reasons from [1957] Ex. CR 1. *British Columbia Electric Railway Company Limited v. The Minister of National Revenue* – SCC Cases (scc-csc.ca). The Exchequer Court decision is at *B.C. Electric Ry. Co. Ltd. v. Minister of National Revenue* – Office of the Commissioner for Federal Judicial Affairs Canada (fja-cmf.gc.ca).

[93] *Symes v. The Queen*, [1993] 4 SCR 695. *Symes v. Canada* – SCC Cases (scc-csc.ca).

[94] The historical period in which Vancouver Power acquired the franchise is notable for the advancement of the "social gospel" and the related movement that sought to bring order to a chaotic municipal infrastructure including public transportation.

[95] *British Columbia Electric Railway Co., supra* note 92, with the Exchequer Court indicating that in 1949, the freight service netted a profit of $779,183 and the passenger service incurred a loss of $309,094.

the *B.C. Public Utilities Act*, the company could not do so unless an alternative passenger service was made available and it obtained the approval of the affected municipalities, which were objecting strenuously to the change. To get approval, the company agreed to operate a bus service and to pay the five affected municipalities $220,000 in total. BCER deducted $5,499 of the $220,000 payment (in its 1950 tax year) and $22,000 of the $220,000 (in its 1951 tax year) when computing its income for tax purposes.

The Minister maintained that the deductions should be disallowed because the $220,000 was a capital outlay for which no deduction was expressly allowed under the 1948 ITA.[96] The statutory income tax law precludes taxpayers from using accounting methods to amortize depreciable capital outlays and instead provides for capital cost allowance (CCA). The Minister maintained that the taxpayer never acquired depreciable property when making the capital outlay, and the outlay was therefore non-deductible.

Based on pre-1950 case law, the Exchequer Court upheld the Minister's assessment on the basis that the outlay was not made primarily for the purpose of earning business income, and that it was a capital outlay for which no deduction was allowed. The taxpayer appealed.

Justice Abbott agreed with the Exchequer Court result but not with its approach. Therein exists the importance of the decision. He set out the methodology to take when determining whether the deduction of a commercial outlay is allowed or denied under the statutory law.

Abbott's first point was that outlays must be tested against paragraphs 12(1)(*a*) and (*b*) (current paragraphs 18(1)(*a*) and (*b*)) of the ITA. They provide that no deduction is to be made in respect of an outlay or expense except to the extent that it is incurred for the purpose of gaining or producing income from a business or property source. If a capital outlay, the outlay must also be of a type for which the statute expressly permits a deduction, such as

[96] *Ibid.*

for depreciable property. Abbott italicized the text of the *Income War Tax Act* that no longer applied. That Act denied the deduction of outlays not "*wholly, exclusively and necessarily*" incurred for the purpose of earning income.

Next, Abbott cautioned that British and Canadian precedent interpreting the former wording no longer necessarily applied. He then related the purposes of Canada's modern income tax law to the presumed purpose of a business undertaking:

> The less stringent provisions of the new section should, I think, be borne in mind in considering judicial opinions based on former sections. Since the main purpose of every business undertaking is presumably to make a profit, any expenditure made "for the purpose of gaining or producing income" comes within the terms of s. 12(1)(*a*) whether it be classified as an income expense or as a capital outlay.
>
> Once it is determined that a particular expenditure is one made for the purpose of gaining or producing income, in order to compute income tax liability it must next be ascertained whether such disbursement is an income expense or a capital outlay. The principle underlying such a deduction is, of course, that since for tax purposes income is determined on an annual basis, an income expense is one incurred to earn income of the particular year in which it is made and should be allowed as a deduction from gross income in that year. Most capital outlays on the other hand may be amortized or written off over a period of years depending upon whether or not the asset in respect of which the outlay is made is one coming within the capital cost allowance regulations under s. 11(1)(a) of the *Income Tax Act*.[97]

At least five points should be made about Abbott's methodology. First, it confirms that the statutory approach taken in the 1948 ITA and its successors is less stringent than the previous approach.

[97] *Ibid.*, SCC pp. 136–37.

This must be borne in mind when considering precedent in respect of the *Income War Tax Act* and the British statutory tax law.

Second, even a capital outlay should be tested to determine the extent to which it is incurred "for the purpose of gaining or producing income." As Abbott noted, normally this purpose test will not be an impediment in deducting the cost of an outlay because one can presume that a business outlay is incurred to make a profit; but this is a *presumption.* That presumption is not met, for example, if an expenditure is incurred in whole or part for an ineligible purpose such as a personal purpose with the ineligible portion being non-deductible.

Third, to the extent the purpose test is satisfied, it is necessary to determine whether the outlay is a deductible expense incurred on income account or a capital outlay.

Fourth, Abbott found that an outlay is a deductible expense in the year it is incurred only if it results in current-year income. Strictly speaking, the provision's text does not say this, and Abbott's *obiter* caused a split in the views of the Supreme Court eight years later in *Premium Iron Ores.*[98] The Court reconciled the split discussed below in its 1967 decision in *Farmers Mutual Petroleums.*[99]

Fifth, a capital outlay is deductible only to the extent the statutory law allows it.

Having formulated the method applicable, Justice Abbott applied the law to the facts. He found that BCER's $220,000 payment was "connected" to its profit-making operations.[100] The evidence showed that it relieved the taxpayer of an obligation to operate an unprofitable passenger service, while retaining the

---

[98] *Premium Iron Ores Limited v. MNR,* [1966] SCR 685. *Premium Iron Ores Ltd. v. Minister of National Revenue* – SCC Cases (scc-csc.ca).

[99] *Farmers Mutual Petroleums Limited v. MNR,* (1967), [1968] SCR 59, dismissing the taxpayer's appeal from [1966] Ex. CR 1126. *Farmers Mutual Petroleums Limited v. Minister of National Revenue* – SCC Cases (scc-csc.ca). The Exchequer Court decision is at https://reports.fja-cmf.gc.ca/fja-cmf/j/en/item/399192/index.do?q=Farmers+mutual.

[100] *British Columbia Electric Railway Co., supra* note 92, SCC p. 137.

right to operate a profitable freight service. Abbott found that the taxpayer's "profits were increased substantially"[101] and the outlay "was clearly one made for the purpose of gaining or producing income."[102] Thus, Abbott found that the connection of an outlay to a business is not enough and that it is deductible only to the extent it also satisfies the income-producing purpose test. In this case, 100 percent of the outlay satisfied then paragraph 12(1)(*a*).

With respect to the outlay being capital, Abbott noted that BCER's $220,000 expenditure was not depreciable property for which the statutory law provided a deduction. He therefore dismissed the taxpayer's appeal.[103] (Chief Justice Kerwin and Justice Fauteux concurred.)

Justice Charles Locke, in his minority opinion, focused on the payment being a non-deductible capital outlay. (Justice Cartwright concurred.) Locke concluded that there was no need to consider whether the outlay was incurred "for the purpose of gaining or producing income," and he expressed no opinion on the matter. Earlier in his opinion, he stated that it is not "decisive of the question whether the payments … resulted in an increase of income." Locke did so in response to the taxpayer's argument that the payment increased its income.

The result in *British Columbia Electric Railway Co.* showed that there were commercial outlays incurred 100 percent for the purpose of earning income that were so-called *tax nothings* in the sense the taxpayer could not claim a deduction. It would take until 1972 for Parliament to legislate the now former eligible capital allowance regime to fill in the gap that existed in the statutory law for amortizing some capital outlays.

Abbott's majority and Locke's minority opinions differ on an important detail with respect to the extent to which the modern deductibility test is more generous than the former test—whether

---

[101] *Ibid.*

[102] *Ibid.*

[103] *Ibid.*

and when an expense must result in income. The parameters of that detail flowed forward in varying ways through the subsequent income tax decisions of the Supreme Court and the lower courts; one such way is discussed below.

The next year, Chief Justice Kerwin decided the already profiled *Bannerman* case, which followed Abbott's methodology without citing it. Instead, Kerwin cited his 3–2 majority 1939 decision in *Riedle Brewery*,[104] for the proposition that the judiciary enjoys latitude when deciding whether expenses are incurred for the purpose of earning income, stating, "with the object and intent that they should earn the particular gross income … for the taxation year."[105]

Despite *British Columbia Electric Railway Co.* and *Bannerman*, taxpayers continued to argue that making an outlay to preserve or protect a source was sufficient to deduct it as an expense; in 1960, a widow did so successfully in *Evans* when the Supreme Court split 3–2.[106] Evans incurred legal fees to establish her legal right to income as a beneficiary of an estate and sought to deduct them from income.

Justice John Cartwright, for the majority in *Evans*, traced the preserve-the-source argument to the Supreme Court's 1940 ruling in *Dominion Natural Gas* where the Court found that incurring an outlay to preserve a source is an alternative basis: for bringing into existence an asset or advantage with an enduring benefit, and for explaining why the outlay should be classified as a capital outlay.[107] But, after reviewing the deductibility test citing Abbott in *British Columbia Electric Railway Co.*, Cartwright distinguished *Dominion Natural Gas* on the basis that Evans' right to income was not a capital asset. He held that Evan's legal fees were deductible because

---

[104] *Riedle Brewery Ltd. v. MNR*, [1939] SCR 253. *Riedle Brewery Ltd. v. Minister of National Revenue* – SCC Cases (scc-csc.ca).

[105] *Bannerman, supra* note 67, p. 564. *Bannerman v. Minister of National Revenue* – SCC Cases (lexum.com).

[106] *Gladys Evans v. MNR*, [1960] SCR 391. *Evans v. Minister of National Revenue* – SCC Cases (scc-csc.ca).

[107] *Dominion Natural Gas Ltd. v. MNR*, (1940), [1941] SCR 19. *Minister of National Revenue v. Dominion Natural Gas Co. Ltd.* – SCC Cases (scc-csc.ca).

she incurred them to collect income owed to her. The reasoning is weak on Evans' right to income not being a capital asset, but the widow did have a sympathetic case. (Justices Taschereau and Ritchie concurred; Justices Fauteux and Judson dissented.)

The *Evans* decision was a prelude to the Supreme Court's splitting on the parameters of Justice Abbott's methodology. The split pitted the requirement that for an outlay to be a current expense, it must produce gross income in the current year against allowing a deduction if the outlay preserves or protects the source of income regardless of producing any income in the year.

The Supreme Court split arose in *Premium Iron Ores* when considering the deductibility of certain legal expenses. Premium Iron Ores paid American counsel in the 1950s to defend a reassessment of tax the Internal Revenue Service (IRS) made against it. The IRS maintained Premium Iron Ores received a taxable benefit in the form of valuable shares issued to it for one cent per share—which were worth US$1.67 a share.

Premium Iron Ores won its case before the U.S. Tax Court and the U.S. Court of Appeals, 6th Circuit.[108] It then deducted the legal fees when computing its Canadian income despite the fact they related to an American tax dispute and did not result in any current-year Canadian gross income. The Minister denied the deduction.

Essentially, the Supreme Court split with no majority consensus for why the legal fees should be deductible, although a majority was

---

[108] *Commissioner of Internal Revenue Service v. Consolidated Premium Iron Ores Limited et al.*, 59 DTC 1112 (U.S. Court of Appeals, 6th Circuit), dismissing the Commissioner's appeal from 57 DTC 1146 (U.S. Tax Court). Although issued to the company, the stock may have been beneficially owned by leading industrialist Cyrus Eaton and an associate (and his spouse), who resided in Cleveland and against whom the IRS issued alternative reassessments. Premium Iron Ores was found neither to carry on business nor to have a permanent establishment in the United States. It acted as sales agent for high-grade iron ore sourced from a mine developed in Ontario during the Second World War. Eaton, who was from Nova Scotia, arranged the financing necessary to develop the mine.

cobbled together to hold for deductibility. Justice Martland conceded that the legal fees were not paid solely for the purpose of gaining Canadian income but found that they "were made with a view to protecting" the Canadian source from an American incursion that could deplete the source if successful; he then applied the Court's 1960 decision in *Evans*.[109] (Justice Spence concurred.) Martland neither cited nor followed Abbott's methodology, although he noted the ITA's deductibility test is more generous than under the British approach taken in the former *Income War Tax Act*.

Justice Roland Ritchie issued a stinging dissent. (Justice Abbott concurred.) The cost of legal fees to defend a domestic income tax dispute was non-deductible, so why would the cost of defending an American dispute be deductible? It made no sense.[110] Ritchie also applied Abbott's methodology and emphasized in italics the *dicta* that required the outlay to result in current-year income in order for a current expense to be allowed.

Justice Emmett Hall issued the swing opinion. Although Hall distinguished several British decisions by citing Abbott's methodology on deductibility, he scrutinized the statutory text and held the following: "the income … referred to may be the income of the taxation year under review or of a succeeding year."[111]

---

[109] *Premium Iron Ores, supra* note 98. When commenting on the Supreme Court's decision in *MNR v. The Kellogg Company* ([1943] SCR 58), Martland J. stated (p. 703): "They [the legal fees] did not directly result in the earning of income at all. They were made with the view to protecting the income earning capacity of the company, since it must be assumed that the loss of the right to the use of the words [in Kellogg's registered trademarks] in connection with its sales would have indirectly resulted in a reduction of its income, not only in the year in which they were incurred, but also in future years as well." *Kellogg* is at *Minister of National Revenue v. The Kellogg Company of Canada Ltd.* – SCC Cases (scc-csc.ca).

[110] But Parliament legislated in 1965 a deduction for amounts paid to object to, appeal or litigate an assessment, interest or penalty imposed under the 1952 ITA, which amendment was made before the dispute reached the Supreme Court. See SC, 1964–65, c. 13, s 3(5) adding para. 11(1)(*w*) to the 1952 Act, applicable to 1964 and later tax years.

[111] *Premium Iron Ores, supra* note 98, SCC p. 711.

The Supreme Court returned to the dispute the following year in *Farmers Mutual Petroleums.*[112] The protagonist behind Farmers Mutual was William Harrison Riddle, an American promoter experienced in the oil industry. He organized a business whereby farmers in southeastern Saskatchewan were vigorously solicited into pooling their rights to oil and gas inside Riddle's Farmers Mutual.[113] The transfers turned out to be a poor financial decision for many farmers, and they sued Farmers Mutual on the basis that they had been defrauded.

Although Farmers Mutual successfully defended these actions, the affected farmers organized and managed to get the Legislative Assembly of Saskatchewan to establish the *Royal Commission on Certain Mineral Transactions* to investigate their allegations. The Commission recommended the creation of a Board to allow for the re-negotiation of the contracts. The Legislature enacted the *Mineral Contracts Re-negotiation Act,* 1959, to accomplish this objective. Farmers Mutual incurred additional legal expenses, all of which it attempted to deduct in computing its business income. The Minister denied the deductions, and Farmers Mutual appealed.

Justice Martland rejected Farmers Mutual's assertion that it could deduct the legal fees on the basis that they were incurred to protect its income source. (Justices Cartwright, Ritchie, Hall and Spence concurred.) He cited with approval Abbott's methodology in *British Columbia Electric Railway Co.* to determine the deductibility of expenditures. After doing so, he held the legal fees were non-deductible capital outlays because they were incurred to defend the taxpayer's capital interest in its acquired mineral leases.

---

[112] *Farmers Mutual Petroleums, supra* note 99.

[113] *Ibid.* Farmers Mutual acquired title to oil and gas resources from farmers who had previously granted an oil company a 10-year lease of their resource title (with each farmer earning 10 cents per acre leased from the oil company and a 12.5 percent royalty from any production during the 10-year term). In return for transferring their resource title, each farmer received one share of Farmers Mutual and a trust certificate indicating it held 20 percent of the rents payable in trust for the farmer. Approximately 2,500 certificates were issued.

The result meant that Abbott's methodology applied when testing the deductibility of an expense or outlay in the context of computing income from a business or property source, subject to an expense not having to result in current-year gross income. It should also have relegated the preserve-the-source intent argument back to its relevancy for why an outlay is, or is not, on account of capital.

While the Supreme Court was sorting out the parameters of Justice Abbott's deductibility methodology, he decided for the Court a dispute concerning Canada's mining sector. By the summer of 1934, Sir Harry Oakes was perhaps the wealthiest man in the British Empire. A prospector from Maine, Oakes struck gold at Kirkland Lake in 1912, where he developed and operated over the next three decades one of the most productive gold mines in the world, Lake Shore Mines. Charlotte Gray told the story of Oakes' life and unsolved murder in her acclaimed 2019 book *Murdered Midas*.[114] She indicated that Oakes' "fuse blew" over taxes in 1934.[115]

PM Richard B. Bennett is generally perceived to be Oakes' antagonist, with their dispute connected in an obscure way to Justice Abbott's unanimous 1963 decision in *Hollinger North Shore Exploration*.

Hollinger North Shore Exploration (1963)

At the dawn of the 20th century, a mining syndicate was formed by two brothers from Mattawa, Ontario, which is in the upper Ottawa Valley.[116] Brothers Noah and Henry Timmins would emerge to become Canadian legends. The Timmins boys located rich ore bodies across northern Ontario and Quebec; they began by buying mining claims, one of which became a great gold mine at Porcupine, Ontario. That mine was the Hollinger Gold Mine, and

[114] Charlotte Gray, *Murdered Midas: A Millionaire, His Gold Mine, and a Strange Death on an Island Paradise* (Toronto: HarperCollins Publishers Ltd., 2019).

[115] *Ibid.*, p. 89.

[116] D.M. LeBourdais, *Metals and Men* (Toronto: McClelland & Stewart Limited, 1957), pp. 130, 155, 159–61 and 360–72.

it was the mother lode. By the 1950s, Henry's son, Jules, was continuing the family tradition.

The dispute in *Hollinger North Shore Exploration* concerned interpreting the parameters of a so-called *temporary* exemption from income tax extended to Canada's mining sector in the wake of the 1935 election.[117] The Liberals won that depression-era election with Liberal PM Mackenzie King replacing Conservative PM Bennett. It took another 35 years for Parliament to repeal that temporary measure. Before considering the dispute, it should be explained the exemption was the result of *realpolitik*.

The story behind how the tax exemption for mining profits came about begins in 1930 with rumours that Sir Harry Oakes had contributed a significant sum to Mackenzie King's Liberals in the lead-up to the 1930 election; King's lure was a promised appointment to the unelected Senate or as the Lieutenant Governor of Ontario.[118] Neither happened once Bennett and his Conservatives won the election.

In 1934, Bennett riled up the mining sector in general and Oakes in particular by imposing a special tax on windfall gains realized by gold miners when U.S. President Franklin D. Roosevelt's administration revalued gold to US$35 an ounce from US$20.67.[119] This change created an instant profit of US$14.33 per ounce for those holding gold reserves. The gold-mining sector held significant gold reserves, and Bennett decided that all Canadians should share in the sector's windfall.

Harry Oakes and the Timmins brothers were side-swiped by Bennett's changes. The Bennett government proposed a 10 percent tax on windfall gains realized by gold mines in its 1934 Budget. Representatives of the sector immediately descended on Ottawa, but

[117] *MNR v. Hollinger North Shore Exploration Company, Limited,* [1963] SCR 131. *Minister of National Revenue v. Hollinger North Shore Exploration Co., Ltd.* – SCC Cases (scc-csc.ca).

[118] Gray, *Murdered Midas, supra* note 114, pp. 88–89.

[119] J. Harvey Perry, *Taxes, Tariffs, and Subsidies: A History of Canadian Fiscal Development,* Volume I (Toronto: University of Toronto Press, 1955), p. 277.

the best they could do was get the tax changed to a 25 percent tax imposed on the difference between US$20.67 per ounce and gold's prevailing market value, with that tax credited against any income tax payable by affected companies.[120] The tax on windfall gains was to raise $10 million, but with the changes, it panned out at somewhat less than $5 million and was meant to be temporary expiring May 31, 1935.

To compensate for the expiry of the tax, the Bennett government proposed in its 1935 Budget that the tax on gold gains be replaced by a reduction in a precious-mining company's depletion allowance to 33.33 percent from 50 percent coupled with a reduction in a shareholder's depletion deduction to 20 percent from 50 percent in respect of dividends received from such companies. The government justified these changes on the basis that the depletion provisions were "unduly generous" and that one such provision was allowing both a corporate mine and its shareholders to claim depletion, which "cannot be defended."[121] Soon after, the Conservative Bennett government was defeated in the 1935 election.

Thomas Crerar, the Liberals' incoming Minister of Mines and Resources, was the on-the-ground politician linked to the King government implementing a three-year exemption from income tax on profits earned from a new mine's production commenced after 1935.[122] Crerar was the former Unionist Agriculture Minister in Sir Robert Borden's War Cabinet during the First World War. He then became the breakaway leader of the Progressives in the 1921 election, only to turn up as an incoming Liberal minister in 1935.

---

[120] *Ibid.*

[121] *House of Comms Debates*, March 22, 1935, p. 1986.

[122] James Edgar Rae, *T.A. Crerar: A Political Life* (Montreal-Kingston: McGill-Queen's University Press, 1997), pp. 178–79; and Bryce, *Maturing in Hard Times*, *supra* note 8, p. 114. Rae is relied on for Crerar's role in the King government's decision to extend new mines a tax exemption on their profits during the first three years of commercial production. For the amendment, see SC, 1936, c. 38, s. 20 adding Part XIII (Metalliferous Mines), s. 89 to the *Income War Tax Act*. The exemption was supposed to expire at the end of 1939.

Throughout it all, Crerar was a master at winning special preferences for important sectors of the economy—those that could pay off big politically. This started with the farming sector during the First World War, and by 1935, he had turned his attention to the mining sector. During the election, Crerar made 12 radio broadcasts about the importance of mining and secured favourable newspaper coverage in the *Globe and Mail, Winnipeg Free Press* and *Northern Miner.*[123] The sector's scions, including the Timmins family, were elated and presumably followed up with proposals.

The result was a sector-specific tax haven provided by the King government. R.B. Bennett was not amused. After the Liberals announced their tax haven for mining, now Opposition Leader Bennett asked members sitting in the government benches in the House of Commons, "Is it not right and just and fair that, so far as possible, everybody in Canada should stand equal under our taxation laws?"[124] He believed that his government had been "abused" by the mining sector,[125] a sector that was associated with the brokerage houses that raised capital for mining and promoted and traded mining stock.

Bennett also advised the House of Commons that his government cut depletion allowances because the sector was paying tax on its profits at half the 1933 general corporate tax rate of 12.5 percent. The reduction was meant, he contended, to ensure that the sector paid at least two-thirds of the 12.5 percent rate and was combined with an increase in the corporate rate to 13.5 percent of profits. Enraged, the mining sector turned to King in its deep need for special treatment, and King complied. Bennett summed up his experience with the mining sector by saying, "I think we paid a rather high price" for doing what was right in tax policy terms, if not politically.[126]

---

[123] *Ibid.*

[124] *House of Commons Debates*, May 5, 1936, p. 2521.

[125] *Ibid.*

[126] *Ibid.*

In other words, the Mackenzie King government turned Bennett's attempt to ensure the mining sector paid at least 8.3 percent corporate income tax on its mining profits into a 100 percent exemption from tax on such profits during a new mine's first three years of production.

The Exchequer Court and the Supreme Court decided several disputes over the next 35 years about various aspects of the mining sector's tax exemption. Most concerned whether the mine was really a new mine, an extension of an existing mine, or the reopening of a mine shuttered when commodity prices were low. The disputes were decided based on their facts, and the mining companies were often successful but not always.[127]

The dispute in *Hollinger North Shore Exploration* concerned a mine that everyone agreed was new. It was a great high-grade iron-ore mine in northern Quebec on its border with Labrador. The people behind the mine and its 350-mile railway from Schefferville to the port of Sept-Îles were leading businessmen in Canada and the United States. Jules Timmins had secured control of the concession by the early 1940s. But he needed a partner with access to deep amounts of capital.

If the Timmins family was the royalty of Canadian mining during the first half of the 20th century, members of the Hanna family were the founding fathers of Cleveland. The Hanna empire was front and centre in feeding America's expanding steel industry as the post–Second World War economy boomed. It included extensive interests in mining, shipping, real estate, and a host of other ventures. Originally formed as a partnership in the 1880s, M.A. Hanna Company became a limited liability company in the roaring 1920s. It reorganized itself in the 1960s and became

[127] For taxpayer success, see (1) *North Bay Mica Company Limited v. MNR,* [1958] SCR 597; and (2) *MNR v. Bethlehem Copper Corporation Limited,* (1974), [1975] 2 SCR 790. The Crown was successful in *MNR v. MacLean Mining Company Limited,* [1970] SCR 877. See (1) *North Bay Mica Co. Ltd. v. The Minister of National Revenue* – SCC Cases (scc-csc.ca); (2) *M.N.R. v. Bethlehem Copper Corp. Ltd.* – SCC Cases (lexum.com); and (3) *Minister of National Revenue v. MacLean Mining Company Limited* – SCC Cases (scc-csc.ca).

Hanna Mining Limited. Calling Hanna a mining company simply obscured the extensive nature of its holdings.[128]

By the early 1950s, the Timmins and Hanna empires were interlocked in a great mining adventure on the Quebec north shore that spilled into Newfoundland and Labrador. Located in the Labrador iron-ore range, the venture would eventually involve a host of companies in Canada and the United States, including the ever-present Cleveland-Cliffs Iron Ore Co. and The Iron Ore Co. of Canada, which would later be headed by a future Prime Minister, the late Brian Mulroney. George Humphrey led the Hanna empire in the early 1950s until he became the United States Secretary of the Treasury in President Dwight Eisenhower's administration.

The mine opened to great acclaim in the summer of 1954, with numerous dignitaries in Canada and from the United States travelling to see the first tons of ore loaded onto ships at Sept-Îles. *Life Magazine* in an editorial focused on the mine as representative of an unprecedented economic boom that put paid to arguments raised in the 1930s that America's economy had matured and its expansion had ended. The roles played by Jules Timmins, M.A. Hanna Co., Premiers Maurice Duplessis and Joey Smallwood in advancing the adventure were mentioned; special tribute was given to George Humphrey, who had made it his mission that there would be "Iron Ore by 54."[129]

In time, nature would reveal that the mother lode of iron ore was in Labrador, with the feasibility of mining the ore made possible by one of the most fascinating characters in the colourful history of the promotion of North American mining stocks, John Christopher Doyle. Doyle was a "crook," according to the Honourable John Crosbie, but with the aid of his good buddy Premier Joey Smallwood, Doyle's mining venture at

---

[128] Peter Newman, *The Establishment Man* (Toronto: McClelland & Stewart Limited, 1982; 1983, Seal ed.), p. 244. Also see Terry S. Reynolds and Virginia Dawson, *Iron Will: Cleveland Cliffs and the Mining of Iron Ore* (Detroit: Wayne State University Press, 2011).

[129] "The Saga of Ungava," *Life Magazine*, as re-printed by the *Globe and Mail*, August 23, 1954, p. 6.

Wabush got off the ground.[130] His public company, Canadian Javelin Ltd., sold the venture in return for royalty rights to an international consortium of steel companies put together by interests in Cleveland.[131]

The tax dispute was fought for the taxpayer by two of the top tax litigators in Canada's history, H. Heward Stikeman and Paterson (Pat) Thorsteinsson. They established two of Canada most prominent tax law firms, Stikeman Elliott in Montreal and Thorsteinssons in Vancouver. Assisting them in the case was future Liberal Cabinet Minister Donald Johnston.

The joint venture participants were from the Hanna and Timmins empires. The taxpayer Hollinger North Shore was part of the Timmins empire, and it held the mining lease Quebec granted in 1953. It then sublet the lease to The Iron Ore Co. of Canada, which was part of the Hanna empire. In effect, The Iron Ore Co. became the mine operator for the joint venturers.

The profits that the joint venture participants earned from ore production were tax exempt for the first three years of production. But as explorer, Hollinger North Shore Exploration also had a right to royalties from production. It was this royalty right that became the focus of the tax dispute. The royalties exceeded $3 million in 1956 alone (about $34 million in 2024 dollars).

The Minister maintained that the royalties Hollinger North Shore Exploration received were not eligible for the three-year exemption from tax. It did not "operate" the mine, the Minister argued, and the issue was whether the royalties met the statutory requirement of being income "derived from the operation of a mine." Only if they were, would the income be exempt from income tax.

Justice Abbott first noted that "the ordinary meaning of the words 'derived from the operation of a mine' is broader than that contended … [and] the word 'derived' in this context is broader

---

[130] John Crosbie (with Geoffrey Stevens), *No Holds Barred: My Life in Politics* (Toronto: McClelland & Stewart Inc., 1997), pp. 111–12.

[131] Philip Smith, *Brinco, The Story of Churchill Falls* (Toronto: McClelland and Stewart Ltd., 1975), pp. 99–100.

than 'received' and is equivalent in meaning to 'arising or accruing.'"[132] The mine was being operated as one unit by The Iron Ore Co. of Canada for the co-venturer's "joint benefit." The royalties as a return on capital could only be realized "through the operation of the mine" and were eligible for the exemption during the first three years of production.[133] (Justices Cartwright, Fauteux, Martland and Ritchie concurred.)

Abbott's decision in *Hollinger North Shore Exploration* on the meaning of "derived" has broader implications for those who draft arcane income tax provisions that affect all Canadians. It reflected a breadth in meaning that, in the right circumstances, would allow a tax provision to look through legal form to reach an amount for the purpose of taxing it or preventing tax avoidance.[134]

Back in 1934–35, Sir Harry Oakes left Canada because of Bennett's tax on windfall gold gains and the curtailment of depletion allowances, which had the ricochet political effect of incenting the Mackenzie King government into exempting from tax a new mine's profits during its first three years of production. It is worth parsing the Oakes situation because he complained to the press that he was facing income tax rates of 80 percent or more.

Citing a top marginal tax rate can be deceptive because it needs to be grounded not only by the amount of income at which it begins to apply but also by the way in which it is integrated into the overall scheme for imposing tax on income and the reality

---

[132] *Hollinger North Shore Exploration*, *supra* note 117, p. 134.

[133] *Ibid.*, pp. 134–35. Five years later, Spence J. found in *Gunnar Mining Ltd.*, [1968] SCR 226, that the meaning of the phrase "derived from the operation of a mine" did not exempt from tax the interest income the company earned in the three-year period from investments acquired with its tax-exempt mining income. Gunnar Mining was also denied a depletion allowance it claimed in respect of that interest income. Justices Cartwright, Abbott, Hall and Pigeon concurred. *Gunnar Mining Limited v. Minister of National Revenue* – SCC Cases (scc-csc.ca).

[134] For example, see the use of the word "derived" in paras. 212(1)(c) to (e) of the ITA, which provisions concern the imposition of a 25 percent withholding tax on certain amounts paid or credited by a person in Canada to a non-resident person (but also see ss. 212(9)).

that some politicians love to extend major tax breaks. The special tax on windfall gold gains is an example; the tax rate went up to 25 percent from the proposed 10 percent rate, but the tax payable was cut in half because the tax became a credit against income taxes. Bennett could take credit for taxing the sector's windfall gains at a 25 percent tax rate, while the sector would be relieved by the cut in the tax take because the tax was a credit against income tax, to the extent otherwise payable by the mine. Bennett's tax on gold gains essentially imposed a minimum corporate tax on a mine's profits from gold during its application.

While Charlotte Gray indicated Oakes' "estimate of Ottawa's tax grab is unreliable," she agreed it was "punitive," which provides no sense of what the tax take from Oakes would have been if he stayed.[135] Oakes also told the press that Lake Shore Mines was already subject to corporate income tax, which does not give a sense of the extent to which it was paying income tax, if any.

To better understand whether Bennett acted punitively, it is necessary to distinguish the tax on gold gains and the tax imposed on income; they taxed different things and different persons. Oakes' reaction suggests that Lake Shore Mines was not paying much, if any, income tax and was caught by the tax on gold not being fully offset by corporate income tax, and even more likely that both Lake Shore Mines and Oakes were caught by Bennett's decision to have Parliament curtail depletion allowances.

Gray mentioned that one reliable estimate was that Oakes' mining stock earned him $10.7 million between 1925 and 1932, or about $1.33 million a year, exacting personal income tax of $5.3 million for the period, or almost 50 percent.[136] Presumably, this included paying Ontario's then municipal income tax. In 1933, he earned $3 million from the shares and paid $1 million of personal taxes.

[135] Gray, *Murdered Midas, supra* note 114, p. 90.
[136] *Ibid.*, p. 88.

The Bennett government increased the top marginal tax rate to 56 percent for federal purposes in 1933 on taxable income above $500,000, to which was added a 5 percent surtax on the tax imposed on taxable income above $5,000. Total taxes payable on $1 million were $527,131, being a $50,473 increase from 1932. Yet Oakes' tax of $1 million was 33.33 percent of his $3 million in dividends. Increasing the top marginal rate without more is therefore not necessarily effective in raising taxes.

The federal rates did not change in 1934; yet in 1935, the Bennett government had Parliament cut the depletion allowance that shareholders of precious-metal mining companies could claim to 20 percent from 50 percent, and imposed an additional progressive tax on investment income, with the rates increasing from 2 percent to 10 percent. The changes increased the top marginal federal tax rate on investment income to about 69 percent (56% + 10% + 5% of the tax on income over $5,000). The 69 percent tax rate on investment income like dividends was backstopped by a new tax on gifts to prevent tax avoidance (e.g., income-splitting by gifting to a relative income-producing property such as shares).

It appears that Prime Minister Bennett recognized by 1935 that, as part of his New Deal for Canadians, increasing the top tax rate in 1933 had not been effective, although making it effective should be expected to encounter significant political pushback. Cutting depletion and imposing a special tax on investment income in 1935 changed things significantly, and the changes applied to Oakes, who could not avoid it on his dividends, given the new tax on gifts.[137]

---

[137] Like the tax on investment income, the new tax rates on gifts began at 2 percent of the value of gifts up to $25,000 and ended at a 10 percent rate for gifts in excess of $1 million, which was in addition to a top marginal rate of about 69 percent on taxable income (56% + 10% on investment income + the 5% surtax). Former senior Finance official Robert Bryce indicated that these were low rates for gifts, which to him suggested the Bennett government did not have its heart in the matter (Bryce, *Maturing in Hard Time, supra* note 8, pp. 112–13). Bryce does not appear to have appreciated that the gift tax prevented obvious avoidance of the tax on investment income; but for the gift tax, wealthy individuals

The combined effect of the 1935 changes would have been a tough pill for Oakes and others in a similar position to swallow, so to speak, after having been allowed to claim a 50 percent depletion allowance on their dividends previously. A rough estimate of $1.04 million would be the federal tax take if Oakes earned $2 million of dividends, or 52 percent plus additional amounts to Ontario.[138]

The above estimate suggests two things. First, the 1935 changes reveal the extent to which Bennett skewered a major tax preference for wealthy owners of gold-mining corporations when he curtailed their depletion claims. In that sense, the top marginal tax rate of 56 percent (plus a 5 percent surtax) that applied to taxable income above $500,000 in 1933 and 1934 was illusory; it applied only after high-income individuals claimed their tax benefits such as capital gains not being taxable, a 50 percent depletion allowance on dividends received from precious-metal stock and their charitable deductions.

Second, as suggested, while posted top marginal tax rates can be illusory, they can become real if there is the political will to act and face the political pressures that result. Those pressures can include

---

could have gifted their property to close relatives to avoid the combined taxes on their investment income. Bryce went so far as to suggest that the gift tax was "ineffectual" because it raised only a "small increase in revenues," which misses the purpose of the tax. This led him to further speculate that Bennett may have wanted to be perceived to be making reforms in the context of his New Deal measures. Some historians make similar speculations about Bennett's New Deal proposals. It is amazing the extent to which Bennett has been subjected to such speculative broadsides in the historical record, and anyone reading that record should exercise caution. The number of income tax changes the Bennett government made during the Great Depression is startling; for example, it had Parliament enact a withholding tax regime that imposes tax on non-resident persons receiving Canadian-sourced dividends, interest and royalties and several anti-avoidance rules that applied to different types of tax avoidance.

[138] The $1 million estimate of federal income tax in 1935 assumes Oakes made no charitable donations (or gifts to relatives) and is based on the Bennett government's curtailing depletion and imposing additional progressive tax at rates up to 10 percent of investment income. However, Oakes donated to charity—especially, in the Niagara Falls area.

driving people with significant amounts of income offshore, thus making them so-called *tax refugees*.

Oakes believed that the Bennett government was punishing him, presumably for supporting Mackenzie King, and Gray notes that an earlier biographer of Oakes claimed that Ottawa—which means Bennett—had acted with malice against him when enacting the tax on gold and curtailing depletion. But Oakes was a wealthy person fully capable of having friends in the press help shape the public narrative. One such friend was a former prospector co-venturer who also struck it rich in Kirkland Lake. He owned a substantial interest in the *Globe and Mail*, which Gray notes was sympathetic to Oakes, as the liberal press barons raked him over the coals as a two-time tax dodger who recoiled at paying Canadian income tax after previously renouncing his American citizenship presumably to avoid the income tax that Uncle Sam has imposed on American citizens since 1911.

When acting, Bennett had a distinct advantage over almost all politicians in that he knew the tax code and how to legislate against preferential tax treatment. The change to depletion was part of a broader stream of tax-raising changes he ensured Parliament enacted during the Great Depression, which was the last thing wealthy Canadians expected, given that Bennett was one of Canada's wealthiest citizens and the country's top corporate-commercial lawyer. His political mistake was acting without addressing a too-high top marginal tax rate, rather than curtailing tax preferences enjoyed by Sir Harry Oakes and several other high-income Canadians.

Bennett's previously quoted explanation of why he curtailed depletion does not support the view that he acted with malice or to punish wealthy Canadians such as Oakes; it suggests that he tried to correct an obvious tax policy deficiency but, in doing so, failed to fine-tune the marginal rate structure. For doing so, he became a target of the wealthy, their friends in the press and his political enemies to such an extent that no statue of R.B. Bennett has ever been placed on Parliament Hill.

Once Mackenzie King replaced Bennett as prime minister in 1935, it is instructive of the way in which he and his government operated: the mining sector secured the Holy Grail for mining profits. We will never know the total sum that the sector donated to the Liberals in the lead-up to that election in return for that tax preference. It is likely the Timmins' family knew.

All of this makes it a bit rich for Mackenzie King to express moral outrage in his diaries about the lifestyle of tax refugees inhabiting the Bahamas when he visited Nassau in 1938. Gray quoted King's diaries: "[T]he atmosphere of the place is mostly unhealthy. It has been built up out of excessive money made from rum-running and expenditures of millionaires who had gone to reside there to escape taxation in their own countries." Her interpretation is that King was upset by the fact that almost 150 of the tax refugees were Canadians not resident in Canada for more than 183 days a year.[139] What is notable is that King never expressed moral outrage about why wealthy Canadians who remained in Canada, and their corporations and trusts, were escaping income tax because of his government's tax policies aiding and abetting the rumrunners and those who operated new mines and brokerages in the name of a higher calling—ensuring Mackenzie King was prime minister. Is this why there is a statue of Mackenzie King on Parliament Hill and a conspicuous lack of one for Bennett?

In the next decision, Justice Abbott returns to the subject matter of computing business income.

Joseph Irwin (1964)

In *Irwin*, Abbott considered the computation of the gross profit of a trading business that buys and sells inventory.[140] He stated the methodology in the context in which Irwin was trying, through

---

[139] Gray, *Murdered Midas*, *supra* note 114, pp. 116–117.

[140] *MNR v. Joseph Irwin*, [1964] SCR 662, allowing the Minister's appeal from (1962), [1963] Ex. CR 51, which partially allowed the taxpayer's appeal (to treat adventure property as inventory of a business with an inventory write-down) from (*sub nom* No. 672) (1959), 60 DTC 26, 23 Tax ABC 233 (TAB). *Minister of National Revenue v. Irwin* – SCC Cases (scc-csc.ca). The Exchequer Court's decision is at https://reports.fja-cmf.gc.ca/fja-cmf/j/en/item/397405/index.do.

finesse, to avoid taxation on his gains under the Supreme Court's adventure tax precedent.

The Minister's auditors reassessed Irwin, who was a petroleum engineer, on the basis that he was engaged in adventures in the nature of trade when he bought and sold prospective oil lands. His gains were treated as taxable business income rather than tax-exempt capital gains. Irwin successfully argued before the Exchequer Court that if he was carrying on a business, his business should be allowed to write down the cost of its retained-land inventory to market value each year, which reduced the assessed income.

But it should be noted that an adventure in the nature of trade is not a business *per se*; it is included in the meaning of "business" by statutory definition. Drawing this nuance is important because 30 years later a Supreme Court panel would divide 3–2 on whether Abbott's holding in *Irwin* found that adventure property cannot be inventory.

The Minister appealed in *Irwin* on the basis that Irwin was not entitled to an inventory write-down. That is, he never maintained an account of inventory in his records nor reported that he had inventory in his tax return. If correct, the costs of Irwin's oil and gas properties were not deductible until each disposition.

Justice Abbott's decision enunciates a clear principle for computing the gross profit of a trading business that buys inventory and writes its cost down to market value before selling it: "The law is clear therefore that for income tax purposes gross profit, in the case of a business which consists of acquiring property and reselling it, is the excess of sale price over costs, subject only to any modification effected by the [statutory] 'cost or market, whichever is lower' rule."[141] Once that gross profit is computed, the taxpayer's net income (or loss) from the business is computed as the difference between gross income that is based on accrued revenue (received or receivable) for the year less expenses incurred to earn that income

[141] *Ibid.*, SCC pp. 664–65.

for the year. Best commercial principles are to be applied as modified by the statutory law.

Irwin's difficulty was not with best commercial principles. His difficulty was his failure to comply with a statutory provision in the 1952 ITA that required that he adopt a method for valuing inventory of a business. Practically speaking, Irwin had not adopted a method because he maintained he was not carrying on a business with his receipts from dispositions being tax-free capital gains. Rather, Irwin was ensnared by his tax position of exemption, and the Supreme Court was having none of his equivocation.

Abbott began the core of his decision by expressing doubt about whether the rules related to deducting the cost of business inventory before a sale applied if the inventory has a known cost and sale price for each specific property, which would be especially the case for adventure property. He reversed the Exchequer Court and held that Irwin had, if he carried on a trading business, failed to adopt an inventory method, which could have been done only if he obtained ministerial permission. Not only was no permission sought, but Irwin also failed to put forward his market values for the purported inventory until trial. If he had in fact inventory of a trading business, he had not been reporting income. (Justices Cartwright, Martland, Judson and Spence concurred.[142])

Justice Abbott was a senior member of the Supreme Court by 1968 when he decided a novel but important aspect to whether a group of persons has legal control of a corporation.

Vina-Rug (Canada) Limited (1968)

The issue in *Vina-Rug* is whether more than one "group of persons" can have simultaneous control of the same corporation, or group of corporations.[143] If they can, the associated corporation rules applied to associate the taxpayers Vina-Rug and Stradwick's

---

[142] *Ibid.*, SCC p. 666.

[143] *Vina-Rug (Canada) Limited v. MNR*, [1968] SCR 193. *Vina-Rug (Canada) Limited v. Minister of National Revenue* – SCC Cases (scc-csc.ca).

Limited, and the two corporations had to share one small business deduction.

The facts are straightforward, subject to the math. Stradwick's Limited's share structure is the key to unravelling the mystery of whether a "group of persons" combination could form a voting majority to control both it and Vina-Rug. In 1961 and 1962, both corporations had various shareholders.

Stradwick's Limited had four shareholders. They were John Stradwick Sr. (30 percent), son 1 (25 percent), son 2 (25 percent) and H.D. McGilvery (20 percent)—an apparent stranger to Stradwick Sr. and his two sons in a family and tax sense. While no two shareholders had more than 50 percent of the votes, a combination of any three of the four shareholders could readily assemble a voting majority: (1) Stradwick Sr. plus his two sons, (2) Stradwick Sr. plus one of his sons and McGilvery and (3) the two sons and McGilvery. While the latter voting majority appears unlikely, as it could pit the two sons against their father, it is not so unlikely if a juicy tax benefit were available.

Vina-Rug had several shareholders, but the key shareholders were son 1 (15.3325 percent), son 2 (15.3325 percent), McGilvery (15.3325 percent) and Stradwick's Limited (13.125 percent). Others held the remaining shares (40.8775 percent). Once again, while no two shareholders had more than 50 percent of the votes of Vina-Rug, a combination of any three of the key four shareholders could form a group of persons in control. Since Stradwick Sr. was not one of the four key shareholders of Vina-Rug, the issue narrowed down to whether son 1, son 2 and McGilvery could form a group of persons in control of both Vina-Rug and Stradwick's Limited.

Other key facts are that McGilvery had been a shareholder of Stradwick's Limited since 1950, and he and Stradwick Sr. owned shares of two other companies, which were engaged in the manufacturing, wholesaling or retailing of flooring.

Son 1 testified that he, his brother, and their father Stradwick Sr. controlled Stradwick's Limited as a group of persons. This would mean that they formed a group of persons that controlled only one of the two corporations. But, at trial, the Exchequer Court held that son 1, son 2, and McGilvery were also a group of persons in control of Stradwick's Limited. This finding doomed Vina-Rug's position that it and Stradwick's Limited were not associated. Vina-Rug appealed.

Justice Abbott's approach in income tax disputes was to write a crisp judgment that focused on the issue before the court; he did not wander off topic. His unanimous decision in *Vina-Rug* follows that pattern. It comes in at just over three pages despite the complex matter of simultaneous control by two or more groups of persons of one or more corporations being incredibly important in terms of income tax and company law for the country's future. In the 21st century, it would not come as a surprise if the Supreme Court were to issue a 40-plus-page judgment on such a topic.

Vina-Rug opened with a straightforward statement that described the issue, and it quoted the relevant provision, subsection 39(4) of the 1952 ITA. Abbott then listed shareholdings of each company, based on their share registries. This was followed by a tight statement of the relevant facts as determined at trial. In doing so, Abbott stated without any fanfare that, in 1956, "John Stradwick, Jr., W.L. Stradwick, H.D. McGilvery and Stradwick's Limited acquired control of Vina-Rug."[144] Thus, Abbott did not include Stradwick Sr. in that group of persons in control.

Abbott then noted certain facts that he indicated were irrelevant in the context of how he was deciding the case. Those facts were that: (1) son 1 had testified that he, his brother and their father Stradwick Sr. controlled Stradwick's Limited as a group of persons; and (2) McGilvery attended and voted his shares at all meetings.

In reaching his decision, Justice Abbott cited with approval the Supreme Court's then leading precedent on corporate control, its

[144] *Ibid.*, SCC p. 196.

1967 unanimous decision in *Dworkin Furs et al.*[145] It held that a person or group of persons has legal control of a corporation if it has a voting majority to install a board of directors, thereby gaining effective control of the company's affairs. Given this, Abbott held that "once it is established that a group of shareholders owns a majority of the voting shares of a company, and the same group a majority of the voting shares of a second company, that fact is sufficient, in my opinion, to constitute the two companies associated" under the tax law.[146]

It did not matter whether another group of persons could form a majority: "In my view, it is immaterial whether or not other combinations of shareholders may own a majority of voting shares in either company, provided each combination is in a position to control at least a majority of votes to be cast at a general meeting of shareholders."[147] (Justices Fauteux, Judson, Hall and Spence concurred.)

From the late 1950s to mid-1970s, either Justice Abbott or Justice Wilfred Judson wrote the unanimous or majority decisions in a series of disputes that concerned the application of Canada's international tax treaties, which are meant to prevent double taxation. Abbott decided two of these disputes: *Furness, Withy & Company Limited,*[148] in 1968 and *Tara Exploration and Development Company Limited,*[149] in 1972. The first concerned interpreting the *Canada-United Kingdom Tax Treaty*, and the second the *Canada-Ireland Tax Treaty*.

---

[145] *MNR v. Dworkin Furs (Pembroke) Ltd. et al.*, [1967] SCR 223. *Minister of National Revenue v. Dworkin Furs (Pembroke) Ltd. et al.* – SCC Cases (scc-csc.ca).

[146] *Vina-Rug, supra* note 143, SCC p. 197.

[147] *Ibid.*

[148] *Furness, Withy & Company Limited v. MNR*, [1968] SCR 221. *Furness, Withy & Company Limited v. Minister of National Revenue* – SCC Cases (scc-csc.ca).

[149] *MNR v. Tara Exploration and Development Co. Limited,* (1972), [1974] SCR 1057. *Minister of National Revenue v. Tara Exploration and Development Co. Ltd.* – SCC Cases (scc-csc.ca).

Furness, Withy & Company (1968)
In *Furness*, the taxpayer was incorporated, and resided in the United Kingdom but had offices at Canadian ports where it carried on agency and stevedoring work. It acted as an agent for and serviced its own ships and those of other companies. Furness sought to sweep all its profits from these two activities in Canada into tax-exempt status, based on a treaty benefit. The Minister sought to tax the profits from both activities.

Article V of the treaty stated: "[P]rofits which a resident of one of the territories [U.K.] *derives from operating ships* or aircraft shall be exempt from tax *in the other territory*" [emphasis added]. The issue for decision was whether none, one, or both of the taxpayer's activities in Canada resulted in profits derived from operating ships.

In a two-page decision, Abbott reviewed the trial judge's findings and affirmed them. The exemption did not apply to profits derived from servicing the ships of other corporations. It did apply to profits from servicing its own ships. A related portion of head office administration expenses incurred to manage its taxable Canadian activities was deductible in computing its Canadian income. (Chief Justice Cartwright and Justices Judson, Richie and Pigeon concurred.)

International shipping companies pay little, if any, taxes on income derived from operating ships in international waters. Under treaties, this can be accomplished by not residing in a country that taxes profits derived from operating ships in international waters. Canadian waters are international waters in a tax sense to other countries.

Tara Exploration and Development (1972)
In *Tara Exploration and Development*, the taxpayer was incorporated in Ontario to explore for minerals in Ireland, where control of the corporation and its management resided. As a resident of Ireland, the taxpayer realized a large profit from buying and selling shares of a related mining company in Canada. The Minister sought to tax the profit, which was allowed only if such profit was attributable to a "permanent establishment" that the taxpayer had in Canada.

Tara Exploration and Development had no employees, had an office in Ontario only to satisfy corporate registry requirements, and retained an accountant and a lawyer who would obtain any necessary approvals from Ireland in respect of the company's Canadian activity.

Justice Abbott reviewed the facts and law and held the profit was not taxable in Canada because the taxpayer had no Canadian permanent establishment as required by the treaty. This meant the profit was taxable only to the extent that Ireland imposed a tax in the circumstances. (Justices Martland, Judson, Ritchie and Laskin concurred.)

By the late 20th century, it was common for a multi-national corporation to avoid creating a permanent establishment in one or more countries from which it derived income. That income would be included in the income of a taxpayer in a country that would impose a low or zero tax on the income.

The last decision of Justice Abbott considered is his unanimous 1969 decision in *J. Harold Wood*.

J. Harold Wood (1969)

Abbott's decision in *J. Harold Wood* does not have significant value as a precedent, but there are three aspects to the decision that make it worthy of consideration in the context of his approach to income tax and its avoidance.

First, *J. Harold Wood* is a federal income tax case in which a taxpayer obtained leave to appeal prior to the implementation of the Supreme Court's leave requirement in 1975. Normally, an appeal of a federal tax dispute to the Court occurred as a matter of right—that is, where the taxes in dispute met a modest dollar threshold. For most of the pre-1975 period, the threshold was $500, which increased to $10,000 in the early 1970s.

Second, the Supreme Court provided written reasons during the period for why it was granting or denying leave, as in the *J. Harold Wood* case.

Third, Abbott was known to be pro-Crown in most tax disputes—especially ones that concerned tax avoidance. The Supreme Court had considered several disputes just like *J. Harold Wood* in the prior decade, which were decided for the Crown in an income tax avoidance context. Yet, Abbott reversed the Exchequer Court and allowed the taxpayer's appeal in a unanimous decision.

Why? It went against Abbott's perceived pattern when deciding income tax disputes. Abbott's 1969 decision in *J. Harold Wood* suggests that his approach to income tax factored in the question of whether a taxpayer's actions were, or were not, based on tax avoidance intent.

In 1968, J. Harold Wood, a lawyer, petitioned the Supreme Court to grant leave to appeal a federal dispute over the taxability of $700 of receipts. Justice Louis-Philippe Pigeon heard the petition in Chambers on October 4. Three days later, Pigeon issued his decision granting leave to appeal.[150]

Over several years, Wood acquired at a discount 11 mortgages. Under such a transaction, the person purchasing the mortgage pays the lender-owner less than the principal the borrower owes. How much less is a matter of negotiation and risk calculation, but significant sums can be made on such transactions. Wood had in effect assumed the position of lender and received interest and principal owing on the mortgages over their terms. The interest receipts are taxable income. The tax issue is whether the receipt of principal above the discounted price is taxable income.

Very astute people had been purchasing discounted mortgages since at least the late 1940s and claiming tax-exempt status in respect of the receipts of principal under the mortgages. Many of these taxpayers were lawyers. But the Supreme Court had held in a series of disputes beginning in 1962 that the principal amount received above the discounted price was a taxable profit. The Court reasoned that the holders of the discounted mortgages either were

---

[150] *J. Harold Wood v. MNR*, [1968] SCR 957. Leave to appeal granted. *Wood v. Minister of National Revenue* – SCC Cases (scc-csc.ca).

involved in a business trading in mortgages or had undertaken an adventure in the nature of trade. Either way, the gains were taxable income. The disputes include *Curlett* (1962),[151] *Scott* (1963),[152] *MacInnes* (1963),[153] *Lloyd Estate* (1965),[154] and *Curlett* (1967).[155] In some of the disputes, the Court reversed the Exchequer Court.

But Wood's situation was different despite the cumulative weight of Supreme Court precedent disallowing tax-exempt treatment in respect of gains from discounted mortgages. The Exchequer Court had followed Supreme Court precedent and denied Wood's appeal. Originally, by mistake, both Wood and the Minister's counsel thought Wood had a right to appeal. But this was incorrect because the tax in dispute was below $500. At the last minute, Wood realized he needed leave, notified the Crown, and organized his petition.

Justice Pigeon in his written decision considered the point of law in issue too important not to grant leave. But he noted that the justice who heard a petition for leave had the sole discretion to decide whether to grant leave, and not the Supreme Court. This was a concern to Pigeon in addition to the last-minute petition not being in keeping with the Court's need to manage its caseload. Nine days later, a Supreme Court panel of five heard oral argument. On January 28, 1969, less than four months after leave had

---

[151] *Harry Graves Curlett v. MNR*, [1962] SCR vii, 62 DTC 1320, affirming [1961] Ex. CR 427. The Exchequer Court decision is at https://reports.fja-cmf.gc.ca/fja-cmf/j/en/item/397414/index.do?q=curlett.

[152] *James Scott v. MNR*, [1963] SCR 223. *Scott v. Minister of National Revenue* – SCC Cases (scc-csc.ca).

[153] *MNR v. William MacInnes*, [1963] SCR 299. *Minister of National Revenue v. MacInnes* – SCC Cases (scc-csc.ca).

[154] *Estate of Dr. William J. Lloyd (Clara M. Lloyd, Executrix) v. MNR*, [1965] SCR v, 65 DTC 5031, affirming (1963), [1964] Ex. CR 566. The Exchequer Court decision is at *Lloyd v. Minister of National Revenue* – Office of the Commissioner for Federal Judicial Affairs Canada (fja-cmf.gc.ca).

[155] *MNR v. Harry Graves Curlett*, [1967] SCR 280. *Minister of National Revenue v. Curlett* – SCC Cases (scc-csc.ca).

been granted, Justice Abbott issued the Court's unanimous decision in *J. Harold Wood.*[156]

J. Harold Wood had been practicing law in Toronto since 1928. His law practice included a substantial component of handling mortgages for lenders. In 1957, he and an associate acquired for $7,100 a mortgage on which $8,500 of principal was owing at an interest rate of 6.5 percent annually. In 1962, the borrower had fully repaid the mortgage with Wood receiving in that year a $700 gain.

Wood had purchased an interest in 13 mortgages from 1956 to 1963 inclusive, two of which were not purchased at a discount. This was a modest total, given his active practice of handling mortgages for lenders. Wood's action and circumstances were not suggestive of a speculative trading operation; they were more in keeping with an older person's acquisition of safe investments for retirement.

In a three-page decision, Justice Abbott reviewed the facts and distinguished the Supreme Court's prior precedent. (Justices Judson, Ritchie, Hall and Pigeon concurred.) Abbott contrasted the situation to the facts in Justice Judson's unanimous decision in *Scott* six years earlier. In that case, the taxpayer-lawyer had purchased 149 agreements between 1947 and 1953. (Justices Taschereau, Fauteux, Ritchie and Hall concurred.)

Justice Douglas Abbott resigned on principle over an internal dispute occurring within the Supreme Court in December 1973 (he resigned together with Chief Justice Gérald Fauteux with the internal dispute discussed later).[157] They were replaced as members of the Court by Justices Jean Beetz and Louis-Philippe de Grandpré. Douglas Abbott died in 1987.

---

[156] *J. Harold Wood v. MNR*, [1969] SCR 330. *Wood v. M.N.R.* – SCC Cases (scc-csc.ca).
[157] Ian Bushnell, *The Captive Court: A Study of the Supreme Court of Canada* (Montreal-Kingston: McGill-Queen's University Press, 1992), pp. 400–04.

RONALD MARTLAND: A LEGAL PURIST

Prime Minister John Diefenbaker appointed Ronald Martland to the Supreme Court in January 1958, replacing Justice Henry Nolan, a decorated veteran of the First and Second World Wars, who died prematurely a year after being appointed to the Court.[158]

Legal scholars describe Justice Martland—a conservative justice—as being "a legal purist who adhered staunchly to the strict traditions of the British common law."[159] He also was a person that "had good humour and openness,"[160] and who came to the Supreme Court from Alberta with a broad range of legal experience and knowledge that included criminal defence work, corporate law and oil and gas law, following the completion of a prestigious Rhodes scholarship and an outstanding academic performance at Oxford. Martland, who had been a Chancellor of the Anglican Church of Canada, was a judicial force of increasing influence over his long tenure on the Supreme Court.[161]

The Pierre Trudeau government bypassed Martland—in line to be appointed chief justice after Chief Justice Fauteux had resigned in 1973—for Bora Laskin, a liberal justice and former academic. Laskin's appointment is clouded by intrigue because the Prime Minister's office had already telephoned Martland to advise that he would be appointed the new chief justice.[162] It should be noted in this context that a number of legal academics, at least at Dalhousie

---

[158] See Colonel Henry Gratton "Harry" Nolan, Military Commander, Calgary Alberta, University of Calgary Digital Archives. https://digitalcollections.ucalgary.ca/archive/Colonel-Henry-Grattan–Harry–Nolan–Military-Commander–Calgary–Alberta–2R3BF1OYCXWT.html.

[159] Balcome, McBride and Russell, *Supreme Court of Canada Decision-Making, supra* note 17, p. 247.

[160] Philip Slayton, *Mighty Judgment: How the Supreme Court of Canada Runs Your Life* (Toronto: Penguin Canada, 2011), p. 32.

[161] Balcome, McBride and Russell, *Supreme Court of Canada Decision-Making, supra* note 17, p. 248.

[162] Robert J. Sharpe and Kent Roach, *Brian Dickson: A Judge's Journey* (Toronto: University of Toronto Press published for The Osgoode Society for Canadian Legal History, 2003), p. 142.

Law School, took issue during the late 1970s and early 1980s with Martland's conservative approach to the law and advocated in their lectures for a more activist judicial approach. The decision to bypass Martland would remain contentious in the years that followed, although academia welcomed the appointment of one of its own as chief justice.[163]

Court insiders credit Martland with being the judge who eight years later blocked Prime Minister Pierre Trudeau's attempt to repatriate the constitution without the agreement of a substantial number of the provinces.[164] Legal scholars were surprised by his style and "creative statements" in his 1981 partial dissent in the constitutional law dispute known as *Patriation Reference*,[165] and maintained that Martland was "at his best" when deciding administrative and constitutional law disputes.[166]

In 1967, Sydney Peck published a study in the *Canadian Bar Review* that applied scalogram analysis to test the personal policy preferences of Supreme Court justices.[167] (Scalogram analysis is a psychometric technique used to examine whether a set of items or variables measure a single underlying construct or dimension. The basic thrust is that if the set of judgements, or statements, truly measures dimension, then a person or group's responses should

[163] Philip Girard, *Bora Laskin: Bringing Law to Life* (Toronto: University of Toronto Press published for The Osgoode Society for Canadian Legal History, 2005), pp. 408–11.

[164] Balcome, McBride and Russell, *Supreme Court of Canada Decision-Making, supra* note 17, p. 247.

[165] *Reference re Resolution to Amend the Constitution of Canada*, [1981] 1 SCR 753; and (Nos. 1, 2, 3), (1981), 125 DLR (3d) 1. Re: Resolution to amend the Constitution – SCC Cases (scc-csc.ca).

[166] Balcome, McBride and Russell, *Supreme Court of Canada Decision-Making, supra* note 17, p. 247.

[167] Sydney Peck, "The Supreme Court of Canada, 1958–1966: A Search for Policy Through Scalogram Analysis," (1967) 45:4 *Canadian Bar Review* 666. For scalogram analysis, Louis Guttman's work advanced this technique and the description of such analysis in the following two sentences in the narrative is based on his work. See Stouffer, S.A., Guttman, L., Suchman, E.A., Lazarsfeld, P.F., Star, S.A., Clausen, J.A. (1950) *Measurement and Prediction*: Princeton University Press and https://en.wikipedia.org/wiki/Louis_Guttman.

follow a predictable pattern based on their overall score or scale value on that dimension.) He analyzed non-unanimous decisions from 1958 to 1966, including 28 tax decisions. Peck identified which of the justices during the period tended to side for or against the government in tax disputes.[168] He classified Judson as being strongly pro-government, with Abbott being as pro-government as Cartwright was pro-taxpayer. But Peck classified Martland as neutral between government and taxpayers.[169]

Despite Peck's classification, quantitative and qualitative analysis of Martland's income tax decisions suggest he was pro-Crown, especially if the matter concerned tax avoidance. However, this analysis focuses on income tax cases and does not distinguish unanimous from non-unanimous outcomes.

Justice Martland heard 123 income tax cases, of which 45 concerned tax avoidance during his 24 years as a Supreme Court judge.

In late June 1958, newly appointed Justice Ronald Martland issued his first unanimous income tax decision for the Supreme Court. That first decision concerned a company the previously mentioned William Harrison Riddle owned with his wife.

Minerals Limited (1958)

Minerals Limited reveals the extent to which some farmers made the poor financial decision to get involved with Riddle, after which many farmers alleged they were defrauded—allegations that failed in the courts of Saskatchewan.[170]

Riddle began the promotion in December 1949 when he incorporated Farmers Mutual Petroleums Ltd. It granted Riddle the exclusive right to solicit farmer participation and the sale of shares of Farmers Mutual during the next five years. It also paid Riddle's

---

[168] *Ibid.*, pp. 683–84. Peck's database included 14 federal income tax cases, six federal excise cases, three federal succession duty cases, one federal customs case, three municipal tax cases and one provincial social service tax case. His list of federal income tax cases is at his footnote 41.

[169] *Ibid.*, pp. 688–89.

[170] *Minerals Limited v. MNR*, [1958] SCR 490. *Minerals Limited v. The Minister of National Revenue* – SCC Cases (scc-csc.ca).

expenses and gave him a 20 percent interest in the rents earned from oil and gas leases farmers assigned to the company.

Riddle employed agents who swarmed southeast Saskatchewan, soliciting farmers to assign their leases with oil and gas exploration and production companies to Riddle's Farmers Mutual. In return, for each acre covered by a lease, a farmer would receive one share of the company and a 20 percent interest in the rents Farmers Mutual earned from those leases. This meant Riddle earned 20 percent of the rents personally, which was the same amount each farmer would earn from his transferred leases. Farmers Mutual retained the remaining 60 percent.

The dispute reveals that participating farmers had given up 80 percent of the rent entitlements to the value of oil and gas production from their acreage for one share of Farmers Mutual per acre. It was a poor financial decision for farmers whose acreage produced oil or gas.

Riddle's agents soon learned that some farmers had never agreed to lease their acreage to an oil and gas exploration and production company. This surprised Riddle, and he quickly developed a plan to exploit the situation. He decided that Farmers Mutual could not acquire such leases. Instead, he sought to lease the acreage personally from such farmers for 10 years, which gave him the right to pursue oil and gas exploration and production. To get the leases, he printed up a form document in which he agreed to pay a farmer ten cents per acre, subject to an additional ten cents per acre each year no exploration occurred. Many farmers agreed. Riddle assigned the leases, which covered 81,000 acres, to Farmers Mutual on the same terms other farmers assigned their leases for shares of Farmers Mutual and 20 percent of the revenues produced by the assigned leases. Presumably, Riddle also received his 20 percent promotion interest in any revenue from the assigned leases.

In May 1950, Riddle and his wife incorporated Minerals Limited, which Martland indicated became Riddle's "alter ego." Canadian judges used this terminology in older cases to taint the effect of the related transaction, although Martland did not clarify whether he used the phrase in that sense.[171] Martland then referred to Riddle's sale in June 1950 of his promotion business to Minerals Limited for $10,000, which included his rights and obligations under his agreement with Farmers Mutual.

At that point, Minerals Limited assumed operation of Riddle's promotion. As part of the transactions, Riddle assigned to Minerals Limited his residual interest in the leases he personally acquired from farmers, covering 81,000 acres, which acreage was in addition to 750,000 acres covered by the leases other farmers assigned to Farmers Mutual. Soon oil and gas companies approached Riddle and Minerals Limited, expressing an interest in exploring for oil and gas on the 81,000 acres.

Minerals Limited sold its residual interest in the 81,000 acres in 1951 for a flat $2 per acre to an exploration company. The profit after all expenses was $140,000 (about $1.65 million in 2024 dollars). Minerals Limited claimed tax-exempt capital gains treatment. It maintained that it acquired the leases "unwillingly" and the leases were an "ordinary investment" sold in a group as an "isolated transaction."[172]

Justice Martland found that there was no evidence to support the contention that Minerals Limited had any intention to work the leases or retain them as an investment. He distinguished one leading British precedent and considered other British and Supreme Court precedents. Martland also applied Kerwin's unanimous decision in *McIntosh*, where he found that a transaction that is an isolated sale does not prevent the resulting gain from being taxable as income.[173] Minerals Limited had realized the profit in the operation of its business.

---

[171] *Ibid.*, p. 493. With respect to a corporation being the "alter ego" of another person, see Hudson J. of the Supreme Court in *Pioneer Laundry*, *supra* note 20, and Noël J. of the Exchequer Court in *Foreign Power Securities*, *infra* note 309.
[172] *Ibid.*, pp. 495–97.
[173] *McIntosh*, *supra* note 63. *McIntosh v. Minister of National Revenue* – SCC Cases (scc-csc.ca).

Perhaps Martland's most famous income tax decision is the next from 1962.

Irrigation Industries (1962)

Martland led a 3–2 majority in deciding *Irrigation Industries* for the taxpayer, on reversal. The decision is a rare and fascinating exception in that the Supreme Court allowed a tax avoidance result in the pre-*Charter* era. Even more surprising, the unlikely duo of Justices John Cartwright and Wilfred Judson dissented, which raises the question of why they agreed in their dissent.[174]

The dispute concerns whether gains from selling stock were taxable income or tax-exempt capital gains in circumstances where it can be said the corporation lacked a *bona fide* investment intent. But Martland's decision fails to reveal this lack of *bona fide* investment intent. For that, one needs to read the 1959 Tax Review Board decision because the people behind the stock's purchase and sale are not identified in the Supreme Court's decision.

Brian Locke, a leading Toronto-Calgary investment broker, was Irrigation Industries' directing mind. A wealthy client tipped Locke about acquiring shares of a New Brunswick mining company being promoted by Jim Boylen, a high-flying mining stock promoter in the 1950s and 1960s. Boylen later enticed New Brunswick billionaire K.C. Irving into investing to build a smelter. Irving came to regret doing so. His biography dedicates a chapter to the investment, which opens with his late-in-life lament, "I should have raised hell."[175]

Tipped early about Boyle's promotion, Locke stuffed four thousand shares of the mining stock into Irrigation Industries. He did

---

[174] *Irrigation Industries Limited v. MNR*, [1962] SCR 346, allowing the taxpayer's appeal from 60 DTC 1232, [1960] CTC 329 (Ex. Ct.), which affirmed 59 DTC 446, (1959) 22 Tax ABC 335 (TAB). *Irrigation Industries Ltd. v. The Minister of National Revenue* – SCC Cases (scc-csc.ca).

[175] Douglas How and Ralph Costello, *K.C.: The Biography of K.C. Irving* (Toronto: Key Porter Books Limited, 1993), p. 166.

so by having it acquire the stock at $10 per share on February 23, 1953. Locke and his associates then sat back and watched Boylen's handy work. It led to a rapid price rise on the Toronto Stock Exchange (TSE).

New Brunswick Mining and Smelting Corp. Ltd. opened on the TSE at $10.50 a share in March 1953 and quickly rose to $23.75 per share. Within three weeks, Irrigation Industries sold 2,400 of its shares. The rest were sold in June 1953.

Irrigation Industries unloaded its four thousand shares at an average sale price of $16.72 per share ($66,897 in total) for juicy quick-flip gains of $26,897. The stock's sleigh ride soon dropped with pace down the TSE board, resting at $3.40 a share by 1955. Boylen's promotion work lugged his stock-sleigh back up the hill, and he later lured Irving into riding it back down.

The Tax Appeal Board and Exchequer Court had no difficulty holding that the gains were taxable income from an adventure in the nature of trade. R.S.W. Fordham, Q.C., for the Board dismissed the appeal after noting the stock market was an "open book to him [Locke]."[176] He added that Irrigation Industries had no money of its own to purchase the stock; the funds came from Locke and his associates. The so-called *bona fide* investment was to make a "fast dollar," which it did.[177]

Justice Martland resorted in *Irrigation Industries* to British precedent (and a lower-court Canadian decision) to allow the taxpayer's appeal. (Justices Taschereau and Locke concurred.) By 1962, Supreme Court precedent, including Martland's unanimous decision in *Minerals Limited*, was invariably finding gains of this type to be taxable income, including when the taxpayer's initial intent was investment and the secondary intent was resale.

Two years earlier, in 1960, Justice Judson led a 4–1 Supreme Court majority in *Regal Heights*. (Justices Fauteux, Martland and

[176] *Irrigation Industries, supra* note 174, TAB at 59 DTC p. 448.
[177] *Ibid.*

Ritchie concurred.[178]) He applied a "secondary sale intent" guideline to a case where the taxpayer claimed that a *bona fide* investment intent on purchase had been frustrated by events beyond its control—i.e., it intended to develop land in Calgary into a shopping centre for rent. But it sold the land instead. Judson's approach allowed the lower judiciary to side step questioning the credibility of leading businessmen on their purported *bona fide* investment intent. Cartwright dissented, rejecting the Court's secondary intent guideline.

In *Irrigation Industries*, Martland provided a judicial-policy justification for why investing in stock should be treated differently for tax purposes from investing in real estate followed by a quick sale. He stated:

> Corporate shares are in a different position because they constitute something the purchase of which is, in itself, an investment. They are not, in themselves, articles of commerce, but represent an interest in a corporation which is itself created for the purpose of doing business. Their acquisition is a well-recognized method of investing capital in a business enterprise.[179]

With this, Justices Cartwright and Judson found themselves joined in dissent. Cartwright cited and applied two Supreme Court

---

[178] *Regal Heights Limited v. MNR*, [1960] SCR 902. Regal Heights Ltd. v. Minister of National Revenue – SCC Cases (lexum.com). Also see *Gairdner Securities, Ltd. v. MNR*, [1954] SCR x, 54 DTC 1015, [1954] CTC 24, wherein Rand J. stated (DTC p. 1016): "It is then urged that the particular purchase of Dominion Malting stock in 1944 was an exceptional transaction, designed to obtain a working control of that company in order to enable Gairdner to introduce his sons to industrial management. I will assume that he had such an object in mind, but it was only one of *at least two purposes*, the other of which was made evident, i.e., that if at any time a sufficiently favourable opportunity to sell arose it would be seized upon" [emphasis added]. Locke and Fauteux JJ. concurred, and Kerwin C.J. found the matter was a question of fact, adopting Rand's reasons. Cartwright J. found the matter was a question of fact, adopting the trial judge's reasons.

[179] *Irrigation Industries*, *supra* note 174, SCC p. 352.

decisions: (1) Kerwin's unanimous 1958 holding in *McIntosh*,[180] and (2) Judson's majority 1960 holding in *Regal Heights*. For good measure, Cartwright applied a leading British precedent from 1904 that Martland had distinguished. While Cartwright had dissented from Judson's secondary intent guideline in *Regal Heights*, unlike in that decision, Irrigation Industries' original and sole intent was to earn an adventure profit from selling the shares.

The Supreme Court issued its decision in *Irrigation Industries* in March 1962. Shortly afterward, Gwyneth McGregor at the *Canadian Tax Foundation* described the possible effect of Martland's decision in her case comment. It is "in the nature of a hundred-megaton bomb, since it appears to widen the capital gains area beyond anything previously done by the courts."[181] In September 1962, PM John Diefenbaker appointed *The Royal Commission on Taxation*, which would publish its seminal six volumes of proposals for tax reform in 1966.

In 1970, Martland confronted a different type of situation regarding gains from selling shares.

Samuel Ciglen (1970)

Samuel Ciglen was a lawyer based in Toronto. He was also active with Morris Black in promoting Canadian oil and mining stock in sketchy circumstances to American investors. One such promotion was the Great Sweet Grass stock scandal.

By 1956, Ciglen and Black gained listings for Great Sweet Grass stock on the TSE and the American Stock Exchange, but the U.S. Securities and Exchange Commission (SEC) suspended U.S. trading in 1956. It accused Ciglen of being the man behind Great Sweet Grass stock, which was illegally promoted from boiler rooms in New York. Canadian regulators initially reacted by doing

---

[180] *McIntosh, supra* note 63, SCC p. 119. *McIntosh v. Minister of National Revenue* – SCC Cases (scc-csc.ca).

[181] Gwyneth McGregor, "About the Courts: Bombshell," (1962) 10:3 *Canadian Tax Journal* 166. But see *Ronald Fraser*, *infra* note 271.

nothing, and trading continued in Toronto. The scandal attracted the attention of leading newspapers and magazines across North America and is discussed in Professor Christopher Armstrong's 2001 book *Moose Pastures and Mergers*.[182]

In Washington, an SEC official testified in the fall of 1956 that Ciglen was "the motivating force and driving genius" behind the scheme.[183] By March 1957, the SEC claimed Ciglen had made a $6 million profit from the promotion (about US$70 million in 2024 dollars). Not amused about the unfolding testimony, Ciglen told the Canadian press that he was considering legal action. He compared his unfriendly treatment at the hands of the SEC to the friendly treatment accorded by the Ontario Securities Commission, which he stated, "perform[s] an excellent function."[184]

Ciglen and Morris had netted large U.S.-denominated profits on their Great Sweet Grass promotion while remaining in Toronto. Given this, a Canadian investigation of security law irregularities would, even if it occurred, have relatively minimum consequences. Such activity was, and remains, pursued invariably by provincial regulators in a civil law context with little or no criminal law enforcement. It is white-collar crime, and Canada is well known internationally as a haven for criminals who commit white-collar crime and launder their profits.

But Ciglen and Morris miscalculated. National Revenue investigated their cross-border activities and brought in special counsel

---

[182] Christopher Armstrong, *Moose Pastures and Mergers: The Ontario Securities Commission and the Regulation of Share Markets in Canada, 1940–1980* (Toronto: University of Toronto Press, 2001), pp. 124–25. Also see "Gt. Sweet Grass Trade to Stay on Market Here," *Globe and Mail*, October 27, 1956, p. 28; "Boiler Rooms: The Pressure Is Up," *Business Week*, November 10, 1956, pp. 145–48; and "Say Sweet Grass: Kroy Sold Stock Illegally," *Globe and Mail*, November 28, 1956, p. 24. Also see James Fieldon, "Sam 'Sweet Grass' Ciglen: All-American Headache," *Saturday Night Magazine*, October 26, 1957, pp. 7, 34 and 38.

[183] *Ibid.*, "Say Sweet Grass: Kroy Sold Stock Illegally," p. 24.

[184] "Charges Rile Ciglen: May Take Legal Action," *Globe and Mail*, March 9, 1957, p. 30.

and prosecuted the pair for tax evasion in respect of $8 million. Arrested by the RCMP in 1961, they were tried after a 15-month preliminary hearing. Their first trial ended after 68 days of hearings in 1963 when the trial judge died. The second trial began in late 1964 and spanned 115 days of testimony and considered 1,632 exhibits and 11,000 pages of documents.[185]

At the time, the trial of Ciglen and Morris by judge without a jury was the longest in Canadian history under an indictment for income tax evasion. Although the trial judge acquitted both, the Ontario Court of Appeal convicted Ciglen after the Crown appealed, based on an error of law; the Court of Appeal affirmed Black's acquittal. That error of law is more than just interesting.

In the indictment, Ciglen was charged with conspiracy to willfully evade income tax by "suppressing taxable income" through a diversion of profits from selling shares of Great Sweet Grass (and Kroy) to another person (the "company"). The company sold the shares for gains as if they were its own and recorded them in its books. [If a promoter such as Ciglen sold the shares for a gain, it would be taxable income. But if an investor sold the shares, which it owned, the gain would be a capital gain to it unless the investor engaged in an adventure in the nature of trade. Consequently, who owned the shares could be critical when determining whether the gains were taxable as ordinary income.]

Trial Judge W.F. Rogers found the recording to be a falsification—they were Ciglen's gains. But this falsification was not sufficient to convict. "Only a total failure to account would be enough."

Rogers found a reasonable doubt, based on whether the gains were income or tax-exempt capital gains to Ciglen. He did so after indicating that National Revenue had "traditionally" not treated gains from selling shares as "income," which was described as an "anomaly" arising because of the distinction between income and

---

[185] "Longest in Canada: $8 Million Income Tax Trial Nearing Conclusion," *Globe and Mail*, November 16, 1966, p. B10; and "Ciglen and Black acquitted of tax conspiracy," *Globe and Mail*, March 1, 1967, p. B1.

capital gains. Rogers also noted in his 117-page decision that the courts appear to encourage taxpayers to employ devices to reduce tax: "Indeed, the courts appear to recognize and even encourage devices and stratagems by taxpayers which are designed to reduce the tax load upon them."[186] He then wielded the British *Duke of Westminster* principle for the proposition that Ciglen was entitled to reduce tax and acquitted him.

The Supreme Court upheld the Court of Appeal's conviction of Ciglen but splintered 4–2–1–2.[187] Justice Martland, for a minority of four, found that the trial judge "erred in law in holding that the determination as to whether the profits were income or capital gains was for the Minister, and beyond the purview of the Court, and that he was unable to make a decision on the evidence before him." The following is one of the rare occasions when a Supreme Court judge actually cited the *Duke of Westminster* principle in an income tax decision before 1984, when Martland stated the following:

> In the penultimate paragraph of his judgment, the trial judge, dealing with the issue of a guilty mind, said this:
>
> > Since a taxpayer is entitled to adopt a position that will not attract any tax as opposed to wilfully evading payment of tax imposed by the Act, and if such a course of conduct is open to a taxpayer, it has a direct bearing on the issue of a guilty mind.
>
> He approaches that issue by relying upon the proposition which was stated by Lord Tomlin in *The Commissioners of Inland Revenue v. The Duke of Westminster* [footnote omitted]:
>
> > Every man is entitled if he can to order his affairs so as that the tax attaching under the appropriate Acts is less than it otherwise would be.

[186] "Ciglen and Black Acquitted of Tax Conspiracy," *Globe and Mail*, March 1, 1967, p. B1.

[187] *Sam Ciglen v. The Queen*, [1970] SCR 804. Ciglen v. R. – SCC Cases (scc-csc.ca).

> But in relation to the Kroy-Fulton deal, that can have no relevance, when, on the trial judge's own finding, records were deliberately falsified in order to allocate profits accruing to the appellant to Torny.
>
> The trial judge concluded his reasons by saying, immediately after the paragraph above quoted:
>
>> I am unable to establish by inference from the conduct of the accused and the cumulative effect of the evidence herein, any agreement to conspire as charged in the indictment, the accused Samuel Ciglen is acquitted.
>
> For the appellant it is urged that this is a finding of fact or of mixed fact and law, and, therefore, not subject to appeal by the Crown. But when the trial judge reached that conclusion, for the reasons already outlined, he was considering the evidence under a misconception of law as to what was necessary to be proved in order to establish the Crown's case. The error in this case was as to the legal effect of facts which he had found, and that is an error of law.[188]

For Martland, tax evasion includes having a record falsified intentionally to have another person treat a taxable amount as if it were their amount. To treat it as tax avoidance is an error of law; the Crown had a right to appeal the trial judge's acquittal of Ciglen to the Ontario Court of Appeal. (Justices Fauteux, Abbott and Judson concurred.)

In his minority of opinion for two, Justice Ritchie agreed with Martland and separately with Justice Spence that the trial judge's acquittal was founded on an error of law and a misapplication of the law of evidence. (Justice Pigeon concurred.)

Justice Spence in his minority opinion found that the Court of Appeal considered three questions of law and could come to its own conclusion to convict based on the trial judge's findings of fact.

[188] *Ibid.*, pp. 818–19.

Chief Justice John Cartwright dissented with Justice Hall. The Court of Appeal should have dismissed the Crown's appeal because it concerned three grounds, none of which were solely questions of law.

Martland considered in the next case whether certain transactions should be struck down as a sham.

James A. Cameron (1972)

In the early to mid-1960s, Mr. J.K. Campbell was the president and owner of J.K. Campbell & Associates Limited (Campbell Limited), a roofing and contracting company in the four western provinces with its head office in Edmonton. Besides Mr. Campbell, Campbell Limited had three key employees: Robert Steele managed the Calgary branch, Gordon Symon managed the Edmonton branch, and James Cameron was the superintendent of roofing operations at the Edmonton branch. As managers, they earned salaries and a bonus based on a percentage of profits. For example, Cameron received 5 percent of profits from the Edmonton and Calgary branches.

Campbell, who was nearing retirement, entered discussions with Steele, Symon and Cameron to determine whether, as a group, they wanted to purchase Campbell Limited. On April 17, 1964, Steele, Symon and Campbell incorporated Independent Management Ltd.; its purpose was to provide management services to Campbell Limited and to acquire Mr. Campbell's shares. James Cameron was appointed president.

By September 1964, the three managers ceased to be employees and acted through their new management services company. Independent Management Ltd. charged 15 percent of Campbell Limited's net annual profits, before taxes, from its operations across western Canada. Campbell Limited also agreed to reimburse Independent Management for its salary payments, plus sundry expenses. But Campbell continued to control Campbell Limited as a transition in ownership occurred over time. Campbell began selling his shares to Independent Management in amounts that it could afford to pay. This process continued in 1965 and 1966.

At no time were customers or lower-level employees informed of the transition that continued to occur. Further, the transition plan had changed what had been employment income into business income in a context in which Steele, Symon and Cameron continued to do the day-to-day functions that they had done as employees. But the new arrangement allowed them to avoid tax on employment income, which had been converted into corporate small business income, eligible for a preferred corporate tax rate, to the extent their company did not pay them salaries and a bonus.

The Minister's auditors attacked the transition plan on the basis it was a tax sham. In general terms, a tax sham is a transaction or arrangement that disguises or masks the true legal arrangement. If the transactions were masking what remained an employment relationship, they would be ignored for tax purposes, meaning the income would be taxable employment income. Justice Martland, quoting the English Court of Appeal's 1967 decision in *Snook*, described a sham as follows:

> As regards the contention of the plaintiff that the transactions between himself, Auto-Finance, Ltd. and the defendants were a "sham," it is, I think, necessary to consider what, if any, legal concept is involved in the use of this popular and pejorative word. I apprehend that, if it has any meaning in law, it means acts done or documents executed by the parties to the "sham" which are intended by them to give to third parties or to the court the appearance of creating between the parties legal rights and obligations different from the actual legal rights and obligations (if any) which the parties intend to create.[189]

[189] *MNR v. James A. Cameron,* (1972), [1974] SCR 1062 (pp. 1068–69). The quote is from the opinion of Lord Justice Diplock of the English Court of Appeal in *Snook v. London & West Riding Investments, Ltd.*, [1967] 1 All E.R. 518, p. 528. https://decisions.scc-csc.ca/scc-csc/scc-csc/en/item/5239/index.do.

But Justice Martland immediately turned his attention to the trial judge's findings of fact as to whether a tax sham existed under Canadian law. Those findings of facts were as follows: (1) the purpose of inserting the management services company was not to create a more effective Campbell Limited; (2) Campbell wanted to deal with one corporate entity in the transition of ownership and not three individuals, who could bring others into the plan through the company; (3) in fact, Symon ceased to be an owner of the management services company, and a new corporation became a partial owner; and (4) tax savings were incidental to the overall transition plan.

Based on these findings, Martland held that he was not prepared to find the management services contract (and management corporation) to be a sham because the trial judge determined that the tax savings were "incidental to the overall plan." (Justices Abbott, Ritchie, Pigeon and Laskin concurred.[190]) That is, the decision rested on tax avoidance not being the main purpose of the plan.

The *Cameron* decision should be compared to Justice Martland's oral decision in a tax sham context less than one year later—*The Deltona Corporation*. The profile of that decision below is followed by three other oral decisions from 1977 and 1978. In each decision, Martland stated the Supreme Court's brief unanimous reasons for dismissing the appeal. While profiling such decisions may surprise some readers, the fact that a decision is decided orally does not mean it is insignificant. The Court for unknown reasons may not comment in detail when deciding a dispute. In four income tax cases, it has reversed the lower court orally. Two occurred before 1982, and two

[190] *Ibid.* What is not mentioned in *Cameron*, and which appears to be percolating below the surface of the dispute, is that the plan provided Campbell with an excellent personal tax result. The proceeds of sale received for his shares result in tax-exempt capital gains, which were being funded over time from the portion of his company's revenues being paid to Independent Management for services, which presumably Campbell Limited deducted in computing its income. One does not get the sense from the facts as decided that the ex-employees were acting as facilitators of a "surplus stripping" plan. They were transitioning to ownership from their perspectives, while Campbell was transitioning to retirement.

after 1982; two concerned tax avoidance, with the first reversal for the Crown in 1968 and the other for the taxpayer in 1996.[191]

The Deltona Corporation (1973)

A long-standing Canadian corporation and its non-resident parent corporation, The Deltona Corporation, sought in 1966 to avoid a 15 percent tax on a $2.5 million dividend about to be paid offshore to Deltona. To do so, it undertook a complex reorganization that culminated with a distribution of corporate assets to Deltona, purportedly without being taxable. To achieve this result, a preordained series of transactions was executed, which hinged on an election to create a "non-resident-owned corporation" under s. 70 of the 1952 ITA.[192] That definition included a condition that the corporation derive income from certain listed activities taxable under Part I of the 1952 ITA.

The Crown argued in *The Deltona Corporation* that "the cumulative effect of the election was that it was a sham, there never being any intention to derive income from investments."[193] The Exchequer Court agreed in 1971 holding on this point:

> My conclusion that the amalgamated corporation was not, at the time of payment of the dividend in question, a non-resident-owned corporation is based on my finding that it never "elected" to be "taxed" …

[191] The four Supreme Court oral reversals are: (1) *MNR v. C.I. Burland Properties Ltd.*, [1968] SCR v, 68 DTC 5220 (for the MNR); (2) *Canfor Ltd. v. Minister of Finance (B.C.)*, (1977), [1978] 1 SCR 1047 (for the taxpayer); (3) *Wally Fries v. The Queen*, [1990] 2 SCR 1322 (for the taxpayer); and (4) *Mara Properties Ltd. v. The Queen*, [1996] 2 SCR 161 (for the taxpayer).

[192] *The Income Tax Act*, RSC, 1952, c. 148.

[193] *The Deltona Corporation*, (1971), Exchequer Court (May 10, 1971, Cattanach J.), 71 DTC 5186 (at p. 5197), [1971] CTC 297; with the Supreme Court affirming the trial judge's opinion 73 DTC 5180, [1973] CTC 215. The Exchequer Court's judgment is in the Supreme Court's file 12396 (see "Appeal Case" document), pp. 503–37 (citation at p. 526). The factums for the taxpayer (appellant) and Crown (respondent) are also in the file, with the taxpayer's valid-election argument at paras. 34–35 and the Crown's sham-election argument at para. 43 of its factum.

> ... I say it never "elected ... to be taxed" under section 70 because such an election would be a decision to pay income tax under Part I ... . In this case, in my view, there is no actual decision to pay tax ... . While it is true that there was a resolution of the Board of Directors at 11:00 a.m. on March 28, 1966, which purported to be an election under section 70, ... there was a shareholders' resolution at 3:30 p.m. on the same day to distribute the amalgamated corporation's assets to its shareholders and to surrender its charter and, at 3:45 p.m., the directors executed a general deed of conveyance whereby all assets of the amalgamated corporation were conveyed to the appellant, its sole shareholder. When these three acts ... are looked at as acts that were practically speaking simultaneous, it is apparent that there was never a decision ... to pay tax under Part I of the *Income Tax Act.* Any apparent decision to pay tax was nullified by the simultaneous decision to wind up and the immediate implementation of that decision by distributing all the corporation's assets to its shareholders.[194]

Before the Supreme Court, the taxpayer maintained that it could, among other things, rely on the *Duke of Westminster* principle to strictly interpret the text of the election provision,[195] and that the trial judge's decision depended on the insertion of words not in that text. It claimed a statutory right to elect under the provision. The Crown argued the election was a sham because the taxpayer had no intent to carry on the type of business required under the provision.[196] It cited the English Court of Appeal's

---

[194] *Ibid.* See Appeal Case document, pp. 535–37; 71 DTC p. 5201.

[195] *Duke of Westminster, supra* note 2.

[196] *The Deltona Corporation, supra,* note 193, SCC. The Crown argued in the Supreme Court the election was "in fact and at law, ... nothing more than a sham or pantomime. At no time did the amalgamated company have any intention of carrying on any of the types of business operation referred to in section 70." Crown's factum at para. 43.

decision in *Snook* and the Supreme Court's decisions in *Cameron* and *Smythe.*[197]

On the second day of the hearing, Justice Martland dismissed the taxpayer's appeal orally from the bench, stating the Supreme Court was of the "opinion that the judgment of the Exchequer Court was correct" (with Justices Judson, Ritchie, Spence and Laskin).[198] The Court has never commented on, in the context of articulating the parameters of a tax sham, the differences in the facts and tax avoidance intent under the income tax law in *Cameron* and *The Deltona Corporation.*

John Christopher Doyle's income tax affairs dating to the early 1950s came before Justice Martland in 1977 and 1978.

John Christopher Doyle (1977, 1978)

The son of a coal dealer from Guelph, Ontario, John Christopher Doyle was born in Chicago in 1915. In 1949, the multilingual Doyle settled in Montreal after being a captain in the United States Army during the Second World War. He claimed to have been in counter-intelligence while in Italy, which is consistent with his effecting later intrigues. Doyle's comet blazed across the front pages of leading North American newspapers and magazines from the mid-1950s to the late 1980s in the context of manipulating stock markets, political events—and the American and Canadian justice systems.

John Doyle was in serious legal trouble by the summer of 1962. At New Haven, Connecticut, a grand jury indicted him for committing numerous criminal offences under U.S. securities laws including fraud. But in February 1965, Doyle ended the resulting trial in Hartford by pleading guilty to the non-extraditable offence of failing to register with the Securities and Exchange Commission 50 shares for sale in Connecticut. Federal Court Judge T. Emmet

[197] *Cameron, supra* note 189; *Smythe, infra* note 248. *Smythe* concerns corporate surplus stripping.

[198] *The Deltona Corporation, supra* note 193, SCC. The file also contains the Supreme Court's transcribed oral judgment.

Clarie fined Doyle $5,000 and sentenced him to a three-year prison term (reduced to three months subject to probation).

Doyle sought to withdraw his plea and appealed his conviction after he was sentenced to a term in prison. The U.S. Court of Appeals, 2nd Circuit, dismissed his appeal in late June 1965, and Doyle was ordered to surrender to the U.S. Marshall for Connecticut on July 15, 1965.

On July 14, 1965, Justice John Harlan of the U.S. Supreme Court denied Doyle's request to extend bail past July 15; Doyle absconded a fugitive from U.S. justice to his penthouse suite in Ottawa, which had a commanding view of the Parliament buildings across the street.[199] Inside the House of Commons, Opposition Leader John Diefenbaker and PM Lester Pearson were engaged in an acrimonious struggle for power as the country teetered towards its second election within three years.

Doyle had been executing intrigues to scuttle U.S. law enforcement since the summer of 1962. Not shy about being in the public spotlight, he proceeded to grant interviews sought by leading newspapers and magazines. Doyle led off inviting a reporter from the *New York Times* to his suite in late July 1965; the resulting story hit the front page of its financial section on July 26 with a photograph of Doyle playing his organ.[200] While the maestro of manipulations was having a grand old time in Ottawa, in Washington, the United States Supreme Court denied Doyle's petition to hear his appeal.

Leading political figures caught up in Doyle's intrigues include Prime Ministers John Diefenbaker and Lester Pearson, Newfoundland and Labrador Premier Joey Smallwood and U.S. Attorney General Robert (Bobby) Kennedy. In the case of Diefenbaker and Pearson, Doyle was accused of orchestrating an affidavit in which six elected Social Credit members agreed to vote

[199] "Nationwide FBI Alert Prepared for Missing Stock Fraud Figure," *Hartford Courant*, July 16, 1965, p. 25.

[200] John M. Lee, "John Doyle Tells Why He Fled to Canada," NYT, July 26, 1965, pp. 1 and 34 (Financial Section).

for Pearson to form a Liberal-minority government in the wake of the political uncertainty that arose after the April 1963 "hung" federal election,[201] with the result being that PM John Diefenbaker conceded his Progressive Conservatives could not form a new minority government.

In the case of Smallwood and Kennedy, after Pearson formed a minority government, Smallwood met Kennedy in Washington in late April 1963. He asked Kennedy to stop Doyle's prosecution before it became public knowledge. (Doyle and Smallwood both learned of the indictment, although it was sealed.[202]) The outcome was that the U.S. Department of Justice moved in the summer of 1963 to have the Federal Court unseal the indictment with Justice prosecuting Doyle, which ended with his 1965 conviction and flight to Canada a fugitive from justice.

While Murray Teigh Bloom devoted a portion of his 1971 book, *Rogues to Riches: The Trouble with Wall Street*,[203] to Doyle's then-exploits, he failed to penetrate in any significant way the web of intrigue Doyle spun over the prior two decades.

In June 1972, the RCMP transferred Staff Sargent Richard "Sandy" MacGibbon to St. John's from Toronto. MacGibbon–who specialized in investigating commercial crime–led a 14-member team created to investigate whether John Doyle committed offences under Canada's *Criminal Code*. MacGibbon's team executed search warrants in four provinces on Friday, December 15, 1972. While they knew the media response would be intense, they could not have appreciated in full the extent to which their action would engage the legal, political, business and media worlds in Canada and the United States during the next 15 years.

---

[201] Norman Webster, "Doyle Linked to Darabaner, Marcoux Says," *Globe and Mail*, November 6, 1965, p. 3.

[202] "Smallwood Intervened For Doyle, Court Told," *Globe and Mail (Report on Business)*, October 29, 1963, p. 1.

[203] Murray Teigh Bloom, *Rogues to Riches*, *Rogues to Riches: The Trouble with Wall Street* (New York: G.P. Putman's Sons, 1971), pp. 95–104.

Arrested in Montreal on December 7, 1973, Doyle was transported by airplane to St. John's, charged and incarcerated. The charges concerned Doyle's alleged bribery and kickback schemes relating to his past dealings with the Government of Newfoundland and Labrador, which came to the attention of the incoming Finance Minister, John Crosbie who would later become a leading federal Progressive Conservative politician. But Doyle was granted bail despite being a fugitive from American justice. If that were not enough, a magistrate in St. John's ordered the return of Doyle's passport in October 1974. That magistrate had been a cabinet minister in an earlier Smallwood government. Doyle promptly boarded a jet and absconded to Panama City, a fugitive from Canadian justice.

The drama continued for subsequent years. In December 1975, the RCMP charged–in absentia–Doyle with fraud.[204] It next laid 406 charges against Doyle in early March 1976.[205] The Crown alleged he had engaged in "wash trading." That involves executing buy-sell orders to create an impression of an active market at inflated price levels.[206] Doyle fought the charges while resting comfortably in his luxury-penthouse suite in Panama City.

Next, Doyle and his Canadian Javelin were the subject matter of a special investigation under federal company law in the late 1970s and early 1980s.[207] The related litigation to frustrate that probe was unrelenting with disputes reaching the Supreme Court. Doyle finally succeeded in 1985 when the Federal Court of Appeal

---

[204] *Canadian Press*, "Doyle Sought on Warrant of Fraud," *Globe and Mail*, January 14, 1976, p. 14.

[205] "Five in Javelin Case Face 406 New Counts," *Globe and Mail*, March 10, 1976, p. B 6.

[206] *Special*, "Dealer Charged in Doyle Case Returns Home," *Globe and Mail*, September 1, 1977, p. 9.

[207] The Restrictive Trade Practices Commission, *An Investigation of the Affairs and Management of Javelin International Limited [formerly Canadian Javelin Limited]*, 1977–83.

nullified the Commission's 1983 report detailing Doyle's activities, and its remedial recommendations.[208] But that probe included detailed findings against Doyle with Canadian Javelin shareholders suing him and his company in the Quebec Superior Court.[209]

Justice John Gomery of the Quebec Superior Court presided over the trial, with the Court travelling to Panama so Doyle could testify.[210] Gomery stripped Doyle of his control of the company by ordering the cancellation of his shares at a set price, which funds were to be used to pay millions in damages.[211]

Throughout it all, Doyle proclaimed his innocence. As the curtain was closing on Doyle's almost five-decade long public performance, *The Globe and Mail*'s Paul Knox profiled Doyle from Panama City on April 14, 1999. That front-page story was titled: "A fugitive dreams of clearing his name; Millions disappeared–and the so did he. But 25 years later, John C. Doyle denies doing

---

[208] *John C. Doyle v. Restrictive Trade Practices Commission and F. H. Sparling and Canadian Javelin Ltd./Javelin International Ltd.*, [1985] 1 *Federal Court Reports* 362 (Federal Court of Appeal); with the Commission being denied leave to appeal to the Supreme Court of Canada, [1985] 2 *SCR* vii. The Commission's findings were nullified because a commissioner was not present during a portion of the hearings.

[209] *Sparling. v. Javelin International Ltd. [Canadian Javelin changed its name to Javelin International]*, [1986] *Recueils de Jurisprudence du Québec* 1073 (Quebec Superior Court); affirmed with variations to the Orders. The related litigation and appeals went into the 1990s.

[210] William Marsden, "Doyle faces Panama Quiz in Bid to Clear Name," *Montreal Gazette*, June 8, 1985, pp. 1&2.

[211] Gomery J. ordered Doyle to pay Javelin $15,419,382 plus interest for shareholder abuses and over $9 million in legal costs. In partial payment of the damage award, Doyle was to be stripped of 1,064,766 Javelin shares at the price credited to Doyle of $4.50 per share. The evidence suggested Doyle also held over 500,000 Javelin shares through interposed corporations. Gomery froze those shares pending later hearings to determine if Doyle was their beneficial owner. The Court of Appeal reduced the damage award against Doyle to $9.5 million in 1991. It confirmed Gomery's order cancelling Doyle's Javelin shares for compensation.

anything wrong."[212] Although Knox provided an outstanding recap of what had played out in public, below I explain how Doyle financed his rise to prominence by recounting his income tax disputes from the early 1950s.

In 1977 and 1978, Justice Martland dismissed orally from the bench Doyle's separate income tax appeals from a 1970 decision of the Exchequer Court (in the 1977 decision,[213] with Justices Ritchie, Spence, Pigeon and Dickson, in the 1978 decision,[214] with Justices Ritchie, Dickson, Beetz and Pratte). The two cases concern three different tax issues dating to 1950 and 1954, which the Minister reassessed in the late 1950s to impose personal income tax on Doyle.

The first issue involved a complicated series of transactions in which Doyle realized a substantial gain in 1950 from selling used coal-mining equipment he'd acquired in his native Illinois to a coal mine in Saskatchewan. To do so, Doyle formed a syndicate with Sir Harold Mitchell and his brother who resided in Bermuda and controlled a coal empire. While Doyle's actions in closing the deal would burn his bridges with the Mitchells, the outcome was that the Mitchells allowed him to acquire, as his share of the gain, ownership of the Montreal coal-sales agency he had moved to Canada to operate on behalf of a leading American coal company, which the Mitchells appear to have controlled. The Supreme Court found Doyle was taxable on his share of the gain because it was from an adventure in the nature of trade. That 1950 gain gave Doyle the financial means to pivot to stock market intrigues and away from selling coal.

In the second issue, which dates to 1954, Doyle earned a large gain from selling Chilean iron-ore mining claims to a public company he incorporated, Canadian Javelin Ltd. The gain arose

[212] Paul Knox, "A Fugitive Dreams of Clearing His Name," *Globe and Mail*, April 14, 1999, pp. 1 and 19.
[213] *John Christopher Doyle v. MNR*, (1977), [1978] 1 SCR 547.
[214] *John C. Doyle v. MNR*, [1978] 2 SCR 837.

because he caused Canadian Javelin to pay him in excess of $2 million of its shares for the Chilean mining claims, which others later alleged were almost worthless. Doyle was found to be taxable on the gain.

It was those shares that Doyle used over the next three decades to retain *de facto* control of Canadian Javelin and to manipulate American and Canadian stock markets for his own benefit. The shares were also the subject matter of a Montreal lawsuit a former Doyle associate in New York brought against him in the late 1950s after they had parted company on acrimonious terms. On settlement, the associate ended up with approximately 50 percent of the 1954 shares, subject to Doyle's obtaining a first option to acquire them back if the associate decided to sell them; the associate also agreed not to vote the shares against Doyle's interests in Canadian Javelin. The associate moved to Europe.

National Revenue had also taxed Doyle's former associate on 50 percent of the gain in the late 1950s before the Montreal lawsuit was settled, letting them coordinate the extent to which each should be taxable on the gain. They failed to do so, and the Exchequer Court and the Supreme Court found Doyle was taxable on 100 percent of the gain.

A few months after the Supreme Court's decision, the Federal Court (which replaced the Exchequer Court) found in a separate trial that Doyle's former associate, who returned to Canada from Europe for the trial, was taxable on 50 percent of the gain. Once Doyle learned of this holding, he sued the Crown to re-open the Supreme Court's decision to ensure he was taxable on only 50 percent of the gain. But the Federal Court dismissed his lawsuit because the issue was subject to *res judicata*: the Supreme Court had decided the dispute and he was therefore barred from relitigating the same dispute. Doyle's further appeals were denied. In the third issue, also from 1954, Doyle was found to be taxable on the appropriation of certain corporate assets for his own benefit.

Justice Martland's final oral decision considered is from 1978 and it is significant taxwise historically for at least four reasons.

The first and most obvious reason in this context is that it concerns tax avoidance transactions in which the taxpayer was successful in the Supreme Court in the pre-*Charter* era. Second, at each level, the judiciary confronts a long-standing regime that applied to the resource sector. The extent to which the regime effected a tax preference, as distinguished from allowing cost recovery of commercial outlays incurred for the purpose of gaining income, is debatable.

Third, by the mid-to-late-1970s, Parliament added several tax preferences to the *Income Tax Act*, despite tax reform effective 1972, that had nothing to do with taxing income; they sought to achieve a positive economic or social result by offering up tax incentives. At the time, the economy was in disarray, the national debt was piling up, and one never had a sense the prime minister had a firm understanding of commercial or economic reality.

Fourth, the decision occurred in the middle of a political crisis that raged over several years concerning the oil and gas sector of the economy, pitting the Province of Alberta against Ottawa. The central characters in the drama were two very astute and smart politicians: Conservative Premier Peter Lougheed and Liberal Prime Minister Pierre Trudeau. You had to be there, so to speak, to understand the drama that accompanied these two political titans engaging each other on the national stage. At that very moment in history, Pierre Trudeau was also engaged in a drawn-out and testy fight for the nation, with a smart and popular separatist Premier René Lévesque of Quebec.

Also, keep in mind that Justice Martland had grown up and practised law in Alberta and that his appointment to the Supreme Court filled one of the two seats on the court that are, by custom, reserved for the four western provinces of Alberta, British Columbia, Manitoba, and Saskatchewan. As such, Martland might reflect a western-Canadian view of the dynamics in which the interests of Ontario-Quebec tend to dominate national public policy decisions.

Alberta & Southern Gas Company Limited (1978)

Alberta & Southern Gas Company Limited was incorporated in Alberta on March 25, 1957. Its parent corporation, Pacific Gas and Electric Company Limited of the United States, was a significant distributor of natural gas and electrical power in California.[215]

Pacific Gas was also a majority owner of Pacific Gas Transmission Limited, which operated a natural gas pipeline from the Washington side of the British Columbia border with the United States down through Washington, Oregon and into California. On the Canadian side of the border, Pacific Gas Transmission owned a 45 percent interest in Alberta Natural Gas Company Limited, which transmitted natural gas from Alberta to the British Columbia border with the U.S.

Alberta & Southern existed for the purpose of buying natural gas in Alberta and selling it to Pacific Gas Transmission for delivery in the U.S. to their respective parent corporation, Pacific Gas. To accomplish this purpose, it signed hundreds of gas purchase contracts with producers in Alberta.

Prime Minister John Diefenbaker's Progressive Conservative Government had Parliament enact in the early 1960s a regime under which taxpayers could deduct the cost of an acquired right, licence or privilege in petroleum-producing land. This regime was a closing event in a decade-long controversy that traces to the issue litigated in the Supreme Court's 1955 decision for the taxpayer in *Home Oil,* which was referred to when considering Justice Abbott's influence.

The basis of the Home Oil Controversy is the extent to which deductible resource-related expenses reduced depletion allowances, and it involved tax on significant amounts of income from oil

[215] *The Queen v. Alberta & Southern Gas Company Limited,* (1978), [1979] 1 SCR 36, dismissing the Minister's appeal from 77 DTC 5244, [1977] CTC 388 (FCA), dismissing the Minister's appeal from 76 DTC 6362, [1976] CTC 639 (FCTD). *R. v. Alberta and Southern Gas Co. Ltd.* – SCC Cases (scc-csc.ca).

and gas production. The controversy was fueled by: (1) a major discovery of oil at Leduc in 1947, which transformed the Alberta economy; (2) Americans' operating Canadian oil and gas companies and assuming the Canadian tax regime for deducting oil and gas outlays operated like the American tax regime; (3) federal government action from a distant Ottawa, which, industry would argue, did not understand or appreciate the western Canadian oil and gas sector of the economy; (4) Finance Minister Abbott's having the executive pass a 1951 regulation clarifying depletion calculations; and (5) the related Supreme Court precedent in *Imperial Oil*,[216] curtailing depletion allowances the oil sector successfully litigated before the court in *Home Oil*.

In 1972, Alberta & Southern resold approximately 86 percent of its natural gas purchases to Pacific Gas. It also provided risk capital to domestic producers for their use in exploration activity. Alberta & Southern did so to maintain a sufficient supply of natural gas. It prepaid for gas deliveries, thereby providing funding to the producers for exploration activity, and loaned funds to producers, in the expectation that they would sell their production to Alberta & Southern.

To generate the needed capital—the seed funds advanced to producers—Pacific Gas paid Alberta & Southern a premium of three cents per cubic thousand feet of natural gas deliveries. This premium resulted in an excess profit margin that Alberta & Southern

[216] *Imperial Oil*, *supra* note 90. For a discussion of the "Home Oil Controversy," see Jacques Barbeau (ed.), "The Rationale of the Canadian Treatment," *Oil and Gas Production and Taxes*, Tax Paper Number 33, Canadian Tax Foundation, 1963, pp. 263–65; and for the changes affecting the oil and gas sector, see W.C. Shakespeare, "Canadian Income Tax Amendments in 1962," (1963), 11:1 *Canadian Tax Journal* 19 (pp. 23–29). For a discussion of the Canadian tax treatment of resource outlays differing from the American approach, see A. Gordon Burton, FCA, "Comments re Taxation of the Oil and Gas Industry," *Studies of the Royal Commission on Taxation*, Number 12, 1966 (Queen's Printer) at p. 16. The effect of the Canadian approach was to tax only two-thirds of the net income from a producing well. The result for a corporation was an effective marginal tax rate of 33.33 percent, which was lower than the American rate.

used to establish commercial relations with gas producers. It received a $4 million premium in each of its 1972 and 1973 taxation years, which was fully taxable to the extent that Alberta & Southern did not incur offsetting expenses.

Parliament's 1972 ITA was interfering with this commercial objective by taxing Alberta & Southern's premium, which would not have existed but for the supply needs of the American parent. Its response was to enter a tax avoidance scheme that ran the risk the judiciary would deny the tax benefit it sought under the tax law. This was quite possible at the time, given that very few taxpayers were successful before the Supreme Court in a tax avoidance case.

The *Alberta & Southern Gas Co.* tax avoidance gambit was relatively straightforward. Justice Angus Cattanach of the Federal Court–Trial Division described it this way: "The device adopted, as was aptly put by the witnesses, to 'remove these amounts [the $4 million premium] from the grasping reach of the tax collector and so preserve the funds for the purpose to which they were dedicated' …, was to enter into 'carve-out' agreements with Amoco Petroleum Company …, a gas producing company with which the plaintiff had also entered into gas purchase agreements."[217]

Under a carve-out agreement, a person acquires a percentage interest in another person's "working interest," which is a right, licence or privilege to produce petroleum substances. The person acquiring such a right is provided a deduction for the cost of the interest and earns a royalty in any resulting production, which would be taxable as income.

A regime that had been put in place for the benefit of the oil and gas sector was about to be used to avoid tax. To do so, Alberta & Southern entered into a carve-out agreement with Amoco Petroleum Company under which it paid Amoco $4 million for a working interest in certain lands (i.e., a right to produce and dispose of petroleum substances), with the outlay being deducted by

[217] *Alberta & Southern Gas*, *supra* note 215, FCTD at 76 DTC p. 6365.

Alberta & Southern under s. 66 of the 1972 Act. Amoco would also deduct the amount as an expense incurred to explore for natural gas—a double dip of deductions, so to speak.

Amoco located, extracted, refined and provided Alberta & Southern $4 million of production under the carve-out agreement, with Amoco bearing all costs of extraction, processing and refining. Alberta & Southern would include the $4 million in its income when it received the production. However, the commercial substance of the carve-out was that Alberta & Southern was receiving interest from a temporary $4 million loan. Loans normally are not deductible in computing income.

The Minister reversed Alberta & Southern's $4 million deductions in 1972 and 1973 on the basis it did not satisfy the "principal-business corporation" condition necessary to benefit from the resource provisions and because the arrangement was really a temporary loan; it failed to acquire a "Canadian resource property [i.e., the right or licence]." In the alternative, the Minister contended that the carve-out agreement was a sham or an artificial transaction subject to reversal under the artificial income reduction anti-avoidance rule in then s. 245 of the 1972 ITA.

Justice Cattanach found that Alberta & Southern met the principal-business corporation test under the marketing of natural resources heading in the statutory test, and rejected the Minister's contention that marketing requires one to search out customers. Alberta & Southern was found to be buying gas and marketing it to its three main customers. With respect to whether the $4 million was a loan or the purchase price for a Canadian resource property, Cattanach rejected the view that the funds were a loan. He found Amoco was not obligated to repay the amount. Further, Alberta & Southern could legally acquire the petroleum under the contract,[218]

[218] *Ibid.*, FCTD at 76 DTC pp. 6366–67. Cattanach J. found that Alberta & Southern satisfied the definition because it had a right under the agreement to take petroleum worth up to $4 million from the land plus interest.

albeit Cattanach referred in his opinion to the $4 million being an indebtedness of Amoco.[219]

Also, the transactions were not a sham; Cattanach cited the 1967 British definition of a sham Lord Justice Diplock enunciated in *Snook*: "all the parties thereto must have a common intention that the acts or documents are not to create the legal rights and obligations which they give the appearance of creating."[220] Cattanach stated: "Put another way and in more succinct and colloquial language if the parties to a contract do precisely what they contract to do there is no sham. As a corollary of that if the parties do as they contract to do then that is the substance of the contract. The agreements were realities and not fictitious."[221]

Cattanach next considered whether the artificial income reduction rule in s. 245 applied to deny the deductions. He found that s. 245 did not apply because, as a general rule, it was subject to the more specific rules, which in this case allowed the deductions.[222] As a result, Alberta & Southern kept the funds from the tax collector and employed them in their intended commercial purpose.

With respect to questions of the morality of the matter, Cattanach stated: "It is not my function to make any moral judgment.

---

[219] *Ibid.*, FCTD at 76 DTC p. 6366.

[220] *Snook*, *supra* note 189, p. 528.

[221] *Alberta & Southern Gas*, *supra* note 215, FCTD at 76 DTC p. 6370.

[222] *Ibid.* There were also two side issues relating to Alberta & Southern's deduction of certain interest charges and its depletion allowance claim. It borrowed the $4 million, as it had not yet received the funds from Pacific Gas. The interest rate paid exceeded the 3 percent received on the funds from Amoco. Although the Minister denied the interest expenses, Cattanach J. allowed the deduction. The receipts were treated as income, and the outlays as the cost of earning that income, with a resulting loss. It was suggested that a profit "may have resulted," but it is unclear how this could have been the case. With respect to depletion allowance, Alberta & Southern claimed a 25 percent allowance on the basis of its "royalty" receipts from Amoco—the royalty amount appears to be the $4 million as it circled back to Alberta & Southern. For example, it claimed $4,074,050 in its fiscal 1973 year. If allowed, Alberta & Southern would be achieving a continuous one-year tax deferral on its $4 million with the additional advantage of a 25 percent allowance deduction. This deduction was also allowed.

My function is limited to determining if the plaintiff by those transactions has brought itself within the four corners of section 66. For the reasons given I think that the plaintiff has been successful in doing so."[223]

The Minister appealed to the Federal Court of Appeal. Counsel focused the appeal on the artificial income reduction anti-avoidance rule and dropped all other arguments, including the sham argument. The panel hearing the appeal was Chief Justice Jackett, and Justices Pratte and Urie.

Jackett delivered a unanimous decision for the taxpayer. The first point the Chief Justice made in his reasoning was that the trial judge was wrong to find that the artificial income reduction rule could not apply because it was a general rule subject to the more specific provision allowing the expense in s. 66. He also reviewed the tax law and set out the types of deductions that can occur in a business.

First-level deductions relate to current expenses incurred for the purpose of earning business income. The Chief Justice in a footnote referred to Justice Abbott's 1958 majority opinion in *British Columbia Electric Railway Co.* for the methodology to be applied. Second-level deductions concern amounts allowed as capital allowances, such as CCA and depletion. These deductions are allowed only to the extent they satisfy the express provisions providing for the deductions. Third-level deductions concern amounts of an unusual nature that the ITA expressly allows to obtain an equitable result, having regard to abnormal results created by ordinary commercial rules for computing business profits. Fourth-level deductions relate to amounts Parliament has seen fit to allow to achieve some end, which Chief Justice Jackett referred to as "incentive allowances."

With respect to resource deductions under then s. 66, Jackett found that it provided for carryovers of current resource exploration expenditures, a special scheme for the deduction of capital outlays

---

[223] *Ibid.*, FCTD at 76 DTC p. 6372.

relating to pre-production costs and incentives to explore for and to develop natural resources. The amounts were deductible, and the artificial income reduction rule did not apply to deny the deductions claimed based on a contextual reading of s. 66 and the related income inclusion rule for royalties received in para. 12(1)(*g*). Taken together, these provisions had the "obvious purpose of encouraging taxpayers to put money into such resource properties and keep it there. That being what the provisions seem to have been intended to encourage, … a transaction that clearly falls within the *object and spirit* of section 66 cannot be said to unduly or artificially reduce income merely because the taxpayer was influenced in deciding to enter into it by tax considerations" [emphasis added].[224]

The Chief Justice's decision is based on the object and spirit of the contextualized provisions in issue and it recognizes that if the funds were deductible under s. 66, the value of the production sent back to Alberta & Southern was income to it under para. 12(1)(*g*). This meant that the $4 million it paid had to be continually invested in the exploration sector in order to continue the deferral. Thus, once so encouraged, the Federal Court of Appeal found that the artificial income reduction rule did not apply to deny the tax deferral merely because the taxpayer was influenced by tax considerations when entering the transactions.

Canada Tax Cases recognized the significance of the decision immediately and devoted more than one and a half pages to it in an editorial note.[225] It emphasized at least two points. First, the Court of Appeal found that the more general anti-avoidance rule could deny a tax benefit allowed under a specific provision. Second, the Court allowed the deductions with one effect being uncertainty as to whether the Court considered a tax avoidance motive irrelevant or merely inconclusive when considering whether a transaction was artificial. The Minister appealed.

[224] *Ibid.*, FCA at 77 DTC p. 5249.

[225] *Ibid.*, Carswell's editorial note on the FCA's decision is at [1977] CTC pp. 389–91.

In a brief judgment, Justice Martland dismissed the Minister's appeal (with Justices Pigeon, Dickson, Beetz and Pratte): "We have not been persuaded by the arguments of counsel for the appellant that there is error in the conclusions reached by the Federal Court of Appeal. The appeals are dismissed with costs."[226]

Subsequent to the decision, a massive tax avoidance scheme swept out of Alberta across Canada until Parliament shut it down in 1986. The scheme extended out from the resource sector to include loss companies and the tax-exempt sector such as pension funds. Under the scheme, a producer of oil or gas would separate the income from the deduction by selling a carve-out of the resource income to a loss company or a tax-exempt person thus transferring the right to the income to persons who would not pay income tax on it.[227]

By separating the income from the deduction, the revised scheme was distinguishable from the "object and spirit" of the contextualized interpretive approach Chief Justice Jackett had taken and which was upheld by the Supreme Court. This revised scheme turned the *Alberta & Southern Gas Co.* tax deferral into an absolute loss of expected tax revenues for the federal and provincial governments because, while the transferor's resource expenses continued to be deductible, they were no longer offset by the resulting royalty income that was transferred to persons who paid no tax on it. Also note the fine line that separates that avoidance scheme to divert the right to the royalty income to a loss company or pension fund, which earned the income, from Samuel Ciglen's tax evasion scheme, which relied on a false statement in the records of the recipient company as to who earned his stock promotion gains.

Justice Martland's final decision profiled is especially important in terms of the Supreme Court's evolving approach to income tax avoidance although it does not concern income tax.

---

[226] *Ibid.*, SCC at [1978] SCR p. 36.

[227] John V. Krukowski, *Canadian Taxation of Oil and Gas Income*, 2nd ed. (CCH Canadian Ltd., 1987), p. 318.

Rather, the dispute concerns provincial succession duties imposed after Parliament ended its estate and gift tax regime upon the enactment of an income tax on capital gains applicable to 1972 and later tax years.

There are several fascinating aspects to the Supreme Court's 1980 decision in *Frank M. Covert et al. v. Minister of Finance of Nova Scotia*.[228] First, the Court divided 4–3 for the Crown in a tax avoidance context with the dissenting three expressly citing the 1935 *Duke of Westminster* principle.

Second, the dispute turns on interpreting the words "beneficially entitled." In a non-tax context, those words have a relatively settled meaning under the historic principles of the courts of equity, which courts and principles were merged in the 19th century with those of the courts of common law in most jurisdictions in the British Empire including many of its former colonies in the United States. But that merger never occurred in Quebec nor Louisiana because their civil law is grounded in the traditions of the Napoleonic civil code.

Third, while the Oxford-educated Justice Martland led the majority, all three concurring judges were from Quebec. Unlike under the merged common and equitable law, Quebec's civil code does not distinguish between the concepts of "legal" and "beneficial" title to property.

Fourth, Martland who perhaps is the greatest conservative judge to sit on the Supreme Court, was matched against perhaps the greatest liberal judge to sit on the Court, the dissenting Justice Brian Dickson. Their dual unfolded over 47 pages as they countered each other's analysis of the relevant precedent grounded in the principles of the courts of equity, corporate law, and the differences in the underlying precedent in succession duty and estate tax cases.

Along the way, Justice Martland unexpectedly cites two of Lord Denning's decisions that "pierced the corporate veil," one of which

[228] *Frank M. Covert et al. v. Minister of Finance of Nova Scotia*, [1980] SCR 774. https://decisions.scc-csc.ca/scc-csc/scc-csc/en/item/5972/index.do.

denied an income tax avoidance gambit. For some who studied the Common Law, Lord Denning is the greatest judge to sit in the 19th and 20th centuries as a member of the British House of Lords and the English Court of Appeal. Justice Dickson counters with the *Salomon* principle (that corporations are separate persons whose legal form must be respected in the absence of improper conduct) citing the Privy Council's 1939 reversal of the Supreme Court's 1938 decision in *Pioneer Laundry*.

Fifth, Justice Martland rested his opinion on Justice Dickson's majority Supreme Court opinion in a succession duty case decided four years earlier. Dickson is left struggling to get out from under that opinion and distinguished it.

In what is perhaps most surprising about their dual, Martland wrote the opinion that reflects the reasons and result in a tax avoidance context that many in the 21st century might expect would be reached by a liberal justice, while Dickson wrote the opinion that reflects the reasons and result that many in the 21st century might expect would be reached by a conservative justice. Why so?

All of which suggests that something significant is occurring in the judgment in terms of the judicial function and I will speculate on that after profiling the decision in question.

Frank M. Covert et al. (1980)

Frank Covert was one of three executors for the Estate of Roy A. Jodrey. Thinking about the interests of the citizens of Nova Scotia, author Peter Newman spilt more ink on Covert and Jodrey than on any other persons in Nova Scotia in his 1973 best-selling book, *The Canadian Establishment*.[229] More than on the Sobey family; more than on the Oland family; that is telling.

Covert who was a lawyer, and Jodrey who was a businessman, operated on the national stage with little or no fanfare. Covert's home base was his law firm in downtown Halifax, with frequent sojourns to the boardrooms of the Upper Canada Establishment.

[229] Newman, *The Canadian Establishment*, *supra* note 73, pp. 203–06.

Jodrey and his empire resided in small town Hantsport, which sits next to the Avon River and its access to the Bay of Fundy. Jodrey took field trips to Bay Street where he checked up on his investments and to attend his directorships in over 50 major corporations, including the Bank of Nova Scotia for which he was one of the largest shareholders.

Newman described Jodrey as "one of the most successful investors of his generation." He described Covert as "one of the few Maritimers who has been accepted by every branch of the Upper Canadian Establishment."[230]

On May 15, 1972, *An Act Respecting Succession Duties* became law in Nova Scotia. That law taxed the "successor" in Nova Scotia on the value of property inherited from a deceased person. In the case of corporate shares inherited beneficially by a corporation not resident in Nova Scotia, a section deemed the shareholders of the acquiring corporation to be the successor of the shares to the extent of the value of the shares.

Roy Jodrey was soon presented with a plan that sought to avoid succession duties owing on 4,600 shares of his R.A. Jodrey Investments Limited, which would otherwise pass under his will to his 12 grandchildren each of whom resided in Nova Scotia.

In September 1972, three corporations were incorporated in Alberta. Corporation 1 was the parent of its subsidiary Corporation 2. The third corporation was White Rock Investments to which Roy Jodrey sold 4,600 shares of J.A. Jodrey Investments for a promissory note of $3,735,200. Jodrey held one share of White Rock Investments personally and its other issued shares were held in trust for him.

Next, Jodrey revoked his decision to leave his grandchildren the 4,600 shares of J.A. Jodrey Investments. Instead, he left the residue of his estate to Corporation 2 (including the $3,735,200 owing to him under the note issued by White Rock Investments).

---

[230] *Ibid.*

Here's the key. On Jodrey's passing, Corporation 1 as the shareholder of Corporation 2 would be the deemed successor for the residue of Jodrey's estate under the legislation. But successor Corporation 1 was not a resident of Nova Scotia even though the 12 grandchildren owned it. If instead they owned Corporation 2, the duty would clearly have been payable by them as deemed successors residing in Nova Scotia.

It is noteworthy that Jodrey's 12 grandchildren had complete control in law under the tax avoidance plan to avoid tax on *their* inheritance upon the passing of their grandfather. Since they owned Corporation 1, they had the share voting rights and held the power of corporate control under law to cause a wind up of both Corporation 1 and the subsidiary Corporation 2 and to have either Corporation 1 or themselves receive the property that was the subject of their inheritance.

Roy Jodrey passed less than one year later, on August 12, 1973. At that time, Corporation 2's White Rock Investments owed him $2,999,000 under the note and presumably the value of its 4,600 shares of J.A. Jodrey Investments had increased since September 1972. Although the value of neither property appeared to be caught by the statute, Nova Scotia assessed the value of the Jodrey estate subject to succession duties to be $3,784,273. The duty rate was 48.5 percent, or tax of $1,534,421.96.

As suggested, the dispute turns legally on whether only Corporation 2 was "beneficially entitled" to the inherited property, or whether Corporation 1 was also beneficially entitled to the property, by reason of the power under law that the 12 grandchildren had over both corporations.

Justice Martland found that the meaning of "beneficially entitled" should not be based on the meaning given by the courts of equity, which presumably would have held that the subsidiary Corporation 2 was the only person beneficially entitled to the property. Instead, after canvassing various Canadian and British authorities, he held that the parent Corporation 1 also was beneficially entitled to the property. Justices Pigeon, Beetz and Chouinard concurred.

In Martland's view, the case should be decided based, using a phrase taken partially from Lord Denning on "the realities of the situation … [which were] the subsidiary company was bound hand and foot to the parent company and had to do whatever its parent said. It was a mere conduit pipe linking the parent company to the estate."[231]

After analyzing the precedent cited by the litigants, Martland noted that unlike Lord Denning, he saw no need to pierce the corporate veil; among other things, he found that the Supreme Court should not be "rigidly bound … [to the] rules of equity … in connection with trusts,"[232] applying Justice Dickson's majority 1976 decision on a similar issue in *Minister of Revenue (Ontario) v. McCreath et al.*[233]

In *McCreath*, the taxpayers argued the settlor of property under a trust did not have a property interest in the trust property at the time of her death and therefore no succession duties applied. The settlor, Myrtle McCreath, created the trust in 1948. Under its terms, the trustee National Trust Co. had the discretion to pay the whole annual income of the trust to the benefit of McCreath and her children, or to the benefit of any one or more of that group. When she passed in 1968, she was survived by her husband and four young children. The trust property was worth $25 million.

While McCreath had retained the power to direct in her will what portions of the trust property should go to which of her children, she had failed to do so. Instead, the trust distributed the property to them equally under the terms of the trust. The taxpayers argued that no succession duties were payable because McCreath's children did not inherit the property from her.

Justice Brian Dickson led a majority of four in *McCreath* in denying the tax avoidance plan. He noted in his opening remarks that there was an "ongoing struggle between taxing authorities, casting

---

[231] *Frank M. Covert et al., supra* note 228, p 796.

[232] *Ibid.*, p. 794.

[233] *Minister of Revenue (Ontario) v. McCreath et al.*, (1976), [1977] 1 SCR 2. https://decisions.scc-csc.ca/scc-csc/scc-csc/en/item/4323/index.do?site_preference=normal.

an ever wider net to garner succession duties or estate taxes, and taxpayers adopting ever more sophisticated means of escaping that net."[234]

Although McCreath had disposed of the property to the trust in 1948, it remained "property passing on her death" because she retained a lifetime stake in the trust property by reason of her being a beneficiary of the income. Dickson held: "I do not believe that the niceties and arcana of ancient property law should be fastened upon with mechanical rigidity to determine the effect of a modern taxation statute whose purpose is plain."[235] He added later that "the policy of the Act … is to tax all *inter vivos* gifts from which the donor failed to detach" themselves after the gift.[236] Justices Martland, Spence and Laskin concurred.

Accordingly, both Dickson's 1976 opinion in *McCreath* and Martland's 1980 opinion in *Covert* focus on the legal and commercial realities of the plans, not their legal form. Myrtle McCreath and the trust she created for the benefit of herself and her children, and Roy Jodrey and the tiered corporate structure he created for the benefit of his 12 grandchildren, cleverly ensured that the destiny of the property subject to the inheritances was secured by a power existing in trust law (McCreath) or corporate law (Jodrey). It did not matter if it that power was property; succession duties applied.

But, in *Covert*, Justice Dickson in dissent indicated that the Supreme Court was being asked to determine if Roy Jodrey's "acts constitute (a) reprehensible tax evasion or (b) legitimate tax planning."[237] This is a surprising way to frame a tax avoidance issue as distinguished from tax evasion. By doing so, he sought to distinguish

[234] *Ibid.*, p 4. Justice Wilfred Judson wrote a brief opinion in *McCreath* reaching the same result for different reasons. Judson held that McCreath had reserved a testamentary power of appointment in respect of the trust property and that power was "squarely within the concluding words" of the relevant provision.
[235] *Ibid.*, p. 15.
[236] *Ibid.*, p. 20.
[237] *Frank M. Covert et al.*, *supra* note 228, p 800.

situations where a taxpayer seeks to (1) *disguise or (2) alter the character of a transaction* caught by a tax statute from cases where a taxpayer finds a gap in the law that allows the taxpayer to "validly take his income wholly outside the express wording of the statute."[238]

Dickson determined that the purpose of Jodrey's tiered corporate structure was to move the residue of the estate beyond the reach of the statute. On this, he noted the person who drafted the provision in issue recognized that the property could be gifted to a non-resident corporation, but failed to cover off the possibility it could have a non-resident parent corporation owned by residents of Nova Scotia.

Justice Dickson next drew a fine distinction after citing the *Duke of Westminster* principle, which he indicated is not open to challenge. While it is impermissible to bring to the construction of a fiscal statute a "bias in favour of the Crown," there are no "special principles of construction governing the interpretation of fiscal legislation."[239] A judge must be neutral when deciding disputes.

The correct interpretive approach, according to Dickson in 1980, is "to construe the legislation with reasonable regard to its object and purpose and to give it such interpretation as best ensures the attainment of such object and purpose." In the case of succession duty legislation, its primary purpose is "to capture such amounts for the fiscal coffers as the words of the statutory net can catch."[240]

Somewhat out of character, Dickson applied two British decisions for discerning his correct approach for interpreting fiscal statutes. In 1904, the Privy Council discerned the main and obvious purpose and object of the legislation to be to validate the sale of property done to collect unpaid taxes and held that object should be given effect if the words permitted. In a 1976 decision, a judge of the courts of equity denied the Crown's submission that the

[238] *Ibid.*, p. 799.
[239] *Ibid.*, p. 807.
[240] *Ibid.*

British Finance Act be given a strict interpretation when taxing capital gains from selling a person's first home. Instead, the court based its broader interpretation on the statute's general scheme being to exempt from tax any proceeds from selling homes, with it being fair and reasonable to do so to the extent the wording permitted.

Next, Dickson considered many leading estate and succession duty cases but ultimately discerned the meaning of "beneficially entitled" based on the principles of the courts of equity and the well-recognized corporate law principle that a parent corporation is not the beneficial owner of property its subsidiary owns.

Justice Dickson ended his dissent in *Covert* by noting that the statute had no section dealing with improper tax avoidance, illegal transactions, frauds or shams; nor did Jodrey's acts create a sham. These findings were used to distinguish his 1976 holding in *McCreath.* In comparison, McCreath "sought to create the impression through the language of the gifting instrument that she had disposed wholly and irrevocably of the subject-matter of the gift … [where] the degree of control retained defeated characterization of the transaction as a gift."[241] Justices Ritchie and McIntyre concurred.

For me, Justice Ronald Martland's 1980 majority opinion in *Covert* reflects a consistent judicial policy response to tax avoidance that dated to the Supreme Court's 1938 majority opinion in *Pioneer Laundry.* He followed the Supreme Court's precedent unlike Justice Dickson in his dissent, which is significant dissent including because of his citation of the 1935 British *Duke of Westminster* principle.

But the principle itself benefits tax avoiders, and Dickson appears to acknowledge this by expressing a more balanced approach that discerns the object and purpose of a fiscal statute or provision from its schemes and words, which object and purpose should then be used to determine the extent to which a judge may give a broad and liberal meaning to the scheme and text in issue.

[241] *Ibid.*, p. 825.

Dickson also meant to exclude from his correct approach acts that concerned tax evasion, frauds and shams, which he extends not only to transactions that disguise a transaction (a sham) but also to those that alter the character of a transaction. For example, where a settlor of a trust retains a degree of control over a gift that defeats the characterization of the transaction as a gift.

What is suspect about the legal form of the tax avoidance plans McCreath and Jodrey effected is that they relied on self-dealing transactions to achieve a particular legal result under the principles of trust and corporate law to avoid a fiscal statute's object and purpose. Were they acting in bad faith when they created that legal form, which they intended to enforce against the Crown? Is the government an innocent third party acting on behalf of all taxpayers when it is responding to self-dealing taxpayer specific transactions and documents executed with tax avoidance intent?

For the three judges from Quebec, we will never know why they concurred with Martland's opinion. But it is noteworthy that provinces unlike Parliament cannot impose indirect taxes, and that too was before the Supreme Court in *Covert*. The Martland majority applied Dickson's unanimous opinion issued three weeks earlier, which reversed the British Columbia Court of Appeal, with the Supreme Court holding that an analogous statute imposed a direct tax on the person who inherited property.[242]

The above suggests a nuance about Martland adhering staunchly to the traditions of the British common law. He obviously considered and followed precedent when applicable, but not the British *Duke of Westminster* principle in income tax avoidance disputes under Canadian fiscal law. It was in conflict with the Supreme Court's judicial approach to tax avoidance. Martland's approach rarely applied British precedent inconsistent with the Supreme Court's precedent.[243]

[242] *Attorney General of British Columbia v. Canada Trust Co. et al.*, [1980] 2 SCR 466.

[243] Martland J.'s 1962 majority opinion in *Irrigation Industries* (*supra*, note 174) is an obvious exception.

Brock Martland, who is a high-profile criminal defence lawyer in Vancouver and who clerked at the Supreme Court, when asked to comment on his grandfather, said:

> My grandfather was, like most of us, a product of the time and context that he grew up in. He was an amazingly smart young fellow who skipped so many grades as a kid that the University of Alberta required him to wait one year before he would be allowed to start university. He then became a Rhodes Scholar, studying law at Oxford University. He was trained in the English common-law tradition, and spent his career as a lawyer and judge in that mould, respectful of tradition and the need to adhere to precedent. His timing was such that he retired from the Supreme Court of Canada in early 1982, almost exactly timed with the arrival of the *Charter of Rights and Freedoms*, and the start of an entirely different role for the courts. That timing symbolically aligned with the role he played as a judge. By background, training and temperament, he sought to decide cases based on a careful assessment of the relevant law, rather than any broader political type of view about societal norms or aspirations.

Justice Ronald Martland retired in 1982. He was replaced by Justice Bertha Wilson. Ronald Martland died in 1997.

WILFRED JUDSON: TERSE, VERY TERSE

Progressive Conservative Prime Minister John Diefenbaker elevated Wilfred Judson to the Supreme Court from the High Court of Ontario in 1958, replacing Justice Roy Kellock.

Born and raised in England, the working-class Judson immigrated to Canada in 1923 to teach Latin at a High School in Toronto. He graduated from Osgoode Hall Law School in 1932 and practised law over the next 19 years before being appointed to the Ontario High Court in 1951.

Justice Judson had the ability to take complex income tax issues and put them into concise understandable terms when writing a judgment. He also had an eye for identifying and articulating the key facts that, in his opinion, turned an income tax issue.

His colleague Justice Wishart Spence once described Judson as being "terse, very terse."[244] Philip Slayton, Judson's law clerk during 1969–70, described him as "austere ... with a narrow conception of a judge's role."[245] His income tax opinions do not fit Slayton's description and suggest Judson's perception of a judge's role in deciding income tax disputes was more nuanced.

Justice Judson's inclusion in the nine is based on both the quantitative and qualitative aspects of his decisions in income tax cases. In less than 20 years, he heard 125 income tax cases, of which 50 concerned tax avoidance—more than any other judge in the history of the Supreme Court.

Rarely in dissent in an income tax dispute, Judson was a conservative judge who came to the court as an expert in the law of equity,[246] and this may have influenced his approach to taxation. Academics who scrutinize the opinions of Supreme Court judges may be surprised to

---

[244] Girard, *Bora Laskin*, *supra* note 163, p. 371.

[245] Slayton, *Mighty Judgment*, *supra* note 160, p. 32.

[246] Snell and Vaughan, *The Supreme Court of Canada*, *supra* note 85, p. 202.

learn that Judson, normally a strict constructionist,[247] emphasized commercial substance over legal form to deny tax avoidance from 1958 until his retirement.

Judson's most famous precedent-setting income tax avoidance decisions concern the similar schemes he rejected for a unanimous Supreme Court in the 1969 companion cases *Smythe,*[248] and *Craddock.*[249]

There is no better place to begin considering the way Judson approached income tax than his decision in *Smythe,* which was the lead case.

Conn Smythe (1969)

Smythe and *Craddock* concern corporate surplus stripping—converting what would be taxable dividends if distributed, into amounts that are tax exempt or tax preferred such as capital gains. Multiple individuals and corporations participated in the scheme.

Heward Stikeman at the law firm Stikeman Elliott developed the original scheme in the 1950s, and it went national. Leading tax litigator and former Olympian Richard Pound wrote about the scheme in his 2002 book, *Stikeman Elliott.* Stikeman modified a business model Walter Gordon perfected while a leading accountant at the firm Clarkson Gordon.

Gordon was a Canadian nationalist concerned about foreign persons' acquiring control of Canadian corporations. He set up a

---

[247] Frederick Vaughan, *Aggressive in Pursuit: The Life of Justice Emmett Hall* (Toronto: University of Toronto Press published for The Osgoode Society for Canadian Legal History, 2004), p. 172.

[248] *Smythe et al. v. MNR,* (1969), [1970] SCR 64, dismissing the taxpayer's appeal for different reasons from (1967), [1969] Ex. CR 189. *Smythe et al. v. Minister of National Revenue* – SCC Cases (scc-csc.ca). The Exchequer Court decision is at *Smythe et al v. Minister of National Revenue* – Office of the Commissioner for Federal Judicial Affairs Canada (fja-cmf.gc.ca).

[249] *Wilbour Lee Craddock and Stanley Curtis Atkinson v. MNR,* 69 DTC 5369, [1969] CTC 566, dismissing the taxpayers' appeal from (1968), [1969] 1 Ex. CR 23, 68 DTC 5254, [1968] CTC 379. The Exchequer Court decision is at *W.L. Craddock v. Minister of National Revenue and Stanley Curtis Atkinson v. Minister of National Revenue* – Office of the Commissioner for Federal Judicial Affairs Canada (fja-cmf.gc.ca).

holding company after the Second World War to undertake *bona fide* acquisitions of corporations holding significant amounts of surpluses. Once a target corporation was acquired, its surpluses could be distributed as tax-free intercorporate dividends to the holding company for its use to pay the vendor for the acquisition.[250]

Vendors of shares earned tax-free capital gains. Gordon's holding company would keep the acquired corporations out of the hands of foreign entities and operated them with positive results.[251] Gordon sold the company to other Canadians in 1986 before his death in 1987. As for his former accounting firm, as part of its 125th year celebration in 1989, it published *The Clarkson Gordon Story* and promptly merged with American interests to become Ernst & Young Canada.

Stikeman, who learned of Gordon's takeover enterprise in 1949, established a similar business with his partner Fraser Elliott, which they eventually operated with success.[252] They also appear to have taken the business model one step further, by developing a tax avoidance plan. Under the plan, the twist was that the vendor shareholders essentially kept the underlying business while extracting its surpluses tax free. To do so, they transferred their shares to one or more facilitator corporations, which charged a fee for facilitating the tax-free strip. The vendors continued to own the business that produced the surpluses through a new corporation. To accomplish this, Stikeman's scheme circumvented the designated surplus rules, which were enacted when Douglas Abbott was the Minister of Finance.

In general, the designated surplus rules sought to deny the tax-free distribution of a target corporation's surpluses computed before the acquisition of control. Among other things, the rules helped ensure that a person did not acquire a Canadian corporation by

---

[250] Walter Gordon, *A Political Memoir* (Toronto: McClelland & Stewart Ltd., 1977), pp. 25–26; and Pound, *Stikeman Elliott*, *infra* note 253, pp. 38–39. Also see David MacKenzie, *The Clarkson Gordon Story: In Celebration of 125 Years* (Toronto: Clarkson Gordon, 1989), p. 41.

[251] *Ibid.*, p. 26.

[252] *Ibid.*, Pound, *Stikeman Elliott*, pp. 38–43.

using its surpluses to pay for the acquisition on a tax-free basis. The rules were supplemented by s. 105 of the 1952 ITA, which allowed a corporation to elect to pay a special 15 percent tax on all, or a portion, of its pre-1949 "undistributed income on hand." If done, the tax-paid amount could be paid as dividends to individual shareholders in Canada, free of personal income tax.

In Stikeman's scheme, no dividend was paid, and this appears to be why the designated surplus rules did not apply. Pound indicated that Stikeman's scheme drove federal tax authorities "mad" and National Revenue mustered all resources it could spare to ferret it out and reassess participants.[253]

National Revenue's response was to wield the full force of any provision that could apply to prevent the result, subject to the judiciary agreeing it applied. The chosen route was to apply, in the alternative, three anti-avoidance rules: (1) subs. 81(1) of the 1952 Act on the basis that the corporation had "undistributed surplus on hand" that the individuals had "otherwise appropriated in any manner whatsoever … on a winding-up, discontinuance or reorganization" of the corporate business [the precursor to current subs. 84(2)]; (2) subs. 8(1) on the basis the individuals appropriated an amount otherwise than pursuant to a *bona fide* business transaction or as a shareholder taxable benefit [the partial precursor to current subs. 15(1)]; and (3) subs. 137(2) on the basis a benefit had been conferred on the individuals as a result of one or more sales or other transactions not done *bona fide* in an arm's length transaction [the precursor to current s. 246].

---

[253] Richard Pound, *Stikeman Elliott: The First Fifty Years* (Montreal-Kingston: McGill-Queen's University Press, 2002), pp. 63–65. Pound explained the reason the designated surplus rules were enacted and Stikeman's role in trying to avoid them. The designated surplus rules included ss. 28 and 105A of the 1952 ITA. Subsection 28(2) denied the intercorporate dividend deduction; s. 105B imposed a tax of 15 percent on dividends paid out of designated surplus to a non-resident corporation or a tax-exempt person, and a 20 percent tax on dividends paid to a trader in securities. Section 105 allowed a corporation to elect to pay a 15 percent tax on its "undistributed surplus on hand" as of the end of 1949, which amount was not taxable to the recipient per subs. 81(4). Also, s. 105C imposed a 20 percent tax on certain amounts on a post-acquisition amalgamation.

There was a practical difference in the three proposed positions. If the deemed dividend rule in subs. 81(1) applied, the individual shareholders were entitled to a dividend tax credit to reduce the personal tax payable. Otherwise, they faced the full impact of tax at marginal tax rates—then in excess of 50 percent of their receipts. This seemed harsh to some in a context where surpluses could be accessed at a 20 percent federal tax rate under another rule discussed later. But shareholders had chosen to seek a 100 percent exemption. In other words, they were too greedy. Many of the participants would eventually settle their disputes rather than risk going to court for reasons discussed below.[254]

As National Revenue was digging in for a protracted fight, newly elected Liberal Prime Minister Lester Pearson appointed Walter Gordon Minister of Finance. Knowing the tax-planning mechanics underlying the stripping schemes, Gordon recommended in his 1963 Budget that Parliament amend the tax law to expressly preclude corporate surplus-stripping schemes. The new law was not retroactive in effect. Gordon stated the following about the abuse in the House of Commons:

> Another type of tax avoidance about which the government is particularly concerned is the proliferation of methods of moving undistributed income from a corporation into the hands of its shareholders without payment of tax. This abuse, and it is an expensive abuse to the public treasury, has become increasingly prevalent in recent years. It is time something was done about it.[255]

Walter Gordon's proposal shocked many tax professionals at the time because it reverted to the pre-1949 approach of constraining tax avoidance by granting the Minister of National Revenue the

[254] *Ibid.*

[255] *House of Commons Debates*, June 13, 1963, p. 1004. Parliament enacted the rule despite the outcry of tax professionals. The rule went against the principle that taxpayers have fiscal rights and should be able to structure their affairs without being subject to a discretionary power to deny the results.

discretionary power to deny the stripping schemes. Articles soon followed in the tax literature and articles in newspapers critical of the proposal.[256]

In a 1963 *Globe and Mail* article titled "Ministerial Discretion in Tax Cases Assailed," Stuart Thom, a Toronto tax lawyer at Osler, Hoskin and Harcourt, and Gwyneth McGregor, editor of the *Canadian Tax Foundation*, agreed Gordon's move represented a "backward step." They suggested that a better approach "would be for Canadian courts to abandon the strict interpretation of the letter of the law and begin to apply its spirit."[257]

The *Smythe* tax avoidance gambit occurred in late 1961, before the new rules applied. The judiciary was left to determine whether income tax was payable on those transactions.

By 1966, Ray Magladry of the *Toronto Daily Star* reported that the Minister of National Revenue E.J. Benson, a chartered accountant and the Member of Parliament for Kingston, gave taxpayers involved in the pre-1963 schemes a stark choice. Magladry reported that Gordon's new discretionary rule had stopped the strippers cold. But there was an ongoing brawl between National Revenue and the strippers about the legality of pre-existing strips. That brawl was so hot that Benson told the strippers that they either settle their disputes by paying a 20 percent tax on their dividends or go to court and risk having to pay the full rate applicable. Magladry also noted that Revenue officials were describing the scheme as a "sham" or "artificial" tax avoidance.[258]

---

[256] For example, see P.N. Thorsteinsson, "Ministerial Discretion Resurrected," (1964), 10:3 *McGill Law Journal* 256. Also see Jacques Barbeau and Derek H. Parkinson, *Dividend Stripping in Canada: An Analysis of Section 138A(1) of the Income Tax Act* (Toronto: CCH Canadian Ltd., 1964).

[257] Ruth Worth, "Ministerial Discretion in Tax Cases Assailed," *Globe and Mail*, November 21, 1963, p. 32. While the quote appears to be inconsistent with the narrative, the focus here is on the Supreme Court and not the Exchequer Court or the Tax Review Board. On appeal, the Supreme Court invariably reversed Exchequer Court decisions that allowed tax avoidance gambits. But when doing so there was an economy of reasons with no grand statements assailing tax avoidance.

[258] Ray Magladry, "Heat's on 'Strippers,'" *Toronto Daily Star*, October 3, 1966, p. 11.

The issue distilled in the *Smythe* and *Craddock* cases is whether the taxpayers made a *bona fide* sale of their shares to another corporation thereby realizing tax-exempt capital gains.[259] The taxpayers in *Smythe* were associated with the Toronto Maple Leafs franchise in the National Hockey League.

Conn Smythe had served with distinction during the First World War in the trenches at Ypres, the Somme, Vimy Ridge and Passchendaele and was awarded the Military Cross for his actions during the Canadian infantry's capture of Vimy Ridge in 1917. Smythe ended the war as a POW in Poland after attempting to escape near the Rhine. After the War, he acquired the Toronto St. Pats in 1927 and changed its name to the Maple Leafs.[260]

C. Stafford Smythe, Conn Smythe's son, moved into management with the Maple Leafs. He became entangled with Harold Ballard in the early 1960s when they each purchased some of Conn Smythe's shares. They were charged with tax evasion in March 1968 for defrauding the Leafs. Stafford Smythe died 12 days before the trial, and Ballard was convicted and sent to prison—but he gained Leafs ownership. To the chagrin of almost all Leafs fans and players, there never seemed to be an end to the debacle of Ballard's ownership throughout the 1970s and 1980s.

Clarence "Hap" Day, who was the St. Pats' captain in 1927, continued as the captain of the Maple Leafs, which became a Toronto institution over the next decade under Smythe's inspired ownership. A Stanley Cup followed, and as Day neared retirement, Smythe traded him to the New York Americans in 1938, where he played one final season.

Maple Leafs owner, Major Conn Smythe, re-enlisted during the Second World War and was maimed near Caen in the summer of 1944 after the D-Day landings. He was invalided home to

---

[259] *Ibid.*

[260] Kelly McParland, *The Lives of Conn Smythe* (Toronto: Fenn/McClelland & Stewart Ltd., 2011). This and the next three paragraphs rely on McParland's account of Conn Smythe's life.

Toronto, where he sought to rebuild his Maple Leafs. As a side business, the Smythes and Day operated a successful sand and gravel business in Toronto through a corporation. Its owners were Conn Smythe (52 percent), C. Stafford Smythe (30.8 percent), Hap Day (16 percent) and A. Boyd (1.2 percent).

The Smythe, Smythe and Day sand and gravel business accumulated significant corporate surplus by 1960, which would be taxable as dividends if distributed. Conn Smythe was aging, and much of his wealth was tied up inside the corporate business, including his shares of Maple Leaf Gardens Limited. He wanted to free up some of that wealth and undertake estate planning. Smythe and the others were advised they could do so in ways that were taxable, one of which would involve a dealer in securities, which would result in a 20 percent federal tax under s. 105B of the 1952 ITA. Conn Smythe considered the tax too high when combined with provincial tax and chose a scheme that sought to avoid all tax.[261]

The tax avoidance plan, while complex, had five key steps. First, the taxpayers' corporation transferred its business assets to a new corporation they owned, for a promissory note of $2,611,769. Second, the new corporation obtained a bank loan that it used to purchase shares of two facilitator corporations in Vancouver. Third, the two facilitator corporations used the cash they received for their shares to purchase the taxpayers' shares of the original corporation. Fourth, the taxpayers' claimed tax-exempt capital gain treatment. Fifth, the taxpayers reinvested some of their cash back into the new corporation by purchasing its debentures.

For their services, the facilitator corporations charged a fee of $41,431. In the process, Smythe, Smythe and Day sought to extract $728,852 of their corporation's "undistributed surplus on hand" as tax-exempt capital gains (about $7.5 million in 2024 dollars).[262]

---

[261] *Smythe, supra* note 248, with the Exchequer Court decision having the details concerning Conn Smythe's objectives.
[262] *Ibid.*, SCC p. 66.

Conn Smythe and the others were soon caught up in a national audit project. Surrender was not a word that came easy to Major Smythe. It took almost a decade to decide the matter, which came before the Exchequer Court in September 1967. In late December 1967, the Court held that a taxable benefit had been conferred on the Smythes and Day applying the anti-avoidance rule in subs. 137(2), to which there was no dividend tax credit. They appealed.

Stikeman, with Bruce Verchère assisting, litigated the dispute in the Supreme Court on behalf of Conn Smythe and Hap Day. Stikeman is said to have stepped in and taken on a weaker case out of professional duty, having designed the general nature of the scheme.[263] Canada's then leading criminal defence counsel John J. Robinette represented C. Stafford Smythe, who was at risk under unrelated federal charges of tax evasion.

Justice Judson denied the tax avoidance albeit he did not follow the Exchequer Court's approach. He applied the anti-avoidance rule in then subs. 81(1) instead of subs. 137(2). In doing so, he established two significant precedents.

First, the "winding-up, discontinuance or reorganization of a business" terminology, in the modern version of an anti-avoidance dividend-stripping rule dating to the 1920s, is to be applied

[263] Pound, *Stikeman Elliott*, *supra* note 253, p. 64. Pound did not explain why the *Smythe* case was weaker. It may have been weaker because the plan was more aggressive than in *Craddock*. In *Smythe*, the shareholders sought to convert $2,570,336 of value (over $26 million in 2024 dollars) into tax-exempt capital gains of which $728,652 was "undistributed surplus on hand." The shareholders appear to have undertaken a so-called *forward* strip of anticipated future corporate surplus. They contributed about $2.25 million back into the new corporation by purchasing its debentures, which could be redeemed over time tax free. In *Craddock*, Craddock and Curtis owned a corporation that had $101,000 of "undistributed income on hand," and they sold their shares of that corporation for $101,000, thereby limiting their conversion of the surplus into tax-exempt capital gains to $101,000. They never tried to convert and extract tax free the value of all the assets and business operations inside the old corporation, which presumably exceeded $101,000 when factoring in accruing capital appreciation in respect of the business.

based on the commercial substance of the transactions. On this point, Judson adopted the reasons of President Maclean of the Exchequer Court in his 1941 decision *Emily Merritt.*[264] In that dispute, Justice Kerwin affirmed that aspect of Maclean's decision for the Supreme Court in 1942 while allowing the Crown's appeal, thus reversing Maclean on another point.

Second, Judson made clear that the commercial substance of a legal sale of a share in a dividend-stripping context is not to be based on its legal form under that anti-avoidance rule. He did so despite many private-sector planners' arguing the rule did not apply because the taxpayers' receipts for selling their shares of the original corporation traced through the facilitator corporations to a bank loan obtained by the new corporation and technically did not come out of the surplus. That is, the planners sought to separate the share-sale receipts from the corporate surplus and say, "Look judge, there was no distribution of surplus." This is a distinction without a difference in terms of commercial substance and reality. Judson focused on the share sales and stated:

> … there was no sale of the shares of the old company to the dividend-stripping companies. The shares were transferred to these companies, with a fee of $41,433, for the purpose of enabling them to perform certain shuffles with the cheques and bank drafts to produce the result stated in these reasons. Taxation cannot be avoided by the transactions that were put through in this case.[265]

---

[264] *Smythe, supra* note 248, pp. 69–71 (pp. 70–72 if PDF version, online), citing Maclean of the Exchequer Court decision (it's p. 181) in *Minister of National Revenue v. Merritt* – SCC Cases (scc-csc.ca). The Exchequer Court decision is at *Emily L. Merritt v. Minister of National Revenue* – Office of the Commissioner for Federal Judicial Affairs Canada (fja-cmf.gc.ca).

[265] *Ibid.*, SCC p. 72 (p. 73, if PDF version, online). Subsection 81(1) of the 1952 ITA was in issue [subs. 84(2) of the 1985 ITA]. The 1952 provision applied: "Where funds or property of a corporation have, at a time when the corporation had undistributed income on hand, been distributed or otherwise appropriated in any manner whatsoever to or for the benefit of one or more of its shareholders on the winding-up, discontinuance or re-organization of its business."

(Justices Abbott, Martland, Ritchie and Pigeon concurred.) These were legal sales of shares, which Judson refused to recognize for tax purposes as capital gain sales because the sales (transfers) were made to a facilitator rather than for a *bona fide* commercial purpose. Their sole purpose was to avoid income tax. While the funds received traced to bank loans, this effected a distribution of corporate surplus in "any manner whatsoever." The $728,865 deemed dividend was eligible for a dividend tax credit, but it would have been taxed at high marginal tax rates.

Judson's decision in *Smythe* is the type that drives many a tax planner to distraction with claims that the judge imposed a personal smell test on the transactions, rather than the law. Another view is that Lord Tomlin in the 1935 British *Duke of Westminster* decision made it clear that his decision to apply a strict interpretation approach to the text of tax law (because taxpayers are entitled to arrange their affairs to minimize tax) was subject to the transactions being done with *bone fide* intent.[266] The Duke honoured those annuities in cases where a servant left his service after obtaining the annuity. But Smythe, Smythe and Day kept (or reacquired control over) the business they supposedly sold. Another way of looking at this is that, as suggested in the context of profiling Justice Martland's 1980 majority opinion in *Covert*,[267] bad faith intent taints a person's legal rights when that person seeks to enforce them against innocent third parties, and Justice Judson was an expert in the principles of the courts of equity.

In short, where Justice Judson came out on an income tax issue, he was normally decisive for a panel he sat on. Justice Abbott was often nearby, and he believed that Judson "had the best legal mind of any judge of his day."[268] There are limited exceptions where Judson dissented, as with Justice Cartwright in the 1962 tax avoidance dispute won by the taxpayer in *Irrigation Industries*.[269]

266 *Duke of Westminster, supra* note 2, Lord Tomlin p. 21.

267 *Frank M. Covert et al. (1980), supra* note 228.

268 Girard, *Bora Laskin, supra* note 163, p. 371.

269 *Irrigation Industries, supra* note 174.

Five months before Judson's next decision, the *Globe and Mail* reported in May 1964 that two recent Exchequer Court decisions appeared to be taking a new approach when deciding whether a taxpayer's gain from selling an asset was business income or tax-exempt capital gains. Referring to an article by Gwyneth McGregor, the *Globe* reported that the new approach appeared to differ from the Supreme Court's primary and secondary intent sale guidelines under the adventure in the nature of trade case law and that it may expand tax-exempt capital gains treatment.[270] The two cases were decided after the Supreme Court's 1962 decision in *Irrigation Industries*. McGregor indicated the irony was that the trend could result in a tax on capital gains.

Ronald Fraser (1964)

Justice Judson brought agreement back to the Supreme Court on share sales in his unanimous 1964 holding in *Ronald Fraser*.[271] The facts are straightforward. Two individuals, experienced in the real estate sector, formed a corporate group in 1950 to develop land and construct buildings as the post-war economy began to boom. Dominion Stores Ltd., a national grocery chain, sought their assistance in locating a store in Hamilton.

A company in the Fraser corporate group acquired 123 acres near Aldershot and began constructing a Dominion Store located on a portion of the acreage. When the store was 80 percent complete, Fraser sold his shares to Dominion Stores. He then sold his shares of another company holding vacant land. Fraser claimed tax-exempt capital gains treatment on both sales.

Judson dismissed Fraser's appeal for a unanimous Supreme Court in 1964 without citing or distinguishing *Irrigation Industries*. (Justices Martland, Ritchie, Hall and Spence concurred.) He held that the way in which Fraser and his associate realized the gains from selling

---

[270] Bruce MacDonald, "Will Courts Point Way to Capital Gains Tax?," *Globe and Mail*, May 12, 1964, p. B5.

[271] *Ronald K. Fraser v. MNR*, [1964] SCR 657. *Fraser v. Minister of National Revenue –* SCC Cases (scc-csc.ca).

their shares was "merely an alternative method that they chose to adopt in putting through their real estate transactions." Further, the "fact they incorporated companies to hold the real estate makes no difference."[272] Placing the emphasis on commercial substance and not legal form resulted in the gains being taxable business income and not tax-exempt capital gains.

A complex tax avoidance scheme was under audit in Toronto at the time the litigation in *Ronald Fraser* was percolating up the judicial hierarchy. It is the next decision considered.

Oakfield Developments (1971)

Oakfield Developments concerns the meaning of corporate control and whether two or more corporations were under common control and thus "associated corporations." The associated corporation rules are meant to stop corporations under common control from multiplying a tax benefit called the "small business deduction," which reduces the corporate tax rate below the general corporate rate on business income.

Without the associated corporation rules, corporations could simply subdivide business activities into as many corporations as required to ensure the small business tax rate applies to their total business income; but associated corporations must share one corporate small business deduction. The case law is rife with decisions that consider plans that attempt to multiply the small business deduction.

Progressive Conservative Finance Minister Donald Fleming addressed in his 1960 Budget the ease with which corporations could divide into multiple corporations with each qualifying for the then small business tax rate on their first $25,000 of corporate business income. The technical deficiency in the rules was that their application turned on common *ownership* of corporate shares, and a person or group of persons in control of a corporation does not legally own the shares owned by the corporation. As such, the

[272] *Ibid.*, SCC p. 661.

test could be avoided by simply tiering corporations down a corporate structure. In response, Parliament enacted Fleming's recommended change to the associated corporation rules applicable to 1961 and subsequent tax years.[273] Under it, association would be determined based on common *control* of corporations.

Alerted to the change by its tax accountant, a corporate group in Toronto began plans to avoid the proposals. Originally called Polestar Developments Limited, it became Oakfield Developments (Toronto) Limited under a corporate restructuring that included amalgamating with other companies. It aimed to, by the end of 1960, multiply access to the small business deduction on a go-forward basis despite the new rules.

By amalgamation and related steps, the number of corporations of the Okun family (Okun Group) controlled through Polestar (Oakfield Developments) was reduced to 32 from 42. As this was

---

[273] SC, 1960, c. 43, subs. 11(1), amending subs. 39(4) of the 1952 ITA. The Supreme Court identified a similar deficiency in the 1948 ITA litigated in *Army & Navy Department Stores Ltd. et al.*, [1953] 2 SCR 496. Locke J., for the majority, allowed the appeal of one of the two corporations (denied the low corporate tax rate preference) because the trial judge had failed to apply the legal principle that a shareholder of a corporation does not own the property it owns (e.g., shares of another corporation). The result was that the taxpayer corporation was allowed to benefit from the low corporate tax rate. Justices Taschereau and Fauteux concurred. Justice James Estey dissented and in doing so stated that the matter did not concern "that a corporation is a distinct and separate legal entity"; the issue was the meaning of "directly or indirectly," and he found that a shareholder could have "indirect" ownership of corporate property. Cartwright J. issued a minority opinion directed at Estey's dissent. Cartwright cited the British decisions *Macaura* ([1925] AC 619, p. 626) and *Salomon* (*infra* note 293) for the proposition that a shareholder does not have "indirect" ownership of the corporation's property and that it is not the agent or trustee of its shareholders. The result was one of a handful of pre-*Charter* Supreme Court successes for a taxpayer in a tax avoidance context under the modern ITA; it rests on the bedrock nature of the separate personality of a corporation under the *Salomon* principle and not the *Duke of Westminster* principle, which was not cited. All five judges agreed the corporate taxpayer in the second case did not qualify for the deduction. *Army & Navy Department Stores Ltd. v. Minister of National Revenue / Army & Navy Department Store (Western) Ltd. v. Minister of National Revenue* – SCC Cases (lexum.com).

occurring, the Okun Group restructured a separate group of corporations. These restructurings occurred based on a legal opinion obtained by the group's tax accountant.[274]

The share capital of all 32 companies held through Polestar (Oakfield Developments) was restructured so that the Okun Group ultimately held only 50 percent of the votes necessary to elect the various boards of directors (but holding 100 percent of the common shares). The remaining 50 percent of the votes were held by strangers to the Okun Group, Toronto lawyer Mr. Lionel H. Schipper and his wife Carol (who together owned 100 percent of the preferred shares).[275] With a 50–50 vote split, the 32 corporations were supposedly not under common control; no person (or group of persons) had control of any of the 32 corporations. As such, each could claim a separate small business deduction.

But at no time did the Okun Group want to forgo effective control of the numerous corporations in its group. To ensure effective control, Oakfield Developments could be wound up by a 50 percent vote. If this happened, 100 percent of Oakfield Developments' surplus would be paid to its common shareholders (the Okun Group), and the preferred shareholders (the Schippers) would be repaid only their invested capital and any amount owing on their guaranteed 10 percent annual return.

The Minister's auditors associated all corporations, based on a technical deficiency in the plan; the issuance of the preferred shares to the Schippers was invalid because it occurred before Polestar (Oakfield Developments) had the legal authority to issue

---

[274] *Oakfield Developments (Toronto) Limited v. MNR*, [1971] SCR 1032, dismissing the taxpayer's appeal for different reasons from (1968), [1969] 2 Ex. CR 149. *Oakfield Developments (Toronto) Ltd. v. Minister of National Revenue* – SCC Cases (scc-csc.ca).

[275] *Ibid.* Mr. Meyer Okun, the head of the Okun Group, approached Mr. Schipper's father for assistance. He recommended his son, and he acquired 4,999 preferred shares and his wife 1 preferred share. They were guaranteed a 10 percent annual return on their preferred shares and repayment of the capital used to purchase the shares.

the shares. Oakfield Developments lost at trial and appealed to the Supreme Court.

Wilfred Judson decided not to affirm the Exchequer Court's reasons and instead decided the dispute, based on the meaning of legal control of a corporation rather than on the technical deficiency that any tax planner could fix in a similar scheme.

In his unanimous decision, Judson cut through the complexity and found the Okun Group had legal control despite not having more than 50 percent of the votes. Okun Group could cause a winding-up of Oakfield Developments and be "entitled to all of the surplus after return of capital and the payment of a 10 per cent premium to the preferred shareholders." Judson concluded: "[T]hese circumstances are sufficient to vest control in the group when the owners of non-participating preferred shares hold the remaining 50 per cent of the voting power."[276] The panel comprised seven judges rather than the normative five judges before the 1990s: Justices Abbott, Martland, Ritchie, Hall, Spence and Pigeon concurred.

Justice Judson's 1971 decision in *Oakfield Developments* was controversial in the tax community because he found the Okun group had legal control despite not having more than 50 percent of the votes. In doing so, he distinguished the Court's then leading precedent on corporate control, which is its 1967 unanimous decisions in five companion cases known collectively as *Dworkin Furs et al.*[277] Judson did so because in "*Dworkin Furs*, the voting was also split equally between two groups, but there was only one class of shares." There, each "group had the same *de jure* rights, and each shareholder was entitled to share proportionally in the profits and assets of the company by dividends or on winding up. In addition, neither group could itself wind up the company."[278]

---

[276] *Ibid.*, p. 1037.

[277] *Dworkin Furs et al., supra* note 145. *Minister of National Revenue v. Dworkin Furs (Pembroke) Ltd. et al.* – SCC Cases (scc-csc.ca).

[278] *Oakfield Developments, supra* note 274, SCC p. 1037.

In 1983, Richard Miner suggested in his text *Associated Corporations*,[279] that Judson's decision in *Oakfield Developments* "adds little to the general law on control but rather represents a concerted effort by the court to derail what it viewed as an elaborate tax avoidance scheme and appears to have no application beyond its particular facts."[280] Despite this, the precedent became of central importance in two subsequent Supreme Court decisions on the meaning of corporate control.

The Supreme Court was considering another corporate legal control issue when the Court decided *Oakfield Developments*. The Court appears to have had more difficulty deciding its outcome. Although the oral hearing was held before the Court released its decision in *Oakfield Developments*, it took several more months to decide the dispute, and there was a dissent.

Consolidated Holding Company Limited (1971)

Judson's majority decision in *Consolidated Holding Co.* concerns a conflict between the powers granted in a will to executors to vote shares held in trust and the company law requirement of unanimity in the decision to vote shares held by joint owners. Judson was an expert in the law of equity, which includes trusts. The issue was whether Consolidated Holding and Martin & Robertson Ltd. (M&R Ltd.) were associated corporations in the 1963 and 1964 taxation years.[281] If so, they had to share one small business deduction.

Consolidated Holding had two shareholders who were cousins (Harold Duncan Gavin and Robert Duncan Gavin). They each owned 1,651 of 3,302 issued shares and formed a group of persons in control. Through Consolidated Holding, they also had a substantial minority interest in M&R Ltd.[282]

---

[279] Richard B. Miner, *Associated Corporations* (Toronto: The Carswell Company Limited, 1983).

[280] *Ibid.*, p. 17.

[281] *MNR v. Consolidated Holding Company Limited*, (1971), [1974] SCR 419, allowing the Minister's appeal from 69 DTC 5429, [1969] CTC 633 (Ex. Ct.). *Minister of National Revenue v. Consolidated Holding Co.* – SCC Cases (scc-csc.ca).

[282] *Ibid.*, Ex. Ct. at 69 DTC p. 5429.

M&R Ltd. had 30,000 issued voting shares. The two cousins each owned 1 voting share and controlled 13,110 voting shares through Consolidated Holding.[283] Duncan Gavin Sr. owned 13,777 voting shares of M&R Ltd., but when he died these shares went to his executors: the two Gavin cousins and the Montreal Trust Co.

Two possibilities existed:
First, Consolidated Holding disputed its association with M&R Ltd., based on its articles of association and the corporate law principle that exists in respect of voting shares held jointly. The principle provides joint holders of shares must agree when exercising the right to vote shares. Thus, while the Gavin cousins controlled directly and indirectly 13,112 votes in M&R Ltd. shares, they could not control the 13,777 votes the three executors had, as Montreal Trust could disagree on how to vote the shares on an issue. On this basis, the two corporations were said not to be associated.

Second, based on Duncan Gavin Sr.'s will, the two cousins had the power to decide how to vote his 13,777 shares of M&R Ltd. as two of three trustees—binding on all other trustees. When combined with the votes on the 13,112 shares of M&R Ltd., they controlled directly and indirectly both corporations. The Minister assessed on this basis.

Consolidated Holding was successful before Deputy Justice Sheppard of the Exchequer Court. He held that the corporate articles of association provided that the shares had to be voted unanimously and that the two Gavin cousins did not control the executor votes on the 13,777 shares of M&R Ltd. because Montreal Trust could vote differently. The Minister appealed.

Justice Judson found that the two corporations were associated. (Chief Justice Fauteux and Justices Abbott and Hall concurred.) He posed the issue in terms of conflicting theories about what to consider in determination of legal control of a company by a person or group of persons: the first considered the M&R Ltd.'s share

[283] *Ibid.*

registry only, while the second considered the *legal realities* existing under Duncan Gavin Sr.'s will.[284]

Judson held that legal control of a corporation cannot be determined by merely looking at its share register and its legal indicia (articles of association) if it has issued shares that are trust property. Although under the corporate law a trust had to vote its shares as a unit, if the trustees were not unanimous, the shares could not be voted. In that event, Judson found that the two Gavin cousins would control M&R Ltd. through their minority shareholdings held by Consolidated Holding, which became a majority voting block if the executor-trustees could not vote due to a lack of unanimity.[285]

Justice Spence dissented. He relied on the corporate law principle that the corporation could require the trustees to achieve unanimity before voting trusteed shares.

The result was that the Supreme Court looked to the legal realities effected by the trust, and not merely the share registry and articles of association, to determine legal control of the corporation. The unanswered question at the time was: Would the Court extend its legal realities approach to non-trust arrangements that fetter shareholder voting rights?

As previously mentioned, either Judson or Abbott wrote the unanimous or majority decisions in a series of disputes that concerned the application of Canada's international tax treaties, which are meant to prevent double taxation. Judson decided three disputes regarding the *Canada-United States Tax Treaty: Interprovincial Pipe Line Company v. MNR* (1959),[286] *Interprovincial Pipe Line Company v. MNR* (1968)[287]

---

[284] *Ibid.* SCC p. 422.

[285] *Ibid.*

[286] *Interprovincial Pipe Line Company v. MNR*, [1959] SCR 763, allowing the taxpayer's appeal from 59 DTC 1018, [1959] CTC 1 (Ex. Ct.). *Interprovincial Pipe Lane Co. v. Minister of National Revenue* – SCC Cases (scc-csc.ca).

[287] *Interprovincial Pipe Line Company v. MNR*, [1968] SCR 498, dismissing the taxpayer's appeal from (1967), [1968] 1 Ex. CR 25. *Interprovincial Pipe Line Company v. Minister of National Revenue* – SCC Cases (scc-csc.ca). The Exchequer Court decision is at https://reports.fja-cmf.gc.ca/fja-cmf/j/en/item/398970/index.do?q=Interprovincial+Pipe+Line.

and *MNR v. Stickel.*[288] Limited space allows sole consideration of the third, *Stickel.*

Ernest Stickel (1974)

Toward the end of his tenure on the Supreme Court, Judson encountered an income tax dispute that concerned an American academic who moved with his family to Edmonton to teach at the University of Alberta.

Ernest G. Stickel was born, raised and educated in Ohio. He graduated from Case Western Reserve University in Cleveland where he was employed from 1953 to 1957 while working to obtain his doctorate in Philosophy in 1957. His wife was born in the Dominion of Newfoundland and Labrador and moved to the United States before meeting her future husband. In the early 1960s, they resided in Washington, D.C., north of the College of William & Mary in Virginia where Stickel taught. They later moved to Maryland where Stickel worked for the Board of Education. They had four children.

In late 1966, Stickel applied for and was offered a position with the University of Alberta. Mrs. Stickel was said to be reluctant to move because she was not familiar with western Canada. They agreed to a temporary posting for two years. It just so happened a tax benefit was available to professors and teachers in temporary positions not exceeding two years. Stickel's two-year contract ended on June 30, 1969.

Article VIIIA of the *1950 Canada-U.S. Tax Treaty* provided, in general, that a professor or teacher who resided in one country (in this case the U.S.) who temporarily visited the other country (Canada) to teach for a period not exceeding two years was not subject to income tax on the resulting teaching income during that two-year period by the other country (Canada).

---

[288] *MNR v. Ernest Stickel*, (1974), [1975] 2 SCR 233, dismissing the Minister appeal from 73 DTC 5178, [1973] CTC 202 (FCA), which allowed the taxpayer's appeal from 72 DTC 6178, [1972] CTC 210 (FCTD). *M.N.R. v. Stickel* – SCC Cases (scc-csc.ca).

The Stickels moved to Canada on July 1, 1967, and they did not return to the U.S. until March of 1970, residing in Canada for almost three years. After his lecturing contract expired in June 1969, Stickel held two non-teaching jobs in Canada between July 1969 and March 1970. He claimed that he was not taxable on his Canadian teaching income during the two-year period, based on the treaty benefit.

The Minister assessed tax on Stickel's salary received as a lecturer, and Stickel appealed. He lost at trial on the basis he stayed in Canada for more than two years and therefore did not satisfy the requirements of the treaty benefit rule. No determination was made as to whether Stickel continued to reside in the U.S. during this period while living and working in Canada. He appealed.

The Federal Court of Appeal found that Stickel met the meaning of the expression "temporarily visits" when he moved to Canada for the purpose of lecturing for a period not exceeding two years. Since Stickel met that purpose test, it did not matter that he had stayed in Canada longer than two years. The Court of Appeal also found that on the facts established at trial, Stickel remained a resident of the U.S. He continued to own property in the U.S. although he brought his family with him, closed their home in the U.S. and dispersed some belongings. This finding of fact was critical because Stickel could claim the treaty benefit in Canada only if he also resided in the U.S. The Minister appealed.

Justice Judson agreed Stickel could claim the treaty benefit. (Justices Ritchie, Spence, Pigeon and Dickson concurred.) He added that he had not overlooked the fact that Stickel had successfully claimed that his income was not taxable in the U.S. because he had ceased to reside there during the period. Judson stated the problem was "the treaty giving him exemption for Canadian tax on his Canadian income."[289]

In the dispute, two purposes in respect of the treaty benefit were in conflict. The first purpose was to encourage cross-border

[289] *Ibid.*, SCC p. 235.

movements of professors and teachers on a temporary basis without income tax affecting its purpose. Stickel satisfied this purpose, and the resulting teaching income was exempt from Canadian income tax for the allowed period. The second purpose was of the treaty itself, which was to provide relief from double taxation rather than a no-tax windfall. Stickel did not satisfy this purpose, as he claimed he was not a resident of the United States for the purpose of paying U.S. income tax on his salary from lecturing.

While U.S. residency was a necessary condition for Stickel to qualify for the treaty benefit, both the Federal Court of Appeal and the Supreme Court agreed that he was a resident of the U.S. despite the view of the U.S. Internal Revenue Service. It is this latter aspect of Judson's decision that is most surprising because it meant that professors and teachers could arbitrage the two tax systems as they crossed the border on temporary assignments.

Nevertheless, the benefit professors and teachers obtained under the tax treaty is immaterial in the bigger picture. More significant tax benefits are at stake in the context of wealthy people and multi-national corporations navigating the international network of tax treaties established by countries to avoid double tax, seeking to benefit from no tax. Nothing should come as a surprise in this world of high-stakes tax avoidance.

The Supreme Court has decided numerous resource-related tax cases since the enactment of federal income tax in the fall of 1917. One such case is Judson's 1974 majority decision in *Jack Appleby*.[290]

Jack Appleby (1974)

Canada has a long history of extending tax benefits to participants in the primary sector of the economy—be it farming, oil and gas exploration and development, mining exploration and

[290] *Jack Appleby v. MNR*, (1974), [1975] 2 SCR 805, dismissing the taxpayer's appeal from 72 DTC 6275, [1972] CTC 317 (FCA), affirming 71 DTC 5438, [1971] CTC 728 (FCTD). *Appleby v. M.N.R.* – SCC Cases (scc-csc.ca).

development, forestry or fishing. Much of the wealth that makes Canada a prosperous country is the direct result of this underlying economic activity. Although this seems not to be appreciated by those who grow up and live in an increasingly urbanized Canada.

The issue before the Supreme Court in *Jack Appleby* was whether the taxpayer, as a financier of a prospector tasked to locate mineral reserves, could benefit from a tax preference. In general terms, that preference exempted from tax the financier's resulting income from a successful prospecting if (1) the financer exchanged his rights under the prospecting agreement for an interest in the mineral reserve, or (2) shares of a corporation were acquired in return for the interest in the mineral reserve.

Jack Appleby was entitled to this tax benefit unless the shares he acquired under rule (2) above occurred "while on or after carrying on a campaign to sell shares of the corporation to the public." Since Appleby owned and sold the shares personally, the issue was whether he could be denied the benefit in circumstances where his corporation undertook the promotion campaign.

Appleby owned J. Appleby Securities, which acted as an agent, broker and promoter. He personally arranged for a prospector to strike certain mining claims, which he transferred for shares of Winston Mines Ltd. On that same day, Winston Mines and J. Appleby Securities agreed that the latter would underwrite the issuance of shares of Winston Mines into the market.

The prospectus indicated that Appleby agreed to promote Winston Mines and that he beneficially owned 75,000 of its shares (with any sale proceeds accruing to him personally). Once regulatory approval to issue the shares was obtained, J. Appleby Securities began a promotion campaign recommending to prospective buyers that they purchase shares of Winston Mines.

J. Appleby Securities also entered a "support the market" agreement under which it and another broker agreed to purchase and sell shares of Winston Mines at prices set by J. Appleby Securities, which also agreed to purchase any Winston Mines stock that the other broker failed to sell back into the market. This included shares whose price fell below the market price when purchased, with J. Appleby paying the other broker what it had paid.

Appleby sold his 75,000 shares in Winston Mines, which he acquired free under the promotion, into the market through other brokers that knew of the arrangement under which the other broker was purchasing shares at fixed prices, which were then acquired and paid for by J. Appleby Securities. The other broker's actions were described as "running the box" for J. Appleby Securities.

Jack Appleby repeated this type of activity with two other mining companies he incorporated. Among other facts, it was ruled that Appleby personally set the daily prices at which the other broker was to buy and sell shares of the three mining companies.

Judson reviewed the facts and the lower court holdings against Appleby. Although Judson noted the taxpayer argued that the other broker ran the box for the company J. Appleby Securities, he considered it "obvious … that it was running the box on the sole instructions of Appleby, who at the same time had his own shares to dispose of."[291] Appleby had done so "while carrying on a campaign to sell shares of these companies to the public … [and his brokerage was] completely under his domination." Taken together, this meant Appleby could not claim the benefit because para. 83(4)(*a*) of the 1952 ITA excludes "a person who disposes of the shares while or after carrying on a campaign to sell shares of the corporation to the public."[292] (Justices Ritchie and de Grandpré concurred.)

Justice Judson had just used a judicial knife to slice through the seminal decision of the British House of Lords in *Salomon,*[293] dating to the late 19th century, under which a corporation has separate personality from its shareholders. Beyond this, many questions remain, including whether Appleby was denied the exemption because he lacked a *bona fide* intent under the exemption.

---

[291] *Ibid.*, SCC p. 811.

[292] *Ibid.*

[293] *Aron Salomon (Pauper) v. A. Salomon & Company, Limited*, (1896), [1897] AC 22 (HL).

Did Appleby act in a manner that the Supreme Court considered, in a general sense, to be improper conduct that was abusing the purpose of the exemption? The answer appears to be, "*yes.*" Was the Judson-led majority offended by the nature of the stock trading—running the box? His taking the time to describe the nature of running the box suggests that this was the case.

In dissent, Justice Pigeon found that Jack Appleby was entitled to the exemption. J. Appleby Securities was a separate person, and it carried out the marketing campaign. For Pigeon, to decide otherwise required that the Crown justify piercing the corporate veil or the scheme be a sham.

Although the Crown argued that Jack Appleby participated in the promotion to the extent of taking advantage of the market created, Pigeon was not of the view this was enough to deny Appleby the exemption. He also disagreed with the trial judge's decision that the "obvious" purpose of the denial rule in respect of marketing was to ensure that a person benefiting from the exemption was rewarded for his financial participation in prospecting and not for the activities of a dealer in shares. Pigeon added: "Unless there is ambiguity, it is to be applied literally in accordance with the general rules of law including the effect of the incorporation of limited companies."[294]

All of which makes Justice Martland's minority decision in *Jack Appleby* interesting in the context of considering whether it charts an approach between the extremes reflected in Judson's majority decision and Pigeon's dissent. Although Martland agreed with the majority result, he stated this did not extend to concluding "when the agents of a corporation carry on a promotion campaign—they do so personally." He made it clear that he was respecting the *Salomon* principle that a corporation is a separate person at law from any of its shareholders.

For Martland, the distinguishing fact was that Jack Appleby owned 75,000 shares of Winston Mines and promoted its shares, using

[294] *Appleby*, *supra* note 290, SCC p. 819.

another company under his control. Such a person "can be found to have carried on a campaign for the sale of shares if he causes his own company to carry it out on his behalf."[295] In essence, Appleby could not cleanse the personal benefit he sought to derive from selling his shares in Winston Mines through personal actions as owner of J. Appleby Securities by relying on its separate corporate personality.

David Judson, who is a capital markets and mergers and acquisitions lawyer with Torys LLP in Toronto, when asked to comment on his grandfather, said:

> Justice Judson was born in 1902 in the Town of Todmorden England in Yorkshire. Todmorden was, essentially, a one industry town dominated by a large iron works. Those were not prosperous times in that part of England. It was generally expected that men as young as 12 or 13 would leave school and work at the foundry in order to contribute to family finances. Young Wilfred bucked that trend. He taught himself to speak Latin fluently by the time he was 10 years old and immersed himself in studies graduating from Manchester University with an MA at age 20. He was denied entry to Oxford and Cambridge due to not having the correct accent or pedigree. As a result, he emigrated to Canada and settled in Parkdale in Toronto as a very young man. He taught Latin at Parkdale Collegiate High School for a number of years and scraped together enough money to put himself through law school at Osgoode Hall, graduating as the gold medalist. He went on to practice in Toronto and became a Bencher of the Law Society of Upper Canada before being appointed to the Ontario Supreme Court and, subsequently, to the Supreme Court of Canada. He was an intellectual and very serious about his work—some would say a bit dour. I found him to be a very articulate and straightforward man. He was certainly

[295] *Ibid.*, SCC p. 807.

> a doting and wonderful grandfather to me. He introduced me to all the judges on the Court in the early 1970s and we would often visit with Justices Martland and Ritchie in particular. I would, as a young man, listen rapt to those weighty discussions and take it all in. One thing is for certain. Wilfred Judson had little tolerance for those who attempted to evade or avoid paying tax. He was a letter of the law man, and was firmly of the view that a judge's role is to interpret and apply the law, not to create it, as that was solely within the purview of the elected legislature. I was very proud to have known him.

Justice Wilfred Judson retired from the Supreme Court in July 1977. He was replaced by Justice Willard Estey, whose father was Supreme Court Justice James Estey. Wilfred Judson died in 1980.

JOHN CARTWRIGHT: BORN TO THE LAW

Chief Justice John Cartwright was not selected, even though a convincing argument can be made for his inclusion. He has the quantitative numbers in terms of cases decided, having heard 95 income tax cases of which 29 concerned tax avoidance. Cartwright was also a liberal judge who often led the Supreme Court in disputes where the Court decided the matter for the taxpayer.

John Cartwright left Osgoode Hall Law School in 1914 and enlisted during the First World War; wounded twice, he was awarded the Military Cross in 1917. After the war, he finished his studies at Osgoode Hall and practised law in Toronto. Cartwright was appointed a counsel to the Government of Canada for the 1946 *Royal Commission on Soviet Spying Activities* and was the lead prosecutor in the resulting trials. Liberal Prime Minister Louis St. Laurent appointed him to the Supreme Court in 1949 when the Court expanded to nine justices.

Philip Slayton, who was Wilfred Judson's law clerk during 1969–70 suggested the extent of the cultural shift that occurred for youth during the 1960s when he described Cartwright as having "impeccable manners and grooming, conservative and old-fashioned."[296] The ways of an older generation were receding as the ways and values of their grandchildren ascended.

A notable decision of Chief Justice Cartwright in favour of the taxpayer is his 1954 precedent-setting commercial substance decision in *Dominion Taxicab Association.*[297]

Dominion Taxicab Association (1954)

In the dispute, taxi drivers had to pay $40,500 to the Dominion Taxicab Association when joining; $40,000 was applied to payment for services, and $500 was refundable on leaving. The tax

[296] Slayton, *Mighty Judgment, supra* note 160, p. 32.

[297] *Dominion Taxicab Association v. MNR*, [1954] SCR 82. *Dominion Taxicab Association v. Minister of National Revenue* – SCC Cases (scc-csc.ca).

issue was whether the association's $500 receipts were gross revenue or repayable loans. Justice Cartwright, for the majority, held that the amounts were neither gross revenue nor loans; they were non-taxable deposits. (Justices Kerwin, Locke and Fauteux concurred; Justice Rand issued a minority opinion.)

On substance, Cartwright stated: "It is well settled that in considering whether a particular transaction brings a party within the terms of the *Income Tax Acts* its substance rather than its form is to be regarded."[298] It is disputed whether Cartwright meant legal or commercial substance.[299] The distinction can be significant in a tax avoidance context. Legal substance is a narrower concept that takes its meaning from the true legal relationships created under a contract. Commercial substance is a broader concept that includes commercial principles and realities although it is not necessarily as broad as economic substance.

It appears Cartwright meant commercial substance. His reference to substance when interpreting the contract in light of the statutory law follows in the same paragraph in which he stated: "The expression 'profit'… has not a technical meaning and whether or not the sum in question constitutes profit must be determined on ordinary commercial principles unless the provisions of the *Income Tax Act* require a departure from such principles."[300] In this rendition of substance, commercial principles and reality are not divorced from legal principles when the issue concerns computing commercial profit (or loss).

---

[298] *Ibid.*, SCC p. 85.

[299] For example, see Deen Olsen and Perry Derksen, "The Historical Legal Context for the Enactment of the General Anti-Avoidance Rule: Judicial Anti-Avoidance Doctrines and Statutory Anti-Avoidance Rules," pp. 53–75, in Brian J. Arnold (Editor), *The General Anti-Avoidance Rule: Past, Present, and Future* (Toronto: Canadian Tax Foundation, 2021), where they cite (p. 60) *Dominion Taxicab Association* when referring to the "substance over form" doctrine although they do not say what type of substance is referred to in that case; instead, they cite the *Duke of Westminster* principle for the proposition the substance referred to is "legal substance."

[300] *Dominion Taxicab*, *supra* note 297, p. 85.

Chief Justice Cartwright confronts in the next decision how best to balance taxpayer rights and obligations in an income tax context.

Highway Sawmills (1966)

Highway Sawmills Limited carried on a logging operation on Vancouver Island in the 1940s and 50s. During this time, it purchased land that included merchantable timber from the Esquimalt and Nanaimo Railway Company. Highway Sawmills planned to abandon the land after it was logged for its merchantable timber, intending that the local government sell the land due to the company's failure to pay property taxes. The land's purchase price was based on cruises conducted by qualified assessors of merchantable timber, and no value was assigned to the land at the time of acquisition.[301]

The company logged the merchantable timber and deducted CCA in respect of its timber limits, which are depreciable property under the CCA regime. The deduction of CCA for both "timber limits" and "a right to cut timber from a timber limit" is computed on a depletion basis under a separate schedule to the *Income Tax Regulations*, which enunciates the computations.[302] In general, the annual CCA deduction is the portion of the cost of a timber limit that is prorated to the taxation year, based on the quantity of timber cut from the limit in the year.

In 1957, instead of abandoning the stripped land, Highway Sawmills sold it for $22,620 to the Alaska Pine and Cellulose Company Limited, which wanted to operate a tree farm. As the price received for the land exceeded the timber limit's depleted tax

---

[301] *Highway Sawmills Limited v. MNR*, [1966] SCR 384, dismissing the taxpayer's appeal from [1965] Ex. CR 297, 65 DTC 5080, [1965] CTC 142, which allowed the Minister's appeal from 63 DTC 453, (1963) 32 Tax ABC 161 (TAB). Also see *Avril Holdings Limited v. MNR*, (1970), [1971] SCR 601. *Highway Sawmills Limited v. Minister of National Revenue* – SCC Cases (scc-csc.ca). For *Avril Holdings, Avril Holdings Ltd. v. Minister of National Revenue* – SCC Cases (scc-csc.ca).

[302] The *Income Tax Act*, 1985, see Regulation 1100(1)(e) and Schedule VI to the *Income Tax Regulations*.

cost, Highway Sawmills had deducted more CCA than its net tax cost. Such excess CCA is normally recaptured as income.

Highway Sawmills maintained that the recapture of excess CCA into income rule did not apply because land is not depreciable property under the CCA regime. As such, the $22,620 received for selling the land was treated as a windfall free from tax. The Minister reassessed Highway Sawmills and included the $22,620 in its income for the 1957 taxation year on the basis that the land was part of the timber limit. Highway Sawmills objected and was successful before the Tax Appeal Board, which the Exchequer Court reversed. Highway Sawmills appealed.

Justice Cartwright reviewed the various statutory and regulatory definitions and provisions in issue and contrasted the phrase "a timber limit" with a "right to cut timber from a timber limit." He assigned a meaning to a timber limit that included the land upon which merchantable timber grows. (Justices Abbott, Judson and Spence concurred.[303])

When doing so, Cartwright went beyond the text and context in which the phrase "a timber limit" was found under the CCA regime. He indicated that the purpose of the scheme was to provide taxpayers with an allowance in respect of timber limits and equated a taxpayer's "right" to deduct CCA to the taxpayer's "obligation" to add excess deductions to income.

> Without these statutory provisions the owner would have no right to make such deduction from income. The right to make the deduction is subject to the obligation, if he disposes of the asset, to add to his income the proceeds of that

[303] *Highway Sawmills*, *supra* note 301, SCC p. 393. Cartwright J. stated: "I think it plain that when those lands were acquired by the appellant they were properly described as 'timber limits' both in ordinary popular language and in the sense in which those words are used in the statutory provisions. In my opinion, the phrase 'timber limits' describes a parcel of land with merchantable timber standing upon it. … The phrase 'a timber limit' is used in … contradistinction to the phrase 'a right to cut timber from a limit', which is one apt to describe a profit à prendre."

> disposition to the extent that such proceeds do not exceed the capital cost to him.[304]

In 1975, Dale Gibson stated in the *Canadian Bar Review*: "[It] is unlikely that anyone will ever feel nostalgic about the Supreme Court's performance in the 1960's."[305] Gibson was writing in the context of constitutional law, but I feel nostalgic for equating statutory rights with obligations in an income tax context.

Two liberal jurists, Cartwright and Spence, and two conservative jurists, Abbott and Judson, formed this majority and, in doing so, paid heed to the rules of statutory interpretation and precedent. At the end of his judgment, Cartwright noted in *obiter* that Highway Sawmills would have been allowed to deduct, under its construction of the provisions, all its capital cost for the timber limits "although it had already recovered $22,620 of that cost."[306]

Justice Ritchie, the third conservative judge on the panel, dissented. He found it "to be plain that the phrase means the 'timber within defined limits or boundaries'" thus excluding the land upon which the timber grows.[307] Ritchie did not consider this result to run contrary to the expressed intention of Parliament, and he found that an amendment would be required to "include land stripped of timber in the prescribed class of depreciable property."[308]

Chief Justice Cartwright also wrote the opinion in the Supreme Court's unanimous 1967 decision in *Foreign Power Securities*;[309] his judicial policy approach to tax avoidance reveals the importance

---

304 *Ibid.*, p. 393.

305 Dale Gibson, "And One Step Backward: The Supreme Court and Constitutional Law in the Sixties," (1975) 53 *Canadian Bar Review* 621, p. 622.

306 *Highway Sawmills*, *supra* note 301, SCC p. 394.

307 *Ibid.*, p. 396.

308 *Ibid.*, p. 398.

309 *Foreign Power Securities Corporation Ltd. v. MNR*, [1967] SCR 295, aff'g [1966] Ex. CR 358. See *Minister of National Revenue v. Foreign Power Securities Corporation Ltd.* - SCC Cases (scc-csc.ca). The Exchequer Court decision is at *Foreign Power Securities Corp. Ltd. v. Minister of National Revenue* - Office of the Commissioner for Federal Judicial Affairs Canada (fja-cmf.gc.ca).

the Court took during the period to a finding of fact for or against the presence of taxpayer *bona fides*.

Foreign Power Securities (1967)

The *Foreign Power Securities* decision is important in several respects, including its relationship to one of the most heated debates in the history of the House of Commons. For this reason, time is taken to detail the facts and to consider the way in which Justice Cartwright approached the dispute, which was decided at trial by Justice Camil Noël.

Foreign Power Securities Limited was incorporated in 1927 for the purpose of investing in public utilities primarily outside Canada. A public corporation, it incurred significant losses during the Great Depression. By the Second World War, Foreign Power's main asset was a facility located in France. The French government nationalized that asset during the war. Payment was in francs that were blocked from leaving France, which Foreign Power received after the war over many years. By the mid-1950s, Foreign Power had reinvested about $3.3 million of this money in Canadian bonds and similar securities.

Persons involved in a national pipeline project acquired control of Foreign Power shortly after the Louis St. Laurent government passed the necessary legislation in June 1956 to make the project commercially viable. Shares of the company that would own the national pipeline were then transferred to Foreign Power, which sold them into the market at a substantial profit on which it claimed tax-exempt capital gains treatment. The sequence is detailed below.

In the early 1950s, Nesbitt Thompson & Company Limited was a dealer and underwriter of securities when it advanced $85,000 to Western Pipe Line Limited and Alberta Interfield for the purpose of funding a national pipeline project. After changing its name to N.T. Investments Limited, it became an investor in securities, ceasing to be a securities dealer. It transferred its trading assets and underwriting business to a new company, except its interest in the pipeline project.

In 1954 and 1955, N.T. Investments acquired 72,624 common shares of Trans-Canada Pipe Lines Limited in return for assisting the pipeline project. It also acquired another 10,712 shares of Trans-Canada Pipe Lines for making advances to Canadian Delhi Oil Limited, which was a partner in the pipeline project.[310] Since these shares were acquired in respect of its former trading and underwriting activity, N.T. Investments should have been taxable on any profits realized when selling the shares.

The Warnock Hersey Company Limited, which was controlled by Peter Thomson, acquired control of N.T. Investments on December 22, 1955. It next acquired control of Foreign Power on June 28, 1956; the acquisition occurred 22 days after the Pipe Line Debate ended in the House of Commons with the Liberals voting to close debate—the arrogance of which sealed the fate of the Liberal government's re-election prospects.

The Pipe Line Debate ended on June 6, 1956, followed by the *Northern Ontario Pipe Line Crown Corporation Act* becoming law. At the end of 1956, Foreign Power was a controlled subsidiary of N.T. Investments.

The first key non-arm's length transaction involved N.T. Investments transferring 11,225 shares of Trans-Canada Pipe Lines to Foreign Power on July 6, 1956, one month after the debate ended and mere days after The Warnock Hersey Company acquired control of Foreign Power. A second transfer of 7,142 shares to Foreign

[310] In a related development, Quebec Natural Gas Corporation was incorporated in June 1955 for the purpose of acquiring Hydro-Quebec's gas distributing business. The incorporators included N.T. Investments Limited and Canadian Delhi Oil Limited as well as various investment houses and the International Utilities Corporation. N.T. Investments immediately transferred a majority of its 750 shares of Quebec Natural Gas Corporation to Foreign Power, with the remainder being transferred in January 1957. Also, the incorporators, including Foreign Power, entered into an agreement in September 1956 to finance Quebec Natural Gas Corporation in proportion to their interest. In return, they received additional shares of Quebec Natural Gas Corporation.

Power occurred on February 18, 1957.[311] The price set on the transfers was $8 per share. This price made no allowance for the fact the value of the shares was enhanced by the Liberal Government's decision to extend up to $80 million of financing toward the construction of the western section of the project.

Trans-Canada Pipe Lines' stock was $24.50 per share in the over-the-counter market as of March 1957, less than one month after the second transfer of 7,142 shares at $8 per share to Foreign Power on February 15, 1957. Speculators were running rampant in the market. At $24.50 per share, unrealized profits of about $16.50 per share had been diverted to Foreign Power.

The price of Trans-Canada Pipe Lines' shares rose to $47.50 per share by mid-June 1957 before it fell back to $20.50 a share at the end of 1957. On January 2, 1958, the shares were listed on the TSE.

The outcome of the Pipe Line Debate made several taxpayers small fortunes. By the end of 1957, Foreign Power realized about $703,600 in gains from selling 16,000 shares of Trans-Canada Pipe Lines together with shares of Quebec Natural Gas Corporation. In 1958, it realized additional gains of about $64,000. Foreign Power maintained that its gains were tax-free capital gains.

The Minister's auditors issued assessments against Foreign Power on the basis that its gains were taxable as ordinary income from an adventure in the nature of trade. Counsel for Foreign Power relied on several factors, including that Foreign Power was a *bona fide* public investment company under s. 69 of the 1952 ITA, whose gains were normally tax exempt.

Immediately before trial, counsel for the Minister brought a motion to amend his reply to Foreign Power's pleadings. He sought to add a paragraph that listed several facts the Minister would rely

[311] Before and after June 1956, N.T. Investments transferred 83,336 shares of Trans-Canada Pipe Lines to various persons. The transfers included transfers to P. Thomson (November 1954: 14,500); to Power Corporation (May 1955: 14,000); and to Nesbitt, Thomson and Company Limited (March 1957: 3,750).

on at trial. These additional facts are lengthy, but their thrust was that the persons in control of Foreign Power engaged in a deliberate scheme that sought to cloak the profits with non-taxability, with the transfers executed at a below-market price of $8 a share. Although Foreign Power objected strenuously, the Exchequer Court allowed the motion on the condition that Foreign Power could object to the relevancy of the facts at trial and to the presentation of any document that dealt with any person other than Foreign Power.

The tone of the hearing before the Exchequer Court was set. Counsel for the minister was preparing to argue that the adventure in the nature of trade case law should apply to a situation where The Warnock Hersey Group effected a diversion of profits from taxable to non-taxable status pursuant to a blatant tax avoidance scheme. Besides claiming a *bona fide* investment intent, counsel for Foreign Power would be relying on (1) its separate personality under the *Salomon* corporate law principle, (2) the Minister's failure to rely on any anti-tax avoidance rule and (3) the *Duke of Westminster* principle.

Justice Noël of the Exchequer Court opened his analysis with a discussion about the *Salomon* principle. Relying on the Privy Council's 1939 decision in *Pioneer Laundry*,[312] Noël found that the Minister cannot disregard the separate legal existence of a corporation unless there is the presence of fraud or improper conduct. But Noël also stated, relying on Chief Justice Kerwin in *Atlantic Sugar Refineries* and Justice Judson in *Regal Heights*,[313] that "the true nature of the transactions involved must always be considered and where motives are important, the interconnection or interrelationship of companies dealing with each other as well as the motives and acts of a company's manager and directors must be explored because a corporation is but a legal entity which cannot have purposes separate from those of its managers and directors."[314]

[312] *Pioneer Laundry, supra* note 20.
[313] *Regal Heights, supra* note 178.
[314] *Foreign Power Securities, supra* note 309, Ex. CR p. 361.

In essence, Justice Noël had just noted that in Canada, a transaction involving corporate intent is subject in an income tax context to the approach taken by Chief Justice Kerwin and Justice Judson.

The final introductory point Noël made about the separate *persona* of a corporation is that a corporation could be a sham under the tax law. While this does not affect the corporation's legal existence, it allows the judiciary to ignore its sham aspects.[315]

The rub, if you will, for Justice Noël was that he considered the Minister's assessments to be unusual in that "he is seeking to have these profits held taxable as resulting from an adventure in the nature of trade on the basis of its shareholder's (N.T. Investments Ltd.) activities and intentions and as being a means used by it to transfer its profits."[316] Noël was concerned that Foreign Power was being taxed on profits on the basis that the share sales had an income character to N.T. Investments. The Minister could have taxed the profits in the hands of N.T. Investments by applying the non-arm's length fair market value transfer rules in the 1952 ITA, but he did not.

In concluding that the profits were not taxable to Foreign Power, Noël made the following findings: (1) Foreign Power was a *bona fide* public investment company; (2) it was never an underwriter of securities; (3) the non-arm's length nature of the transfer was not of much assistance in determining whether the profits were taxable profits to it; (4) the shares were acquired for less than their market value; and (5) the company sold the shares after a short holding period to take

---

[315] *Ibid.*

[316] *Ibid.*, Ex. CR pp. 362–63. Noël J. stated: "And, finally, in some cases in matters of taxation it is necessary for the Court to go beyond the corporate entity in order to determine whether a transaction was at arm's length or not or artificial … [citing the Exchequer Court decisions in *Shulman* (1961) and *Rivershore Investments Limited* (1964)] … or to find out whether the corporation should be characterized as a 'paper sham' a 'simulacrum', cloak or alias or *alter ego* or an artificial vehicle, … [citing the Exchequer Court decision in *Rolka* (1962)] and thereby in some cases establish whether the transaction entered in by it be given legal effect or not. Before parting with this matter I should add that even if a corporation set up as a sham cannot, however, be disregarded, although … [citing British precedent, Noël indicated the corporation can be found to be acting for the people who called it into existence]."

advantage of an unrealistic high market price, and in such circumstances a short holding period was of little assistance to the Minister, given the Supreme Court's 1962 decision in *Irrigation Industries.*[317]

Justice Noël concluded by discussing three points about tax avoidance:

First, the *Duke of Westminster* principle entitles every person to structure their affairs to pay the least amount of tax payable. Nevertheless, "there is much to be said in favour of preventing the ingenuity expended by certain people to devise in some cases elaborate and artificial methods of disposing of income in order to avoid the payment of taxes because it thereby increases *pro tanto* the load of the tax on the shoulders of those who do not desire or know how to use such methods."[318]

Second, Noël found that if Parliament wants an effective deterrent to tax avoidance, it should legislate a rule to block it rather than have its Minister ask the judiciary to squeeze the transaction into the adventure case law.[319]

Third, Noël noted that the-then ITA did not have a provision under which the Minister could deny a tax avoidance result based on one of the main purposes being the intent to avoid income tax.[320]

---

[317] *Ibid.*, Ex. CR pp. 383–85.

[318] *Ibid.*, Ex. CR pp. 385.

[319] *Ibid.*, Noël J. stated (p. 386): "I would think that if it is desired to have an effective deterrent to a tax avoidance practice which is considered to be against the public interest, Parliament should legislate it … so as effectively to block it. The Court should not be asked to accomplish the task, as it is being asked to do here, by squeezing into the notion of an adventure in the nature of trade, a transaction which is a *bona fide* investment and nothing else. Nor is the situation any different if such a *bona fide* investment was entered into with the knowledge that the capital value of the *res* would surely increase …."

[320] *Ibid.* Noël J. stated (pp. 386–87): "There is indeed no provision in the *Income Tax Act* … [that constrains tax avoidance where the main, or one of the main, purpose(s) is to avoid tax]. The only authority of this character conferred by the statute is conferred on Treasury Board by section 138." That rule granted the Executive the power to deny tax avoidance transactions for which one of the main purposes was the "improper avoidance or a reduction of tax." Parliament repealed the power in 1985 on the basis it was inconsistent with the *Charter*.

The Minister appealed. Cartwright found that Noël gave full consideration to the facts and held that "the primary activities of the respondent are those of a bona fide investment company" and that the decision to sell so soon after acquisition was based on the taxpayer's opinion the shares reached an unrealistic high price.[321] Once this "finding of fact is accepted, no question of law arises. A perusal of the record in the light of the full and able arguments addressed to us satisfies me that this finding was right."[322] (Chief Justice Taschereau and Justices Fauteux, Martland and Spence concurred.)

The result in the Supreme Court's decision in *Foreign Power Securities* is an anomaly. The Court invariably upheld or reversed decisions of the Exchequer Court to ensure that taxpayers did not escape the tax net through tax avoidance schemes. What explains this anomaly if it can be explained? It appears that many factors came together for the taxpayers that assisted them in their objective.

First, the Minister's auditors failed to take the direct route in taxing the profits by assessing N.T. Investments under ss. 16–17 of the 1952 ITA on the basis that the price Foreign Power paid for the transferred shares was less than their fair market value and understated a taxable profit. Second, counsel for the Minister sprung the tax avoidance allegations on the judiciary at the last moment. This allowed the taxpayer to object to the relevancy of the new allegations at trial, and this could have undermined the Minister's case. Third, the 1950s' pipeline controversy was still alive by the mid-1960s with rumours involving Liberal politicians and their financial backers flying about the public domain.

Before mentioning one of those rumours, the most important point is that the result in *Foreign Power Securities* flowed from Justice Cartwright's determination that the key matter in issue—whether the taxpayer was a *bona fide* investment company and why it sold the shares quickly—was a question of fact rather than law.

[321] *Ibid.*, SCC p. 297.

[322] *Ibid.*

From at least 1938 until the early 1980s, the Supreme Court placed significant weight on whether a taxpayer acted with *bona fides*, when deciding income tax avoidance disputes.

This makes sense because the Supreme Court liberally, without much citation or notice, applied Lord Tomlin's *caveat* in the *Duke of Westminster* decision that taxpayers need *bona fide* intent in income tax matters. Even in the Supreme Court's 1955 tax avoidance holding for the taxpayer in *Sheldon's Engineering*, where Justice Charles Locke applied the strict interpretive approach, he noted before doing so: "The good faith of the respondent in the matter is not impugned, the only questions between the parties being as to the true construction of the relevant provisions of the statute."[323] (In that case, Chief Justice Kerwin and Justices Taschereau, Estey

[323] *MNR v. Sheldon's Engineering Ltd.*, [1955] SCR 637, p. 643. Also consider by way of counter example to *Foreign Power Securities* the Supreme Court's 1970 decision in *First Torland Investments Limited et al.*, which concerns three disputes like the one in *Foreign Power Securities.* In that case, numerous farms in western Canada under private-sector administration since the Great Depression were transferred to three corporate taxpayers that sought *bona fide* investment company status, and tax-exempt capital gains from sales. Unlike in *Foreign Power Securities*, the trial transcript shows that the three companies did not qualify for investment company status and, in any event, carried on a trading business. The Supreme Court relied on these findings at trial to dismiss the taxpayers' appeal: *First Torland Investments Limited, et al. v. MNR,* 70 DTC 6354, [1970] CTC 634, dismissing [1969] 2 Ex. CR 3, 69 DTC 5109, [1969] CTC 138. Although that was not clearly stated in the Exchequer Court decision, Stanley Edwards counsel for the taxpayers conceded to the court that the companies "don't qualify under Section 69" and focused his argument on the farms being investment property with the gains being tax-exempt capital gains (see p. 200 of the Supreme Court's case file, case files 11475, 11476, 11477). The Exchequer Court held for the Crown. On appeal, Abbott J. stated for the Supreme Court (November 3, 1970): "We agree with the finding made by the learned trial judge that, on the facts, the profits realized by the appellants on the sales of the farmlands in issue in this appeal were profits from a business. The appeals are dismissed with costs." Abbott, Martland, Spence, Pigeon and Laskin JJ. *Minister of National Revenue v. Sheldon's Engineering Ltd.* – SCC Cases (lexum.com). The Exchequer Court decision in *First Torland* is at https://reports.fja-cmf.gc.ca/fja-cmf/j/en/item/398784/index.do?q=First+Torland.

and Cartwright concurred.) Similarly, Foreign Power was a *bona fide* investment company.

What is also instructive about Justice Cartwright's holding in *Foreign Power Securities* is that he was not drawn into discussing the parameters of legal and illegal tax avoidance in an adventure case.[324] His approach is consistent with the Supreme Court's not discussing in *obiter* the parameters of the judicial function in a tax avoidance context during the period.

Two final non-tax observations are in order about three companies on the periphery of the decision. First, Peter Newman wrote in *The Canadian Establishment* in 1973: "When Warnock Hersey International had closer ties with Power Corporation, it owned a luxurious beach villa in Jamaica. In the early sixties, several Liberal cabinet ministers used to pass the key quietly around themselves and spend free time there. Montreal Trust, another Power operation, acts as the main depository for financing Quebec's federal and provincial Liberal parties."[325]

Second, Quebec's Union Nationale Premier Maurice Duplessis had several of his cabinet ministers exposed in the 1958 "Natural Gas Scandal" for owning and selling for-profit shares of Quebec Natural Gas Corporation to which Quebec sold its Hydro-Québec natural gas distribution company.[326] In Ontario, the Conservative Minister of Mines was exposed as earning significant profits from selling shares in Northern Ontario Gas Co., and he resigned.[327]

---

[324] *Foreign Power Securities, supra* note 309. See paras. 4 and 17 of the Crown's factum at Supreme Court case file 10515.

[325] Newman, *The Canadian Establishment, supra* note 73, p. 58.

[326] Gerard Filion, *Documents de l'histoire du Québec/Québec History Documents*, "Le scandale du gaz natural," Marianopolis College. Filion wrote the story for *Le Devoir*, June 14, 1958, p. 4. For an article in English, the posted material includes "Gas Attack," *Time Magazine (Canada)*, June 30, 1958. Quebec appointed a commission of inquiry, which reported in 1962 (those who acquired shares included 31 civil servants). http://faculty.marianopolis.edu/c.belanger/quebechistory/docs/Scandaledugaznaturel-NaturalGazScandal.html.

[327] *Ibid.*, see "Gas Attack." Philip Kelly was the Minister who resigned.

Chief Justice Cartwright is not included in the chosen nine because he was an outsider to a conservative block that invariably decided income tax disputes from the late 1950s to the mid-1970s. That block included Justices Abbott, Judson, Martland, Ritchie and Chief Justice Fauteux.

James Snell and Frederick Vaughan, in their 1985 book on the history of the Supreme Court of Canada, described John Cartwright as being a person who "seemed to have been born to the law and to a position of social prominence."[328] Vaughan also described Cartwright as a "man of uncommon virtue" in his biography of Justice Emmett Hall.[329]

Chief Justice John Cartwright retired in 1970. He was replaced as a member of the Supreme Court by Justice Bora Laskin. John Cartwright died in 1977.

The next part provides the selection of a chief justice for the hypothetical panel of nine Supreme Court judges.

[328] Snell and Vaughan, *The Supreme Court of Canada*, *supra* note 85, p. 198.

[329] Vaughan, *Aggressive in Pursuit*, *supra* note 247, p. xi.

PART III

The Chief Justice

ONE JUDGE STOOD OUT to be selected the chief justice of the hypothetical nine-member bench that consists of the most influential Supreme Court judges in income tax disputes during the 1920–2019 period. His selection is based on the qualitative aspects of his opinions and the fact his tenure is the most balanced between the pre-*Charter* and *Charter* eras.

BRIAN DICKSON: A JUDGE'S JOURNEY

Liberal Prime Minister Pierre Trudeau elevated Brian Dickson to the Supreme Court in March 1973, replacing Justice Emmett Hall. Before being elevated, he had been a member of the Manitoba Court of Appeal.

The son of Irish Protestant immigrants, Dickson spent his teen years during the Great Depression on the prairies, where his father was a banker. He graduated from the University of Manitoba Law School in 1938. Despite being its Gold Medalist, he was unable to find a law position. There simply were no legal positions on the prairies at that time. He took a non-legal position at Great West Life and was a part-time member of the active militia.

With the declaration of war, Dickson enlisted and entered officer training with the Royal Canadian Artillery in 1940. On a mission to salvage equipment in heavy fighting, he and his convoy were hit by Allied bombers, falling short of German lines. Over 150 Canadian troops were killed, and many more severely wounded. Dickson barely survived the surgery in which his right leg was amputated under a tent near Caen.

Invalided home to Manitoba in late 1944, Dickson embarked on a distinguished legal career in Winnipeg after being discharged from the Army in 1945. He practised business law at a leading firm, Aikens MacAulay, and like Ronald Martland, was a Chancellor of the Anglican Church of Canada. In 1963, Brian Dickson was appointed to the Manitoba Court of Queen's Bench.

Justice Robert Sharpe and legal scholar Kent Roach wrote in their biography titled *Brian Dickson, A Judge's Journey* that Dickson on retirement "was revered in the legal community as a judge with exceptional ability," that his writing style was "lucid" and his opinions "crafted strong and enduring precedents in Canadian law notable for their compassion."[330]

---

[330] Sharpe and Roach, *Brian Dickson, supra* note 162, p. 5. Sharpe and Roach's account of the life Brian Dickson is relied on in the introductory paragraphs.

Chief Justice Dickson was a liberal justice who tended to join the old-guard conservative justices in denying income tax avoidance. He heard 45 income tax cases of which 14 concerned tax avoidance. Dickson also tended to be in dissent with Justices Laskin and Spence in contentious non-tax disputes until the late 1970s.

Before considering several of Brian Dickson's opinions, it should be noted that he appears to have preferred deciding tax disputes that involved individual taxpayers rather than corporate taxpayers; his leading tax opinions concern individuals, although he sat as a member of panels in which corporate tax was at issue. When contentious income tax issues involved ordinary (and not so ordinary) individuals, Dickson often wrote a unanimous or majority opinion on the matter. In corporate tax cases, others tended to write those opinions even though Dickson practised business law in Manitoba before he was appointed a superior court judge.

During the 1970s, Justice Dickson was a bridge between the liberal minority and the conservative majority. This is exemplified in his 1974 majority income tax decision in *Angle*, which concerns an action the Minister took to collect a tax debt owed by a related company.[331]

Ethel Annabelle Angle (1974)

Ethel Annabelle Angle was no ordinary Canadian. She and her fellow American husband, Richard Angle, were successful promoters of Canadian mining stock. Murray Teigh Bloom devoted almost five pages to Richard Angle's stock promotion activity in his 1971 *Rogues to Riches, The Trouble with Wall Street.*[332] Angle's husband, who grew up in Kansas City, was connected familywise to the Republicans and President Harry Truman. After his post-war discharge from the United States military, he successfully traded grain

[331] *Angle v. MNR*, (1974), [1975] 2 SCR 248. *Angle v. M.N.R.* – SCC Cases (scc-csc.ca).
[332] Murray Teigh Bloom, *Rogues to Riches*, *supra* note 203, pp. 113–17. The following paragraphs include facts Bloom wrote about, as well as from newspaper articles.

in the United States until an American stock-fraud artist operating out of a Toronto boiler room conned him out of $40,000.

Angle hopped in his car and drove straight to Toronto to confront the crooks, who had disappeared with his money. He returned to Kansas City, started an investment newsletter and eventually landed back in Toronto, where by the late 1950s, he had transformed himself and his newsletter into "The Canadian Forecaster."

In the early 1960s, Angle was promoting a mining stock that ramped up to a $1.45 a share. Bloom indicated that after someone started shorting the stock, Angle pumped $200,000 of his own money into the promotion to maintain the stock's price. He also paid the *Cosa Nostra* $2,500 to determine who was shorting the stock, but it then threatened him and demanded an additional $17,500. Terrified, Angle through his lawyer turned to Samuel Ciglen, who advised them to involve the police, which investigated. Later, Angle was wired to record conversations with the *Cosa Nostra.*

Since the late 1930s, Toronto had been a haven for rogue American promoters' intent on peddling dubious Canadian mining, oil and gas stocks into the United States.[333] In the early 1940s, the SEC obtained evidence that named provincial officials who allegedly were bribed by ex-patriate American stock promoters.[334] While this was never proven, Ontario provided little or no substantive help to the Americans during most of the ensuing years.

---

[333] Lund (Anthon H.) of the U.S. Securities and Exchange Commission, *The Canadian Problem: Illegal Securities Offerings, 1933–1955,* "Draft" Confidential [SEC] Staff Report, March 30, 1955. The report's circulation was limited to 15 officials. It is posted at Virtual Museum and Archive of the History of Financial Regulation (sechistorical.org).

[334] *Ibid.*, p. 36. The SEC obtained secret indictments beginning in 1941 against some of the rogue American brokers in Toronto, hoping they would return home for a visit. Early on this paid off when it apprehended a boiler-room operator named Niditch at the Quebec-Vermont border. Niditch ended up being sentenced to serve 10 years in prison. In 1945, he asserted in an affidavit that the rogue group of broker-dealers in Toronto made "pay-offs" to officials at the Ontario Securities Commission, whom he named.

In 1955, the Americans prepared a secret study of the situation in Toronto, which they titled their "Canadian Problem."

By the early 1960s, the *Cosa Nostra* was muscling in on penny-stock promotions, and the situation was turning violent. In the extortion attempt of Angle, four were charged in Toronto, including brothers Paul, Eugene and Albert Volpe. Three mistrials occurred. In one, a jury member was approached with a bribe. In the fourth trial, the jury returned an acquittal for all charged. But Justice Cartwright for a unanimous Supreme Court in 1967 reversed the acquittal and sent the matter back for retrial.[335]

Paul and Eugene Volpe pleaded guilty during their retrial in 1968. Richard Angle testified against them and stated that he would have "sold my soul to hell" to get out of the room in which a Volpe associate confronted him demanding 100,000 shares of a stock that Angle had promoted.[336] Albert Volpe, who at the time was operating a casino in Greece, was acquitted after he returned to Canada for his trial. Angle did not testify at that trial; his testimony from the earlier trial was read to the jury.

The fourth accused was serving a 20-year prison sentence in the United States for a $500,000 jewel heist from a hotel in Beverley Hills and an attempted heist of a Brink's truck.[337] Paul Volpe would become a leading figure in Canada's criminal underworld after beginning his career involved in penny-stock promotions out of Toronto. He was murdered in 1983.

---

[335] *The Queen v. Natarelli et al.*, [1967] SCR 539. Justice Cartwright, with Chief Justice Taschereau and Justices Fauteux, Judson and Spence concurring. *The Queen v. Natarelli et al.* – SCC Cases (scc-csc.ca).

[336] "Volpe Brothers Plead Guilty to Threat against Stockholder," *Globe and Mail*, May 15, 1968, p. B4. Three years earlier, the Minister seized $120,000 from a bank account to pay an income tax debt Richard Angle owed. The funds were about to be transferred to a Bermuda bank account. Angle argued the funds were property of a company he promoted and thus the Minister could not seize them to collect his tax. In 1968, the Ontario courts declared Angle the legal owner of the funds, making them subject to seizure to pay his tax debt. See "Angle Gets $120,000 Seized on Tax Claim," *Globe and Mail*, July 11, 1968, B2.

[337] Bloom, *Rogues to Riches*, *supra* note 203.

The legal issue and the facts are disjointed in *Angle* because the matter concerns two distinct tax cases, only one of which was decided by the Supreme Court. In the first case, the Exchequer Court decided whether Ethel Angle owed tax on the basis of her receiving a taxable shareholder benefit of $50,000 for a pool addition made to her home by a related company called "Transworld Co."

In the second case, the Supreme Court decided whether the Minister could collect tax that another company owed the Minister by seizing part of the money Angle was owed for selling her home that included the pool addition. The facts are complicated, but the Minister could collect only if Angle's $50,000 debt for the pool addition existed in law after the Exchequer Court decision in the first case.

In the first case, to avoid a $50,000 taxable shareholder benefit, Angle agreed to owe Transworld Co. a $50,000 debt as part of granting it a lease of her property. The debt was to pay the company for surrendering the pool addition to Angle, but she already owned the addition because it was built on her land. She then tried to get out from under the Minister's taxable benefit assessment by borrowing $50,000 from Mr. Angle to pay the debt. This occurred while Angle was in the process of moving with her children to be with him in the state of Washington.

In 1969, in Vancouver, the Exchequer Court held in the taxable shareholder benefit case that among other things, Ethel Angle's purported payment of the debt set up when agreeing to the lease was not genuinely paid by her; later, Justice Dickson stated that the trial "judge rightly concluded that this trumpery did not amount to payment for the pool house."[338] As a result, Angle owed income tax on a $50,000 taxable benefit. But Angle maintained that, as a result, she was no longer indebted to Transworld Co. for the pool addition.

---

[338] *Angle, supra* note 331, p. 252. Also see *Angle v. MNR*, 69 DTC 5423, [1969] CTC 624 (Ex. Ct.), which concerns the taxable benefit.

Meanwhile, by October 1970, Kansas City Traders, a company related to Angle, owed $40,266 in unpaid taxes. At the end of that month, the Minister obtained a writ of extent in the third and second degrees that applied to $34,612 owed to Angle (the third-degree creditor) by the purchasers of her home; $34,612 she owed Transworld Co. (the second-degree creditor) that built and paid for the pool addition (on which there was a sham repayment); $40,266 Transworld owed Kansas City Traders (the first-degree creditor, tax debtor), which owed the Minister $40,266.[339]

Angle appealed. The Supreme Court heard oral argument on November 7, 1973, while it was in turmoil over how to handle two criminal law cases: *Doré,*[340] and *Kienapple.*[341] It issued two decisions in *Doré,*[342] the second of which applied *Kienapple* to overturn the first. The Court decided *Angle* after its *Kienapple* decision and before its second decision in *Doré.*[343] Professor Ian Bushnell, who wrote about the internal dispute in *The Captive Court* in late 1992, never discussed *Angle*, and it is unclear why.[344]

---

[339] *In re Kansas City Traders Ltd.*, 71 DTC 5061 (Ex. Ct.). The Minister executed the writ against Adolf Franz Bauer and Anne Bauer, the purchasers of Angle's home, with the Bauers being the fifth-degree debtor. They owed a law firm (the fourth-degree creditor) to whom Angle assigned the agreement of purchase and sale. On motion in the Exchequer Court, after the 1969 Exchequer Court judgment in the *Angle* taxable benefit case, the Court confirmed the writ against Angle and Transworld Co.

[340] *Doré v. Attorney General (Canada)*, (1974), [1975] 1 SCR 756. *Doré v. Attorney General of Canada* – SCC Cases (scc-csc.ca).

[341] *Kienapple v. The Queen*, (1974), [1975]1 SCR 729. *Kienapple v. R.* – SCC Cases (scc-csc.ca).

[342] *Doré, supra* note 340.

[343] The sequence in hearings and decisions is as follows: The Supreme Court (1) heard oral argument in *Doré* in October 1972; (2) heard *Kienapple* in October 1973; (3) heard *Angle* in November 1973; (4) issued its first decision in *Doré* and its *Kienapple* decision in February 1974; (5) ordered in April 1974 a rehearing of *Doré*; and (6) released its *Angle* decision on May 27, 1974. It then re-heard *Doré* and reversed the first decision based on *Kienapple.*

[344] Bushnell, *The Captive Court, supra* note 157, pp. 402–4.

Five points about the internal dispute are relevant when considering *Angle*.

First, Brian Dickson was newly appointed to the Supreme Court, and it was experiencing a significant internal dispute. How he handled himself in that context could be critical for him moving forward.

Second, the five-member panel hearing *Angle* (Justices Martland, Judson, Laskin, Spence and Dickson) were on the nine-member panels hearing the two criminal cases. But the panel in *Doré* increased to nine members from five only after Chief Justice Fauteux and Justice Abbott, who were on the five-member panel that rendered the original decision in *Doré*, resigned office on principle. As mentioned, the second decision applied *Kienapple* and reversed the first decision.

Third, Martland had criticized in his *Kienapple* dissent, leave having been granted. This brought the internal dispute into the open.[345] When Martland made his comment directed at Laskin in February 1974, Laskin was the Chief Justice having been appointed on December 27, 1973. The former academic Laskin had wanted to change the criminal law, and Chief Justice Fauteux, who had the same matter before him in *Doré*, knew nothing about Laskin's plan until notified, presumably by Martland. Martland is the only judge

[345] *Kienapple, supra* note 341, p. 731. Martland J. stated: "Presumably, when leave to appeal to this Court was granted it was felt that the outcome of the appeal, if successful, would have some practical favourable consequences for the appellant. However, in the course of his argument, counsel for the appellant conceded that if the appeal succeeded the appellant would not be entitled to obtain a new trial in respect of both the charges against him. He was still subject to the sentence on the charge of rape, which sentence was exactly the same as, and concurrent with, the sentence on the other charge. In the result, therefore, the appeal to this Court constituted an academic exercise, the only result of which, if successful, will be to prevent the addition to the appellant's already lengthy criminal record of a conviction for the crime of sexual intercourse with a female under the age of fourteen, not being his wife, which crime it is clear that he committed." Subject to a clarification, Fauteux C.J. concurred with Martland and with the dissent of Ritchie J. (Fauteux C.J. and Martland and Abbott JJ., concurring). Laskin J. for the majority (Judson, Spence, Pigeon and Dickson JJ., concurring).

to sit on all four panels that heard *Doré* (twice), *Kienapple* and *Angle*. The departed Fauteux and Abbott came from the conservative wing of the court, and Martland's comment suggests the extent to which Laskin had undermined his relationship with it. Chief Justice Laskin was in dissent in many of the contentious cases that followed.

Fourth, the parameters of *res judicata* were in issue in the two criminal cases, and in *Angle* in a civil law context.

Fifth, Justices Laskin, Spence and Dickson (the so-called *LSD* dissent block) formed a liberal majority on the panel that could have allowed Angle's appeal if it formed. It didn't. The Supreme Court's newest member at the time of the 1973 oral hearing in *Angle* formed a majority in the spring of 1974 with Court's most tenured members, Justices Martland and Judson. Laskin, who heard the *Angle* appeal before he became Chief Justice, issued his *Angle* dissent as Justice Laskin.

In the Supreme Court, Angle argued that the Minister's collection action on the debt she owed Transworld Co. for the pool addition was *res judicata* by issue estoppel based on the debt being found not to exist when the lease was struck down. Justice Dickson rejected this argument on the basis that the debt's legal existence was distinct from the amount of the taxable benefit. After noting Angle had sworn an affidavit confirming she owed the debt, Dickson held: "[the] question not being *eadem questio* [the same question], I am of the opinion that this is not a case for application of the principle of issue estoppel."[346] (Justices Martland and Judson concurred.)

---

[346] *Angle, supra* note 331, p. 257 (Dickson J.'s analysis is at pp. 253–57). Dickson also stated (p. 252): "Her husband arranged for the Toronto-Dominion Bank to loan her $50,000 on December 27, 1967. The proceeds of the loan were deposited to the credit of Transworld but, as the money was assigned to the bank as security for the loan, it could not be withdrawn by Transworld until the loan was paid. In February 1968 Mr. Angle gave Mrs. Angle a cheque for $50,000 drawn on the Transworld account and signed by him as agent for the company with which she repaid the bank loan. The judge rightly concluded that this trumpery did not amount to payment for the pool house."

There was no *res judicata* by issue estoppel in respect of the debt because the underlying precedent established that issue estoppel does not arise unless the issue is fundamental to the resulting decision, which was not the case. In law, Angle had a legal obligation to pay the debt because striking down the lease did not mean she repaid the debt.

> If Transworld or its shareholders were suing Mrs. Angle for recovery of corporate funds expended on the construction of the pool house, the … proceedings in the Exchequer Court *would afford her no defence*. It is true that one of the leases contained a clause whereby Transworld purported to surrender to Mrs. Angle all its interest in the improvements for $49,768.51 and when the lease was struck down this clause suffered a similar fate. *But that was not, and was not tantamount to, a finding that Mrs. Angle was not indebted to Transworld. Transworld was not a party to the proceeding and the Exchequer Court did not have jurisdiction to make the finding* [emphasis added].[347]

Justice Laskin agreed Angle's "attempted evasion of tax liability through a leasing scheme was exposed as a sham," but he dissented for other reasons. (Justice Spence concurred.[348]) The Supreme

[347] *Ibid.*, SCC p. 256.

[348] *Ibid.*, SCC p. 262. Laskin J. in his dissent stated (pp. 268–69) the Minister's position that "the pool house transaction can be both a benefit and a loan or debt at the same time ignores the basis upon which he sought and succeeded in his reassessment of the appellant. There are two related points here which call for comment. First, the Minister founded his claim against the appellant upon s. 8(1)(*c*) and not upon s. 8(1)(*a*) or (*b*) or s. 8(2). Any question of a loan, arising from the arrangements for a bank credit to Transworld which was ultimately repaid by a Transworld cheque (leaving Transworld and the appellant where they were before), was negated by Sheppard J. as having been dependent upon a lease which was ineffective to support it. A device which failed as a defence to a reassessment, and so determined by a final judicial decision, cannot, in my view, be later reactivated as between the same parties to provide a different basis upon which to attempt to capture the same sum twice." Comment: The lease was not being reactivated; the question was whether Angle owed Transworld the debt for the pool addition, which added value to her home that was realized on

Court has never cited nor considered its *Angle* decision in the context of determining the parameters of a sham.

While Ethel and Richard Angle were engaged with legal issues in Vancouver and Toronto, William Moldowan of Vancouver was active in the *Sport of Kings*—thoroughbred horse racing and breeding. Moldowan was also the co-owner, and employee, of Active Trading Limited until 1967. He sold his interest and started two new companies, one of which distributed horse-racing forms.

William Moldowan (1977)

In the years 1962–69, Moldowan bought 53 horses at a cost of $183,463 and sold horses for $121,091. He raced his horses at major tracks located in British Columbia, eastern Canada, the western United States and Florida. Moldowan's horses won $184,018 in prize money, including $29,558 in 1966.[349]

Despite this, Moldowan incurred significant losses from his farming activity in 1968 and 1969, which he used to shelter his other income from tax. (Horse racing and breeding are "farming" as defined in the ITA.) He lost $21,097 in 1968 and $20,810 in 1969. How could a person who won more than $17 million in 2024 dollars, racing horses over eight years in the 1960s, incur tax-deductible losses? There are at least two reasons, with the obvious being that the *Sport of Kings* is an expensive sport to pursue.

---

its sale, and for which proceeds were about to be received. Dickson J. noted (pp. 258–59): "On discovery October 6, 1969, Mrs. Angle said she was indebted to Transworld. The books of account and records of Transworld were taken out of the country by Mrs. Angle and her husband on leaving Canada in 1968 to reside in Las Vegas, Nevada and Mrs. Angle has since refused to produce those books and records. It is not alleged and there is no evidence to suggest that since October 6, 1969, she paid Transworld the amount of her debt to that company. There is an affidavit of a Las Vegas chartered accountant stating that the decision of the Exchequer Court eliminated the character of the indebtedness of $34,612.33 as a debt or loan, and a similar affidavit of a Vancouver solicitor, but as I have indicated, I am of the opinion that the decision of the Exchequer Court did not have any such effect."

[349] *William Moldowan v. The Queen*, (1977), [1978] 1 SCR 480. *Moldowan v. The Queen* – SCC Cases (scc-csc.ca).

The less obvious reason is that taxpayers who earn income from a farming business may compute their farming income using the cash method under the ITA, which is not an acceptable method under commercial principles. In other words, the cash method is a special tax benefit available to those who carry on a farming business;[350] it extends a tax benefit because it does not seek to accurately compute commercial income. A farmer is allowed to time when to "receive" amounts earned into income for tax purposes and when to "pay" for expenses incurred to earn income—for example, a farmer may defer receiving in the current tax year a revenue amount until the next year to create a loss for the current year. As well, Moldowan was able to deduct the cost he paid in a year for each acquired thoroughbred horse immediately in computing his farm income (or loss) for the year despite using the horse to earn revenues over several years.

Some wealthy and high-income Canadians have also, since at least the 1930s, acquired rural estates for personal use, and they use the cash method to compute income from marginal farm activity, which results in losses, used to shelter other income from taxes. The quintessential taxpayers were Robert Samuel McLaughlin, owner of the McLaughlin car company in Oshawa, which he sold to General Motors, and E.P. Taylor, Canada's leading industrialist during the middle decades of the 20th century. Both McLaughlin and Taylor were active in the *Sport of Kings*, with Taylor's undersized filly, Northern Dancer, being one of the great thoroughbreds of all time and a prized breeding mare.

Parliament enacted by the early 1950s a rule that limits the deductibility of farming losses incurred by a person whose chief

[350] The cash method in s. 28 of the ITA can also be used to compute income from commercial fishing. But it does not provide a significant lifestyle tax benefit to commercial fishermen. The tax benefit for farmers was narrowed somewhat in the 1980s with the addition of the mandatory inventory adjustment rules to s. 28, which rules in general reduce a farming loss by the value of inventory (which is defined to include all livestock) on hand at the end of the fiscal year. A special rule applies to horses and certain bovine animals.

source of income is neither farming nor farming in combination with another source. The latter exception is awkwardly worded, with the intent of not applying the restriction to full-time farmers who supplement their farming income with secondary income-earning activities such as driving a local school bus. The rule's direct target is high-income Canadians such as those in business, dentistry, medicine, law and accounting looking for a lifestyle tax shelter.

William Moldowan was such a taxpayer. Between 1960 and 1972, Moldowan earned employment, investment, business and rental incomes in addition to farm income and losses. In 1968, Moldowan's total income from all sources (other than racing and breeding horses) was $23,073; in 1969, $34,882. After deducting farming losses, his net income was $1,976 in 1968 and $14,072 in 1969.

Moldowan did not apply the restricted farm loss rules, which would have limited his farming losses to no more than $5,000 in 1968, and $5,000 in 1969. The Minister applied the rules, and Moldowan appealed. He maintained his chief source of income in 1968 and 1969 was farming or farming in combination with some other source. Moldowan was unsuccessful before the Tax Review Board, the Federal Court–Trial Division and the Federal Court of Appeal. Moldowan appealed for relief.

Justice Dickson set about interpreting and applying the restricted farm loss rule in s. 13 of the 1952 ITA [s. 31 in the 1985 ITA] to the facts as established at trial.[351] He clarified three important matters.

First, Dickson clarified that a source of income could include an activity that incurs a loss if the activity has a reasonable expectation of profit (REOP). Prior to *Moldowan*, the judiciary sent mixed signals on whether an individual's commercial activity resulting in a loss could be a source of income. An individual's activity that has a REOP is a source of income, and thus a taxpayer's farming source could be, in the right circumstances, the taxpayer's chief

[351] *Moldowan, supra* note 349.

source of income. The loss from such a chief source is deductible from other sources of income.

The first aspect of Dickson's opinion was thus relieving—especially, for full-time farmers. But the *caveat* was that the activity would not be recognized as a business source if there were no REOP, *objectively* determined.[352] Dickson set down a non-exhaustive list of factors to consider when determining whether an activity has a REOP.

With this, the Minister's auditors saw a green light to deny the deductibility of suspect losses that failed the objective test of having the intent of gaining income. This aspect of the decision was especially contentious among tax professionals over the next 25 years. Numerous articles were written on the subject matter questioning the REOP test although I published one in support of it. The dispute culminated with the Supreme Court's reviewing its REOP test in a real estate tax shelter context in 2002, which decision is considered in Part IV.

Second, Dickson clarified there are three categories of farmers:

1. Unrestricted full-time farmers: Taxpayers for whom farming may reasonably be expected to provide the bulk of income.
2. Restricted farmers: Taxpayers who do not look to farming, or to farming and some other subordinate source of income, for their livelihood.
3. Hobby farmers: Taxpayers who carry on some farming activities as a hobby, and who therefore cannot deduct any losses from the activity.

This approach was a win for full-time farmers. For other taxpayers, the results were unfavourable because their farm losses could be restricted or denied in full, depending on the facts.

[352] *Ibid.* Dickson J. indicated that the following criteria should be considered: the profit and loss experience in past years, the taxpayer's training, the taxpayer's intended course of action, and the capability of the venture as capitalized to show a profit after charging capital cost allowance. The list was said not to be exhaustive.

Third, Dickson clarified that the "combination of income" test (farming in combination with some other source) required that the non-farm source or sources must be in respect of *subsidiary* interests of the taxpayer. The combining source is generally a sideline employment. This test is applied relatively and objectively to the facts. This was a bad result for those living on rural estates with marginal farm revenues and those who raced or bred horses. It was a particularly bad result for high-income professionals looking for a lifestyle tax shelter, such as doctors, dentists, lawyers, accountants and judges. (Justices Martland, Judson, Spence and Pigeon concurred.)

This third aspect of the decision also was contentious with tax professionals, and it culminated in the Supreme Court's reviewing the matter in a horse-racing context in 2012, which decision is considered in Part IV. Given this, it should be noted that Brian Dickson kept a stable of horses, which he loved raising and riding. He rode one each dawn along the Ottawa River from his large rural estate 40 kilometres west of Ottawa.[353]

While Brian Dickson was riding one of his horses at dawn each morning in eastern Ontario without the benefit of a lifestyle tax shelter, Mr. Gene Nowegijick was going to work as a logger in northwest Ontario. In 1975, he was employed by Gulf Bay Development, which was a corporation without share capital that had its head office and administrative office on the Gulf Bay Reserve on Lake Nipigon northwest of Lake Superior.

Gene A. Nowegijick (1983)

Gene Nowegijick was a status Indian within the meaning of the *Indian Act* as a member of the Gulf Bay Band. All directors of Gulf Bay Development resided on the Gulf Bay Band's Reserve.

[353] Sharpe and Roach, *Brian Dickson, supra* note 162, p. 140. Also see Marina Strauss, "Dickson Sets Course for Social Justice," *Globe and Mail*, November 9, 1985, p. A8.

The trees were cut about 10 miles off reserve, which the Gulf Bay Development sold to third parties.[354]

Each day, Nowegijick left the reserve to go to the logging site and returned to the reserve after work. In the 1975 taxation year, Nowegijick earned $11,057 from this work. Nowegijick's assessed taxable income after deductions and exemptions was $8,698 upon which the Minister found him to be liable for income tax of $1,965.

Nowegijick appealed the assessment as a test case to the Federal Court–Trial Division, maintaining that his logging income was exempt from tax under s. 87 of the *Indian Act*, which states that "the personal property of an Indian or Band situated on a reserve" is exempt from tax. One difficulty in applying this exemption to income is that income tax is assessed on a person rather than on the person's property; this is a basic tenet of income tax law.[355] The tax is a personal income tax.

The matter came before Justice Mahoney in March 1979 and he found that wages, once received, become a negotiable instrument or

---

[354] *Gene A. Nowegijick v. The Queen*, [1983] 1 SCR 29. *Nowegijick v. The Queen* – SCC Cases (scc-csc.ca).

[355] In *James B. McLeod v. Minister of Customs and Excise*, [1926] SCR 457, Mignault J. stated: "All this is in accord with the general policy of the [*Income War Tax*] Act which imposes the income tax on the person and not on the property. In other words, it is the person who is assessed in respect of his income." In *Frank Sura v. The Queen*, [1962] SCR 65 [for unofficial English translation, see 62 DTC 1005 and [1962] CTC 1], Taschereau J. for an unanimous Supreme Court held that income tax under the modern ITA is a personal tax, citing with approval, Mignault J.: "Rien dans les amendements subséquents apportés à la loi, ne change le principe que ce n'est pas la propriété d'un bien qui est taxable, mais que la taxe est imposée sur un contribuable, et est déterminée par le revenu que l'emploi, les entreprises, les biens, ou la propriété procurent à celui qui en est le bénéficiaire légal. Comme l'a dit M. le Juge Mignault dans la cause de *McLeod v. Minister of Customs and Excise*: 'All of this is in accord with the general policy of the Act which imposes the Income Tax on the person and not on the property.'" This was critical in *Sura* because it resulted in the Court's denying a husband the ability to split his income with his wife for income tax purposes (he claimed such a right, based on his wife's legal interest in their communal property, including his income under Quebec's then matrimonial property law). https://decisions.scc-csc.ca/scc-csc/scc-csc/en/item/6535/index.do?q=sura.

money in the recipient's hands. Mahoney held that the wages had to be determined by reference to taxable income and "in respect of" Nowegijick's wages *as property* on the reserve. He did not cite or distinguish the precedent to the contrary. The Minister appealed.

In a brief three paragraph judgment released in late September 1979, the Federal Court of Appeal reversed Mahoney based on the established precedent. Nowegijick appealed and he was joined by various groups representing the interests of Indigenous Canadians, as interveners.

The Supreme Court would take more than three years to release its unanimous decision in January 1983. Justice Dickson wrote the decision. (Justices Ritchie, Beetz, Estey, McIntyre, Chouinard and Lamer concurred.) He opened his analysis by noting that the Indigenous are Canadian citizens and, in the affairs of life not governed by treaties and the *Indian Act,* are subject to all the responsibilities of other citizens, including the payment of taxes.

Dickson framed the question for decision as follows: "[T]o construe the words 'no Indian … is … subject to taxation in respect of any such [personal] property'. Is taxable income personal property? [Bracketed word "personal" in original."[356]] The next step was to hold that income tax was imposed on Nowegijick's *property.* This was said to be the case because the words "in respect of" in the exemption were to be given their widest meaning possible.

> They import such meanings as "in relation to", "with reference to" or "in connection with." The phrase "in respect of" is probably the widest of any expression intended to convey some connection between two related subject matters.[357]

In doing so, Dickson found that there was no compelling reason to apply the Supreme Court's prior precedent that established income tax is a tax on the person and not on property. He did so on the basis that the prior precedent resolved constitutional law issues, and income-splitting under Quebec's communal property regime.

---

[356] *Nowegijick, supra* note 354, p. 38.
[357] *Ibid.*, p. 39.

Instead, Justice Dickson focused on the exemption. He indicated that the suggestion in the case law that exemptions from taxes must be clearly expressed in a statute was "legal lore."[358] This suggestion appears to be directed at a statutory interpretation rule the British judiciary established under which a person cannot benefit from a tax exemption unless its text clearly applies to the person. In contrast, Dickson found that treaties should be construed liberally and doubtful expressions should be resolved in favour of Indigenous people. If the wording of the exemption can be reasonably interpreted in favour of an exemption, this approach should be favoured over a more technical construction.

With respect to the exemption, Dickson held that s. 87 of the *Indian Act* provides an exemption from tax for both the Indigenous as individuals on a reserve and their income as property situated on the reserve. The following somewhat cryptic *obiter* suggest there were unexplained limits to the breadth of the decision:

> I conclude by saying that nothing in these reasons should not be taken as implying that no Indian shall ever pay tax of any kind. Counsel for the appellant and counsel for the interveners do not take that position. Nor do I. We are concerned here with personal property situated on a reserve and only with property situated on a reserve.[359]

How broad is the exemption? The Supreme Court is working out the limits over time.

Eleven months after *Nowegijick*, Justice Dickson issued his majority 1983 opinion in a dispute over the tax treatment of a $300 prize that an employer awarded a research assistant in 1976.

Elizabeth Savage (1983)

Mrs. Elizabeth Savage was awarded a prize after she voluntarily took and passed insurance industry courses to further her career.

---

[358] *Ibid.*, p. 36.

[359] *Ibid.*, p. 41.

The tax issue initially appeared to be whether the $300 was employment income or other income under the ITA. The Act includes sections that apply to both types of income; "other income" expressly applies to scholarships, bursaries and prizes. Savage treated the $300 as a prize to which the other income section applied; under it, the first $500 was excluded from such income. The Minister maintained that the prize was a benefit Savage received from her employer, and the relevant employment-income section did not provide an exception for a prize regardless of its amount.

The taxpayer won her case in the Tax Review Board but lost before the Federal Court–Trial Division. The Federal Court of Appeal reversed the trial court, and the Crown obtained leave.

Justice Dickson's decision in *Savage* is important despite the modest amount of income and tax in issue.[360] At its core is the way s. 3 of the ITA applies to compute a resident taxpayer's overall net income from all sources of income worldwide before that net income is reduced by deductions allowed to compute taxable income. Several fundamental income tax issues are present in the case.

Section 3 totals income, including specific types of income computed under the ITA's more detailed rules that apply to certain listed sources. Detailed rules apply for the purpose of computing income or loss from an office or employment; income or loss from a business or property source; taxable capital gains net of allowable capital losses; and for special deductions that are allowed when computing s. 3 net income, including alimony payments, childcare expenses and moving expenses.

Dickson opened with the observation that the "$300 minnow has escaped the taxman's net in two of three tribunals" that had heard the dispute.[361] He first considered whether Savage's $300 prize was employment income under ss. 5–8, and in doing so he distinguished a British case that took a narrow approach to determine

---

[360] *The Queen v. Savage*, [1983] 2 SCR 428. *The Queen v. Savage* – SCC Cases (scc-csc.ca).

[361] *Ibid.*, p. 435.

whether an amount is an employment benefit. The British law was inapplicable:

> Our Act contains the stipulation, not found in the English statutes referred to, "benefits of any kind whatever . . . in respect of, in the course of, or by virtue of an office or employment." The meaning of "benefits of whatever kind" is clearly quite broad; in the present case the cash payment of $300 easily falls within the category of "benefit."[362]

When doing so, Dickson also applied *Nowegijick* to the expression "in respect of" in the above excerpt. It had the widest possible meaning that could reasonably be construed. The $300 minnow was therefore employment income.

The fact Savage's employer-awarded prize was employment income did not end the dispute. This is because s. 3 also applies to income from a source inside or outside Canada "without restricting the generality" of it being income from an employment, business or property. In general terms, this wording acknowledges the existence of income from other sources.

The next issue was whether Savage's $300 prize was also "other income" to which s. 56 applied. Justice Dickson found that the $300 was the type of achievement prize listed as other income in s. 56. This meant that the $300 was both employment income and other income.

Given this, how does s. 3 apply to an income that is both employment income and other income? A related issue is whether s. 3 applies to an amount received that has the character of income but that is not income from an employment, business or property source and is not expressly listed as being other income in s. 56.[363]

To determine how s. 3 applied to an amount that was both employment income and other income, Dickson put s. 56 in context

[362] *Ibid.*, p. 440.

[363] The answer should be yes, including because the wording of s. 3 of the ITA indicates this is the case.

and noted that it opens with the expression "Without restricting the generality of section 3." This wording meant: "Income can still be income from a source if it does not fall within s. 56." Dickson also stated: "[Section] 56 does not enlarge what is taxable under s. 3, it simply specifies."[364] Although this was *obiter*, its implication is that the wording of s. 3 applies to other income in its entirety; its application to unlisted other income is not limited by s. 56. (Also see *Curran*, 1959.)

The *obiter* provides further context to Justice Dickson's finding that the $300 was other income under s. 56 that could not be included in s. 3 as employment income—because to do so would defeat the purpose of the $500 exclusion for prizes. (Justices Ritchie, Lamer and Wilson concurred.)

Justice William McIntyre issued a minority opinion that agreed the prize "was a prize 'for achievement in a field of endeavour ordinarily carried on by the taxpayer' within the meaning of s. 56(1)(n) of the *Income Tax Act*."[365] He refrained from discussing any other matter the majority considered.

Chief Justice Dickson's next decision concerned a trust Samuel Bronfman established for his second daughter in the 1940s.

Bronfman Trust (1987)

Dickson delivered the Supreme Court's unanimous 1987 decision in *Bronfman Trust.*[366] Instead of selling assets earning income, the trust borrowed to make a capital distribution to the beneficiary of the trust. It deducted the interest that arose on the loan as being incurred for the purpose of earning income from a source. The Minister's auditors disallowed the deductions on the basis the funds were not borrowed to earn income from a source—they were borrowed to distribute capital.

---

364 *Savage*, *supra* note 360, pp. 445–46.

365 *Ibid.*, p. 447.

366 *Bronfman Trust v. The Queen*, [1987] 1 SCR 32. *Bronfman Trust v. The Queen* – SCC Cases (scc-csc.ca).

In reviewing the matter, Dickson denied the trust deductibility of interest on the basis its borrowing was not done for the *bona fide* purpose of earning income. (Justices Beetz, McIntyre, Lamer, Wilson and La Forest concurred.) He noted that the purpose of the interest deductibility section is to allow for the accumulation of capital to produce taxable income; the borrowing to distribute capital did not produce taxable income.

In so finding, Chief Justice Dickson articulated a judicial policy in respect of tax planning that focused on the true commercial nature of transactions. He noted there was a "recent trend in tax cases … towards attempting to ascertain the true commercial and practical nature of the taxpayer's transactions."[367] For Dickson, this trend was a "movement away from tests based on the form of transactions and toward tests based on what [in 1966] Lord Pearce has referred to as a 'common sense appreciation of all the guiding features' of the events in question."[368]

Dickson indicated that emphasizing the true commercial nature of a taxpayer's transactions rather that their legal form could avoid outcomes in which a manipulating sequence results in a mere patina of compliance with income tax law. But doing so had to be consistent with the text, the purposes of the tax statute and commercial realities.[369]

The *Bronfman Trust* decision was controversial in the tax community. The bottom line is that professionals who plan tax avoidance schemes fear the judiciary's emphasizing the commercial substance over the legal form of transactions and requiring taxpayers to have

---

[367] *Ibid.*, para. 39.

[368] *Ibid.*

[369] *Ibid.*, para. 40. Chief Justice Dickson stated the judicial policy as follows (para. 40): "This is, I believe, a laudable trend provided it is consistent with the text and purposes of the taxation statute. Assessment of taxpayers' transactions with an eye to commercial and economic realities, rather than juristic classification of form, may help to avoid the inequity of tax liability being dependent upon the taxpayer's sophistication at manipulating a sequence of events to achieve a patina of compliance with the apparent prerequisites for a tax deduction."

a *bona fide* purpose to earn income from a source under their tax minimization plans.

Chief Justice Dickson's final income tax decision occurred in late 1990, involving spousal income-splitting through a family company. It too was controversial.

McClurg (1990)

In *McClurg*, Dickson led a 4–3 Supreme Court majority whose decision is notable for two holdings. (Justices John Sopinka, Charles Gonthier and Peter Cory concurred.) The first concerned company law principles. The Dickson-led majority held that corporations may issue shares under which corporate directors have a discretion to declare and pay disproportionate amounts of dividends to different common shareholders. Many company-law lawyers believe this to be a contradiction of the equality principle applicable to share rights held by shareholders; it puts the directors in conflict *vis-à-vis* upholding their fiduciary duty to the company and its membership. Justice Gérard La Forest issued a strong dissent holding that such shares are not allowed under company law. (Justices Bertha Wilson and Claire L'Heureux-Dubé concurred.)

Under income tax law principles, Dickson held that the payment of a disproportionate amount of dividends on discretionary shares to Mrs. McClurg did not, in the circumstances of the case, offend the anti-avoidance rule in subs. 56(2). In general terms, that provision concerns a transfer of property made at the direction of a taxpayer for their benefit (or another person) to avoid tax, which amount would otherwise be included in the taxpayer's income. In the case, the company's directors used a discretionary dividend clause to declare and pay a disproportionate share of dividends to Mrs. McClurg. She would pay less tax than her fellow-shareholder husband on the dividends.[370]

Chief Justice Dickson found that the anti-avoidance did not apply to the dividends because Mrs. McClurg made a *quid pro quo*

[370] *McClurg v. The Queen*, [1990] 3 SCR 1020. *McClurg v. Canada* – SCC Cases (lexum.com).

contribution to the company's success. Although normally a receipt of dividends does not require a shareholder to make a *quid pro quo* contribution to the company of personal effort, Dickson articulated in *obiter* an exception for tax purposes applicable to some discretionary dividends. What is especially interesting about his exception, which is described below, is that Dickson was steeped in commercial and company law, dating to his time practising law.[371]

In *McClurg*, Dickson stated in *obiter* that the anti-avoidance rule in subs. 56(2) may apply to dividends paid in a non-arm's length situation where "there is no legitimate purpose to the dividend distribution."[372] He emphasized: "There is no question that the payments to Wilma McClurg represented a legitimate *quid pro quo* and were not simply an attempt to avoid the payment of taxes." He added that "the dividend payment was the product of a *bona fide* business relationship." This *dictum* did not arrive out of thin air in a civil tax law context without a legal underpinning. Although Dickson did not cite precedent, its source is the Supreme Court's approach to criminal fraud in a commercial and company law context.

Twelve years earlier in *Olan et al.*, Brian Dickson used the phrases "*bona fide* business interests," "legitimate business reason" and "*quid pro quo*" in the context of reversing an acquittal of three directors accused of fraud when their purchaser company acquired a target company with its own assets.[373]

---

[371] For Dickson's business-law background, see Sharpe and Roach, *Brian Dickson, supra* note 162, pp. 65–86.

[372] *McClurg, supra* note 370, Dickson C.J. stated (last para. of Part II): "[I]f a distinction is to be drawn in the application of s. 56(2) between arm's length and non-arm's length transactions, it should be made between the exercise of a discretionary power to distribute dividends when the non-arm's length shareholder has made no contribution to the company (in which case s. 56(2) may be applicable), and those cases in which a legitimate contribution has been made. *In the case of the latter, of which this appeal is an example, I do not think it can be said that there was no legitimate purpose to the dividend distribution*" [emphasis added].

[373] *R. v. Olan et al.*, [1978] 2 SCR 1175. *R. v. Olan et al.* – SCC Cases (lexum.com). See *R. v. Zlatic*, [1993] 2 SCR 29, for a more recent case in which the Supreme Court applied *Olan*. *R. v. Zlatic* – SCC Cases (lexum.com).

At trial, the jury convicted the three directors of fraud. They had caused an acquired target corporation to sell blue-chip securities worth more than $1 million, which funds were used to make an unsecured demand loan through a subsidiary to the purchaser corporation. It used the funds to acquire the target despite not having the ability to repay the loan on demand.

While the Ontario Court of Appeal reversed the jury's finding of fraud on the basis there was no proof the three directors acted with deceit, Dickson overturned the acquittal for a unanimous Supreme Court. He emphasized that the acts of the three directors might not have been done in "furtherance of the *bona fide* business interests"[374] of the acquired corporation. The jury could find fraud despite a lack of deceit if there was evidence of a fraud having been committed by "any other fraudulent means."

As mentioned, a company's directors have a fiduciary duty to the company that has members. This is one key reason why Dickson's later majority decision in *McClurg* on company law principles garnered such a strong dissent from Justice La Forest. But in *Olan et al.*, when considering the actions of the three directors in that case, Dickson stated: "It was open to the jury to ask this question—what possible legitimate business reason could have prompted the disposal by Langley's of a portfolio of high quality securities and, in effect, the substitution therefor, as to $790,000, of unsecured demand promissory notes of a company with a working capital deficit of over $1,100,000 and over which company Langley's had no control?"[375] He held: "[I]t was open to a jury to find that the exchange of the portfolio for the loan was something other than a *quid pro quo.*"[376] Instead of confirming the jury's conviction, Dickson ordered a new trial due to a faulty jury instruction. (Chief Justice Laskin and Justices Martland, Ritchie, Spence, Pigeon, Beetz, Estey and Pratte concurred.)

---

[374] *Ibid.*, p. 1189.
[375] *Ibid.*, p. 1191.
[376] *Ibid.*, p. 1193.

Essentially, Dickson's criminal-law decision in *Olan et al.* and his civil-tax law *obiter* in *McClurg* require a company's directors to ensure that there is a *legitimate* business reason or relationship for their actions when they dispose of, loan or distribute company assets, including by declaring discretionary dividends; this is how they ensure that they satisfy their fiduciary obligation to the company. Despite his decision in *Olan et al.*, Chief Justice Dickson's *obiter* in *McClurg*—indicating the possible application of subs. 56(2) to discretionary dividends paid on a non-arm's length basis to avoid tax—was subject to significant criticism from private-sector tax professionals.

Dickson's critics do not appear to have realized that his concern and approach can be traced to *Olan et al.* That decision also shows that deceit need not be present to prove a criminal fraud. This is mentioned because many tax professionals argue deceit must be present in a tax sham. On what basis should deceit be required to be proven in a civil-law fraud including a tax sham? *Olan* thus raises a series of questions that do not appear to have ever been considered in the income tax case law or tax literature in respect of the anti-avoidance rule in s. 56 and tax shams.

Sharpe and Roach ended their biography of Brian Dickson with something his son, Brian Jr., said to them about his father: "Being a fair man was very, very important to him."[377] In income tax, Dickson sought to achieve fairness in disputes between taxpayers and the Crown by emphasizing *bona fide* purposes in a context that was consistent with the statutory text, the purposes of the tax statute and commercial realities.

Chief Justice Brian Dickson retired in December 1990. He was replaced as a member of the Supreme Court by Justice William Stevenson. Brian Dickson died in 1998.

[377] Sharpe and Roach, *Brian Dickson, supra* note 162, p. 482.

PART IV

The Charter-Era Judges

BY 1982, CANADA WAS on the cusp of a great transformation in terms of its cultural, economic, legal, political and social being. The Supreme Court was beginning to reflect this change. Chief Justice Bora Laskin, a Jew and the son of Russian immigrants who eventually settled at Thunder Bay, in northern Ontario, had been appointed to the court a decade earlier. In 1982, Bertha Wilson, an immigrant from Scotland, became the first woman appointed to the Court.

The dominant cultural theme was shifting to emphasize individual rights and liberties. Increasingly, more non-European immigrants were joining a country in which the post–Second World War baby boomers were beginning to exert their influence on the direction taken by the economy, academia, the media, the judiciary, the bureaucracy and politics.

The Supreme Court and its judges had a new law to wield—the *Charter*—to stamp in stone their views on the way in which the state can interact with its citizens in terms of law. The Court was transforming with the anticipated appointment of more academics and women to the Court as the years rolled forward and the country changed.

By 1984, governments led by newly elected conservative politicians—British Prime Minister Margaret Thatcher, American

President Ronald Regan and Canadian Prime Minister Brian Mulroney—were implementing policies that shifted the economy to *laissez-faire*. This shift followed the economic disruptions of the 1970s—an energy crisis, rampant inflation, high unemployment, stagnation and the failed top-down bureaucratic command approach that had contributed to the disruption and failure to return the economy to the boom years of the 1950s and 60s.

The pattern repeats. Government intervention had been the norm since the economic and social devastation of the Great Depression. Then, a shift occurred to address the excesses that had accumulated under *laissez-faire* in the lead-up to the depression, and its inability to correct the economic failures in a timely manner. By the late 1970s, the excesses of top-down government intervention had built up and contributed to significant economic failure. This, in turn, would be followed by a build-up of new excesses under *laissez-faire*, which culminated in the financial crisis of 2007–09. The economic cycle of voters correcting excesses would repeat itself, with a beginning of a shift back to top-down government intervention and new excesses.

But in legal terms, Canada was, in 1982 and especially after 1985 with the coming-into-force of the *Charter's* equality provision, about to be placed under the intensified judicial influence of the Supreme Court of Canada. A majority would form that was intent on giving the new *Charter* a broad and liberal construction and, in doing so, that majority intervened as judicial activists into the cultural and social fabric of the nation.

This meant that, as economic excesses were about to build out of the shift to emphasize rightest economic ideology, those excesses would be accompanied by excesses building out of the shift in constitutional law to emphasize individual rights and freedoms. Parliament was in the process of losing control of political agendas being advanced in *Charter* litigation, in a context in which the Progressive Conservatives would eventually fracture as a viable political party as a key outcome of the advance of Preston Manning's rightest *Reform Party* out of Alberta, into English Canada's rural heartland in the 1993 federal election.

In Atlantic Canada, an economic and social disaster of historic proportions would unfold in 1992, with its epicentre being in Newfoundland and Labrador, on the announcement of a moratorium on the cod fisheries that had sustained for centuries the Atlantic Canadian villages that fished cod on the Grand Banks. After decades of federal mismanagement, the Mulroney government called on one of our own, Minister John Crosbie, to break the devastating news. He did it with his head held high despite the hostile and sometimes violent reception he received at wharfs, fish plants and press conferences; with simple blunt language few politicians would have the guts to say face-to-face to a hostile crowd terrified for their future after their economic livelihoods had just collapsed along with the fisheries. For doing so, he would earn their respect but lose their support.

Overfishing was the cause, all too often done by foreign fishing fleets to which Ottawa had allotted unsustainable quota, and as those fishing villages emptied, thousands upon thousands fled west as economic refugees in their own country. If they were lucky, they eventually found well-paying jobs in the oil and gas fields of Alberta, and at the construction sites advancing in the Alberta oil sands and on the British Columbia mainland, such as in Whistler. Unlike for the professional class, the 1987 *Canada-United States Free Trade Agreement* and its successor 1992 *North American Free Trade Agreement* did not have an article that extended the working class a path south into the United States.

The first two decades of the *Charter* would be tumultuous for many citizens, being a time when traditional values began to come under siege from the *Charter* judgments pouring out of the Supreme Court one-after-another; judgments applauded by legal scholars and social activists who invariably inhabit an urban-secular world dominated by relativism. Deep societal schisms began to form.

From the *Charter* era, five judges were identified as the strongest candidates for selection as most influential in income taxation, other than as the chief justice. They are Chief Justice Beverley McLachlin and Justices Frank Iacobucci, John Major, Marshall Rothstein and Bertha Wilson. They are presented for selection in the order of their appointment to the Supreme Court, concluding with an explanation for why one was not selected.

These judges participated in far fewer decisions than several judges from the pre-*Charter* era who were not chosen. This is explained by the leave requirement in 1975 contracting the number of tax cases the Supreme Court hears. Many of the justices in the *Charter* era do not want to grant leave in tax disputes, as noted by Justice Willard Estey,[378] and suggested by Justice Marshall Rothstein.[379]

[378] Pound, *Stikeman Elliott*, *supra* note 253, pp. 381–82.

[379] Retired Justice Rothstein, who is counsel on tax litigation to the law firm Osler, mentioned this in a 2019 Osler podcast on the GAAR. The podcast is not available at Osler's website.

BERTHA WILSON: BEING A TRAILBLAZER ISN'T EASY

Liberal Prime Minister Pierre Trudeau elevated Bertha Wilson from the Ontario Court of Appeal to become the first woman appointed to the Supreme Court in March 1982, replacing Justice Ronald Martland. Wilson's appointment returned Ontario to having three judges on the Supreme Court, which in 1979 became two with the appointment of William McIntrye of British Columbia.

Bertha Wilson had headed up legal research for one of Canada's most prominent corporate-commercial-tax law firms, Osler. She would be feted on Bay Street for injecting a strong commercial interest outlook into her opinions, including the application of a strict interpretive approach to statutory income tax law. When doing so, Wilson contextualized the interpretation and application of the text of statutory law from the perspective of those to whom it applies rather than from the perspective of the context and purpose of that law. Her contextualized approach in tax cases rests on "the context of business requires certainty" despite the context and purpose of the statutory income tax law.[380]

Born and raised in Scotland, Wilson was the youngest child of parents who obtained lower-middle-class status; her father was a travelling salesman of stationery, a veteran of the First World War and devotedly religious. Her parents stressed advancement through education, and her mother ensured that she, along with her two brothers, would graduate from the University of Aberdeen. Wilson married a fellow graduate ordained as a minister in the Presbyterian Church of Scotland, and they moved to Macduff, Scotland, in early 1946. In 1949, they moved to Canada to serve a congregation in Renfrew, Ontario.

---

[380] Ellen Anderson, *Judging Bertha Wilson: Law as Large as Life* (Toronto: University of Toronto Press published for the Osgoode Society for Canadian Legal History, 2001). The quote is at p. 135, and it reflects the *obiter* that flows through her income tax judgments. Anderson's account of the life of Bertha Wilson is relied on in the introductory paragraphs about the life of Bertha Wilson.

Later, after Reverend John Wilson was posted to Halifax as a Naval Chaplin and served overseas during the Korean War, Bertha Wilson entered Dalhousie Law School as a mature student, graduating in 1958. Wilson did exceedingly well. Upon graduation, she declined a scholarship to pursue a graduate degree in law at Harvard and articled in Halifax. After her husband's discharge from the navy and her admission to the Nova Scotia Barristers' Society, they moved to Toronto. Hired by Osler, Wilson was on the leading edge of the slow rise in women pursuing a legal career in Canada.

Ellen Anderson, Wilson's authorized biographer, described Wilson as "A Conservative Socialist at Work" in a subpart of her biography of Wilson.[381] Wilson, who was steeped in the Scottish Enlightenment philosophy of David Hume, Adam Smith and others, examined and re-examined the world and its issues from that philosophical foundation.

As Wilson's career advanced at Osler, she became a recognized expert in the law of wills and trusts, and offshore tax planning. At the time, Stuart Thom was Osler's tax expert. Wilson would travel offshore; the firm's initial concern was whether it was appropriate for a married female lawyer to travel with male colleagues.

Bertha Wilson was also a member of the socialist New Democratic Party, which is noteworthy because her work at Osler served the interests of the Canadian establishment and their corporations and family trusts. When she joined Osler in 1958, it had a policy of not engaging in corporate tax avoidance for its clients.[382] This policy gave way over time with the firm's having to move, if for no other reason than market pressure, to the business view that tax is a cost of doing business, which should be avoided if legally possible rather than paid.

On a personal level, while Wilson is said to have considered paying taxes the social responsibility of a good citizen, she worked

[381] *Ibid.*, p. 62.
[382] *Ibid.*, p. 59.

for the firm's clients whose interests were their own. Anderson explains: "Wilson did not consider it any part of her role as a lawyer to preach this [social responsibility] gospel to the clients of the firm."[383]

Clearly, Wilson loved the intellectual challenge presented by not only researching tough legal issues but also finding solutions to problems experienced by the firm's clients. She excelled at doing so, knowing that it was her obligation as a practising lawyer to act in their best interest, which for many meant avoiding tax.

But when Bertha Wilson was appointed to the Ontario Court of Appeal in late 1975, her speech at the swearing-in ceremony suggested she might take a broader view of the law in a tax avoidance context: "[W]hen one becomes immersed in the pressures of daily practice, there may be a tendency to emphasize the form over the substance, and the letter of the law over the spirit, and to lose sight of that larger dimension."[384]

Despite the recognition of the existence of something more in the life of the law, Justice Wilson's "black letter law over its spirit" approach to taxation continued as a judge. She was unwilling to impose her own moral standards in taxation. This meant that business could "rely on the letter of the tax statutes for certainty in arranging their affairs," with one result being that the ability to avoid income tax was broadened such that taxpayers can better personalize the imposition of income tax to their own standards of morality. For her, it was Parliament's job to amend the law if it needed fixing;[385] Anderson mentioned this when discussing *Stubart Investments*, which is profiled below.

It is worthwhile to compare Bertha Wilson's approach to that taken by Patrick Kerwin decades earlier, who as a judge faced down British tax avoidance precedent and instead emphasized the spirit of the income tax law over its black letters. They both came to

---

[383] *Ibid.*, pp. 251–52.
[384] *Ibid.*, p. 84.
[385] *Ibid.*, pp. 251–52 and p. 237.

their judicial appointments as long-standing practitioners, with distinct client bases. Both were also religious on opposite sides of the Protestant-Catholic divide.

One was Scottish, while the other Irish. The Protestant Socialist–New Democrat Wilson at Osler had served the interests of its corporate-commercial client base, while the Catholic-Conservative Kerwin at Guthrie & Kerwin had served the interests of the local municipal government. As judges, they contextualized and applied the statutory income tax law from the perspective of (1) for Kerwin, the broader public as enacted by their government through elected representatives; and (2) for Wilson, the particular person(s) to whom an assessment of tax was, or could be, in issue. In judicial terms, it boiled down to emphasising the commercial substance of transactions in light of the object and spirit of the statutory text in issue versus emphasizing the legal form of transactions in light of the literal or plain meaning of that text.

It can be said that Wilson was pro-taxpayer in income tax disputes. But she heard only 20 income tax cases, of which 4 concerned tax avoidance, over almost 9 years as a Supreme Court judge. Despite this, three of her opinions had a significant impact on the Court's approach to income tax; they will be considered in detail.

The importance of Wilson's minority opinion in *Stubart Investments* cannot be overstated and deserves consideration in detail, including the contrast to Estey's majority opinion.

Stubart Investments (1984)

The Supreme Court's decision in *Stubart Investments* is a seminal income tax decision decided by a five-member panel, all holding for the taxpayer but with three justices in the majority (Justice Estey, with Justices Beetz and McIntyre, concurring) and two in the minority (Justice Wilson, with Justice Ritchie, concurring).[386] The tax

[386] *Stubart Investments Ltd. v. The Queen* [1984] 1 SCR 536, rev'g 81 DTC 5120, [1981] CTC 168 (FCA), dism'g 78 DTC 6414, [1978] CTC 612 (FCTD), dism'g (1973), 74 DTC 1209, [1974] CTC 2284 (TRB). *Stubart Investments Ltd. v. The Queen* – SCC Cases (scc-csc.ca).

dispute dated to the 1960s and focused in tax terms on a loss utilization scheme undertaken within a related group of corporations.

The tax avoidance plan in *Stubart Investments* and the issue before the Supreme Court should be considered in light of the times in which it was decided. The scheme diverted profits from a profitable corporation in Quebec to its sister corporation in Ontario, which had unused business loss carryovers. In doing so, the scheme had no *bona fide* commercial purpose, ignoring the avoidance of tax obligations. However, Canada's federal income tax system had begun to accommodate by 1984—legislatively and administratively—such diversions, provided they complied with certain applicable tax provisions, among the most important of which is that the diversion occurs within what can be described in general terms as being a related group of corporations.[387] This accommodation is a federal proxy for what is known as "corporate group consolidation" of income and losses for tax purposes in many countries, including the United States.[388]

---

[387] For example, the corporate amalgamation and winding-up rules in ss. 87 and 88 of the 1972 ITA were amended to accommodate certain corporate group loss consolidations as proposed in the 1977 Budget. The amendments are discussed by Maureen Donnelly and Allister W. Young, "Policy Forum: Group Relief for Canadian Corporate Taxpaysers-At Last?" (2011), 59:2 *Canadian Tax Journal* 239–63. Donnelly and Young noted (p. 244): "The tax community welcomed these amendments as an end to the artificial transaction route that advisers had been using to access losses of related corporations."

[388] Provincial governments would be concerned about allowing any such consolidations across provincial borders because they could seriously compromise provincial revenues as profits earned in the province could be offset by losses incurred in another province. The concern would be especially acute in those provinces that participate in federal-provincial corporate tax agreements (i.e., all provinces except Alberta and Quebec). In *Stubart Investments*, Quebec-based corporate profits were offset for federal purposes by Ontario-incurred losses, with both provinces at the time not participating in federal-provincial corporate tax collection agreements (with Ontario more recently becoming a participant). The Supreme Court never commented on the tax policy implications of allowing corporate loss utilization schemes across provincial borders. It would be a mistake to assume that such consolidations in a province would net out over the long term, including because smaller provinces tend to have fewer large corporations that

As such, *Stubart Investments* was a hard case for the Supreme Court to confront in the sense that an income diversion to utilize loss carryovers within a corporate group was becoming acceptable in federal tax policy terms by 1984, but it was unacceptable when the Minister reassessed it more than a decade earlier. The economic disruptions of the intervening years suggested to many that a new approach was needed, and the Court's decision provides two paths forward in income tax.

In 1973, Chairman K.A. Flanigan of the Tax Review Board found that the transaction in *Stubart Investments* was a sham. He first noted that the taxpayer's lawyer testified that, "to everyone on the street it would appear that nothing had changed." Among other things, the corporate group avoided making certain statements in corporate filings to ensure it did not "red flag" to creditors of the Ontario company it might hold assets from which they could seek recovery. Flanigan found that one of the sister corporations did not have the intent to obligate itself to the executed contracts.[389]

So, the tax avoidance scheme was executed to, as best as possible, camouflage any change in asset ownership from creditors

---

earn significant profits, and their anticipated tax revenues would be vulnerable to being wiped out by a loss consolidation involving significant losses incurred in larger provinces. It is noteworthy that two federal proposals to legislate a federal statutory regime under which corporate group profits and losses are consolidated failed (1985, 2010). To do so could put in jeopardy the federal-provincial collection agreements that concern corporate income tax.

[389] *Stubart Investments, supra* note 386, TRB at 74 DTC pp. 1211–12. Chairman Flanigan stated: "The reason I cannot come to that conclusion, with respect to the agreement [that a genuine sale of the business and assets took place], is that in the Finlayson group of companies there were sufficient common directors and officers in Stuart Brothers Limited and in Grover to reverse those overt acts at any time that it suited them. … I must find, on my interpretation of the definition of Lord Justice Diplock and in view of what took place in this case, that the agreement was never intended to be implemented in the manner in which it reads, but that it was always intended that Stuart would continue to operate the business and merely put money into Grover until the loss was used up and then the property could be put back where it belonged and where, I feel, it had never, in law, left."

seeking recovery from the Ontario loss company and then reverse the transaction once the losses were used to offset profits earned by the Quebec operation. This lack of intent to follow through on a genuine sale of assets is also obscured by the way in which Estey approached the sham doctrine. This is considered below after briefly mentioning the approach the Federal Court of Appeal took, followed by analysing Wilson's approach.

The Federal Court of Appeal indicated that it had a duty to first determine whether the transaction had been completed before determining whether the transaction was a sham. The Court compared the 1966 transaction recorded at book value to the 1968 transaction, completed at its fair market value of $2 million on sale to a third party.[390] After detailing what the Court described to be a "litany of deficiencies,"[391] Justice John Urie found the Minister was correct—the commercial reality pointed to the transaction being a sham, and, regardless the "appellant has, on the evidence, failed to show that this transaction was in all respects a complete, real transaction."[392] (Justice Darrel Heald and Deputy Justice Kelly concurred.)

In the Supreme Court, Wilson broke her analysis into two parts unlike Estey. She first considered whether the transaction was a sham, disguising the taxpayer's true intent. If so, the judiciary would strike down the sham and decide the dispute, based on the true legal result. If not a sham, the second consideration was whether there was a judicial guideline that allowed the judiciary to apply a *bona fide* business purpose test to deny the results of a tax avoidance scheme.

Wilson had no difficulty deciding the transaction was not, in fact, a sham. In a short judgment, she opened with a concise

---

[390] *Ibid.*, FCA at 81 DTC p. 5124. The Federal Court of Appeal also noted that corporate filings in Ontario failed to mention the Ontario loss business operated the Quebec business, nor did they mention two debentures issued to the Quebec company for its assets (i.e., this information could have tipped off its Ontario creditors).

[391] *Ibid.*, FCA p. 5125.

[392] *Ibid.*, FCA p. 5126.

negative: "I cannot see how a sham can be said to result where parties intend to create certain legal relations (in this case the purchase and sale of a business and a nominee arrangement to operate it) and are successful in creating those legal relations." Wilson's framing of this negative focuses directly on whether the legal relations intended were in fact created. Once done, she shifted the focus to Canadian tax cases that considered sham transactions where the transaction "does not have the legal consequences that it purports on its face to have."[393] Again, this is concise and clear.

In forming her opinion, Wilson cited three Canadian sham cases. The first is the 1962 Exchequer Court decision in *Shields*,[394] which held a partnership registered under Ontario law to be a sham. The second was the 1969 Exchequer Court decision in *Susan Hosiery*,[395] which held an employee pension plan the Minister accepted for registration to be a sham. The third decision is the Supreme Court's previously considered 1972 decision in *Cameron*.[396] The Court held in *Cameron* that a contract of management services was *not* a sham in circumstances where the newly created corporation that acquired the contract was owned by three persons who ceased to be employee-managers of the corporation that granted the contract, with their management-services corporation also intending to acquire shares, and eventual control, of their former employer.

But Wilson described the three sham decisions in a way that obscured the implications associated with certain trial court findings. Her *dicta* on each holding are cited after indicating what was not mentioned.

In describing *Shields*, Wilson failed to mention the finding of fact at trial for why the partnership was found to be a sham.

---

[393] *Ibid.*, SCC p. 539.

[394] *MNR v. Shields*, (1962), [1963] Ex. CR 91, 62 DTC 1343, [1962] CTC 548. https://reports.fja-cmf.gc.ca/fja-cmf/j/en/item/397412/index.do?q=shields.

[395] *Susan Hosiery Ltd. v. MNR*, [1969] 2 Ex. CR 408, 69 DTC 5346, [1969] CTC 353. https://reports.fja-cmf.gc.ca/fja-cmf/j/en/item/398796/index.do.

[396] *Cameron, supra* note 189.

Shield's "main purpose" in creating the partnership was—based on all the facts going for or against the existence of a partnership—to secure a benefit for himself by sharing 50 percent of the profits from his contracting business with his minor son.[397] The partnership was set up to split income with a minor son, a *mala fide* main purpose sham intent in 1962.

> Mr. Justice Cameron held that an alleged partnership agreement between the taxpayer and his son was "not a reality, but a mere simulate agreement" (p. 114); the parties never intended that it should give rise to a partnership and in law it did not do so.[398]

In describing *Susan Hosiery*, Wilson failed to cite the finding of fact at trial that the purported trustee of a pension plan did not intend to implement a *bona fide* pension plan.[399] The plan had a *mala fide* sham intent despite the fact the Minister registered the plan and it thus met the technical meaning of the definition "registered pension fund or plan" in the 1952 ITA.[400] The taxpayer's *mala fide* intent not to implement the plan was revealed when it collapsed the plan after making deductible contributions and then made a second deduction on the return of contributions by contributing them to an employee profit-sharing plan.

> Mr. Justice Gibson found a purported employees' pension plan to be a mere "simulate" that was "masquerading" as a pension plan; the actions of the taxpayers in question "never established a pension plan, nor any relationship of trustee, *cestui que trust*, nor any other legal or equitable rights or obligations in any of the parties and none of the parties intended at any material time that there should be any." (pp. 420–21)[401]

[397] *Shields, supra* note 394, Ex. CR pp. 99–100.

[398] *Stubart Investments, supra* note 386, SCC p. 539.

[399] *Susan Hosiery, supra* note 395, Ex. CR p. 418.

[400] The *Income Tax Act*, RSC, 1952, c. 148, s. 139(1)(ahh). Employer contributions were deductible under s. 76.

[401] *Stubart Investments, supra* note 386, SCC p. 539.

In describing *Cameron*, Wilson did not mention why Justice Martland found there was no sham in that case, when she stated:

> Mr. Justice Martland declined to find a contract for services between an employer and a company incorporated by his former employees to be a sham because "the legal rights and obligations which it created were exactly those which the parties intended." (p. 1069)[402]

Martland had held that he was not prepared to find a sham because the judge at trial determined that the tax savings were "incidental to the overall plan." This incidental tax savings intent distinguished *Cameron* from *Shields* and *Susan Hosiery*.

Justice Wilson next rejected the possible existence of a separate and distinct business purpose test by applying the British *Duke of Westminster* principle that taxpayers are entitled to arrange their affairs to minimize tax.

> The question then is whether the Minister is entitled to ignore it on that ground alone. If he is, then a massive inroad is made into Lord Tomlin's dictum that "Every man is entitled if he can to order his affairs so as that the tax attaching under the appropriate Acts is less than it otherwise would be": *Inland Revenue Commissioners v. Duke of Westminster*, [1936] A.C. 1, at p. 19: Indeed, it seems to me that the business purpose test is a complete rejection of Lord Tomlin's principle.[403]

As a result, Wilson held there is no separate business purpose test independent of the sham doctrine (Justice Ritchie concurred). "I think Lord Tomlin's principle is far too deeply entrenched in our tax law for the courts to reject it in the absence of clear statutory authority. No such authority has been put to us in this case." Wilson added earlier that a transaction may have "no business purpose other than the tax purpose."[404]

---

402 *Ibid.*, SCC pp. 539–40.
403 *Ibid.*, p. 540.
404 *Ibid.*

As noted above, Wilson also sought statutory authority for the proposition that the *Duke of Westminster* decision did not apply even though the Supreme Court had not expressly applied it before in a majority income tax decision. It appears that no one, including the litigants, realized that the Court did not follow the principle from 1938 onward in income tax avoidance cases.[405] Meanwhile, in Britain, the principle was being circumscribed in the case law by 1984.

---

[405] For example, see Robert Bertrand, Alice Desjardins and Rene Hurtubise, *Study for the Royal Commission on Taxation*, Study Number 22, "Legislation, Administration and Interpretation Processes in Federal Taxation," Chapter 6 (Judicial Interpretation of Tax Legislation), pp. 340–433, published by The Queen's Printer (Ottawa) for the 1966 *Royal Commission on Taxation* (the "Carter Commission"), which study was done by the University of Montreal's Faculty of Law. What stands out more than 50 years later when reading the 1964 chapter for the Carter Commission on judicial interpretation is the dearth of post-1949 Supreme Court income tax decisions considered, with the bulk of the analysis referring to British and non-Supreme Court Canadian cases pre-dating 1950 and the enactment of the 1948 ITA. The study followed the conventional view that the Canadian judiciary took the strict, literal or plain-meaning approach to interpreting tax law and followed British precedent. On precedent, the authors did not have the benefit of hindsight; the Court's precedent under the modern ITA was building such that it is not until *circa* 1963–66 one might suspect that the Court may not be following the *Duke of Westminster* principle in income tax avoidance cases and was instead emphasizing its own precedent, which is discussed at *infra*, note 465.

More recent articles include the following: (1) Stephen Bowman, "Interpretation of Tax Legislation: The Evolution of Purposive Analysis" (1995), 43:5 *Canadian Tax Journal* 1167–1189; (2) Professor David Duff, "The Interpretive Exercise Under the General Anti-Avoidance Rule," pp. 383–406 p. 384), *supra* note 299; and (3) Deen Olsen and Perry Derksen, "The Historical Legal Context for the Enactment of the General-Anti-Avoidance Rule: Judicial Anti-Avoidance Doctrines and Statutory Anti-Avoidance Rules," *supra* note 299 and *infra* note 679, p 55. But the Supreme Court rarely followed the strict approach when deciding income tax avoidance cases under the modern ITA before 1984. Among other things, the math results in Part V could not be what they are if the strict approach was followed; those results are consistent with a commercial substance approach being followed that is grounded in text, context and object, as E.A. Driedger indicated in 1983.

Stephen Bowman also considered the old British and Canadian precedent (and articles from 1940, 1965 and 1968) but did not cite pre-*Stubart Investments* Supreme Court income tax avoidance precedent in respect of the ITA in support of the strict approach thesis. Interestingly, Bowman cites in his section titled

Further, the *Duke of Westminster* principle has a *caveat* that concerns taxpayer *bona fides*, which Lord Tomlin stated as follows (which is rarely cited): "There may, of course, be cases where documents are not *bona fide* nor intended to be acted upon but are only used as a cloak to conceal a different transaction. No such case is made or even suggested here. The deeds of covenant are admittedly *bona fide* and have been given their proper legal operation."[406] It is unfortunate that Justice Wilson did not comment on the relevance *bona fides* may have when determining a taxpayer's genuine intent, which intent was lacking in *Shields* and *Susan Hosiery* and the Federal Court of Appeal's finding that there was no complete real transaction. The result is a fundamental weakness in her opinion.

In comparison, Justice Estey wrote an elaborate judgment that sought to set down guiding interpretive principles. He first accepted

---

"The Minority View" Judson J.'s 1964 decision concerning municipal charges in *City of Ottawa v. Royal Trust*, [1964] SCR 526, wherein Judson made it clear that there is no basis for taking a strict approach to a taxing Act (to find the by-law was bad); he looked to the scheme and its purpose.

Professor David Duff states that the "strict construction" approach "was the dominant method for interpreting tax statutes in Canada" before *Stubart Investments*, citing his article "Interpreting the *Income Tax Act*–Part 1: Interpretive Doctrines" (1999), 47:3 *Canadian Tax Journal* 464–533, pp. 469–77. Duff's 1999 article cites other authors in its footnote 9 (including Bowman), and he cites and considers certain British and lower-court Canadian income tax cases under the *Income War Tax Act* and the ITA (generally attribution cases) that applied the strict approach. However, he did not cite modern Supreme Court income tax avoidance decisions prior to *Stubart Investments* (although he cited Estey J.'s *Charter*-era decision concerning real estate property taxes: *Morguard Properties Ltd. v. City of Winnipeg*, [1983] 2 SCR 493).

Deen Olsen and Perry Derksen are more circumspect in that they suggest the Canadian judiciary "was informed" by the *Duke of Westminster* principle before 1988, which may be true in certain lower court income tax decisions but for the Supreme Court only if the word "informed" is taken to mean the Court invariably considered but did not follow the principle in income tax avoidance cases before its 1984 decision in *Stubart Investments*. Also see the discussion at *supra* note 299 and *infra* notes 410 and 465.

[406] *Duke of Westminster, supra* note 2; Lord Tomlin, p. 21. It was fundamental to the decision that the Duke not only intended genuine annuities for his servants (to replace their wages) but also honoured them when a servant left his service.

that statutory interpretation in Canada rests on interpreting the text, context and object of income tax legislation. (Justices Beetz and McIntyre concurred.)

Estey sought to balance the text, context and object approach with the *Duke of Westminster* principle, which rests on a strict reading of the text.[407] This is a contradiction. How and when does one apply the textual, contextual and purposive approach in light of the *Duke of Westminster* principle (or *vice versa*)? As detailed when considering the decisions of the remaining selected judges, the Supreme Court appears to have answered the question as follows: it applies the *Duke of Westminster* principle in regular income tax cases; it reserves the textual, contextual and purposive approach for cases involving the general anti-avoidance rule (GAAR). This dichotomy will be critiqued later.

Unlike Wilson, Estey incorporated his sham analysis into the question of whether there needs to be a *bona fide* business purpose for a tax avoidance transaction. He began by describing a sham in terms of whether the transaction is conducted with deceit, such that a façade is created that differs from the disguised reality.

> A sham transaction: This expression comes to us from decisions in the United Kingdom, and it has been generally taken to mean (but not without ambiguity) a transaction conducted with an element of deceit so as to create an illusion calculated to lead the tax collector away from the taxpayer or the true nature of the transaction; or, simple deception whereby the taxpayer creates a facade of reality quite different from the disguised reality.[408]

But Estey failed to consider *Shields* and *Susan Hosiery* in his opinion despite the fact they were cited by Wilson. No one will ever know why, but one plausible explanation is that both decisions undermined the narrative Estey was establishing in his opinion. Both decisions turned on taxpayer's intent and the trial court's

---

[407] *Stubart Investments*, *supra* note 386, SCC p. 579 (guideline 2 of 3).

[408] *Ibid.*, pp. 545–46.

findings that showed beyond doubt that the taxpayer's main intent in *Shields* was to avoid tax and that its sole intent in *Susan Hosiery* was to avoid tax.

Estey's failure to analyze *Shields* and *Susan Hosiery* is compounded by the fact that he cited the *Duke of Westminster* principle without noting Lord Tomlin's *caveat* concerning the requirement of *bona fide* intent when effecting legal relations.[409] The result was a fundamental weakness in his opinion.

It should be reemphasized that prior to 1984 there was no Supreme Court majority income tax avoidance decision that cited with application the *Duke of Westminster* principle. This is not only somewhat startling, but it conflicts with the accepted wisdom since 1984, and myths are especially difficult to put in issue when they are so often assumed to be true without question.[410]

There are more deficiencies in respect of the sham analysis. But before considering them, it is worth mentioning that Estey left on the interpretive table something Wilson rejected. He found that the judiciary could adopt in the context of the then artificial income reduction anti-avoidance rule in s. 137, "the *bona fide* business purpose test; or a step-by-step transaction rule for the classification of a taxpayers' activities which fall within the ban of such a general tax avoidance provision."[411] Estey ranked this as his first interpretive guideline for future tax avoidance cases and as part of his number three guideline, which included cases where the provisions in

[409] *Ibid.*, p. 552.

[410] The Supreme Court's decision in *Pioneer Laundry, supra* note 20, is its only pre-1984 majority income tax decision on point, and it rejected the *Duke of Westminster* principle, although it was overturned. Justice Roy Kellock applied the principle in his minority opinion against the taxpayer in *Dominion Telegraph Securities Limited v. MNR*, (1946), [1947] SCR 45, p. 53. While not cited, the principle appears to form the basis of Justice Ritchie's 1966 dissent in *Highway Sawmills, supra* note 301, and Justice Pigeon's 1974 dissent in *Jack Appleby, supra* note 290. Also, Justice Martland distinguished the *Duke of Westminster* principle in his 1970 minority opinion in *Ciglen, supra* note 187, upholding Ciglen's conviction for tax evasion.

[411] *Stubart Investments, supra* note 386, p. 574. Interpretive guideline 1, p. 579.

issue relate to an identified business function. Estey also made it clear as part of his number three guideline that if a taxpayer claims the benefit of a tax incentive or preference, the claim must "clearly [fall] within the 'object and spirit' of the taxing provisions."[412]

There are at least three prior Supreme Court sham decisions not considered by Justice Estey, who like Justice Wilson, relied on the arguments advanced, and cases cited, by the litigants. The three sham decisions not considered are the Court's 1973 oral decision in *The Deltona Corporation* (discussed in Part II), its 1974 decision in *Angle* (discussed in Part III), and its 1979 decision in *Lipson*, a unanimous decision in which Estey concurred.[413]

In *Lipson*, individual shareholders of a loss corporation that owned a rental building decided to lease the building from the company so that they could incur the losses personally, which they deducted when computing their personal income. The lower courts in Quebec allowed the scheme, finding that the *Duke of Westminster* principle applied. They also found there was no sham nor any artificial reduction of income. Justice Casey in his separate Quebec Court of Appeal opinion summed up the trial judge's finding that Lipson's tax avoidance motive did not taint his good faith, as follows:

> The trial judge concluded that the Respondent and his associates, the Company's only shareholders, had acted openly and in good faith and that their admitted motivation "… *pour pouvoir profiter des toutes les déductions premises par les loi d'impôt* …" did not taint their dealings … nor did they make these dealings transactions that unduly or artificially reduced the income. He also held that the deal between Respondent's group did not offend against sec. 22 and that the expenses charged had been incurred for

[412] *Ibid.*, p. 576.

[413] *Deputy Minister of Revenue (Quebec) v. Lipson*, [1979] 1 SCR 833. *Deputy Minister of Revenue (Quebec) v. Lipson* – SCC Cases (scc-csc.ca).

> the purpose of producing income within the meaning of sec. 15.[414]

Quebec appealed.

Justice Louis-Philippe Pigeon for the Supreme Court disallowed the tax avoidance scheme. In doing so, he did not cite or discuss the *Duke of Westminster* principle nor the trial court's finding that the taxpayer's tax avoidance motive did not taint his good faith. Instead, he held that the outlays and expenses failed Quebec's basic "for the purpose of gaining or producing income" deductibility test because they were not incurred for the purpose of yielding a profit, as distinguished from gross revenue. He underlined the word profit in his written reasons.[415]

With respect to the word "profit," Pigeon quoted s. 5 of Quebec's *Income Tax Act:* "Subject to other provisions of this act, income for a taxation year from a business or property is the profit therefrom for that year." This wording is almost identical to the text in subs. 9(1) of the federal ITA, and although subs. 9(2) refers to a loss from a business or property, that reference is to a business or property "source," which word is not used in subs. 9(1). This in turn raises the question of when a loss from a business or property satisfies the source requirement.

In *Lipson*, Pigeon found that the purpose of the lease was not to earn a profit from a business or property but "to create a deductible

---

[414] *Ibid.* The lower court decisions are in Supreme Court file 14190 (document titled "Application"), with Casey J.A.'s decision starting at p. 34. Also see the decisions in French of Justices Crête and Dubé. The Court of Appeal did reverse the lower court on a matter related to the treatment of the rents received by the shareholders and flowed on to their corporation. The payments were used to reduce the corporate mortgage on the building and were held to be benefits to the shareholders.

[415] *Ibid.* Pigeon J. stated (p. 839): "It is perfectly clear from these provisions that, in order for an expense to be admissible as a deduction from a taxpayer's income, it must have been incurred in order to make a profit. It is not enough that the expense was incurred in order to obtain gross revenue, as counsel argued at the hearing" [emphasis in original].

loss by means of a disadvantageous contract."[416] He noted that the taxpayers could not reasonably have been expected to execute the lease under its terms if they were arm's length shareholders.[417]

Next, Pigeon turned his attention to the Tax Review Board's holding in the federal dispute instead of discussing the lower courts' application of the *Duke of Westminster* principle. The Board considered the same issues in 1972. Unlike the Quebec judiciary, the Board found that the taxpayer never satisfied the "for the purpose of gaining or producing income" test, the lease was a sham and the artificial transaction anti-avoidance rule applied.[418] Pigeon expressed merit in that decision. (Justices Dickson, Beetz, Estey and Pratte concurred.)

> In other words, the true question was: did the members of the syndicate expect in executing the lease to make a profit proportionate to the risk of loss they were assuming? The most optimistic calculations of the real estate brokers hardly succeeded in showing it would be possible to break even. Could the members of the syndicate reasonably have been expected to enter into such a contract if they had not been shareholders? … There is therefore a great deal to be said in support of the decision of the Tax Appeal Board, (1972), DTC 1222 … regarding respondent's federal income tax for the years 1964 to 1967, a decision based essentially on a provision of the federal Act identical with s. 15(a) of the provincial statute [i.e., the "for the purpose of gaining or producing income" test] (parenthetical added).[419]

Although the Supreme Court did not confirm that the lease was a sham device, it never demurred from this position, albeit it did say the decision was based "essentially" on the taxpayer's lacking a profit intent under the income earning purpose test.

---

[416] *Ibid.*, SCC p. 839.

[417] *Ibid.*, SCC pp. 839–40.

[418] *Lipson v. MNR*, 72 DTC 1222, [1972] CTC 2270 (Tax Review Board).

[419] *Lipson*, *supra* note 413, SCC p. 840.

Estey having concurred in *Lipson* knew the lease was found to be a sham in the federal dispute and the Supreme Court's *obiter* on the matter. But perhaps what is most telling about his opinion in *Stubart Investments* is that he cited with approval *obiter* in the Exchequer Court's 1965 judgment in *Foreign Power Securities.*[420]

Justice Estey did so to question and distinguish the American approach to requiring a business purpose, which incorporates a *bona fide* test. After questioning the American approach, Estey stated that its *bona fide* business purpose test was "[i]n sharp contrast to Noël J., … in *Foreign Power Securities Corp. v. Minister of National Revenue,* 66 DTC 5012, at p. 5027, where he stated:

> 'There is indeed no provision in the *Income Tax Act* which provides that, where it appears that the main purpose or one of the purposes for which any transaction or transactions was or were effected was the avoidance or reduction of liability to income tax, the Court may, if it thinks fit, direct that such adjustments shall be made as respects liability to income tax as it considers appropriate so as to counteract the avoidance or reduction of liability to income tax which would otherwise be effected by the transaction or transactions.' "[421]

Since Noël's *obiter* does not deal with the U.S. *bona fide* business purpose test or the U.S. approach to tax shams, Estey really appears to be citing it for the proposition that a main tax avoidance intent is not relevant when determining the existence of *bona fide* intent in effecting legal relations. If so, Estey's reach was judicial manna

[420] *Foreign Power Securities, supra* note 309. *Minister of National Revenue v. Foreign Power Securities Corporation Ltd.* – SCC Cases (scc-csc.ca). The Exchequer Court decision is at *Foreign Power Securities Corp. Ltd. v. Minister of National Revenue* – Office of the Commissioner for Federal Judicial Affairs Canada (fja-cmf.gc.ca).

[421] *Stubart Investments, supra* note 386, SCC pp. 574–75. A reader of *Stubart Investments* would not know that there is a Supreme Court decision in *Foreign Power Securities* unless he or she already knows.

from heaven for those intent on effecting non-arm's length legal relations for the sole purpose of circumventing tax provisions.

Estey was quite open about one reason for rejecting the need for a *bona fide* business purpose test in Canada. He went so far as to cite with seeming approval Toronto practitioners, David Ward and Maurice Cullity, for the proposition that it is "a legitimate business purpose of a transaction to minimize or postpone taxes" with Ward and Cullity arguing that if "taxes are minimized or postponed, more capital will be available to run the business and more profit will result." Right after citing this material, Estey rejected the proposition that a transaction could be disregarded because there is no *bona fide* business purpose:

> I would therefore reject the proposition that a transaction may be disregarded for tax purposes solely on the basis that it was entered into by a taxpayer without an independent or *bona fide* business purpose.[422]

By this, the Supreme Court signalled to taxpayers, the Minister and the lower courts that a main tax avoidance intent had become a *bona fide* commercial and personal intent and purpose. There is no other conclusion to draw, given the juxtaposition of the views of Ward and Cullity and the Court's rejection of the need for a *bona fide* business purpose.

The Supreme Court's decision in *Stubart Investments* represents the start of a dramatic shift in its approach to tax avoidance. The Court pivoted 50 years on back to the 1935 British *Duke of Westminster* principle. It is almost inexplicable unless one keeps in mind that the enactment of the *Charter* in 1982 signaled to the judiciary in legal terms that Canada had shifted to a rights-driven era from a duty-bound era, which shift was being accompanied by an economic shift to *laissez-faire*.

The next decision of Justice Wilson upended National Revenue's post-1948 approach to identifying and reassessing non-compliant

---

[422] *Ibid.*, p. 575.

taxpayers. Although almost all the Minister's discretionary powers to constrain tax avoidance ended with the repeal of the *Income War Tax Act*, the modern ITA granted broad ministerial powers to require persons to produce information for the purpose of administering and enforcing the law.

In 1962, the Supreme Court confirmed the breadth of the Minister's audit powers in *Canadian Bank of Commerce*, which concerned a ministerial requirement demanding that the bank produce a wide range of information and documents related to the clients of a customer Swiss bank.[423] The requirement did not concern the Canadian Bank of Commerce's tax liability but sought information related to the Union Bank's clients the vast majority of whom would have been unknown to the Minister.

The information sought from the Canadian Bank of Commerce included details of Union Bank clients' safety deposit boxes, powers of attorney, telegraph transfers, book entries, vouchers, lines of credit and account statements. The Minister identified that the relevant documents and information included those described in accounts referred to as "Casual, Manager's, Sundry and similar accounts." The litigants agreed that the information related to many corporations and individuals, some of which were resident in Canada. The bank also admitted the Minister acted in good faith when he issued the requirement.

On June 25, 1962, the Supreme Court unanimously ordered the production of the information with the nine-member panel splitting 5–4 on the reasons. Justice Cartwright, for the majority, focused on the requirement seeking information for "a specified person or persons" and noted that the Union Bank (which was named in the requirement) may or may not have been the person under investigation. It did not matter because it was conceded that the requirement related to a genuine inquiry into the tax liability of some specific person or persons. This meant the private information of

[423] *Canadian Bank of Commerce v. Attorney General of Canada*, [1962] SCR 729. *Canadian Bank of Commerce v. Attorney General of Canada* – SCC Cases (scc-csc.ca).

third parties had to be provided to the Minister. (Justices Locke, Fauteux, Martland and Ritchie concurred.) Chief Justice Kerwin for the minority focused on the broad wording of the provision and considered the Union Bank to be the taxpayer under investigation. The fact third-party information would be disclosed did not affect the validity of the requirement. (Justices Taschereau, Abbott and Judson concurred.)

Gwyneth McGregor's takeaway for the *Canadian Tax Foundation* was that Cartwright's majority opinion meant that, provided the Minister "was making a 'genuine and serious' enquiry into the tax liability of specific persons he need not name those persons in the requirement." The decision stoked fear in tax planners and their clients. McGregor noted it could "revive the fears expressed at the time of the first hearing ... that a judgment in favour of the Minister would allow him to embark on 'fishing expeditions' into the affairs of taxpayers."[424] During the next 20 years, the Minister's auditors fine-tuned their approach to the point they became exceptionally good at identifying and reassessing non-compliant taxpayers.

In 1983, one of National Revenue's tactics came back to the Supreme Court for decision; the Court released its decision on June 21, 1984, which was 14 days after it released *Stubart Investments*.

James Richardson & Sons (1984)

In *James Richardson & Sons*, National Revenue, which was becoming better known as Revenue Canada to the public, had demanded in 1980 that a national brokerage firm provide information about its clients' investments in 1978 and 1979.[425] If obtained, the information would be used to identify and reassess non-compliant taxpayers, such as those not reporting capital gains realized from

[424] Gwyneth McGregor, "Around the Courts: Double Judgment," (1962) 10:5 *Canadian Tax Journal* 316–17.

[425] *James Richardson & Sons Ltd. v. MNR*, [1984] 1 SCR 614. *James Richardson & Sons v. M.N.R.* – SCC Cases (scc-csc.ca).

selling investments. Taxpayers who had failed to comply knowingly, where significant tax was in issue, were also at risk for being charged for tax evasion, especially if they were prominent. Revenue Canada at the time made a public example of prominent tax evaders, including federal politicians.

The issuance of the requirement came as a shock to some of the brokerage's clients. By and large, the affected clients would have been upper-middle class and wealthy taxpayers. Tax professionals and the media dubbed the issuance of the requirement a "fishing expedition," and, if an accurate description, the Minister's net was cast to land "tuna and whales" not "minnows."

As the Minister's use of his broad powers began to gain wider notice in media, other taxpayers began to complain. A young Progressive Conservative member of Parliament named Perrin Beatty took up their cause and undertook a cross-Canada political tour in 1983–84 in the lead-up to the 1984 election; affected taxpayers complained directly to him in public hearings, followed by Beatty's releasing proposals for reform in the spring of 1984.

John Ferguson wrote for the *Ottawa Citizen* in January 1984: "[T]he Act allows investigators to go on fishing expeditions." Taxpayers were accusing the Minister's auditors of using the powers to "shake down" taxpayers. In the story, leading criminal defence lawyer and civil libertarian Clayton Ruby noted the breadth of the statutory powers and referred to them as being "draconian."[426]

Ferguson's story discussed criminal and civil audit and collection powers and noted that in *James Richardson & Sons*, the brokerage was arguing the requirement it received was unreasonable search and seizure under the *Charter*. Perrin Beatty weighed in stating, "The department is running amok."

Given this background, it was with surprise for some that the *Toronto Star* reported on May 7, 1984: "Many Find the Taxman

[426] John Ferguson, "Consultant Handy Safety Valve for Taxman under Pressure," *Ottawa Citizen*, January 24, 1984, pp. 45–49.

Helpful, Gallup Says."[427] Canadians (1,059 in total) were asked about their dealings with Revenue Canada in the previous five years.[428] The *Star* noted that "despite all the bad publicity" officials were found to be helpful by 47 percent of all contacts, 35 percent indicated the officials were neutral, 15 percent said the officials were hostile and 3 percent were unable to categorize the officials. Even of those who were subjected to an audit or examination, 75 percent found the officials either helpful (29 percent) or neutral (46 percent). But 23 percent of those subject to an audit or examination indicated the officials were hostile.[429]

What is one to make of these relatively positive results during a period in which there were a litany of complaints directed at Revenue Canada by business, business lobby groups, tax professionals, politicians, editorialists and taxpayers who were audited for potential non-compliance and some of whom had their assets seized for unpaid taxes?

To some extent, the answer may be that most people responding to the Gallup survey were compliant and most likely employees or retirees. But in the case of respondents who had been audited, the likelihood goes up that a minority would answer that the officials were hostile.

Justice Wilson's decision in *James Richardson & Sons* reversed the Federal Court of Appeal and denied the Minister access to the information by reading down the text of the statutory language in the requirement power. (Justices Beetz, Estey, McIntyre, Chouinard and Lamer concurred.) She interpreted the Court's 1962 decision in *Canadian Bank of Commerce* as holding that the Minister's requirement power applies only if the Minister identifies a specific person or persons in the requirement who is/are subject of a genuine and

[427] "Many Find Taxman Helpful, Gallup Says," *The Toronto Star*, May 7, 1984, p. A3. The survey's margin of error was 10 percent because only 20 percent of all respondents had direct contact with Revenue Canada.

[428] *Ibid.*

[429] *Ibid.*

serious inquiry. There was no identified taxpayer in the requirement issued in *James Richardson & Sons*, and the Court ended the ability of tax auditors to demand information for compliance purposes from third parties if the power is being used to undertake a so-called "*fishing expedition*" for information about unidentified taxpayers.

At the *Canadian Tax Foundation's* 1984 tax conference after the fall election, Perrin Beatty, the new Minister of National Revenue, announced several changes to the way in which Revenue Canada administered the tax law. He announced: "[M]y officials are operating under instructions not to take into account the prominence of a taxpayer in deciding whether or not to conduct a tax-evasion investigation." Further, "even after convictions are rendered, our regularly quarterly press releases and summaries of convictions will no longer 'name names,' a practice I consider an unnecessary additional penalty to those who have already been dealt with under the law."[430]

With respect to tax avoidance, Beatty announced that the Rulings Branch had been instructed to expand the ruling process to encompass the business view that taxes are a cost of business to be reckoned with in a context where there was no business purpose test:

> This controversy [the business purpose test] has now been put to rest by the Supreme Court of Canada in the recent case of *Stubart Investments Ltd.* [footnote omitted], which clearly found that there is no such test in Canadian income tax law unless it is specifically required in a statutory provision. The Supreme Court also provided guidelines which the courts may adopt in looking at what in effect constitutes legal tax planning. [Footnote omitted]. Therefore, consistent with that decision and in recognition of the frustration being experienced by those members of the private sector who are unable to obtain certainty with respect to legal tax planning, I believe it is timely to expand the rulings

[430] The Honourable Perrin Beatty, *1984 Conference Report*, Canadian Tax Foundation, "A Perspective from Revenue Canada," pp. 23–32, at p. 24.

services to encompass the business view that taxes are a cost to be reckoned with.

As a tentative step toward ruling on tax planning, I have directed that transactions similar to those in the facts of *Stubart Investments* be considered within the framework of the existing law. This coincides with the comments of my colleague, the Minister of Finance, in the press release of October 25, 1984,[431] stating that transfers of losses within a corporate group should be better accomodated by the tac laws.[432]

In practical terms, Conservative Prime Minister Brian Mulroney's incoming government had just instructed Revenue Canada to grant tax avoiders favourable advanced income tax rulings for transactions done solely to avoid tax if their lawyer or accountant could muster a reasonably sound technical argument that the transactions were legally effective based on *Stubart Investments*. It is unclear to what extent the Mulroney government cared in the fall of 1984 that *Stubart Investments* decision exposed the federal and provincial treasuries to significant adverse results once tax lawyers and accountants advised their clients that Revenue Canada was instructed to be accommodating.

In judicial and political terms, the outcomes of *Stubart Investments* and *James Richardson & Sons* flashed a green light for tax planners to effect aggressive tax avoidance plans for no other purpose than to avoid tax, while circumscribing Revenue Canada's administrative ability to obtain information from third parties to be used against unidentified non-compliant taxpayers.

While two years later the Mulroney government granted the Minister the ability to seek judicial authorization to require third

[431] Canada, Department of Finance, "Transfers of Losses within a Corporate Group," News Release, October 25, 1984. Also see, *A Corporate Loss Transfer System for Canada*, May 1985. In the Preface, the Honourable Michael Wilson (Minister of Finance) states: "I am particularly concerned and aware that the proposal raises issues with respect to provincial income taxation."

[432] Beatty, *1984 Conference Report*, *supra* note 430, p. 29.

parties to provide information on unnamed taxpayers, the provision included two hurdles that rendered it ineffective for obtaining judicial authorization until Liberal Finance Minister Paul Martin recommended in 1995 their repeal, which occurred in June 1996.[433]

As for tax avoidance, it went out of control, with the Mulroney government maintaining that income tax revenues had "significantly and unexpectedly" declined after it took office.[434] By 1986–87, Finance Minister Michael Wilson considered whether Canada needed a GAAR to constrain tax avoidance. He also began constantly issuing press releases announcing targeted tightening rules to address the evolving plans. These developments were coupled with a major tax reform exercise, which would be Wilson's political legacy. Spread over two electoral mandates, it unleashed negative feedback and political pressures—especially, those related to the new Goods and Services Tax.

After *Stubart Investments*, Estey and Wilson renewed their differing visions of how to interpret the ITA. They did so in 1985 and 1986.

Imperial General Properties Ltd. (1985); George Golden et al. (1986)

In 1985, Justice Estey wrote the majority opinion in a 4–3 split (a reversal for the Crown) in the tax avoidance case *Imperial*

[433] In 1986, Parliament amended the *Income Tax Act* (SC, 1986, c. 6, s. 121); see subs. 231.2(2) and (3). The judge has to be satisfied the unnamed person or group is "ascertainable," and the requirement is to verify compliance by the person or persons in the group. Two additional restrictions on such authorizations were repealed in 1996. They related to the judge also being satisfied the information was not readily available and that it was reasonable to expect, based on any grounds, the person or group may have failed or may be likely to fail to provide the information sought. Liberal Finance Minister Paul Martin's *1995 Budget Plan* states (p. 153): "These restrictions, which make it difficult for Revenue Canada in order to obtain timely information to verify compliance with the Act, are being eliminated. The proposed measure will improve Revenue Canada's ability to verify compliance with the self-assessment system with respect to transactions where no information reporting is required."

[434] Brian J. Arnold, "The Tax Policy Development of the General Anti-Avoidance Rule," pp. 81–90; p. 84 in Brian J. Arnold (Editor), *The General Antic-Avoidance Rule, supra* note 299.

General Properties.[435] Justice Wilson wrote the dissenting opinion. The case concerned the meaning of "corporate control" where there is a 50–50 split in voting shares.

Estey refused to take "a highly technical and narrow interpretation of the legal rights attatched to the shares."[436] (Justices Beetz, Chouinard and La Forest concurred.) He noted the lynchpin of the tax avoidance plan was that only one of two groups held the right to wind up the corporation. Estey applied Judson's 1971 unanimous holding on a similar issue in *Oakfield Developments*.[437] Wilson rejected *Oakfield Developments*, based on her view that Judson deviated from legal control to *de facto* control. (Justices McIntyre and Lamer concurred.)

In 1986, Justices Estey and Wilson applied their different interpretive approaches to reach the same result for the taxpayer in the tax avoidance dispute *George Golden et al.*[438] Estey rejected taking a literal interpretive approach;[439] he interpreted an anti-avoidance rule, meant to address unreasonable allocations of proceeds to avoid tax, in the light of the context and object of the legislation. (Chief Justice Dickson and Justices Beetz and La Forest concurred.) While the rule applied to unreasonable allocations of consideration between different types of property, it did not apply in the dispute

---

[435] *The Queen v. Imperial General Properties Ltd.*, [1985] 2 SCR 288. *The Queen v. Imperial General Properties Ltd.* – SCC Cases (scc-csc.ca).

[436] *Ibid.*, Estey J. para. 11.

[437] *Oakfield Developments, supra* note 274. *Oakfield Developments (Toronto) Ltd. v. Minister of National Revenue* – SCC Cases (scc-csc.ca).

[438] *The Queen v. George Golden et al.*, [1986] 1 SCR 209. *The Queen v. Golden et al.* – SCC Cases (scc-csc.ca).

[439] *Ibid.*, SCR p. 214–15 (para. 8). Estey J. stated: "In *Stubart* … the Court recognized that in the consideration of taxation statutes the law is not confined to a literal and virtually meaningless interpretation of the Act where the words will support on a broader construction a conclusion which is workable and in harmony with the evident purposes of the Act in question. Strict construction in the historic sense no longer finds a place in the canons of interpretation applicable to taxation statutes in an era such as the present, where taxation serves many purposes in addition to the old and traditional object of raising the cost of government from a somewhat unenthusiastic public."

because the allocation was reasonable in the case. The Crown's appeal was dismissed.

Justice Wilson led the minority, which applied the plain-meaning approach to the anti-avoidance rule. The text referred to allocations between "any property … [and] something else," and she held that its plain-meaning did not allow an allocation of proceeds between depreciable property and other property. Wilson dismissed the Crown's appeal. (Justices Julien Chouinard and Antonio Lamer concurred.)

The judicial sparring was about to end. Estey retired in April 1988, and the next year he agreed to be the dinner speaker at the *Canadian Tax Foundation's* annual tax conference. The speech provides a fascinating insight into the Supreme Court's decision in *Stubart Investments*. Of particular interest is the perspective from which the Court considered the transaction in *Stubart Investments*. Estey stated:

> The professed purpose and the attained object were to conserve cash in the group by applying the profits in the years in question from the business to the tax loss theretofore admittedly incurred and recognized under the Act; all of this to the end of restoring the cash position of the taxpayer as far as possible, to its pre-loss condition.[440]

The above description focuses on the transaction's commercial purpose, which was to undertake a loss consolidation within the corporate group. That was the objective both the tax planners and the Supreme Court sought to achieve in *Stubart Investments*; to do so, the Court never applied its past commercial substance over legal form precedent. Rather, the Court relied on the *Duke of Westminster* principle to hold the legal form of the transaction effected legal relations sufficient to achieve the desired commercial result.

---

[440] The Honourable W.Z. Estey, "Basic Problems in Taxation," *1989 Tax Conference*, Canadian Tax Foundation, pp. 1–12, at p. 8.

Yet tax planners were about to embark on a course of action that would use the precedent to achieve results that lacked commercial substance and reality; ignoring that the first time, the Supreme Court cited with approval the *Duke of Westminster* principle in a majority income tax decision, the Court did so to reach a commercial result that was within the object and policy parameters of the statutory law.

Parliament enacts the GAAR (1988)

The GAAR was without a doubt introduced in 1988 to address a perceived mischief arising under *Stubart Investments*. The Supreme Court had allowed the tax avoidance result despite the taxpayer's lack of a *bona fide* purpose in circumstances where it camouflaged as best as possible the transactions that it intended to unwind once it obtained the tax benefit, to ensure the Ontario company's creditors could not seize the assets.

More generally, the GAAR contains two main elements of concern to taxpayers: (1) a torpedo and (2) a lifeboat. The torpedo is that the GAAR will apply to a taxpayer's transaction that results in a tax benefit unless the transaction is undertaken primarily for a *bona fide* non-tax reason. This has come to be accepted as a high hurdle for a tax planner to jump. Parliament through this torpedo sought to address the Supreme Court's *Charter*-era drift back to the *Duke of Westminster* principle in general and the Court's direction in particular that the lack of a *bona fide* business purpose is not a basis to disregard a transaction.

The GAAR's lifeboat is that it applies only if a tax benefit results in a misuse of a provision or an abuse of the ITA read as a whole. Without such relief, the GAAR's torpedo presumably would have sunk the intercorporate loss-sharing scheme in *Stubart Investments* even though such loss-sharing within a controlled corporate group was generally acceptable in policy terms as reflected in the provisions of the ITA by the time of the Supreme Court's decision.

As such, it would have appeared that when the GAAR was introduced, a taxpayer's transaction that lacked commercial substance and likewise was motivated by tax benefits would be torpedoed by the new rule. But what remained to be seen was whether the judiciary would require a taxpayer who undertook a transaction devoid of *bona fide* non-tax purpose to establish, for the purpose of effecting an acceptable result, the transaction complied with the object and spirit of the scheme underlying the particular statutory income tax law in issue.

Put another way, if a transaction has no commercial substance or reality, is that relevant when determining whether there is an abuse? As will be shown later, the explanatory notes to the legislative amendments suggest that Parliament expected that the question was relevant. But would the judiciary tender the lifeboat over to well-advised tax avoiders who wave their arms at the lifeboat and yell toward it that everything about income tax is too complicated to understand what is or is not abusive and allow their transactions on the basis the Crown failed to prove they are abusive of a particular provision in the ITA? Would the judiciary allow them to board the lifeboat, despite their having undertaken complex tax-planning transactions few other people are equipped with the knowledge necessary to understand?

Justice Wilson's next decision concerns a provincial corporate income tax case. It's a sleeper case in terms of precedent, which means it is not easy to discern what would make it so important. That detail rests on her view that certainty is the most important "value in the business law context."[441]

Mattabi Mines Ltd. (1988)

Mattabi Mines sought to claim a $736,000 Ontario investment tax credit (ITC) on the cost of acquired mining equipment by amending prior tax returns. The details are technical but need to be articulated in brief because Wilson's unanimous decision would

[441] Anderson, *Judging Bertha Wilson*, *supra* note 380, p. 237.

be cited by the Supreme Court in the 1990s with approval, despite Estey's opinion in *Stubart Investments*.[442]

Although Estey was on the seven-member panel in *Mattabi Mines*, he was ill, and *Supreme Court Reports* notes that he (and Le Dain J.) took no part in the decision. Several tax wrinkles existed in the dispute.

Mattabi Mines opened a new mine that went into production in August 1972 before the federal government announced that Thomas Crerar's 1936 *temporary* exemption from tax for new mine profits would end December 31, 1973. Mattabi Mines' tax-exempt profits were $7.3 million in 1972 and $39.9 million in 1973. Ontario made no announcement on the status of its similar exemption from tax until April 1974. When doing so, it announced the change retroactive to the end of 1973.

With respect to the Ontario tax credit, it arose based on investment costs Mattabi Mines incurred in 1971. Ontario required ITCs to be used in the year they arose unless the taxpayer incurred a net loss that year and each subsequent year until it could be used. Mattabi Mines earned tax-exempt profits until the end of December 1973 and, as such, had not claimed its ITC. But when Mattabi Mines became taxable on its profits in 1974, it requested Ontario Taxation to amend the company's 1971–73 returns to deduct CCA. It did so to achieve a net loss in each year of $100.

Mattabi Mines had not been deducting CCA because to do so would have wasted it in those years. When it made its request to deduct CCA to achieve net losses, it maintained that it did not have to deduct it from its tax-exempt income; rather, it would deduct it simply to create nominal net losses. If allowed, Mattabi Mines would carry forward the ITC to its 1974 tax year and claim it against tax payable on its taxable income.

On its face, Mattabi Mines' request to amend its tax returns is unreasonable because it sought to create nominal losses despite its

[442] *Mattabi Mines Ltd. v. Ontario (Minister of Revenue)*, [1988] 2 SCR 175. *Mattabi Mines Ltd. v. Ontario (Minister of Revenue)* – SCC Cases (scc-csc.ca).

earning significant tax-exempt profits during the period. As might be expected, Ontario refused to amend Mattabi Mines' tax returns. It appealed. At trial, the Ontario Superior Court allowed Mattabi Mines' appeal. The judge placed significant emphasis on the retroactive nature of Ontario's announcement, but the Ontario Court of Appeal made short work of the trial judge's reasons and allowed Ontario's appeal.

Wilson dismissed the taxpayer's appeal for a unanimous Supreme Court, albeit we do not know what Estey would have thought about her reasons. Ontario had argued that Ontario's income tax law did not allow Mattabi Mines to claim an ITC because the income was exempt from tax and the expenditures were not incurred for the purpose of earning income. Wilson's opinion starts with a holding that rejected the Ontario Court of Appeal's finding that the phrase "for the purpose of earning income" means "taxable income" thereby denying the creation of the ITC. Since income and taxable income are distinct tax concepts, Wilson overturned this finding.

But in the course of doing so, Wilson cited with approval (1) a 1957 Exchequer Court decision called *Royal Trust*, in which Justice Thorson laid down a methodology for deducting business expenses,[443] and (2) Justice Martland's 1966 minority Supreme Court decision in *Premium Iron Ores*. Three distinct issues arise with these citations for the proposition that they articulate the methodology applicable to deducting business costs under the modern income tax statutes.

First, Thorson's 1957 approach in *Royal Trust* pre-dates and differs from Abbott's 1958 methodology in *British Columbia Electric Railway Co.*[444] At least two concerns arise about Thorson's approach. When interpreting paras. 12(1)(*a*) and (*b*) of the 1948 ITA, he cited

---

[443] *Royal Trust Co. v. MNR*, [1957] CTC 32, 57 DTC 1055 (Ex. Ct.).

[444] For Abbott J.'s methodology, see the analysis of his 1958 majority decision in *British Columbia Electric Railway Co.*, *supra* note 92, as modified by Hall J.'s 1966 swing opinion in *Premium Iron Ores*, *supra* note 98, and as confirmed by Martland J.'s 1967 unanimous decision in *Farmers' Mutual Petroleums*, *supra* note 99.

and relied on several Canadian, American and British cases that considered legislation predating the 1948 ITA. This is exactly what Abbott cautioned against the next year in *British Columbia Electric Railway Co.*

The related concern is that Thorson found, citing his own 1947 decision, that it is "not a condition of the deductibility of a disbursement or expense that it … should be traceable to it and that it was never necessary to show a casual connection between an expenditure and a receipt."[445] Wilson cited with approval that *obiter*,[446] which is inconsistent with Abbott's *obiter* in *British Columbia Electric Railway Co.*, where he referred to the expense producing income and being connected to the source.

Despite this, *Royal Trust* has been cited with approval by various Canadian judges in the years that followed. This does not make Thorson's approach correct or acceptable under the ITA. By the way, former Prime Minister John Turner with Heward Stikeman argued the case; *Royal Trust* was a major win for businessmen because it allowed the deductibility of their social club membership fees (e.g., golf clubs) and related expenses when computing business income.

Second, and equally important, Wilson failed in *Mattabi Mines* to note that Justice Hall's swing opinion in *Premium Iron Ores* refined

---

[445] *Royal Trust, supra* note 443. Thorson J.'s full statement on the issue is, as cited by Wilson J. in *Mattabi Mines* [citing Thorson from CTC pp. 43–44]: "It is not necessary that the outlay or expense should have resulted in income. In *Consolidated Textiles Limited v. M.N.R.*, [1947] Ex. C.R. 77 at 81; [1947] C.T.C. 63, I expressed the opinion that it was not a condition of the deductibility of a disbursement or expense that it should result in any particular income or that any income should be traceable to it and that it was never necessary to show a causal connection between an expenditure and a receipt."

[446] *Mattabi Mines, supra* note 442, para. 14. Wilson J. stated: "If there is no need to demonstrate a causal connection between a particular expenditure and a particular income, and no need for the income to be generated in the same year in which the expenditure was made, then it would not seem to matter whether Mattabi suffered tax losses in 1971 or that it would have been exempt from tax had it made a profit."

Abbott's methodology in *British Columbia Electric Railway Co.* Hall determined that gross income need not result in the same tax year, as required by Abbott in his majority opinion in that case and by the dissent of Justices Ritchie and Abbott in *Premium Iron Ores*. But Hall did not hold that an expense is deductible, even if it does not result in income or has no connection to the source.

Third, the next year, 1967, Justice Martland confirmed in *Farmers Mutual Petroleums* Abbott's methodology for a unanimous Supreme Court, albeit he did not discuss the detail concerning the expense being connected to the source:

> To be deductible for tax purposes an outlay must satisfy at least two basic tests:
>
> 1. It must be made for the purpose of gaining or producing income (s. 12(1)(*a*)).
> 2. It must not be a payment on account of capital (S.12(1)(*b*)).
>
> Both of these tests must be satisfied concurrently to justify deductibility. In *British Columbia Electric Railway Company v. Minister of National Revenue*, Abbott J. said at p. 137:
>
> > Since the main purpose of every business undertaking is presumably to make a profit, any expenditure made "for the purpose of gaining or producing income" comes within the terms of s. 12(1)(*a*) whether it be classified as an income expense or a capital outlay.
>
> Once it is determined that a particular expenditure is one made for the purpose of gaining or producing income, in order to compute income tax liability it must next be determined whether such disbursement is an income expense or a capital outlay.[447]

[447] *Farmers Mutual Petroleums, supra* note 99, SCC p. 65. *Farmers Mutual Petroleums Limited v. Minister of National Revenue* – SCC Cases (scc-csc.ca).

Abbott's essential point should remain: a deduction of business expenses presumes the source exists; the presence of an expense does not mean a business source exists, nor that the expense is connected to any such source. To say that no connection needs to exist between the expense and the business source, as suggested by Thorson and many others, misses Abbott's point by a wide margin.

It is disappointing to see the extent to which Martland's minority opinion in *Premium Iron Ores* is cited out of context and *Royal Trust* has been relied on through the years as a precedent-setting decision despite its reliance on cases that never adhered to Abbott's methodology, or at least explain in a principled manner why that methodology does not apply. One explanation for this occurrence is that taxpayers cite the decisions seeking a favourable outcome. This appears to show up in *Mattabi Mines* and helps explain how the Supreme Court, post-1990, managed to lower the standard for the existence of a source of income to an *ancillary* profit-earning intent. More on that later.

In this context, it is sufficient to note that Justice Wilson conditioned her opinion about the methodology to use when determining whether amounts are deductible when she stated: "If there is no need to demonstrate a casual connection …" [see footnote 446]. The "if" suggests counsel for the Crown had failed to effectively counter Mattabi Mines' reliance on Thorson's decision in *Royal Trust* (i.e., that no connection is needed between the outlay and the source) and Martland's minority opinion in *Premium Iron Ores.* This should be considered whenever any of the three cases are cited.

Next, Wilson opined that "a taxing statute is a highly technical piece of legislation which requires an interpretation that will ensure certainty for the taxpayer."[448] After stating that value, she confronted, head on, Estey's majority opinion in *Stubart Investments.* Ontario relied on his interpretive guideline concerning the validity

---

[448] *Mattabi Mines, supra* note 442, SCC para. 20.

of a transaction under a provision regarding a deduction or tax preference:

> (c) 'the object and spirit' of the allowance or benefit provision is defeated by the procedures blatantly adopted by the taxpayer to synthesize a loss, delay or other tax saving device, although these actions may not attain the heights of 'artificiality' in s. 137. This may be illustrated where the taxpayer, in order to qualify for an 'allowance' or a 'benefit', takes steps which the terms of the allowance provisions of the Act may, when taken in isolation and read narrowly, be stretched to support. *However, when the allowance provision is read in the context of the whole statute, and with the 'object and spirit' and purpose of the allowance provision in mind, the accounting result produced by the taxpayer's actions would not, by itself, avail him of the benefit of the allowance* [emphasis added].[449]

Wilson rejected the proposition that this guideline applied; the viability of a transaction was not in issue. But it is noteworthy that the object and spirit of a tax preference was in issue, which was what the guideline concerned. The *coup* was her holding that "the 'object and spirit' of the legislation cannot, in my view, overcome a clear statutory definition."[450] The Supreme Court was said to have no choice in the interpretive approach it could take when interpreting the net loss definition.

In fact, Wilson had just made her own judicial choice to make it clear that her approach to statutory interpretation was correct and not that of Estey. She went out of her way to do so when holding for Ontario and dismissing the taxpayer's appeal. While Ontario lost the interpretive argument, it was successful on the basis that the Supreme Court could not compel Ontario to accept Mattabi Mines' revisions to its tax returns.

---

[449] *Ibid.*, para. 22.

[450] *Ibid.*, para. 23. Wilson found that the interpretive dispute was not one where the Court had a choice of interpretations to "put upon the language used by the legislature."

Chief Justice Dickson and Justices McIntyre, La Forest and L'Heureux-Dubé concurred. Not too much should be made of Dickson's concurrence. He was known not to apply a plain-meaning approach in income tax cases, and a practical matter made it difficult for him to devote time to writing separate reasons. The Supreme Court was faced with a backload of cases, many raising new issues under the *Charter*, while several judges were ill. At one point, only four judges were writing opinions, with Dickson under pressure to release decisions. Estey retired in April 1988. The decision in *Mattabi Mines* was released on October 20, 1988. Beetz, Le Dain and McIntyre retired between November and the end of December 1988.[451]

During this period, some taxpayers were relying on Justice Wilson's *James Richardson & Sons* decision, in conjunction with the Supreme Court's broad and liberal construction of the *Charter*, to argue that they could refuse to comply with a requirement to produce information in respect of an identified taxpayer under the Minister's civil audit powers. A taxpayer's refusal to comply with such a requirement is subject to criminal prosecution, but taxpayers argued that the Minister needed "reasonable and probable cause" to issue the requirement. The Provincial Court of Ontario agreed. If allowed to stand, the decision would undermine Canada's self-assessment income tax system and put in jeopardy the primary source of revenues that funds the Canadian state. The Crown was successful on appeal and the taxpayer appealed to the Supreme Court of Canada.

McKinlay Transport (1990)

McKinlay Transport is part of a trilogy of cases the Supreme Court decided in 1990.[452] The lead dispute concerned a federal combine

---

[451] Anderson, *Judging Bertha Wilson, supra* note 380, p. 155 (and her related footnote 17).

[452] *The Queen v. McKinlay Transport Ltd.*, [1990] 1 SCR 627; *Thomson Newspapers Ltd. v. Director of Investigation and Research, Combines Investigations Act et al.*, [1990] 1 SCR 425; and *Stelco Inc. v. The Attorney General of Canada et al.*, [1990] 1 SCR 617.

investigation of Thomson Newspapers Ltd., which owned the *Globe and Mail.* Although *Thomson Newspapers* is the lead case, *McKinlay Transport* provides a clear example for determining when the *Charter* does not apply to a search or seizure of documents. The Court struggled with the difficult issues before it, and it took almost 18 months from the time it first heard the oral argument on November 1, 1988, until the release of the three decisions on March 29, 1990.

In *Thomson Newspapers*, the company and its officers were served with orders under s. 17 of the *Combines Investigations Act* to produce documents, to appear before the Restrictive Trade Practices Commission and to testify under oath. The Government of Canada suspected that Thomson Newspapers had engaged in predatory pricing practices.

The Ontario High Court held that the orders were unreasonable seizure under s. 8 of the *Charter*, although they did not breach the right of those ordered to testify to life, liberty and the security of the person under s. 7 of the *Charter*. The Ontario Court of Appeal reversed the High Court and found the orders did not violate ss. 7 or 8 of the *Charter*. Thompson Newspapers appealed.

In a split decision, in which one issue had no majority decision, the Supreme Court dismissed Thomson Newspapers' appeal. With respect to the right not to self-incriminate under s. 7, Justices La Forest and L'Heureux-Dubé found, each for different reasons, that the orders to testify did not violate the *Charter*; Justices Wilson and Sopinka found they did, each for different reasons. Justice Lamer found that the question should not be answered because the wrong law was constitutionally challenged. (The challenge was to s. 17 of the *Combines Investigations Act*, while it was s. 20 of that Act and the *Canada Evidence Act* that compelled the testimony.) There was

---

R. v. McKinlay Transport Ltd. – SCC Cases (scc-csc.ca); *Thomson Newspapers Ltd. v. Canada (Director of Investigation and Research, Restrictive Trade Practices Commission)* – SCC Cases (lexum.com); and *Stelco Inc. v. Canada (Attorney General)* – SCC Cases (lexum.com).

no majority formed by the panel on that issue (a 2–2–1 split had occurred), resulting in the decision upholding the Ontario Court of Appeal decision that there was no breach of the right not to self-incriminate under s. 7.

On whether the orders to produce documents were unreasonable search or seizure, by a 3–2 split, the orders were found not to violate the right to be secure from unreasonable search or seizure under s. 8 of the *Charter*. Justices La Forest, L'Heureux-Dubé and Sopinka each wrote separate opinions for the finding. La Forest's reasons in *Thomson Newspapers* are important in understanding the outcome in *McKinlay Transport*. He provided a clear basis for ordering the production of documents.

La Forest found the seizure of documents to be reasonable because the conduct being regulated was far removed from what had been traditionally considered criminal. This law was essentially administrative in nature, and there is a low expectation of privacy for documents used in a business context. The conduct was criminal only in a strictly instrumental sense for the purpose of achieving the statute's regulatory goal of a free market. The offences were not real crimes, but regulatory or public welfare offences. La Forest described them as being comparable to some tax offences; he instructed reference to the Court's decision in *McKinlay Transport*.

Ellen Anderson analyzed Wilson's s. 8 dissent in *Thompson Newspapers*. In a section titled "Guaranteed Rights for Corporations," she indicated that Wilson believed the "coherence" of anti-combine legislation related to ensuring competition had "crumbled," based on the public's no longer having the same moral aversion to large business and the related concerns about competition and a fair market that it had in the late 1880s when the legislation was initially enacted.[453] This is a subjective view that existed at a particular time and place in an era of economic *laissez-faire* and a rights-driven culture. It suggests an inherent peril in *Charter* cases in which the

[453] Anderson, *Judging Bertha Wilson*, *supra* note 380, pp. 262–65 at p. 263.

subjective views of judges can decide the constitutionality of statutory law.

The Supreme Court was delineating the parameters of rights that Parliament could not violate without resorting to the "notwithstanding clause" in s. 33 of the *Charter*. Yet, 30-plus years later, the economy and culture have changed from what they were in 1990, and even if Wilson was right in 1990, which is questionable, the public's view of the need for a fair market and competition may have shifted significantly in light of the way in which large cross-border multinational corporations have evolved, including social media conglomerates. Strong moral overtones of concern may exist.

Unlike La Forest, Wilson also considered the competition law to be criminal in nature rather than administrative. She dissented from allowing the testimony of businessmen to be compelled in hearings even through it could not be used in a criminal proceeding against the witness. But Wilson noted that it exposed the witnesses to the indirect use of the testimony to build a case against the witness. She also dissented from compelling the production of documents, which could be used to build a criminal case against the witness.

But in *McKinlay Transport*, Wilson reached a different outcome in respect of compelling the production of documents under the ITA. She wrote the decision for the Supreme Court. (Justice Lamer concurred, and Justices La Forest, L'Heureux-Dubé and Sopinka agreed subject to their opinions in *Thomson Newspapers*.) Wilson began by describing the issue in terms of its national importance: income tax is the chief source of revenue funding the Canadian state and is collected under a self-reporting system.

> A chief source of revenue for the federal government is the collection of income tax. The legislative scheme which has been put in place to regulate the collection of tax is the *Income Tax Act*. The Act requires taxpayers to file annual returns and estimate their tax payable as a result of calculations

> made in these returns. Moreover, the Act requires various third parties such as employers, corporations and banks to file information on wages, dividends, interest payments and the like: see s. 221(1)(*d*) and Part II of the *Income Tax Regulations*, C.R.C. 1978, c. 945. In essence, the system is a self-reporting and self-assessing one which depends upon the honesty and integrity of the taxpayers for its success: see *Search and Seizure Under the Income Tax Act* (1985), a study paper prepared for the Law Reform Commission of Canada by Neil Brooks and Judy Fudge. Nonetheless, it would be naive to think that no one attempts to take advantage of the self-reporting system in order to avoid paying his or her full share of the tax burden by violating the rules set forth in the Act.[454]

Justice Wilson indicated that the result in *James Richardson & Sons* occurred despite Parliament's broad wording in the audit power provision considered in that case. The Supreme Court had the requirement power "narrowed in scope as a result of the common law rules relating to statutory interpretation, [and now] the appellants submit that the provision cannot withstand *Charter* scrutiny." In other words, the Court's judges in 1984 had intervened as judicial activists armed with their own subjectively delineated values to prevent the Minister from collecting information from a brokerage on unnamed clients to ferret out potential non-compliance and reassess.

A lot had changed in six years once the nature of Canada's self-reporting income tax system was put under direct challenge. The enterprise that funds our very democracy was in direct conflict on a significant issue with *Charter* values. The result was that while the Minister's requirement effected a seizure, it did not violate the *Charter*. There was a low privacy expectation for documents in a self-reporting system; spot checks were required to ensure

[454] *McKinlay Transport*, *supra* note 452, Part 4 (Analysis).

its integrity. The Minister was exercising the power to seize documents not to penalize the taxpayer in the criminal sense but to ensure the taxpayer's compliance in the regulatory-administrative law sense. Reasonable and probable cause was not needed.[455]

The selection of Justice Wilson as one of the nine most influential income tax judges in the history of the Supreme Court is based on her minority 1984 opinion in *Stubart Investments* and her unanimous decisions in *Mattabi Mines* and *McKinlay Transport.* They are three of the most important income tax opinions a Supreme Court justice has issued.

Unlike in *James Richardson & Sons*, Wilson's minority opinion in *Stubart Investments*, when combined with *Mattabi Mines*, provided the Supreme Court with the precedent it used in deciding tax avoidance disputes from 1994 on. During this period, the Court shifted sharply to allowing tax avoidance by emphasizing the legal form of transactions and applying the plain-meaning interpretive approach to the text of an income tax provision, based on commercial interests' seeking certainty when managing their affairs, including the right to avoid tax.

[455] *Ibid.*, Wilson J. stated (p. 648): "At the beginning of my analysis I noted that the *Income Tax Act* was based on the principle of self-reporting and self-assessment. The Act could have provided that each taxpayer submit all his or her records to the Minister and his officials so that they might make the calculations necessary for determining each person's taxable income. … However, a self-reporting system has its drawbacks. Chief among these is that it depends for its success upon the taxpayers' honesty and integrity in preparing their returns. While most taxpayers undoubtedly respect and comply with the system, the facts of life are that certain persons will attempt to take advantage of the system and avoid their full tax liability. Accordingly, the Minister … must be given broad powers in supervising this regulatory scheme to audit taxpayers' returns and inspect all records which may be relevant to the preparation of these returns. The Minister must be capable of exercising these powers whether or not he has reasonable grounds for believing that a particular taxpayer has breached the Act. Often it will be impossible to determine from the face of the return whether any impropriety has occurred in its preparation. A spot check … may be the only way in which the integrity of the tax system can be maintained."

Bertha Wilson indicated in her Foreword to Dr. Ellen Anderson's biography of her that Anderson had become her "philosophical alter ego … [and advised the reader:] 'Yes, that is me.'" Anderson concluded in her biography that Wilson saw and experienced our law and society as "a rolling evolution of law and society in which perpetual change is not feared but confidently accepted; a conviction that principle is not eroded but sustained when we pay vigilant attention to contextual fluctuations … ."[456] In income tax, Justice Wilson's opinions arose over a brief period of less than nine years in which strong contextual fluctuations were present, and she sought to achieve a balance between taxpayers and the Crown by emphasizing the strict or plain-meaning approach because business needs certainty in a context in which Parliament can amend the tax law if necessary.

Justice Bertha Wilson retired in 1991. She was replaced by Justice Frank Iacobucci. Bertha Wilson died in 2007.

[456] Anderson, *supra* note 380, p. xi (Foreword) and p. 384 (Life After Judging).

FRANK IACOBUCCI: THE KEY MESSENGER

Progressive Conservative Prime Minister Brian Mulroney elevated Frank Iacobucci to the Supreme Court in 1991 (after appointing him the Chief Justice of the Federal Court of Appeal in 1988), replacing Justice Bertha Wilson.

The son of working-class Italian immigrants, Frank Iacobucci is a native of British Columbia, and he had worked with his father in a steel foundry to help pay for his education. He graduated with a law degree in 1962 from the University of British Columbia. Iacobucci, who also studied at Cambridge, began his legal career practicing corporate law in New York in the 1960s. By 1967, he shifted to teaching corporate-commercial law at the University of Toronto Law School and later became the Deputy Minister of Justice and Deputy Attorney General of Canada.

Soon after his arrival at the Supreme Court in 1991, Iacobucci began writing precedent-setting decisions one after another until his retirement. Strongly pro-taxpayer and commercial interests, especially in tax avoidance matters, Iacobucci heard 43 income tax cases of which 16 concerned tax avoidance. His decisions for the taxpayer include these 10 precedent-setting cases: *Friedberg* (1993),[457] *Antosko* (1994), *Tennant* (1996), *Neuman* (1998), *Duha Printers* (1998), *65302 British Columbia Ltd.* (1999),[458] *Ludco Enterprises* (2001), *Spire Freezers* (2001),[459] *Stewart* (2002) and *Walls* (2002). (Justice Michel

---

[457] *Friedberg v. The Queen*, [1993] 4 SCR 285. *Friedberg v. Canada* – SCC Cases (scc-csc.ca).

[458] *65302 British Columbia Ltd. v. The Queen*, [1999] 3 SCR 804. *65302 British Columbia Ltd. v. Canada* – SCC Cases (scc-csc.ca).

[459] *Spire Freezers Ltd. v. The Queen*, [2001] 1 SCR 391, 2001 SCC 11. Also see *Backman v. The Queen*, [2001] 1 SCR 367, 2001 SCC 10. The two cases concern whether certain American entities were partnerships for the purposes of Canadian income tax law. In both cases there was an allocation of "partnership losses" from the United States to incoming Canadian partners who sought to deduct the losses from their Canadian income. The Supreme Court found for the taxpayer in *Spire Freezers* and for the Crown in *Backman*. *Spire Freezers Ltd. v. Canada* – SCC Cases (scc-csc.ca) and *Backman v. Canada* –SCC Cases (lexum.com).

Bastarache co-wrote the latter three decisions.) Many of the decisions broke from the Supreme Court's pre-1984 precedent.

This break should be expected because Iacobucci emphasized the legal form of transactions in tax avoidance cases, even if that form is questionable in terms of commercial substance and reality. When doing so, he applied a literal or plain-meaning approach to interpret the ITA (usually called "plain meaning" in what follows). But there were limited exceptions as in 1995, when Iacobucci used the purposive approach to interpret an international tax treaty in *Crown Forest*;[460] the Crown succeeded. Two other exceptions are considered below.

When examining Justice Iacobucci's work, we do not have the advantage, unlike with Justice Wilson, of knowing why he emphasized legal form and the plain-meaning approach when interpreting and applying income tax provisions despite its inconsistency with the Supreme Court's pre-1984 failure to adhere to the British *Duke of Westminster* principle in such cases. The answer to why may be in what is arguably Justice Iacobucci's most important income tax decision—his majority 1993 opinion in the nanny expense case called *Symes*, which arose in a *Charter* context.[461] The evidence is both circumstantial and suggestive that Iacobucci may have varied his approach, starting with *Symes*.

The Supreme Court's decision in *Symes* needs context. For almost everyone, income tax is a boring fact of life and death, not a career that inspires, challenges and on occasion frustrates. For that latter rump group, it is easy to fall into the trap of assuming that the Supreme Court decides income tax disputes within the confines of the income tax system, and that the Court's approach should be based on the merits of the cases in the context of interpreting the statutory law and applying it to the facts in a principled manner. But that is too simplistic, as it fails to account for the broader world that is swirling beyond the confines of the income tax system

[460] *Crown Forest Industries Ltd. v. The Queen*, [1995] 2 SCR 802. *Crown Forest Industries Ltd. v. Canada* – SCC Cases (scc-csc.ca).

[461] *Symes, supra* note 93. *Symes v. Canada* – SCC Cases (scc-csc.ca).

and the Supreme Court Building in Ottawa—the world of faith, family, commerce, economics, influence, politics, social conditions and *realpolitik* activism.

In late 1992, University of Windsor law professor Ian Bushnell published *The Captive Court*.[462] For the left, his book on the history of the Supreme Court as an institution was a call to seize the moment and advance social and *Charter* values. Bushnell maintained that the Court as an institution as well as its judges were captive to the needs of commercial interests in the pre-*Charter* era. In this context, the Court was said to be a "captive court," including to British precedent. Bushnell wrote: "In that world, certainty in the conduct of business affairs was the prime requisite. What was not wanted were creative arbitrators who were concerned with notions of justice and able to alter the rules. Changes in the rules should only occur through the actions of the legislature in response to the political power of the commercial world."[463]

Bushnell advanced a theory that was in support of effecting law reform through activist judicial statutory interpretation that incorporates social and *Charter* values into the judicial function. The conceit of some is that their social values are or should be everyone's social values whether they like it or not.

In advancing this activist agenda, Bushnell carved out a safe harbour for commercial and tax law. He noted that the task of giving meaning to a legal rule is commonly described in academic literature as "a choice: to adopt the literal or plain meaning of the words, or to try and determine, as best as can be done, the actual purpose behind the rule and to decide accordingly."[464] Essentially, Bushnell in *The Captive Court* seeks to distinguish public policy needs from the needs of the corporate-commercial world of commerce. He advocated use of the purposive approach instilled with social and *Charter* values while limiting the application of the plain-meaning

[462] Ian Bushnell, *The Captive Court*, *supra* note 157.
[463] *Ibid.*, p. 57.
[464] *Ibid.*, p. 60.

approach to commerce and tax. Bushnell appears to have made a calculated decision to advance a theory that would not upset or confront powerful interests within the commercial world.

There are holes in Bushnell's theory. He never analyzed in any meaningful way the Supreme Court's income tax decisions from the 1950s to 1983. He appears to assume the Court was captive to British precedent and applied the plain-meaning approach in income tax cases during the period. This is incorrect and undermines his theory.[465] However, it began to take hold, and if the Court's 1993–2002 income tax precedent is reflective of what happened in a broader law context, the dispute inside and outside the confines of the Court was and remains contentious.

The analysis of Justice Iacobucci's approach to income tax and its avoidance below opens with two disputes from 1993.

---

[465] Bushnell is not the only academic to suggest that the Supreme Court was captive to British precedent in the pre-*Charter* era. Peter McCormick applied statistical analysis to the Court's decisions from 1944 to the end of 1999, which also suggested the Court was essentially captive to British precedent in the pre-*Charter* era (see McCormick, *Supreme at Last*, *supra* note 84). But neither McCormick nor Bushnell accounted for the modernized 1948 ITA. An analysis of the Court's related income tax decisions shows that their theory does not hold up in an income tax context. For example, while McCormick's statistical analysis suggested the Court never cited its own precedent more than 50 percent of the time before the 1990s, the percentage exceeds 50 percent in income tax cases for the period from April 1963 to the end of March 1973. The Court's percentage of citing its own precedent during that period exceeds all other periods he analyzed except for the 1990–99 tenure of Lamer C.J. But even then, the Lamer Court's citation of the Court (55.8 percent) only narrowly exceeds citations of the Court in income tax cases in the period 1963–73 (53.1 percent). Note: I undertook a manual count of the Court's citations in income tax cases during that period and compared the results to McCormick's results. If one were to pull the income tax cases from McCormick's data base, presumably his statistics would skew even more to his theory. But his and Bushnell's theory does not appear to account for the Court's taking its signal from Parliament, not academics and a social-activist agenda. Once Parliament modernized the income tax law, the Court began to move away from citing British precedent in income tax cases except in certain niche areas where it remained relevant such as in adventure disputes, which date to the 19th century in the United Kingdom. See also the discussion at *supra* notes 405 and 410.

They occur just as Bushnell's theory takes hold for social activists inside and outside Canadian law schools.

Sie-Mac Pipeline Contractors (1993)

In 1984, Sie-Mac Pipeline Contractors Limited (Sie-Mac) entertained clients at a remote fishing lodge in British Columbia that could accommodate up to 24 guests. The facility was the Hoeya Hilton. The breakdown of 14 attendees was as follows: seven customers, five employees of Sie-Mac and two employees of a related company.[466] The retreat's purpose was to show appreciation to customers and to inform them of new equipment and techniques. Business meetings could be held for one to two hours a day, but everyone was there to have a great time at Sie-Mac's expense; the main activity was fishing.

Sie-Mac's guests travelled by commercial airline from Edmonton to Vancouver where the Hoeya Hilton's Twin Otter plane transported them to the facility. The trip cost Sie-Mac $12,800, pocket change for a company the size of Sie-Mac. The expenses consisted of rooms, meals, transportation, fishing guides, fishing licences, alcohol, tobacco and the cost of canning fish. Sie-Mac deducted the $12,800 when computing its business income for its 1984 taxation year.

The Minister denied the deduction. For the Minister, allowing such expenses however modest in the context of a taxpayer's overall commercial expenses would set a precedent under which other taxpayers would deduct similar and larger amounts. Sie-Mac appealed as a matter of principle; for it, the cost of litigation would far exceed the value of the expenses if they were deductible.

Specifically, the issue was whether the expenses were deductible, given an express denial of the deductibility of expenses for using

[466] *Sie-Mac Pipeline Contractors Limited v. The Queen*, [1993] 1 SCR 895, dismissing the taxpayer's appeal from 92 DTC 6461, [1992] 1 CTC 341 (FCA), which allowed the Minister's appeal from 90 DTC 6344, [1990] 2 CTC 8 (FCTD), which affirmed 89 DTC 230, [1989] 1 CTC 2334 (TCC). *Sie-Mac Pipeline Contractors Ltd. v. M.N.R.* – SCC Cases (scc-csc.ca).

certain recreational facilities, one of which is a lodge as referred to in para. 18(1)(*l*). Sie-Mac's position was that it was paying for services and that it did not have the use of the whole lodge, which could accommodate 24 guests, although no other guests were at the facility at the time. The expenses were said to be no different from those paid to hotels for services, and they were incurred for the purpose of gaining income from a source. The Minister maintained that Sie-Mac paid to use a lodge, and the related expenses were disallowed.

The Tax Court allowed Sie-Mac's appeal on the basis the lodge was akin to a hotel that provided services, as Sie-Mac did not rent or have exclusive use of the facility. The Minister appealed. The Federal Court–Trial Division agreed with the Tax Court, and the Minister appealed.

Justice Allen Linden for the Federal Court of Appeal reversed the lower courts. He did so on the basis Parliament had, as a matter of policy, decided to disallow deductions in respect of using certain recreational facilities, including lodges, even if they were incurred for the purpose of gaining income. (Justices Heald and Stone concurred.)

Linden noted the obvious anomaly that entertainment expenses were deductible in most business contexts but not expenses at certain types of clubs, and in respect of yachts and lodges. But he applied Parliamentary intent despite any technical arguments about the meaning of the word "use." In doing so, he respected a policy decision Parliament made, even if its text created anomalies some might consider unfair. Sie-Mac appealed.

Justice Iacobucci's unanimous decision was short and to the point. He dismissed Sie-Mac's appeal, based on the reasons of Justice Linden (with Justices La Forest, Gonthier, Cory, and Major).[467]

---

[467] *Ibid.*, SCC pp. 895–96. Iacobucci J. held for the Court: "We are all of the view that this appeal should be dismissed for the reasons given by Mr. Justice Linden of the Federal Court of Appeal. The expenses in question are clearly precluded by the provisions of subpara. 18(1)(*l*)(i) of the *Income Tax Act, R.S.C.* 1952."

The timing of the Supreme Court's brief decision in *Sie-Mac* on March 23, 1993, is relevant in understanding the Court's decision to affirm Justice Linden's decision. *Sie-Mac* was decided as follows:

- 2 months *after* the Court's *Charter* decision on search warrants in *Baron,*[468] in which Justice John Sopinka, for a unanimous Court, held that the Minister's search warrant power was unconstitutional as written in the ITA (Justices La Forest, L'Heureux-Dubé, Cory, McLachlin and Iacobucci concurred).
- 6 months *before Slattery (Trustee of).*[469]
- 9 months *before Symes.*[470]
- 14 months *before Antosko.*[471]

This timing places *Sie-Mac* within a *Charter*-era period during which the Supreme Court struggled over what approach to take when interpreting the statutory income tax law. By spring 1994, the Court retreated to the plain-meaning safe harbour that Bushnell carved out for commercial and tax law when he argued the judiciary should advance an activist law reform agenda by instilling social and *Charter* values into the rules of statutory interpretation.

From 1982 to at least 1992, *Charter* disputes had clogged the Supreme Court's docket. This delayed Justice Wilson's attempt in her minority opinion in *Stubart Investments* to resurrect the British *Duke of Westminster* principle. But Wilson provided a clear direction

---

[468] *The Queen v. Berl Baron and Howard Baron, C.A.*, [1993] 1 SCR 416. *Baron v. Canada* – SCC Cases (scc-csc.ca).
[469] *Slattery (Trustee of) v. Slattery*, [1993] 3 SCR 430. *Slattery (Trustee of) v. Slattery* – SCC Cases (scc-csc.ca).
[470] *Symes*, *supra* note 93.
[471] *H. Boris Antosko and Stanley F. Trzop v. The Queen,* [1994] 2 SCR 312, allowing the taxpayers' appeals from 92 DTC 6388, [1992] 2 CTC 350 (FCA), which affirmed 90 DTC 6111, [1990] 1 CTC 208 (FCTD), which had allowed the Minister's appeal from an unreported decision of the Tax Court of Canada. *Canada v. Antosko* – SCC Cases (lexum.com).

for doing so, regardless of what one may think about that direction. She had followed up in *Mattabi Mines* by undermining Justice Estey's attempt to find a more balanced approach.

Wilson's decisions were seized on to navigate to open water when interpreting the statutory income tax law despite what Estey may have said in *Stubart Investments* and what had occurred in the Supreme Court's income tax precedent before 1984. Myths were soon created about that precedent's adhering to the plain-meaning approach, based on the *Duke of Westminster* principle.

But, initially at least, Iacobucci relied on the unifying textual, contextual and purposive interpretive approach. The precedent that builds over the 1990s is like a ship that is struggling to break free from its pre-*Charter* commercial substance and reality mooring to glide independently forward away from the shoals denoted by social and *Charter* values. As one reads Iacobucci's decisions in order, one can see the ship setting a course destined for the plain-meaning approach.

Slattery (1993)

On September 30, 1993, Justice Iacobucci led a 6–3 Supreme Court majority in *Slattery (Trustee of)*, holding that Revenue Canada officials can testify about the tax affairs of a taxpayer in a proceeding under the *Bankruptcy and Insolvency Act.* (Chief Justice Antonia Lamer and Justices La Forest, Gonthier, Cory and Major concurred.) The Minister had petitioned the taxpayer into bankruptcy, and the taxpayer's privacy interest gave way to the effective administration and enforcement of the ITA.

Iacobucci began his analysis of the statutory law with a summary of why that law allowed Revenue Canada officials to testify at the proceedings in bankruptcy. He based his decision on the law's policy and purposes, its text and the context.

> An analysis of the history of s. 241, its underlying purposes and policy, its text and context, applicable judicial authority, and the nature of the proceedings involved herein, leads

> me to conclude that the courts below were correct in their holdings and that this appeal should be dismissed.[472]

Justice McLachlin dissented, and Justices L'Heureux-Dubé and Sopinka concurred.

Less than three months later, the Supreme Court decided *Symes* on December 16, 1993.

Symes (1993)

Justice Iacobucci wrote the 7–2 majority opinion, with Justices Claire L'Heureux-Dubé and Beverley McLachlin issuing separate dissents. *Symes* concerns a woman who deducted nanny expenses against her law business income. The Supreme Court's decision is about *Charter* values as much as it concerns the deductibility of nanny expenses. If successful, high-income women (and presumably men) in business could benefit by deducting nanny expenses.[473]

Both Iacobucci, for the majority, and L'Heureux-Dubé, in dissent, cited with approval Wilson's 1988 unanimous decision in *Mattabi Mines* on the approach to take when interpreting business deduction provisions. Wilson's textual approach was gaining support.

It is in this context that Justice Iacobucci in December 1993 held, for the majority, in *Symes* that *Charter* values should not inform the interpretation of statutory law—if no ambiguity exists in the legislation. (Chief Justice Lamer and Justices La Forest,

---

[472] *Slattery (Trustee of), supra* note 469. McLachlin J. dissented; L'Heureux-Dubé, Sopinka, JJ. concurred. The wrinkle for her was that the Trustee, not the Minister, sought to put the testimony of the Revenue Canada officials into evidence. After noting this, McLachlin J. applied s. 241 of the ITA to disallow the testimony (s. 241 allows testimony for administering and enforcing the Act). She did so despite the fact s. 222 of the *Income Tax Act* expressly allows the Minister to resort to a court of competent jurisdiction to collect income tax debts (which Iacobacci J. noted in his decision). *Slattery (Trustee of) v. Slattery* – SCC Cases (scc-csc.ca).

[473] *Symes, supra* note 93. The nanny expenses were found to be non-deductible "personal and living" expenses when computing income from a business source. *Symes v. Canada* – SCC Cases (lexum.com).

Gonthier, Cory and Major concurred).[474] There was no ambiguity because there is a clear regime for deducting childcare expenses, which Symes bypassed when deducting her nanny expenses from business income.

Both Justices Iacobucci and L'Heureux-Dubé speculated on why and when the deductibility test for business expenses is more liberal under the modern income tax statutes when compared to the *Income War Tax Act*. This was discussed earlier when reviewing Justice Abbott's methodology for applying the "for the purpose of gaining or producing income" test in the modern income

---

[474] *Ibid.* Iacobucci J. stated (p. 752): "I agree with this sentiment [that the values embodied in the *Charter* must be given preference over an interpretation that is inconsistent with or contrary to *Charter* values] reflected in both of these quotations, but I fail to see their relevance in this case. In both *Hills* [[1988] 1 SCR 513] and *Slaight Communications* [[1989] 1 SCR 1038], this Court was confronted with statutory language which was ambiguous. In each case, the values of the *Charter* were consulted to resolve the ambiguity. However, each case recognizes that to consult the *Charter* in the absence of such ambiguity is to deprive the *Charter* of a more powerful purpose, namely, the determination of a statute's constitutional validity. If statutory meanings must be made congruent with the *Charter* even in the absence of ambiguity, then it would never be possible to apply, rather than simply consult, the values of the *Charter*. Furthermore, it would never be possible for the government to justify infringements as reasonable limits under s. 1 of the *Charter*, since the interpretative process would preclude one from finding infringements in the first place" [emphasis in original].

In 1995, Iacobucci J. was in the majority that found 5–2 that the payer deduction for alimony and its corresponding recipient inclusion in income rule were not discriminatory under the *Charter*. His opinion was that the rules did not impose a burden or withhold a benefit and therefore were not discriminatory (Cory J. concurred); Sopinka and La Forest JJ. issued a short opinion agreeing with Iacobucci, Cory, and Gonthier JJ. that the rules did not impose a burden or withhold a benefit; Gonthier J. issued an opinion the reasoning of which differed from that of Iacobucci and Cory JJ.; and McLachlin and L'Heureux-Dubé JJ. issued separate dissents. See *The Queen v. Suzanne Thibaudeau*, [1995] 2 SCR 627. *Thibaudeau v. Canada* – SCC Cases (scc-csc.ca).

tax statutes. Neither Iacobucci nor L'Heureux-Dubé traced their analysis back to that methodology.[475]

Iacobucci noted that the childcare expense regime requires the lower-income parent to deduct the expenses. Symes was advocating a result that was free of this limitation and the maximum amount that could be deducted under the childcare expense regime, which would result in a family decision to have the parent with the business income responsible for childcare deduct the full amount of the expenses from their business income.

Justice Iacobucci also found that the child-expense regime was the proper focus for considering Symes' s. 15 right to equality, and under it, there was no distinction made based on a person's sex. While childcare negatively affects women in terms of employment, incurring social costs for childcare exist outside the confines of the statutory income tax law, which does not recognize imputed income or involve itself with imputed expenses.

The Supreme Court split along gender lines, with the two female justices dissenting. They interpreted the law to allow a deduction of nanny expenses in computing Symes' law business income and found that interpreting the law to deny the deduction

---

[475] Although the Supreme Court considered in *Symes* its 1957 decision in *Canada Safeway* ([1957] SCR 717), it did not consider Abbott J.'s 1958 majority decision in *British Columbia Electric Railway Co.* (*supra* note 92) nor Kerwin CJ.'s 1959 decision in *Bannerman* (*supra* note 67), which decisions are profiled. While interest deductions were denied in *Canada Safeway,* the dispute concerned interpreting both the *Income War Tax Act* and the 1948 ITA and the Court's reasoning was splintered. Kerwin CJ. disallowed the deductions after focusing his analysis on the provisions of the *Income War Tax* Act while also indicating the 1948 ITA clarified the situation (Taschereau J. concurred). Rand J. held, after excerpting the relevant provisions of the ITA, that the interest expenses were too "indirect or remote" from the source. While Cartwright J. agreed with the conclusions of both Kerwin and Rand, he did not comment on their reasoning. Locke J. dissented. Essentially the Court's subsequent decisions in *British Columbia Electric Railway Co.* and *Bannerman* require expenses to be "connected" to a source and not be too remote or too indirect from the source. Canada Safeway Limited v. Minister of National Revenue - SCC Cases (scc-csc.ca).

would infringe Symes' right to equality under s. 15 of the *Charter*. In doing so, Justices L'Heureux-Dubé and McLachlin failed to draw any distinction between nanny expenses that higher-income, self-employed parents can afford when compared to the daycare expenses working parents generally pay. This is a class distinction: working-class parents could not benefit from such a class-oriented result unlike female self-employed lawyers.

By conditioning the interpretative role of *Charter* values on ambiguity, Justice Iacobucci protected the ITA from activist justices—wielding *Charter* values as an interpretative aid. Having made his choice, he was normally consistent in his subsequent precedent-setting decisions. The difficulty with his approach is that it allows a judge to determine whether that text is unambiguous without considering the context in which the text is found and its purpose. In other words, the plain-meaning approach can be wielded to cut statutory interpretation off from the unifying textual, contextual and purposive approach. The result when parsing statutory text could not have been better for tax planners, as the meaning of text is dissociated from its context and purpose.

The result in a tax avoidance context was immediate; it showed up less than six months later in the following case in which Justice Iacobucci wrote the unanimous decision.

Antosko (1994)

By March 1971, the New Brunswick Industrial Board, an arm of the Government of New Brunswick, owned 80 percent of Atlantic Forest Products Ltd. The Board guaranteed $3 million of bank loans made to Atlantic Forest. Between 1972 and July 1973, it also made four loans to Atlantic Forest, totalling $1.425 million, receiving promissory notes in return, payable at interest rates varying from 5 percent to 9.5 percent.

In September 1974, Atlantic Forest defaulted on the bank loans, and the Board honoured its guarantee. The loans and four promissory notes (debt instruments) comprised the total that Atlantic

Forest owed the Board. By March 1975, Atlantic Forest owed it about $5 million.[476]

The Board sold its shares in Atlantic Forest in March 1975 for $1 to Boris Antosko and Stanley Trzop, professional engineers and former university classmates with an entrepreneurial flair. Atlantic Forest was debt free except for $5 million plus accruing interest owed to the Board. Repayment of the debt instruments and accruing interest was deferred for two years to give Antosko and Trzop time to turn the enterprise around, saving the jobs of its employees if successful.

Atlantic Forest owned land, plant and machinery. If all went well business-wise, the Board agreed to sell its $5 million of debt instruments (and accruing interest) to Antosko and Trzop for $10.

Paragraph 20(14)(*a*) of the 1972 Act concerns accrued interest on a debt instrument paid after the transfer of the instrument. The rule is meant to prevent an owner of the instrument from avoiding tax on the accrued interest by transferring the instrument before it is received. Without the rule, the transferor could argue that the value of the accruing interest is reflected in the proceeds of disposition of the note, which would generally be a disposition of capital property. Given the paragraph requires the transferor of the debt instrument to include the accrued interest in income, para. 20(14)(*b*) provides the transferee-purchaser a deduction of the interest, based on the assumption its vendor included the accrued interest in its taxable income.

But, in *Antosko*, the transferor of the debt instruments was a tax-exempt provincial Board, which was not subject to income tax on the accrued interest. Antosko and Trzop claimed that did not matter. By July 1977, they satisfied the necessary commitments to New Brunswick and obtained from the Board for $10 the $5 million debt instruments. Interest accrued daily on the debt instruments at a variable rate, depending on the instrument, of 5 percent to 11.5 percent per annum.

---

[476] *Antosko*, *supra* note 471, *Canada v. Antosko* – SCC Cases (lexum.com).

Antosko and Trzop each received $38,335 of interest from the debt instruments in 1977. They included the interest in income and claimed a deduction under para. 20(14)(*b*). In 1980, Antosko and Trzop each received $283,363 of interest, which they included in income and claimed as a deduction.

With respect to their purchases of debt instruments for $10, which had hundreds of thousands of dollars of accrued interest, Antosko and Trzop maintained the transaction was not structured to defeat the intent of Parliament; rather, they acquired the debt instruments to preserve economic control of the company.

Justice Arthur Stone of the Federal Court of Appeal in 1992 held that given economic and commercial reality, the "object and spirit" of subs. 20(14) was such that Antosko and Trzop did not qualify for the deductions.[477] (Chief Justice Isaac and Justice Heald concurred.) Antosko and Trzop appealed.

Justice Iacobucci took issue with the Federal Court of Appeal's reliance on object and spirit and economic and commercial reality. For the Supreme Court, he reversed the Federal Court of Appeal. (Justices La Forest, L'Heureux-Dubé, Gonthier and Major concurred.) In doing so, he read down the context and purpose aspects of the textual, contextual and purposive interpretive approach and read up its text. The text was supposedly "clear" and, henceforth, a plain-meaning approach applied when interpreting statutory income tax law. Iacobucci's citation of Wilson's decision in *Mattabi Mines* coupled with his own decision in *Symes* sticks out like a sore thumb in his reasoning.

> While it is true that the courts must view discrete sections of the *Income Tax Act* in light of other provisions of the Act and of the purpose of the legislation, and that they must analyze a given transaction in the context of economic and commercial reality, such techniques cannot alter the

[477] *Ibid.*, FCA at 92 DTC pp. 6392–94 (economic and commercial reality) and 6394 (object and spirit).

> result where the words of the statute are clear and plain and where the legal and practical effect of the transaction is undisputed: *Mattabi Mines Ltd.* … [1988] 2 SCR 175, at p. 194; see also *Symes* …, [1993] 4 SCR 695.[478]

Antosko and Trzop could rely on para. 20(14)(*b*) read literally, and it did not matter that they purchased their debt instruments from a tax-exempt Board. They did not have to respect the context, purpose and spirit of paras. 20(14)(*a*) and (*b*) when avoiding income tax.

What occurred in *Antosko* confirms a shift in which the Supreme Court emphasized the plain-meaning approach when interpreting statutory income tax law in the face of the alternative—activist judges wielding social and *Charter* values to interpret a statute whose primary purpose is, as indicated by Douglas Abbott in 1948, to impose tax on persons earning income from economic activity.[479]

Justice Iacobucci's next significant income tax decision concerned the deductibility of interest on a loan incurred in 1981 to buy $1 million of shares, which were disposed of at a loss of $999,000 in 1985. In his decision, he veers from the plain-meaning approach despite taking that approach in *Antosko*. Why?

John M. Tennant (1996)

John Tennant borrowed $1 million from the Royal Bank in 1981 to purchase shares costing $1 million from an arm's length private Canadian corporation, Realwest Energy Corporation. Tennant was

---

[478] *Ibid.*, SCC pp. 326–27.

[479] See Part II (Justice Abbott). A wobble in this shift to the plain-meaning approach occurred four months later. Gonthier J., for a unanimous Supreme Court in late September 1994, applied the "teleological approach" in *Québec (Communauté urbaine) v. Corp. Notre Dame de BonSecours*, [1994] 3 SCR. The case concerns property taxes imposed on real estate. In general, under that approach, a strict or liberal interpretive approach should be applied to a provision depending on its purpose, which purpose is to be determined based on the context of the statute, its objective, and the legislative intent. *Québec (Communauté urbaine) v. Corp. Notre-Dame de Bon-Secours* – SCC Cases (scc-csc.ca).

required to pay interest on the loan until he repaid the principal.[480] By July 1985, Tennant's shares were worth only $1,000, and he transferred them to an arm's length company TWL Holdings Ltd. (TWL) for one thousand shares of TWL ($1,000 in total). He realized a capital loss of $999,000.

If certain conditions are met, a capital loss is an "allowable business investment loss"; 50 percent of the capital loss is deductible against ordinary income in the year it is incurred instead of being restricted to reducing taxable capital gains. The underlying policy allowing deductibility of allowable business investment losses (ABILs) is to encourage individuals to invest in Canadian-controlled private corporations, knowing that if a loss ensues, 50 percent of it may be deducted against income.

Tennant continued to deduct interest on his $1 million loan despite selling his Realwest shares for shares of TWL, costing $1,000. By 1987, Realwest was restructured, and after its prospects improved, it paid a large dividend to TWL, which in turn paid a $316,232 dividend to Tennant. He used the dividend to repay in part his $1 million loan from the Royal Bank.

The Minister objected to Tennant's deduction of interest in 1985 and 1986 to the extent it concerned principal that exceeded $1,000 invested in TWL shares. Tennant unsuccessfully appealed to the Federal Court–Trial Division and the Federal Court of Appeal.

The Federal Court refused to look beyond the legal form of the investment. It noted Tennant claimed an ABIL and "he therefore should be precluded from maintaining the position that this original investment vehicle did not disappear, but merely changed its form."[481] The Federal Court applied *Bronfman Trust* on the basis that the interest was not deductible on the excess because there was no direct use of borrowed funds to acquire the TWL shares.

[480] *John M. Tennant v. The Queen*, [1996] 1 SCR 305, allowing the taxpayer's appeal from 94 DTC 6505, [1994] 2 CTC 113 (FCA), which affirmed 93 DTC 5067, [1993] 1 CTC 148 (FCTD). *Tennant v. M.N.R.* – SCC Cases (scc-csc.ca).
[481] *Ibid.*, FCTD at 93 DTC p. 5072.

On appeal, Justice Francis McDonald of the Federal Court of Appeal found Tennant's Realwest shares ceased to be a source of income after their disposition on July 25, 1985. The result was Tennant's interest deductions were limited to interest payable on $1,000—the cost of the TWL shares. Tennant appealed.

Justice Iacobucci, for a unanimous Supreme Court, reversed the lower courts. He indicated that he did so based on the purpose of the interest deductibility provision.[482] But, in doing so, he did not follow the Court's commercial substance precedent. Instead, something unusual occurred in *Tennant* that reveals itself when the decision is analyzed in light of its result. (Justices La Forest, Sopinka, Gonthier, Cory, McLachlin and Major concurred.)

In the first paragraph, Iacobucci stated: "This appeal involves the question of whether interest can be deducted by a taxpayer on a loan to purchase shares when the shares have been disposed of on a rollover transaction."[483] Framing the issue as a rollover is problematic because there was no rollover transaction although Tennant relied on s. 85, which can result in a rollover to the extent the cost of the old shares became the cost of the new shares. The word "rollover" in the *dicta* infers Tenant's $1 million cost of Realwest shares financed with the loan rolled over into the cost of the TWL shares. That is simply not the case, as Tennant realized a $999,000 capital loss meaning the cost of his TWL shares would be $1,000; this raises questions about the resulting judgment.

In the fourth paragraph Iacobucci stated: "In substance, the appellant's economic interest in Realwest did not change subsequent to the disposition of the Realwest shares."[484] By emphasizing substance over legal form, Iacobucci described the issue as being whether Tennant could deduct interest under para. 20(1)(*c*) of the 1972 Act on a loan after disposing of the shares for one thousand shares of TWL.

Next, Justice Iacobucci indicated what he believed is the purpose underlying the interest deductibility provision in para.

---

[482] *Ibid.*, SCC para. XVI.

[483] *Ibid.*, SCC para. I, p. 307.

[484] *Ibid.*, SCC para. IV, p. 308.

20(1)(*c*): "The purpose of the interest deduction provision is to encourage the accumulation of capital which would produce taxable income, as Dickson C.J. noted in *Bronfman Trust*."[485] After reviewing *Bronfman Trust*, Iacobucci found that "implicit" in its principles is that the ability to deduct interest is not lost because a taxpayer sells an income-producing property, as long as he reinvests in an eligible use.[486] He distinguished the Federal Court of Appeal's 1986 decision in *Emerson*, which the lower courts' applied to limit the interest deductions to the $1,000 of the original principal.[487]

Chief Justice Dickson emphasized in *Bronfman Trust* that "the borrowed funds must still be in the hands of the taxpayer, as traced through the proceeds of disposition in respect of the ineligible use."[488] Tennant's $1 million of borrowed funds traced through to $1,000 of proceeds only. In comparison, Iacobucci treated the non-rollover election under s. 85 as if it resulted in a rollover of Tennant's borrowed $1 million cost in his Realwest shares into the TWL shares. The judicial justification was weak; the value of shares fluctuates, complicating the question of interest deductions. He extended interest deductibility to the original amount of the loan despite the realization of a $999,000 capital loss (a $499,500 ABIL).

Justice Iacobucci's 1996 approach in *Tennant* is surprising because he was in the process of entrenching in the Supreme

[485] *Ibid.*, SCC para. XVI, p. 320.

[486] *Ibid.*, SCC para. XX.

[487] *Russell I. Emerson v. The Queen*, 86 DTC 6184, [1986] 1 CTC 422 (FCA). In *Emerson*, the taxpayer borrowed $100,000 to buy shares that were sold for $35,000, with the taxpayer borrowing an additional $63,750 to repay the original loan. The Federal Court of Appeal held that the interest on the second loan was non-deductible and the source no longer existed in respect of the first loan. Iacobucci J. distinguished *Emerson* on the basis that (para. XXI, p. 320): "[T]he proceeds of disposition in that case were not reinvested into a second eligible use property, unlike the case at hand." Comment: But the taxpayer's proceeds of disposition had to be $1,000, not $1 million, to realize a capital loss of $999,000 if those shares cost $1 million.

[488] *Bronfman Trust*, *supra* note 366, SCC p. 47. *Bronfman Trust v. The Queen* – SCC Cases (scc-csc.ca).

Court's jurisprudence the plain-meaning approach when interpreting income tax law, in which legal form trumps commercial substance. The difficulty with emphasizing legal form in *Tennant* is that the statutory text and legal form of the transactions worked against Tennant, and doing so should have meant Tennant would be denied the interest deductions. As such, the *Tennant* decision is result-oriented with the objective of expanding interest deductibility well beyond what was allowed in precedent. Moreover, this view is supported by Iacobucci's *obiter*, which is inconsistent with key aspects of the Court's 1987 decision in *Bronfman Trust*.

The appropriateness of Justice Iacobucci's decision in *Tennant* is a matter of opinion. What cannot be denied is that the Supreme Court steadfastly refused to divert from a plain reading of the statutory text in tax avoidance cases yet in *Tennant* the Court refrained in the non-tax avoidance case from applying the plain-meaning approach. The *Tennant* decision is a marked departure from the general thrust of the Court's income tax precedent beginning in 1994.

The next two decisions concern the meaning of "legal control" of a corporation and tax avoidance through income splitting.

Duha Printers (Western) Limited (1998)

Duha Printers concerns a series of transactions undertaken to circumvent a corporate business-continuity rule that applies on an acquisition of corporate control.[489] Subsection 111(5) is meant to constrain corporate-loss trading by arm's length persons. In general, its text applies where a person acquires control of an arm's length corporation with loss carryovers; the provision denies the deductibility of the business loss carryovers unless the business that incurred the losses continues on with a reasonable expectation of profit. If true, and subject to conditions, after an acquiring

[489] *Duha Printers (Western) Limited v. The Queen*, [1998] 1 SCR 795, rev'g 96 DTC 6323, [1996] 3 CTC 19 (FCA), which reversed 95 DTC 828, [1995] 1 CTC 2481 (TCC). *Duha Printers (Western) Ltd. v. Canada* – SCC Cases (scc-csc.ca).

corporation amalgamates with, or winds up the loss corporation, the acquired business loss carryovers may be deducted in computing income from a "same or similar" business that incurred the losses before the acquisition.

The nuts and bolts of the tax avoidance plan in *Duha Printers* is simple in concept. Rather than have the profitable corporation (Duha Printer) acquire control of the loss corporation, those in control of the loss corporation had to acquire control of Duha Printers. The text of subs. 111(5) applies only if there is an acquisition of control of the loss corporation.

There is a significant practical issue when the owner of an almost worthless loss corporation seeks to acquire control of a valuable profitable corporation if the acquisition is not the commercial purpose of the transaction. Those in control of the profitable corporation for obvious reasons are unwilling to give up effective control. The tax dispute in *Duha Printers* concerns whether this commercial reality was respected and whether the transactions complied with the statutory tax law.

This in turn requires that Justice Iacobucci embark on a tour in *Duha Printers* of the extensive Supreme Court precedent on the meaning of legal control, most of it dating to the pre-*Charter* era; his tour visits at least seven Supreme Court decisions. They include Abbott's unanimous 1967 decision in *Vina-Rug*; Judson's unanimous 1971 decision in *Oakfield Developments*; and both his 1971 majority decision in *Consolidated Holding Co*,[490] and Estey's 1985 majority decision in *Imperial General Properties* together with Wilson's dissent.

Two important non-control decisions cited stand out. They are Iacobucci's 1994 decision in *Antosko* and the Supreme Court's 1984 decision in *Stubart Investments*. *Antosko* was relied on to make it clear that while different techniques can be used to interpret income tax law, none of those techniques "can alter the result" if the words

[490] *Consolidated Holding Co*, *supra* note 281. *Minister of National Revenue v. Consolidated Holding Co.* – SCC Cases (scc-csc.ca).

of the statute "are clear and plain" and the "practical result of the transaction is undisputed."[491] *Stubart Investments* was relied on for the proposition that there is no business purpose test that vitiates transactions done solely to avoid tax. Iacobucci also relied on Wilson's dissent in *Imperial General Properties* to read down and confine the pre-1984 precedent on the meaning of legal control.

Prior to the series of transactions, Duha Printers appears to have been controlled by Mr. Emeric Duha although reference is also made to his wife Gwendolyn's owning a substantial share interest.[492] The loss corporation, Marr's Leisure Holdings Inc., was controlled by William and Norah Marr (Marr group) who held a combined 62.16 percent of the voting control.

The scheme had two essential elements. First, to acquire control of the profitable Duha Printers, the Marr group with the target losses, paid $2,000 to subscribe for two thousand of Duha Printers' preferred shares thereby acquiring more than 50 percent of the votes to elect the board of directors of Duha Printers, a company worth $600,000. A transaction under which control of a valuable profitable corporation worth $600,000 is acquired for $2,000 makes no commercial sense except in a tax avoidance context.

The second essential element to the plan was to ensure that Mr. Duha did not lose effective control of Duha Printers. To accomplish this, a unanimous shareholders' agreement (USA) was executed under which all shareholders of Duha Printers agreed to elect a three-member board of directors from a pre-determined list of four eligible nominees. Duha Printers' board had to consist

---

[491] *Duha Printers, supra* note 489, SCC para. 87.

[492] *Ibid.*, TCC agreed facts 3 and 23 provide the share registry for Duha Printers and other relevant corporations as of February 7 and 10, 1984. On February 7, Emeric Duha appears to have had legal control of Duha Printers. While his wife Gwendolyn Duha held one hundred of four hundred common shares directly and controlled the votes on the remaining three hundred common shares through her control of Emudulis Ltd., he controlled the votes of 1,190 Class A voting shares through a second company called Advanced Typographical Services Limited. On February 10, 1984, Mr. and Mrs. Marr's Marr Leisure Holdings Inc. held two thousand Class C voting shares of Duha Printers.

of three of the following four people: Emeric Duha, Gwendolyn Duha, William Marr and Paul Quinton. Quinton was an unrelated friend of Emeric Duha and William Marr.

The issue is like that in *Oakfield Developments* and *Imperial General Properties*,[493] but there are two key differences. First, the Marr group's $2,000 preferred shares in the Duha group held more than 50 percent of the voting power. Second, its right to vote those shares was subject to the USA. The planning is clever in the way in which it seeks to avoid Judson's decision in *Oakfield Developments*, with the question being whether it effected a legal result with or without a distinction.

Both the Marr group's acquisition of the two thousand preferred shares of Duha Printers and the execution of the USA occurred on February 8, 1984, as part of a pre-ordained series of transactions to avoid the rules meant to prevent the arm's length buying and selling of corporate loss carryovers. Consequently, the USA fettered whatever voting control the Marr group had over Duha Printers because it had a restricted ability to install the board of its choosing.

William Marr is the sole person from the Marr group who could be elected to the three-member board. Assuming the Marr group voted for William Marr, it also had to elect two board members from the remaining eligible persons, being Mr. and Mrs. Duha, and Paul Quinton. As a result, the least favourable result for Mr. and Mrs. Duha would be that one of them was elected to the board with William Marr, with the third director being Quinton. This makes Quinton the key director—and he had been a Duha Printer director for over a decade. Further, no shareholder could dispose of their shares unless at least two of three directors consented.

Once Duha Printers utilized Marr's Leisure's loss carryovers (after an amalgamation), the outsider Marr ceased to be a board member and the Marr group shares were redeemed for $2,000. This was followed by Quinton's ceasing to be a director of Duha Printers.

---

[493] *Imperial General Properties*, *supra* note 435.

Mr. Emeric Duha ensured the Duha corporate group paid the Marr group $34,559 for its loss carryovers, setting their market value at 7.5 percent of $460,786 (the target loss carryovers).

The Federal Court of Appeal denied the tax avoidance although it found the planning was not a sham because of a lack of deceit.

Justice Iacobucci, for a unanimous Supreme Court, allowed Duha Printers' appeal. (Justices L'Heureux-Dubé, Gonthier, McLachlin, Major, Bastarache and Binnie concurred.) He opened his analysis of the legal control issue by finding that the Canadian standard on legal control is the ability to elect a majority of the board of directors. Once done, Iacobucci rejected the view that a finding on legal control is to be determined based on binding instruments that fetter a person's right to vote shares with two exceptions.[494]

To reach the chosen result, Iacobucci used Wilson's dissent in *Imperial General Properties* to question whether Judson reached the correct result in *Oakfield Developments*. He then distinguished it on the basis each group had 50 percent votes in that case. Other pre-1984 decisions distinguished included Judson's majority 1971 decision in *Consolidated Holding Co.*[495] In it, Judson had considered a will to determine the way in which the trustees could vote the shares, in order to give effect to the resulting *legal realities*. Iacobucci confined the precedent to shares held by trustees, rather than share voting subject to other types of agreements, circumscribing the legal realities present.

The result is that external agreements to a corporation that fetter a person's right to vote shares are not to be considered unless they are a trust or a USA. Iacobucci allowed the latter type of agreement to be considered and had written about such agreements when an academic. It became the one non-trust external agreement to consider when determining legal control of a corporation.[496]

---

494 *Ibid.*, SCC Part V (Analysis).

495 *Consolidated Holding Co*, *supra* note 281.

496 Frank Iacobucci, "Canadian Corporation Law: Some Recent Shareholder Developments," *The Cambridge Lectures 1981* (1982), 88, at pp. 92 *et seq*. The article is cited in *Duha Printers*.

Before considering the USA, Justice Iacobucci found that the Marr group acquired legal control of Duha Printers, since it could elect its one nominee as a board member, Quinton and either Mr. or Mrs. Duha. He never questioned whether Mr. Duha retained simultaneous control of Duha Printers by reason of the USA.

Rather, Iacobucci framed the question as being whether the USA caused the Marr group to lose *de jure* control of Duha Printers. This is an odd way to frame the question in the sense it assumes that the Marr group acquired control despite the pre-ordained execution of the USA, and it assumes that Mr. Duha never retained *effective control* of Duha Printers because of the USA and never acquired effective control of Marr's Leisure on their amalgamation. Iacobucci did so despite having conceded in his earlier analysis that "a USA can play a vital role in the *de jure* control analysis … [and the purpose of the judicial control test is] to determine *the locus of the effective control of the corporation*" [emphasis added].[497]

In effect, Justice Iacobucci found that the Marr group acquired *the locus of effective control* of Duha Printers by way of its $2,000 share purchase, and Mr. Duha never retained that effective control of Duha Printers under a USA meant to protect his ability to retain such control. Apparently, Duha gave up legal control of a $600,000 corporation to the Marr group when it subscribed for $2,000 of preferred shares, which $2,000 was returned to the Marr group along with about $35,000 in payment for more than $460,000 of its loss carryovers. The result defies commercial and legal realities.

Throughout the following litigation, Melville Neuman, Barrister and Solicitor of Winnipeg, was forthright about his tax avoidance purpose and how he effected it. Neuman retained Joe Hershfield, a Winnipeg tax practitioner (who became a Tax Court Justice), for his appeals to the Federal Court of Appeal and the Supreme Court. More than 30 years earlier, Neuman "conceived of the plan" used

[497] *Duha Printers*, *supra* note 489, SCC paras. 69–70.

to strip corporate surplus in *Craddock*, which Judson rejected for the Supreme Court along with a similar plan in *Smythe*.[498]

Melville Neuman (1998)

Neuman is a spousal income-splitting case.[499] Melville Neuman owned shares of a family corporation that earned property income; its shareholders were Neuman and his wife Ruby. The corporation's shares were "discretionary" shares in that they were subject to a clause under which the directors of the company could exercise discretion to decide whether to pay a dividend (and how much) to either shareholder. The purpose of this discretion is to allow the owners of the company to stream dividends to individual shareholders whose income is lower or not subject to tax after claiming a dividend tax credit. Neuman was the higher-income taxpayer and advised his wife, a director of the company, to have it declare and pay a disproportionate share of dividends to her.

Eight years earlier in 1990, a Supreme Court panel split 4–3 in *McClurg* on whether discretionary shares were allowed under company law principles. Justice La Forest issued a strong dissent. However, Chief Justice Dickson led the majority in his final income tax decision in accepting this contradiction of company law principles. In doing so, he indicated that an anti-avoidance rule could apply to deny the tax benefit in certain non-arm's length circumstances.

Ruby Neuman never provided *quid pro quo* to the family corporation as Mrs. McClurg had done. Despite this, Justice Marshall Rothstein of the Federal Court allowed the income

---

[498] *Craddock, supra* note 249, Ex. CR par. 2. *W.L. Craddock v. Minister of National Revenue* and *Stanley Curtis Atkinson v. Minister of National Revenue* – Office of the Commissioner for Federal Judicial Affairs Canada (fja-cmf.gc.ca).

[499] *Melville Neuman v. The Queen,* [1998] 1 SCR 770, rev'g 96 DTC 6464, [1996] 3 CTC 270 (FCA), rev'g (1993), (1993) 94 DTC 6094, [1994] 1 CTC 354 (FCTD), which affirmed 92 DTC 1652, [1992] 2 CTC 2074 (TCC). *Neuman v. M.N.R.* – SCC Cases (scc-csc.ca).

splitting.[500] Rothstein was reversed by the Federal Court of Appeal. It held that Dickson's *obiter* in *McClurg* contemplated the situation in *Neuman* and was "binding on the Courts below and on this Court."[501] The Neumans appealed.

Justice Iacobucci rejected Chief Justice Dickson's *obiter* in *McClurg* that a special anti-avoidance rule could apply in a non-arm's length income-splitting case if the recipient of dividends did not provide *quid pro quo* to the corporation. He never considered whether such a finding was inconsistent with Dickson's 1978 finding in *Olan et al.* that a director may be convicted of criminal fraud for not ensuring *quid pro quo* in certain cases where corporate assets are dealt with in a manner not done with a legitimate business reason or relationship.

The result was that subs. 56(2), which targeted directed payments, did not apply in *Neuman*. Iacobucci cited *Stubart Investments* for the proposition: "[T]axpayers are entitled to arrange their affairs for the sole purpose of achieving a favourable position regarding taxation and no distinction is to be made in the application of this principle between arm's length and non-arm's length transactions." He also indicated the Court should not "embellish … [an anti-avoidance rule] when it is open for the legislator to be precise and specific with respect to any mischief to be avoided."[502]

This occurred despite the broadly worded anti-avoidance rule in subs. 56(2) that dated to 1948 and Estey's conditioning his opinion in *Stubart Investments*, at least for the majority, on the fact the Minister did not rely on an anti-avoidance rule. Prior to *Stubart Investments*, subs. 56(2) had been read against taxpayers' engaging

[500] Marshall Rothstein commented on his Federal Court decision in *Neuman* in Marshall Rothstein, "A Judge's Perspective on the General Anti-Avoidance Rule," pp. 553–54), in Brian J. Arnold (Editor), *The General Anti-Avoidance Rule*, *supra* note 299.

[501] *Neuman*, *supra* note 499, FCA at 96 DTC p. 6477.

[502] *Ibid.*, SCC para. 63.

in tax avoidance activity, including diversions of corporate assets.[503] Under *Neuman*, the legislator was instructed to be "precise" about the mischief that the anti-avoidance rule is meant to address, otherwise, the Supreme Court would read it down.

By now, a reader can see the pattern that will follow for income tax disputes Justice Iacobucci decides. He normally, but not always, emphasized the legal form of transactions and used the plain-meaning approach to read down the context and purpose of the statutory text. The taxpayer will invariably succeed, often by way of a reversal of the Federal Court of Appeal.

Therefore, it appears there is no need to review many more of Iacobucci's precedent-setting income tax decisions. But the following three decisions should not and cannot be ignored.

Ludco Enterprises (2001)

In *Ludco Enterprises*, the dispute concerned Canadian resident taxpayers borrowing to invest in two offshore corporations that earned tax-free income in a tax haven.

Each Canadian taxpayer is required to include in computing their income the amount of net income earned from each source, wherever located in the world, in each taxation year. Parliament enacted the foreign accrual property income (FAPI) rules by 1976

---

[503] For example, see *MNR* v. *Allan Bronfman*, 65 DTC 5235 (Ex. Ct.); *MNR v. Abe Bronfman*, 65 DTC 5239; *MNR v. Harry Bronfman*, 65 DTC 5240; *MNR v. Samuel Bronfman*, 65 DTC 5240; and *MNR v. Barnett Aaron*, 65 DTC 5241; reversing (*sub nom* No. 494, 495, 496, 497 and 498) at 58 DTC pp. 149–57, (1957–58) 18 TAB pp. 456–69 (ITAB). The four Bronfman brothers (Allan, Abe, Harry, and Samuel) and their brother-in-law (Barnett Aaron) were five directors of a private company that gifted corporate property to members of their respective families as well as to former employees of the company between 1950 and 1955. The Minister applied the former version of subs. 56(2) to tax each director on 20 percent of the value of the gifts, but the directors successfully appealed to the Tax Appeal Board. The Exchequer Court reversed the Board on the basis that a majority of shareholders could have voted their shares to prevent the gifts and failed to do so (but the Court reduced the amounts of the assessments).

to address plans designed to avoid Canadian income tax on property income by placing Canadian capital in an offshore company.

The FAPI rules require that each Canadian shareholder of an offshore corporation include in their income their proportionate share of FAPI income earned by their foreign corporation. The threshold for application of the rules enacted in 1976 was that the shareholder holds at least 10 percent of the shares of a foreign corporation.

But tax professionals are well paid to design plans under which Canadian tax is avoided, including moving capital offshore to tax havens. *Ludco Enterprises* involves such a plan. Designed *circa* 1976, it took 25 years for the plan to reach the Supreme Court for decision. While the decision tells the tax story arising in respect of one plan, it is but the jurisprudential face of plans in which numerous other wealthy members of Canadian society have participated.[504]

The law firm that designed the plan was Verchère & Gauthier. Mr. Bruce Verchère was a high-profile tax lawyer originally from British Columbia, who ended his own life in tragic circumstances detailed by Stevie Cameron in *Blue Trust*.[505] He started his law career representing the Minister of National Revenue in tax litigation matters.

Verchère left government service in 1967, settled in Montreal and eventually established his own tax law firm. But Stevie Cameron indicated in *Blue Trust* that Mr. Nathan Boidman was the "technical genius" behind Bruce Verchère.[506] Boidman left the firm along with two other very bright young lawyers (Robert Reiche and Jack Bernstein) after Andre Gauthier had left.

Verchère & Gauthier prepared a document titled "Memorandum Respecting the Establishment of a Non-Resident Investment

[504] *Ludco Enterprises Ltd., Brian Ludmer, David Ludmer and Cindy Ludmer v. The Queen*, 2001 SCC 62, [2001] 2 SCR 1082, reversing 99 DTC 5153, [1999] 3 CTC 601 (FCA), which affirmed 98 DTC 6045, [1998] 2 CTC 104 (FCTD), which affirmed 93 DTC 1351, [1993] 2 CTC 2494 (TCC). *Ludco Enterprises Ltd. v. Canada* – SCC Cases (scc-csc.ca).

[505] Stevie Cameron, *Blue Trust* (Toronto: MacFarlane, Walter and Ross, 1998).

[506] *Ibid.*, p. 41.

Organisation for Canadian Investors." The Supreme Court stated that the document:

> … explained that in 1976 the FAPI rules were implemented to eliminate some foreign vehicles for tax deferral and savings, such as foreign-based family investment corporations or trusts. Under the new rules, passive income of closely held foreign holding companies and trusts was attributed to Canadian shareholders or beneficiaries in the year it was earned, even if not distributed. However, it remained open to Canadians to invest in widely held foreign investment vehicles without incurring current taxation on reinvested income provided that the interest of the Canadian investor was less than 10 percent. The Companies were conceived, and their operations planned, in light of these Canadian income tax laws and the proposal for a new investment vehicle contained in the aforementioned memorandum.[507]

The success of this plan partially hinged on a matter of interpretation in respect of the statutory income tax law that concerned the deductibility of interest—whether interest on capital borrowed to fund offshore corporations in a tax avoidance context is incurred for the purpose of producing income from a source. You be the judge.

In general terms two corporations were incorporated in Panama in 1977 and had their operations and management in the Bahamas. Their purpose was to hold Canadian and American debt instruments that were not subject to Canadian or U.S. income or withholding taxes on interest from that debt.

The Verchère & Gauthier tax plan provided that no Canadian shareholder of the corporations could own more than 9.9 percent of their shares, slightly below the 10 percent threshold under the FAPI rules, meaning the rules did not apply. Many tax planners might argue that the tax results of any such plan is intended by

[507] *Ludco Enterprises*, *supra* note 504, SCC para. 5.

Parliament because it expressly chose to set the threshold at 10 percent, thereby intending to allow Canadians to avoid tax by owning less than 10 percent of an offshore corporation.

In many ways, the anti-tax avoidance rules themselves become the road map for achieving a tax avoidance result. This explains why so much is at stake on whether the judiciary subjects the enforceability of transactions against the Minister to a *bona fide* income-earning purpose test.

The Supreme Court indicated in *Ludco Enterprises* that a second document prepared by Verchère & Gauthier, titled "Memorandum Respecting the Formation and Operation of the International Bond Fund" summarized the tax features of an investment. That is as follows: (1) the fund would not be subject to Canadian income tax with respect to either interest income or gains on its sales of fund assets; (2) Canadian shareholders would not be subject to income tax with respect to their investment in the fund except to the extent of dividends received or proceeds of disposition of their shares; and (3) proceeds of dispositions of the shares by the Canadian shareholders, whether by way of sale or redemption, would give rise to taxation as capital gains. Consequently, the plan was to avoid Canadian income tax on investment income by investing capital in offshore corporations, by allowing the interest income to accumulate tax-free offshore and by converting the accumulated income into capital gains from disposing of shares several years later.

The offshore corporations could distribute dividends that would be taxable in Canada if received by a Canadian shareholder. Thus, in theory, all interest earned by a foreign corporation in each year could be distributed to Canadian investors as taxable dividends. Of course, this would be inconsistent with the objective of the avoidance plan and therefore highly unlikely.

As well, if the capital moved to these offshore corporations was borrowed, an additional tax benefit would arise, being the tax-deductible losses that would arise annually to the extent allowable interest deductions exceeded any dividends received. This presumes the shares are a source of income. The tax avoidance plan in *Ludco*

Enterprises occurred about the same time that the Supreme Court decided in 1977 *Moldowan*, establishing the reasonable expectation of profit (REOP) test to determine the existence of a source of income. But that precedent was criticized in the tax literature during the intervening years; Dickson's REOP test for the existence of a source negated such planning.

Although the dividend-paying policy of the corporations changed over the years, since the beginning in 1977, at least $1 of dividends was paid on each share annually. This policy attempted to answer the argument that the shares were not a source of income, to ensure interest outlays in respect of their purchase were deductible. Mr. Ronald Meade managed the companies, and his expertise and success in managing funds were said by the Supreme Court to be "renowned."

The Ludmer family entered this story in 1977 and 1978 when Mr. Irving Ludmer (Ludmer) arranged to acquire shares of one of the offshore corporations on behalf of Ludco Enterprises and shares of the other offshore corporation on behalf of his children.

By late 1978, $2.3 million was invested in one of the corporations and $2.2 million in the other. In 1979, Ludco Enterprises invested $3 million more in one of the corporations. The total invested was about $7.5 million, and about 80 percent of the share investments (about $6.5 million) were financed with borrowings from Canadian banks. The rate of interest floated and was about 10 percent in 1977, reached about 20 percent in 1981, and levelled off to about 14 percent by the mid-1980s.

At trial, Ludmer testified that his decision to invest was based primarily on Meade's performance in investing, with other factors including tax advantages and rumours that Canada would enact foreign exchange controls. (The economy was in disarray, and the separatists were at their apex in Quebec politics.) Ludmer also indicated that he would not have borrowed the funds if he thought the interest outlays were not deductible. He testified that he sought no professional advice but that he considered the dividend policy in the explanatory memorandum mentioned above.

Step back from this situation for a moment to see an offshore investment fund, designed by Canadian tax lawyers, investing in Canadian and American debt instruments to earn interest that is not subject to income or withholding taxes. Removing the tax aspects of the matter, the same investments could have been done directly in Canada.

By 1984, Parliament amended the FAPI rules and ended the above-described avoidance. These amendments resulted in the winding-up of the foreign corporations and resulted in the taxpayers' realizing total capital gains from disposing of the shares of about $9.24 million, with 50 percent of the capital gains being taxable in 1984.

Between 1977 and 1984, the taxpayers collectively received $600,000 of dividends and deducted about $6 million of interest deductions. That is, the taxpayers would have claimed, collectively, about $5.4 million of losses when computing their net income from all sources during the period.

The Minister audited the transactions in 1986 and 1987 and denied the interest deductions on the basis that they were not incurred for the purpose of gaining or producing income from a source, as required under ss. 3 and 9 via para. 20(1)(*c*) of the 1972 Act. For this purpose, capital gains are not income from a source per subs. 9(3) of the ITA. The taxpayers appealed.

The taxpayers were unsuccessful before the Tax Court and the Federal Court–Trial Division. For example, in 1993, the Tax Court found that the reference to "income" in para. 20(1)(*c*) is to "net income" or profit. This holding is consistent with the Supreme Court's 1979 unanimous decision in *Lipson* as well as its unanimous 1977 decision in *Moldowan*. After reviewing all the evidence, Justice Tremblay found that the real or true purpose of owning the shares financed by the borrowings was not to earn income, as there was no REOP. Consequently, the interest claims were not deductible outlays. The taxpayers appealed.

The Federal Court of Appeal, by a 2–1 majority, dismissed the taxpayers' appeal, but the majority was reached by a swing opinion that agreed in almost all respects with the dissenting justice. The opposing judgments were those of Justices Marceau and Létourneau (dissenting) with Justice Desjardins providing the swing opinion.

Justice Alice Desjardins first agreed with the taxpayers that the Minister was attempting inappropriately to import a dominant intent test into the provision. Second, a taxpayer needs only a reasonable expectation of income (not profit) when the investment is made to be entitled to deduct interest. The test was found to be based on "income" and not "profit" because Desjardins was concerned that shares raise a difficult issue—that an investor is always pursuing two purposes: income and capital appreciation.

But Desjardins found that the taxpayers did not have the necessary income-earning intent. The real purpose of their borrowing was to acquire shares that would produce capital gains. The dividends they received were merely a secondary and incidental purpose. This intention was found from the documents, after describing the method and type of tax avoidance sought. Desjardins stated:

> There is nothing scandalous about the fact that the appellants were seeking to minimize their taxes in this way. They were certainly entitled to conduct their businesses in such a manner as to pay the least possible tax. But there is no doubt that they made this investment "for the purpose" of realizing a capital gain. … Their activity was certainly lawful, but where such investments are made with borrowed money, the interest paid is not deductible.[508]

The taxpayers appealed.

Justice Iacobucci delivered the Supreme Court judgment reversing the Federal Court of Appeal. The essential aspect of his reasoning is that the income-earning purpose test in the interest deductibility provision is satisfied if the taxpayer's ancillary purpose is to earn income. The taxpayers were found to have met this test.

---

[508] *Ibid.*, FCA at 99 DTC p. 5162.

(Justices Gonthier, Major, Bastarache, Binnie, Arbour concurred with Justice LeBel's concurrence subject "to my comments on the interpretation of tax statutes in the companion case of *Singleton*.")[509]

The analysis of Iacobucci opened with a quote from E.A. Driedger in *Construction of Statutes* (2nd ed. 1983, p. 97): "[T]he words of an Act are to be read in their entire context and in their grammatical and ordinary sense harmoniously with the scheme of the Act, the object of the Act, and the intention of Parliament."[510] Although Iacobucci listed Supreme Court decisions that cited Driedger, that does not mean the decisions followed the approach

---

[509] Justice LeBel's concurrence subject to his comments on statutory interpretation in *Singleton* (*infra*, note 546) is intriguing. Professor Tamara Larre of the University of Saskatchewan Law School speculated on the matter in her analysis of Label's tax decisions, stating: "[P]erhaps it is simply that Justice LeBel wanted to emphasize the words-in-total context approach to statutory interpretation that he endorsed in *Singleton*." See Tamara Larre, "Justice LeBel's Tax Judgments: Pragmatism, Pluralism and Commitment to the Integrity of the Tax System," pp. 251–82 (p. 261) in Dwight Newman and Malcolm Thorburn (Editors), *The Dignity of Law: The Legacy of Justice Louis LeBel* (Toronto: LexisNexis, 2015). But, LeBel's dissent in *Singleton* went to the heart of the matter: was the interest incurred for the purpose of earning income from a source?

Larre discussed inherent inconsistencies in LeBel's approach in *Singleton* when compared to Iacobucci's approach in *Singleton* and *Ludco* and suggested they might be explained by LeBel considering the "pragmatic effect" of denying the interest deductions in *Ludco*, which pragmatic effect she discussed. Comment: Some argued that a denial of the interest deductions could cause significant adverse uncertainties and effects for investors who borrow to acquire shares. Such an argument deflects away from whether the borrowings were incurred for the purpose of earning income, or whether they were incurred to avoid domestic tax. In that sense of *bona fides*, which pragmatism is more important: (1) the integrity of the income tax system or (2) treating share acquisitions done to avoid tax as being equivalent to investing to earn income from public capital markets or private domestic corporations?

[510] *Ludco Enterprises*, *supra* note 504, SCC para. 36. Justice Iacobucci also maintained that judicial innovation is undesirable, relying on Justice Beverley McLachlin's unanimous decision for the Supreme Court in *Shell Canada Ltd. v. The Queen*, [1999] 3 SCR 622, allowing the taxpayer's appeal from 98 DTC 6177, [1998] 2 CTC 207 (FCA), which reversed in part 97 DTC 395, [1997] 3 CTC 2238 (TCC)). *Shell Canada Ltd. v. Canada* – SCC Cases (scc-csc.ca).

Driedger identified. *Antosko* never took that approach, for example, but Iacobucci cited it. Nor did *Stubart Investments*, which he cited. Estey had sought to incorporate the *Duke of Westminster's* strict approach into guidelines along with considering the text, context and object of the tax law, which cannot and does not work. Wilson in her minority opinion simply rested her approach on the *Duke of Westminster's* strict approach.

Justice Iacobucci also indicated that the judiciary should not embellish statutory language when considering tax avoidance schemes, citing for this proposition his decision in *Neuman*, both Justices Wilson and Estey in *Stubart Investments*, his 1997 decision *Duha Printers*,[511] and McLachlin's 1997 opinion in *Hickman Motors*.[512]

After Justice Iacobucci suggested that Dickson's statement on requiring a *bona fide* purpose test appeared to have been "made as a passing comment and did not result from an analysis of the text of the provision," he applied the plain-meaning approach as limiting the requirement that the purpose be incurred to earn income.[513] Nothing in the text was said to require a primary or dominant income-earning purpose or that the real purpose be to earn income.

What is judicial intervention in this context? It simply appears to be giving credence to the unifying textual, contextual and object approach that existed *circa* 1983 before *Stubart Investments*. Driedger had studied the Supreme Court's approach to statutory interpretation during the 1950s, 1960s and 1970s. He was a senior drafter of legislation with the Justice Department for most of the first half of those years and rose to become its Deputy Minister. In retirement, he began to teach law at Queen's University but shifted by 1971 to Ottawa University where he taught legislative drafting.[514]

---

[511] *Duha Printers*, *supra* note 489 (see SCC para. 88).

[512] *Hickman Motors Ltd. v. The Queen*, [1997] 2 SCR 336 (para. 8). *Hickman Motors Ltd. v. Canada* – SCC Cases (scc-csc.ca).

[513] *Ludco Enterprises*, *supra* note 504, SCC paras. 49–50.

[514] *Pound*, *Chief Justice W.R. Jackett*, *supra* note 91, p. 278.

The lower judiciary was said to have used three different tests for determining the requisite income-earning purpose: (1) the *bona fide* purpose test, (2) the dominant purpose test and (3) the reasonable expectation of income test. But the Tax Court used a "profit" test. Iacobucci found that adjectives such as "*bona fide*," "real or "true" are useful only when determining the existence of a sham or mere window dressing. This rationale is confusing.

While Iacobucci suggested that a taxpayer's *bona fides* are relevant in the context of determining the existence of a sham, Estey and Wilson had failed to make such a finding in *Stubart Investments*, and the Court has repeatedly cited that decision as being correct for the proposition that a *bona fide* income-earning intent or purpose is not required including when determining the existence of a tax sham. Nor has the Court denied tax avoidance plans because a taxpayer lacks a *bona fide* non-tax purpose (except under the general anti-avoidance rule). What Iacobucci was really doing was reading down Dickson's holding in *Bronfman Trust*,[515] which conditioned interest deductions on the taxpayer's borrowing for a *bona fide* income-earning purpose.[516]

The *bona fide* income-earning purpose test was said to have been adopted in several decisions, based on the strength of Dickson's 1987 *obiter* in *Bronfman Trust*, but Iacobucci rejected this as unsupported by the principles of statutory interpretation or the Supreme Court's recent decisions.

After concluding that an ancillary income-earning purpose test suffices for interest deductibility, Justice Iacobucci found the requisite standard to be the reasonable expectation of income. The next question was which income—net or gross? Iacobucci found that the text of the interest deductibility provision did not support a

---

[515] *Bronfman Trust, supra* note 366. *Bronfman Trust v. The Queen* – SCC Cases (scc-csc.ca).

[516] *Ludco Enterprises, supra* note 504. Iacobacci J. stated (para. 49): "In my opinion, Dickson C.J.'s comments fall short of elevating the *bona fide* purpose test to a rule of law. Indeed, ..., the importation of the *bona fide* purpose test into ss. 20(1)(c)(i) is not supported by the principles of statutory interpretation outlined above, especially as applied in our recent tax law jurisprudence."

requirement for "profit," "net income" nor a "judicial assessment of sufficiency of income":

> The plain meaning of s. 20(1)(c)(i) does not support an interpretation of "income" as the equivalent of "profit" or "net income." Nowhere in the language of the provision is a quantitative test suggested. Nor is there any support in the text of the Act for an interpretation of "income" that involves a judicial assessment of sufficiency of income. Such an approach would be too subjective and certainty is to be preferred in the area of tax law. Therefore, absent a sham or window dressing or similar vitiating circumstances, courts should not be concerned with the sufficiency of the income expected or received.[517]

Iacobucci's above *obiter* on the text of the interest deductibility provision in s. 20—for the proposition that there is no support in the ITA that requires a so-called judicial justification of sufficiency of income—fails to acknowledge that the text of para. 20(1)(*c*) depends on the existence of the "source of income," not a source of losses. Was the interest incurred in a business or property source of income? This answer cannot be found by looking at the wording of a deductibility paragraph within s. 20. The question is overarching, directed at connecting the expense to a s. 3 source of income. The answer derives from the parameters of the "source of income" concept in s. 3, not an expense deductibility rule, which presumes a pre-existing business and property source.

The s. 3 net income text refers to "source of income." The separate concepts "income" and "revenue" should not be conflated when the central question is whether there exists a source of income. As for related text in the ITA, a loss from a business and property through which a para. 20(1) deduction must flow to reach the s. 3 net income provision states in subs. 9(2): "… a taxpayer's loss for a taxation year from a business or property is the amount

[517] *Ibid.*, para. 59.

of the taxpayer's loss, if any, for the taxation year from that *source*" [emphasis added].

If a business or property with revenue that results in a loss is automatically a source, there would be no need to refer to the word "source" in the subs. 9(2) loss provision. This seems obvious in the case of owning a property, because if the cited text ended with "business or property" instead of "source," one should expect any number of taxpayers to claim that they incurred expenses resulting in losses from owning property. The source reference gives context and substance to the commercial concepts of profit and loss. It also provides textual support for Dickson's 1977 holding in *Moldowan* that a business or property is not a source unless it has a REOP and Pigeon's 1979 profit test in *Lipson*.

The result in the Supreme Court's unanimous decision in *Ludco Enterprises* requires a reader to believe that the source of income concept in s. 3 of the ITA is subject to the text in a deductibility paragraph relied on in a tax avoidance plan—to receive $600,000 of dividends against $6 million of interest expenses—that magically results in the shares being a s. 3 "source of income."

Ludco Enterprises provided the necessary reasoning for the next two companion decisions decided seven months later about the parameters of a source of income in a tax shelter context.

Brian J. Stewart (2002);[518] *Jack Walls (2002)*[519]

The *Stewart* and *Walls* cases concern the deductibility of losses under ss. 3 and 9, which arose annually after the acquisition of tax shelter property. *Stewart* was the lead case. More generally, the cases concern the Supreme Court's judicial-policy decision to neuter Dickson's unanimous 1977 decision in *Moldowan* that a taxpayer must have a REOP.[520]

---

[518] *Brian J. Stewart v. The Queen*, 2002 SCC 46, [2002] 2 SCR 645. *Stewart v. Canada* – SCC Cases (scc-csc.ca).

[519] *Jack Walls and Robert Buvyer v. The Queen*, 2002 SCC 47, [2002] 2 SCR 684. *Walls v. Canada* – SCC Cases (scc-csc.ca).

[520] *Moldowan, supra* note 349. *Moldowan v. The Queen* – SCC Cases (scc-csc.ca).

In *Stewart*, the tax shelter property consisted of four condominiums built in the London and Surrey areas (two each). The developments had been syndicated as an investment to potential participants and promoted as providing losses to shelter other income from tax. The losses would result from gross rent earned annually being exceeded by expenses, which were mainly interest on financing and CCA as well as other related property management expenses. This continued for years, with the expectation of resulting capital gains from selling the condominiums.

In *Walls*, a storage-park company was incorporated in 1983, in which two promoters respectively held a 33 percent and 25 percent interest through holding companies. It purchased a mini-warehouse a few months later for $1.18 million. The company then sold the warehouse for $2.2 million to a new partnership they established (its initial partners were a corporate general partner that was also a management company owned equally by the two promoters and a corporate founding partner owned by one of the promoters).

At this stage, the cost of the warehouse had been marked up almost 100 percent to $2.2 million from $1.18 million. To acquire the warehouse from the storage-park company, the partnership paid $1, with the balance being an agreement of sale to the above-mentioned management company, with the partnership obligated to pay interest on that $2.2 million balance at a rate of 24 percent per year ($528,000 per year). The promoters negotiated the prices and terms.

The partnership also agreed to pay the management company service fees of $140,000 per year and management fees of $50,000 per year. The company was also entitled to 50 percent of the partnership's net profit, if any. The partnership was then promoted as a tax shelter to potential participants.

These numbers are stark in commercial terms. It is unclear on what basis potential investors could expect a profit. The cost-base mark-up had, in effect, created a cost that the partnership would presumably deduct as CCA, as well as deduct interest at 24 percent interest on that step-up, plus the service fees and management fees.

The promotional lure to potential investors was the tax benefits associated with deducting the resulting losses from real sources of income.

Brian Stewart

Justice Marshall Rothstein of the Federal Court of Appeal denied Stewart's appeal. In brief, he did so because the promoter's plan offered no expectation of profit and promised losses with a projected capital gain in the future. Since there was no source, the taxpayer could not deduct the losses.

In *Stewart*, Justices Iacobucci and Bastarache started by indicating a taxpayer must have a predominant intent to earn a profit for the taxpayer's activities to be a source, but they immediately read that down: "[If] the activity contains no personal element and is clearly commercial, no further inquiry is necessary."[521] By doing so, they restricted judicial application of Chief Justice Dickson's REOP test to cases where there is a personal element to the taxpayer's intent, without considering or distinguishing the Court's 1979 decision in *Lipson*. Iacobucci and Bastarache, for the Supreme Court, allowed *Stewart's* appeal. (Chief Justice McLachlin and Justices L'Heureux-Dubé, Gonthier, Major, Binnie, Arbour and LeBel concurred.)

To reach this result, Iacobucci and Bastarache applied *Ludco Enterprises* and the plain-meaning approach for the proposition that a taxpayer does not need to earn a net profit to deduct interest.[522]

---

[521] *Stewart, supra* note 518, SCC paras. 54 (predominant intent) and 60 (clearly commercial).

[522] *Ibid.*, SCC para. 65. Iacobucci and Bastarache JJ. cited *Ludco Enterprises, supra* note 504: "The plain meaning of s. 20(1)(i) does not support an interpretation of 'income' as the equivalent of 'profit' or 'net income.' Nowhere in the language of the provision is a quantitative test suggested. *Nor is there any support in the text of the Act for an interpretation of 'income' that involves a judicial assessment of sufficiency of income.* Such an approach would be too subjective and certainty is to be preferred in the area of tax law. *Therefore, absent a sham or window dressing or similar vitiating circumstances, courts should not be concerned with the sufficiency of the income expected or received*" [emphasis by SCC in *Stewart*].

Next, they stated: "[A] clear analogy can be drawn between the facts in *Ludco*, and the facts in the case at bar. In *Ludco*, the taxpayer deducted approximately $6 million in interest charges on borrowed money used to purchase shares which yielded some $600,000 in dividends."[523]

Justices Iacobucci and Bastarache also cited their decision in the companion case *Walls* for the position that "a tax motivation does not affect the validity of transactions for tax purposes."[524]

Jack Walls

In *Walls*, the Minister reduced the partners' losses. The partnership's cost of the storage facility was reduced to its original promoter cost of $1.18 million from $2.2 million (for depreciation purposes), interest deductions were denied on the debt above $1.18 million and the interest deductions that were allowed were capped at 16 percent annually instead of 24 percent on the basis the higher rate was "unreasonable."[525]

The trial judge dismissed the taxpayer's appeal on the basis there was no REOP, applying the Supreme Court's 1977 decision in *Moldowan*. The trial judge also stated that "the reduction of tax in this case was the sole reason for the existence of the shelter"[526] and applied the Federal Court of Appeal's 1992 decision in *Moloney v. The Queen*.[527] (*Moloney* is not a REOP case.) On appeal, the Federal Court of Appeal reversed the trial court in *Walls*, holding that the REOP test did not apply because there was no personal element to the investment. Instead, it focused on the ongoing commercial nature of the business carried on by the limited partnership. But what about *Moloney*?

---

[523] *Ibid.*, SCC para. 66.

[524] *Ibid.*, SCC para. 65.

[525] *Walls, supra* note 519, SCC paras. 3–4.

[526] *Ibid.*, FCTD at 96 DTC p. 6146; and [1996] 2 CTC p. 21.

[527] *Moloney v. The Queen*, 92 DTC 6570, [1992] 2 CTC 227 (FCA). The Supreme Court denied leave to appeal in 1993.

In *Moloney*, a promoter of speed-reading courses organized a business that sold territories to individuals including Moloney who deducted losses without any intent to carry on a genuine business. The Federal Court of Appeal rejected Moloney's appeal, holding that a reduction of taxes cannot, by itself, be a business.[528] The Supreme Court denied the taxpayer leave in 1993.

But in *Walls*, Justices Iacobucci and Bastarache distinguished *Moloney*. (Chief Justice McLachlin and Justices L'Heureux-Dubé, Gonthier, Major, Binnie, Arbour and LeBel concurred.[529]) Two matters about their approach stand out.

First, Iacobucci and Bastarache categorized *Moloney* as a sham without reference to the taxpayer's intent, while the partnership in *Walls* was found to be a source of income without reference to the partners' intent. This approach is a deflection from determining whether the taxpayer intended a sham or had a source of income intent. They then resorted to the Court's no inquiry instruction in *Stewart* (do not question taxpayer intent) in a source of income context because the partnership's activity in *Walls* was said to be "clearly commercial." In comparison, *Moloney* was found to be a sham, based on a lack of commercial activity in that case.[530]

Second, Iacobucci and Bastarache indicated that the trial judge found the reduction of tax was the "sole motivation" for the partnership, but the trial judge stated the reduction of tax was the "sole reason" for the partnership. After doing so, they linked the taxpayer's motive to the Court's extensive post-1984 precedent that

---

[528] *Ibid.* Hugessen J.A. stated (92 DTC p. 6570): "While it is trite law that a taxpayer may so arrange his business as to attract the least possible tax [citing the *Duke of Westminster*], it is equally clear in our view that the reduction of his own tax cannot by itself be a taxpayer's business for the purpose of the *Income Tax Act*."

[529] *Walls, supra* note 519.

[530] *Ibid.*, SCC para. 21. Also, "With respect, the case at bar is distinguishable from *Moloney*. There, the taxpayer was not engaged in a commercial activity, but instead was involved in a sham set up to appear as though it was commercial in nature where in fact the only activity actually engaged in was that of obtaining tax refunds. Here, in contrast, the Partnership purchased and maintained an ongoing commercial operation."

holds: "[M]otive does not affect the validity of transactions for tax purposes."[531] Iacobucci and Bastarache appear to have tried to underpin their reasons for why *Walls* was not a sham by linking the concern to tax avoidance *motive*. But how is an activity clearly commercial if the taxpayer's *sole reason* for the activity is to avoid tax?

Referring to a taxpayer's reason as the taxpayer's motive is problematic because the ITA includes many provisions in which a taxpayer's access to a deduction or a tax benefit depends on the taxpayer's satisfying a purpose or reason test; for example, the deduction of interest and CCA in computing income from a business or property source, and in anti-avoidance rules. There is no Supreme Court income tax precedent for the proposition that a taxpayer's intent, purpose or reason for doing something is irrelevant under such a provision. In fact, it is the central focus of the inquiry.

The Supreme Court also failed in *Walls* to recognize that proof of motive is relevant when proving intent under the law of evidence, as articulated by the Court in a non-tax context, including the criminal law such as fraud.[532] Should the fact that income tax is involved change the law of evidence and the role that proof of motive has in proving intent, unless the Court has carved out an exception from that law for tax avoiders? If so, it should expressly justify such an exception in a principled manner.[533]

---

[531] *Ibid.*, paras. 21–22. Iacobucci and Bastarache JJ. stated: "… the reduction of tax was the sole motivation for its existence [the tax shelter partnership]." At para. 22, they stated: "It is a well-established proposition that a tax motivation does not affect the validity of transactions for tax purposes: *Backman v. Canada*, [2001] 1 S.C.R. 367, 2001 SCC 10, at para. 22; *Shell Canada Ltd. v. Canada*, [1999] 3 S.C.R. 622; *Canada v. Antosko*, [1994] 2 S.C.R. 312; *Stubart Investments Ltd. v. The Queen*, [1984] 1 S.C.R. 536, at p. 540. In addition, we reiterate the caution stated in *Stewart*, at par. 65 that, given the specific anti-avoidance provisions in the Act, courts should not be quick to embellish its provisions in response to tax avoidance concerns: see also *Ludco Enterprises Ltd. v. Canada*, [2001] 2 S.C.R. 1082, 2001 SCC 62, at para. 39; *Neuman v. M.N.R.*, [1998] 1 S.C.R. 770, at para. 63."

[532] *Lewis v. The Queen*, [1979] 2 SCR 821. *Lewis v. The Queen* – SCC Cases (scc-csc.ca).

[533] Canada is not the only jurisdiction in which the judiciary tends to treat a taxpayer's tax avoidance motive as being irrelevant when deciding a tax

Further, the limited partners in *Walls* did not necessarily have the same intent as any other partners, including the general partner. This is mentioned because their intent should not be conflated into the intent that any other partner may have had to earn income from the partnership's commercial warehouse activity, with significant revenues flowing directly to the corporate partner (management company) established by the promoters. That is, the partnership's commercial activity may have been a source of income, for some partners, but did the participant limited partners have a partnership source of income under s. 3 of the ITA?

Accordingly, Justice Iacobucci's precedent is central to the Supreme Court's evolving by the early 2000s from its 1972 position in *Cameron* in which it was unwilling to find an arrangement to be a sham because the taxpayer's *primary* intent was to execute a commercial plan, and any tax savings were incidental. The evolved position by 2002 was that activity engaged in for the sole reason to avoid tax is acceptable to the Court in a source of income context

---

avoidance case. For example, see Yitzhak Hadari, "Tax Avoidance in Linear Transactions: The Dilemma of Tax Systems," 15 *U. Pennsylvania J. Int'l* 59 (1994). Hadari discusses this hesitancy in the American, British and Israeli judicial systems in s. 2 of his article (Taxpayer's Motive and Legislative Intent). He considers judicial statements "holding the taxpayer's motive immaterial and the statutory intent relevant to a given transaction, [such that] the examination of the transaction becomes objective rather than subjective" and further states on p. 64 that the "use of the term 'taxpayer's purpose' may be more suitable in this context. Hadari also notes that on occasion the judiciary "strays" into giving some relevance to a taxpayer's motive in a decision and cites one such decision—*Frank Lyon v. United States*, 435 US 561 (1978). Comment: Under the law of evidence, at least in Canada, *Lewis, ibid.*, held that motive is relevant for proving a person's intent, which is the central inquiry when determining what a person's intent was for doing something under the ITA's intent, purpose and reason tests. If a jury can convict an accused based on motive, are judges in civil law trials concerning tax avoidance "straying" from the law of evidence? The Supreme Court of Canada should explain in a principled manner why motive is irrelevant in proving intent when the issue is whether a taxpayer satisfies an intent, purpose or reason test under the ITA; or if a taxpayer effected a tax sham.

because it is unwilling to consider taxpayer intent if there is a link to activity it considers to be clearly commercial.

As noted, the more recent approach raises this question: What should be considered clearly commercial when the sole reason is to avoid tax? The Court has also evolved from its 1977 position in *Moldowan* and its 1979 position in *Lipson* (requiring a taxpayer to have a REOP or net profit expectation in order to have a source of income) to the position that an ancillary income-earning purpose suffices.

Logically, if no intent to earn income is acceptable, an ancillary intent to earn income must also be acceptable to the Supreme Court. This evolution represents two great leaps in judicial rule-making and faith in taxpayer intent under a self-assessment system. The Court changed its judicial policy to articulate guidelines and rules that accede to the view of those who argue for the judiciary to accept blatant tax avoidance intent when determining the existence of possible shams and purported sources of income.

While Justice Iacobucci is the key messenger effecting this shift, he did so for the Supreme Court as a whole. Former Bay Street lawyer and law dean, Philip Slayton in his 2011 book *Mighty Judgment* quoted one former Supreme Court judge as indicating the Court had become a "court of policy" whose job is not to fix "errors of law" but to "decide policy."[534] The Court had decided as a matter of judicial policy to emphasize the legal form of transactions and apply the plain-meaning interpretative approach—as Bushnell argued in *The Captive Court* and commercial interests demanded. They consider tax to be a cost of business, and they should be able to avoid it as a sound commercial purpose. Let someone else pay. This is the history of taxation. Tax the other guy—not me—as I have a good policy reason not to be taxed.

With respect to his decisions, Iacobucci is reported to have said: "I don't have any illusions that my work will endure forever. It has

[534] Slayton, *Mighty Judgment*, *supra* note 160, p. 6.

to get examined and re-examined and modified as we know more about different kinds of issues."[535]

Justice Frank Iacobucci retired in 2004. At the time, two Ontario seats on the Supreme Court were vacant. They were filled by Justices Louise Charron and Rosalie Abella.

[535] "The Honourable Frank Iacobucci, CC, QC [KC], LLD, LDM," Peter A. Allard School of Law, University of British Columbia, www.historyproject.allard.ubc.ca/law-history-project/profile/honourable-frank-iacobucci-cc-qc-lld-lsm. Justice Iacobucci answered a series of questions about his background in that interview, which is relied on in the brief overview of his background.

JOHN MAJOR: A LITIGATOR TO THE CORE

Progressive Conservative Prime Minister Brian Mulroney elevated John Major to the Supreme Court from the Alberta Court of Appeal in 1992, replacing Justice William Stevenson. Justice Major was a civil litigator in Calgary until his appointment to the Alberta Court of Appeal in 1991.

Born in Mattawa, Ontario, John Major attended university in Montreal and law school at the University of Toronto. After graduating, he went west to Alberta, where he was called to the bar in 1958. Major had an esteemed career at Bennett Jones and was a counsel to the 1978–79 Royal Commission of Inquiry into Certain Activities of the RCMP (the "McDonald Commission") and the 1985–86 Royal Commission into the Collapse of the Canadian Commercial Bank and the Northland Bank (the "Estey Commission"). He was also senior counsel to the 1987 Alberta Inquiry into the collapse of the Principal Group of financial companies (the "Code Inquiry").

Justice Major's selection is based on his co-writing four of the most important income tax decisions the Supreme Court has decided post–*Stubart Investments*. He co-wrote with Justice Iacobucci the *Jarvis* and *Ling* companion decisions in 2002, which set down the parameters of when the Crown can and cannot use information that auditors at the Canada Revenue Agency (CRA) obtain under their civil audit powers, in a criminal prosecution of a taxpayer for tax evasion. These decisions tip the balance toward selecting Major. His better-known companion decisions are the 2005 GAAR decisions in *Canada Trustco* and *Mathew*, which he co-wrote with Chief Justice Beverley McLachlin.

John Major was strongly pro-taxpayer and commercial interest, invariably emphasizing the legal form of a taxpayer's transactions while applying the plain-meaning approach when interpreting the statutory income tax law. He heard 43 income tax cases of which 16 concerned tax avoidance. The first three of Major's decisions considered below provide a lead-in to considering the above-mentioned companion decisions on issues of fundamental importance to the integrity of Canada's self-assessment income tax system.

Jake Friesen (1995)

In 1995, Justice Major led a 3–2 majority in *Friesen*; Justice Iacobucci dissented. *Friesen* is one of the rare income tax cases in which Major and Iacobucci differ. The dispute, which occurred early in their tenures at the Supreme Court, turned on whether the taxpayer could deduct a loss before disposing of land acquired as an adventure in the nature of trade.[536] The land had declined in value below its cost before its disposition. The Court often heard adventure disputes during the 1950s and 1960s, usually about whether a taxpayer's realized gain from disposing of property was taxable business income versus tax-exempt capital gains.

Major cited with approval Iacobucci's 1994 holding in *Antosko* that the plain-meaning approach applies when interpreting statutory income tax provisions unless there is ambiguity.[537] But in doing so, Major indicated he also relied on Estey J.'s approach in *Stubart Investments* and Driedger's unifying textual, contextual and purposive approach, which does not support the plain-meaning approach. The reason Major gave for not considering the object and purpose of the provision in issue was that "the object and purpose of a provision need only be resorted to when the statutory language admits to some doubt or ambiguity."[538] The word "inventory" of a business in s. 10 of the ITA was interpreted to apply to adventure property. (Justices L'Heureux-Dubé and Sopinka concurred.)

Justice Major also cited Abbott's 1964 unanimous decision in *Irwin*,[539] which provides the basic formula for computing the gross profit that allows a business to reduce its sales revenue by the cost of inventory. But he rejected Abbott's *dicta* that it is doubtful

---

[536] *Friesen v. The Queen*, [1995] 3 SCR 103. *Friesen v. Canada* – SCC Cases (scc-csc.ca).
[537] *Ibid.*, para. 10.
[538] *Ibid.*, para. 60.
[539] *Irwin*, *supra* note 140, SCC p. 662.

write-downs apply to business inventory that has an "actual cost and sale price [for] ... each particular piece of property," which would be especially the case for adventure property.[540]

In dissent, Justice Iacobucci held that Abbott's comment on inventory was part of the *ratio* of the decision and that it could not be dismissed as being inapplicable when the property is an adventure in the nature of trade rather than inventory of an actual business. (Justice Gonthier concurred.)

After the *Friesen* decision, retired Chief Justice W.R. Jackett of the Federal Court of Appeal was reported to have expressed the following concern about the Supreme Court's ability to handle income tax disputes:

> He [former Chief Justice Jackett] has concern about the Supreme Court of Canada and is convinced that its judges have no understanding of the basic concepts of income tax-law. He was completely amazed at the decision of the court ... in the case of *Jake Friesen* ... Jackett could not understand how the obvious description of inventory in a statute could possibly have been interpreted to mean that a single piece of raw land so qualified. He said the judges pick cases to support their views without knowing what they mean and what was the context of each decision. Cases that really matter are simply ignored.[541]

If true, it could be partly because the Supreme Court and its judges do not handle the volume of income tax appeals that the Court handled in the 1950s through the 1970s when, in some years, the Court decided more income tax disputes than it has decided in some of the decades since the enactment of the *Charter* in 1982. This situation is not conducive to obtaining either judicial experience in income tax or a feel for the ITA, a notoriously difficult

---

[540] *Friesen, supra* note 536, para. 21 and paras. 50–51. Abbott J.'s comment is at *Irwin supra* note 140, p. 665.

[541] Pound, *Chief Justice W.R. Jackett, supra* note 91, p. 285.

statute to consider in the context of facts and complex plans to avoid tax. It is also not a situation easy to remedy. The Supreme Court exists within a context that has changed significantly over time, including the need to decide *Charter* cases. The issue is easy to criticize but difficult to address.

Patterns are predictive but do not always hold. *Will-Kare Paving* is such a case.[542] Justice Iacobucci concurred with Major's opinion, so they both deviated from their suggested plain-meaning interpretive approach.

Will-Kare Paving (2000)

All roads in Nova Scotia lead one way or another to Halifax except the TransCanada Highway in northern Nova Scotia, which heads east from Truro to Sydney and by ferry across the Cabot Strait to Newfoundland and Labrador. Going west, the TransCanada heads to Moncton and across southern New Brunswick to the border with Maine and then north and beyond into the wilderness of Lower Canada and Upper Canada.

Truro is an industrial hub at the crossroads of the TransCanada Highway and Veterans Memorial Highway that goes south to Halifax. It is a perfect place to locate an asphalt-manufacturing facility and paving company with roadwork needed on major highways leading in all directions. That company is Will-Kare Paving & Contracting Limited.

The tax dispute in *Will-Kare Paving* concerned whether it qualified for two of three tax preferences available to Canadian manufacturers of "goods for sale or lease." The three tax preferences were (1) the tax-rate reduction applicable to corporate profits from the manufacturing or processing in Canada of goods for sale or lease, (2) accelerated capital cost allowance (CCA) in respect of

[542] *Will-Kare Paving & Contracting Limited v. The Queen*, 2000 SCC 36, [2000] 1 SCR 915, affirming 98 DTC 6203, [2000] 3 CTC 200 (FCA), which affirmed (1996), 97 DTC 506, [1996] 2 CTC 2426 (TCC). *Will-Kare Paving & Contracting Ltd. v. Canada* – SCC Cases (scc-csc.ca).

certain equipment and buildings used "primarily" in such activity, and (3) investment tax credits (ITCs) in respect of the cost of qualified depreciable property used primarily in such activity.

Mr. William Lake was the businessman behind Will-Kare Paving. Lake founded the company in 1974 and knew its business, market and potential. Will-Kare Paving built an asphalt plant in 1988 and installed related equipment in 1989 and 1990. At the time, Parliament was curtailing tax preferences as part of Finance Minister Michael Wilson's tax reform exercise of the late 1980s.

Everyone agreed Will-Kare Paving qualified for the tax-rate reduction in respect of manufacturing profits because it met the threshold of earning at least 10 percent of its gross revenue from manufacturing asphalt for sale. But the way in which that reduction applied depended on whether Will-Kare Paving was eligible to claim the CCA and ITC tax preferences. It could claim these two preferences only if it used the plant "primarily" to manufacture asphalt as "goods for sale or lease."

Will-Kare Paving treated the plant as qualified property for the purposes of the ITC regime and claimed credits in its 1988–90 taxation years. It appears that Will-Kare Paving claimed an ITC of 15 percent of the cost of the plant and equipment. Those credits directly reduce federal tax payable, and for small businesses a portion is refundable, even if tax is not payable.

Will-Kare Paving also treated the cost of the plant as a Class 39 asset, which applied to qualifying M&P property acquired after 1987 and before February 26, 1992. The Class 39 CCA rate for 1988–91 ramped down from 40 percent in 1988 to 35 percent in 1989, 30 percent in 1990 and 25 percent after 1990.

The Minister's auditors at Halifax reviewed Will-Kare Paving's 1988–90 income tax returns and denied its claims for ITCs and accelerated CCA, and its reliance on the small manufacturers' rule to deem all its profits to be Canadian M&P profits. This meant Will-Kare Paving had to apply a formula to compute the portion of its profits eligible for the tax rate reduction incentive.

The basis for the reassessments was that the asphalt plant was not acquired "primarily" for the purpose of manufacturing or processing "goods for sale or lease." Only 25 percent of the asphalt was sold to third parties. Will-Kare Paving used 75 percent in its commercial paving contracts. Under commercial and provincial law, paving contracts are contracts for "work and materials" and not "goods for sale." The results were significant for Will-Kare Paving. It appealed for relief.

The Tax Court dismissed Will-Kare Paving's appeal in 1996. It held it was bound to apply a Federal Court of Appeal decision in which the "goods for sale or lease" terminology was interpreted based on commercial law principles. This meant the asphalt Will-Kare Paving used in its road and other commercial contracts tainted its eligibility to claim the tax preferences. The Federal Court of Appeal upheld the Tax Court's decision, and Will-Kare Paving appealed.

Justice Major delivered the majority decision for the Supreme Court. He described two divergent interpretations of the phrase "goods for sale or lease" in the case law. In essence, the choice was between the plain meaning of the words or their commercial law meaning. Major favoured the commercial law meaning.

> To apply a "plain meaning" interpretation of the concept of a sale in the case at bar would assume that the Act operates in a vacuum, oblivious to the legal characterization of the broader commercial relationships it affects. It is not a commercial code in addition to a taxation statute.[543]

A sale has a clear commercial and legal meaning, and Major applied it despite Will-Kare Paving's arguments that were described as advocating an economic realities approach.[544] Given the clear

[543] *Ibid.*, SCC para. 31, pp. 933–34.

[544] *Ibid.* Major J.'s reference to economic realities (para. 33) appears to be referring to the fact Lake could have accessed the ITC regime and the accelerated CCA regime if he organized Will-Kare Paving into two companies: one company manufacturing asphalt and the other doing roadwork. If done, the

and unambiguous language, Major found that a reference to economic realities was unwarranted, and dismissed Will-Kare Paving's appeal. (Justices L'Heureux-Dubé, Iacobucci and Bastarache concurred.)

Justice Ian Binnie dissented. He held that Lake and his Will-Kare Paving should be allowed to benefit from a plain-meaning interpretation of the phrase "primarily in the manufacturing or processing of goods for sale or lease" under the ITC and CCA regimes, because "millions of taxpayers who are *not* lawyers cannot be expected to reach for *Benjamin's Sale of Goods* to research the difference between a contract for the sale of goods and a contract for work and materials and to apply these distinctions in the assessment of their own income tax liability" [emphasis in original text]. (Justices Gonthier and McLachlin concurred.)

Bruce Russell and Anne-Marie Lévesque, who represented the Crown in *Will-Kare Paving*, had also represented the Crown with success in *McNichol et al. v. The Queen*, which was the first case the Tax Court decided under the GAAR.[545] Russell handled a number of the Crown's major income tax cases in Atlantic Canada at the time; *Will-Kare Paving* was his last such case. In *Will-Kare Paving*, they managed a 4–3 successful outcome for the Crown despite it having been unsuccessful in most of the income tax cases the Supreme Court decided during the period. Soon afterwards, Russell joined a law firm in Halifax and was appointed a Justice of the Tax Court of Canada in 2016; Lévesque went on to head the Department of

---

company manufacturing asphalt could have sold all its output (i.e., 25 percent to third parties and 75 percent to the other related company) thereby qualifying for all three preferences. But the preferences would have been contained inside that manufacturing company, while 75 percent of revenue came from paving contracts. This distinction is important. It means a separate paving company could have been exposed to higher marginal tax rates under federal and Nova Scotia income tax law. This is best understood by recognizing that Will-Kare Paving sought to deem all its income to be Canadian M&P profits eligible for the tax rate reduction under the small manufacturers' rule in Regulation 5201, including the profits imbedded in providing paving services.

545 *McNichol et al. v. The Queen*, 97 DTC 111, [1997] 2 CTC 2088 (TCC).

Justice's tax litigation group in Ottawa before joining the CRA's senior management.

Justice Major is also the author of the Supreme Court's 2001 majority opinion in *Singleton.*[546] It (and *Ludco Enterprises*) overturned Chief Justice Dickson's opinion in *Bronfman Trust* that a taxpayer needs a *bona fide* income-earning purpose to deduct interest in respect of a loan.

John R. Singleton (2001)

In *Singleton*, Major held that interest is deductible if the taxpayer's borrowing traces to the acquisition of an income-earning property. (Justices Gonthier, Iacobucci, Major, Binnie and Arbour concurred.[547]) *Bona fides* were in issue because the taxpayer withdrew capital from his law partnership, which his wife used to purchase their personal residence. He then borrowed to replace that partnership capital and sought to deduct the interest against his law income.

Justice Major took issue with the approach Chief Justice Donald Bowman of the Tax Court applied when denying the interest deductions. Bowman looked through the "shuffle of cheques" to find that the borrowing was not incurred for the purpose of earning income; rather it was to use money to purchase a personal residence. As noted in Part II, the similar phrase "shuffles with the cheques" is what Justice Judson used in the context of his unanimous 1969 holding in *Smythe*, which looked through the legal form of the transactions to get a commercial substance over legal sale result.

But for Major, it is "this 'shuffle of cheques' that defines the legal relationship which must be given effect."[548] He made a judicial choice when he said the legal relationships must be given effect,

[546] *Singleton v. The Queen*, 2001 SCC 61, [2001] 2 SCR 1046. *Singleton v. Canada* – SCC Cases (scc-csc.ca).

[547] *Ibid.*

[548] *Ibid.*, para. 32.

as Judson held otherwise for a unanimous Supreme Court in both *Smythe* and *Craddock*.

Few taxpayers can deduct interest to finance the purchase of a personal residence; not many have the capital to pull off the Singleton shuffle of cheques. No new income was taxable because of the borrowing. Rather Singleton's taxable law-firm income was reduced by his deduction of interest.

Justices Michel Bastarache and Louis LeBel dissented. They found that the judiciary is required to look beyond a legal instrument where the legal relations are not created with a *bona fide* purpose. In terms of interpreting tax law, Bastarache and LeBel indicated that a "words-in-total context" approach should be used and not Major's plain-meaning approach in *Friesen*. They found that the income-earning purpose test for interest deductibility under the provision had not been met.

In doing so, Bastarache and LeBel indicated that the transactions fell precisely within Chief Justice Dickson's *obiter* in *Bronfman Trust* that such a manipulating sequence "might well … constitute a formality or a sham."[549] They applied this *obiter* presumably on the basis the sequence was a mere formality that failed to satisfy the income-earning purpose test.[550] The effect of the transaction was to finance the purchase of a personal residence and not to accumulate capital for the purpose of earning taxable income.

The facts in *Singleton* represent a good example of why the parameters of taxpayer *bona fides* is relevant when determining if the Minister is bound to accept legal results effected by self-dealing taxpayer transactions that reduce tax. We don't know if Dickson in *Bronfman Trust* meant that a formality or a sham occurs when a taxpayer's intent or purpose in effecting a transaction lacks a *bona*

---

[549] *Ibid.*, para. 55.

[550] Olsen and Derksen, *supra* note 299, do not refer to the "sham" reference in Dickson C.J.'s *obiter* in *Bronfman Trust*, *supra* note 366. They state that he "speculated [it] could be a formality used to conceal the essence of the transaction." See p. 61.

fide (non-tax) purpose. This meaning is possible, given the importance he placed on *bona fides* in the criminal fraud case *Olan et al.*[551]

Also, Dickson was not on the panel that decided *Stubart Investments*,[552] where Estey did not refer to *bona fides* when describing the nature of shams and relied on the Exchequer Court decision in *Foreign Power Securities*,[553] to distinguish the American business purpose test, which incorporates a *bona fide* test. That is why it is important to note that Estey failed to mention that Cartwright J. rested the Supreme Court's dismissal of the Crown's appeal in that case on Foreign Power being a *bona fide* investment company. Further, just because there is no judicial *bona fide* business purpose test in Canada is not the same as the Canadian sham doctrine requiring the presence of a *bona fide* purpose when enforcing legal results against innocent third parties, although 40 years later almost everyone appears to gloss over this detail in a tax context apparently assuming the Minister is not an innocent third party acting on behalf of all other taxpayers.

Regardless, what is clear is that Dickson maintained that the purpose test in the interest deductibility rule requires that the taxpayer have a *bona fide* purpose to earn income from the property acquired with the borrowed funds. It also seems clear that later Supreme Court judges constrained the application of certain fundamental intent and purpose tests in the ITA consistent with Justice Wilson's view that there need be no business purpose but the tax purpose.

The final four decisions of Justice Major put in issue the different consequences of tax evasion versus tax avoidance. Tax evasion is subject to a public shaming and prison time in a provincial facility or a federal penitentiary. If the prison term is two years less a day, the evader is sent to a provincial facility—otherwise to a federal penitentiary. Tax avoidance is often rewarded for its cleverness.

[551] *Olan et al., supra* note 373.

[552] *Stubart Investments, supra* note 386.

[553] *Foreign Power Securities, supra* note 309.

There is no shame in avoiding tax except when the avoidance gets broad public scrutiny accompanied by reputational risk; but many would argue that any such scrutiny should appreciate that there is both a fine line, and a significant distinction, between avoiding and evading tax.

In a trial concerning an indictment for tax evasion, juries delineate that line and distinction if an accused is willing to risk a jury trial instead of being tried by judge alone. Recall that Samuel Ciglen obtained a favourable result from the judge who heard his case although he was convicted on appeal. In a tax avoidance case, judges, not juries, determine the result, and they apply the judicial guidelines set down by the Supreme Court, which differ dramatically in the pre-*Charter* and *Charter* eras.

Warren Jarvis (2002);[554] *Dr. Chee Ling (2002)*[555]

Georgia Jarvis was an Albertan artist who painted rural landscapes. She lived from 1944 to 1990. During her life, Georgia Jarvis filed income tax returns and reported taxable income from art sales. At the time of her death, she owned original paintings and limited-edition prints. More prints of her work were created after her death.

Jarvis was survived by her husband, Warren Jarvis, an Alberta farmer and the Executor of the Estate of Georgia Jarvis. He sold the artwork after her death. By 1992, sales had fallen and Jarvis

---

[554] *Warren Jarvis v. The Queen*, 2002 SCC 73, [2002] 3 SCR 757, dismissing the taxpayer's appeal from (2000), [2002] 3 CTC 226, 193 DLR (4th) 656 (Alta. CA), affirming 98 DTC 6308, [1998] 3 CTC 252 (Alta. QB), rev'g [1997] 7 WWR 757 amending [1997] 5 WWR 461 (Alta. Prov. Ct.). *R. v. Jarvis* – SCC Cases (scc-csc.ca).

[555] *Dr. Chee K. Ling v. The Queen*, 2002 SCC 74, [2002] 3 SCR 814, dismissing the taxpayer's appeal from (2000) 149 CCC (3rd) 127, [2002] 4 CTC 122 (BCCA), which affirmed [1999] 3 CTC 386 (BCSC) rev'g a decision of the British Columbia Provincial Court that convicted the taxpayer. *R. v. Ling* – SCC Cases (scc-csc.ca).

re-located to a log cabin about 80 kilometres north-west of Calgary. His tax troubles were about to begin.

In late 1993 or early 1994, someone typed up a letter and addressed it to the CRA's Calgary office, advising its recipient that Mr. Jarvis had failed to report substantial amounts of income from the sales of Mrs. Jarvis' artwork in the 1990 and 1991 taxation years. The author of that letter was a "confidential informant," and the identity of informants cannot be revealed by agents of the state without the permission of the informant.

In CRA terms, such information is called a *lead*; some leads amount to nothing, while others direct tax auditors to evidence establishing non-compliance with the law. Unsolicited leads are often based on a personal vendetta with the hope that the CRA will turn the life of that person upside down. Auditors know this and are instructed to ensure alleged non-compliance exists in fact and law.

Within two weeks, the assigned auditor, Ms. Donna Goy-Edwards, determined the lead had merit. She calculated sales at nine galleries of Mrs. Jarvis' art totalled $358,409 between October 23 and December 31, 1990. The sales were $221,366 in 1991. At this point, Goy-Edwards arranged to meet Jarvis at his farm on April 11, 1994. She indicated that an assistant would accompany her.

Goy-Edwards' assistant turned out to be Mr. Moriarty, her manager. She introduced him to Jarvis as her team leader, and his presence would later be explained based on his familiarity with the rural area in which Jarvis lived, thus providing navigational assistance to Goy-Edwards. This became a matter of contention.

Goy-Edwards took the lead in interviewing Jarvis, with Moriarty asking questions for clarification purposes. At no time, did Goy-Edwards or Moriarty caution Jarvis on April 11 about his constitutional rights. He answered all questions posed, which primarily concerned the sales of art.

Essentially, Jarvis indicated that all sales were reported in his record books, and he provided information about his banking arrangements. Jarvis provided an authorization to Goy-Edwards to obtain details held by the bank, but she agreed to allow Jarvis to obtain the documentation directly. Goy-Edwards also asked questions concerning the number of paintings and prints in existence at the time of the death of Georgia Jarvis to compare to the list she prepared from attending the galleries.

By late April 1994, Goy-Edwards determined a discrepancy of about $700,000 between reported income and actual income for the two taxation years; obviously, this is a large discrepancy. She concluded that Jarvis grossly understated the net income from sales, and the understatement suggested the possibility of tax fraud. Goy-Edwards referred her audit file to Special (Criminal) Investigations, which assigned the file to Ms. Dianne Chang, who began a review. She met Goy-Edwards for one to two hours to discuss the file and later contacted her briefly to clarify certain notations in the file. There was no suggestion that Chang or anyone else asked Goy-Edwards to obtain information from Jarvis under the guise of an audit.

Chang performed her own calculations and analysis and gathered additional information from internal sources. Her purpose was to determine whether reasonable and probable grounds existed to obtain a search warrant to further an investigation related to laying possible tax evasion charges. By June 1994, Chang believed such grounds existed and began preparing an Information to Obtain a Search Warrant. She sought approval to seek judicial authorization, but this did not occur until November 1994, despite a lack of new information.

Meanwhile, Jarvis' accountant began seeking clarification as to the status of the file from Goy-Edwards, who did not know what to say. While CRA policy provided that the accountant had to be advised of a referral if he asked, Goy-Edwards advised him that there was nothing to report and that the file was in a "holding pattern due to work demands." The Chief of Investigations was bewildered at that message, but no remedial steps were taken to advise the accountant.

On November 24, 1994, Chang swore an Information to Obtain a Search Warrant, explaining her belief that offences had been committed, based, in part, on analysis she had conducted from the books and records provided by Goy-Edwards. Provincial Court Judge Fradsham authorized the warrants, which were issued under the *Criminal Code.* They authorized searches and seizures at Jarvis' residence, the accountant's residence (his place of business) and the offices of the CRA at Calgary (to seize the books and records that Goy-Edwards obtained). The warrants were executed on November 29, 1994. In early 1995, Chang drew up requirement letters that were issued to financial institutions for information in respect of Jarvis' bank accounts. They complied. The information seized served as the main evidence against Jarvis at his eventual trial.

Jarvis was charged with five offences, including making false statements on tax returns and willfully evading or attempting to evade payment of taxes. His trial occurred in the Alberta Provincial Court–Criminal Division. Coincidentally, the trial judge was Provincial Court Judge Fradsham, who authorized the warrants. At trial, the Crown sought to tender evidence to prove the charges. This was met with an objection as to the admissibility of the evidence.

Judge Fradsham convened two *voir dire.* First, Judge Fradsham found that Goy-Edwards during the April 11 meeting at Jarvis' farm was "seeking out confirmatory proof of her opinion that this was a matter of serious underreporting of income which should be prosecutorily [sic] pursued by Special Investigations."[556] The failure to caution Jarvis of his rights during the meeting at his farm was a breach of his right to life, liberty and the security of the person under s. 7 of the *Charter.* The documents and statements the CRA obtained from Jarvis on April 11 were tainted and could

[556] *Jarvis, supra* note 554, para. 38, p. 782.

not be relied on to obtain the search warrant. The searches and seizures were also invalid as violations of the right to be secure from either an unreasonable search or seizure under s. 8 of the *Charter*, and the evidence was excluded by subs. 24(2) of the *Charter*. What evidence remained was insufficient to establish reasonable and probable cause.

Judge Fradsham held at the second *voir dire* that the CRA could not rely on its civil audit powers to obtain records from banks when investigating a tax offence. He did not believe the explanation that was given for the attendance of Moriarty at the meeting of April 11, 1994. He found the civil tax audit turned into a criminal investigation on March 16, 1994, when Goy-Edwards completed her review of information sourced from galleries. Judge Fradsham excluded banking information obtained after that by the requirement letters.

Next, Judge Fradsham directed a verdict acquitting Jarvis, and the Crown appealed.

The Alberta Court of Queen's Bench and Court of Appeal held that the statements Jarvis made at the April 11 meeting and the banking information obtained under the requirement letters had to be excluded from the information relied on to obtain the warrants, but the remaining information could be used. After deleting the oral utterances Jarvis made at the meeting on April 11, the warrants were validly issued because there remained reasonable and probable cause. The matter was sent back to the trial court. Jarvis appealed to the Supreme Court.

Meanwhile in Vancouver, Mr. James Thatcher of the CRA began a routine audit in November 1994. His audit concerned Dr. Chee Ling, who practised medicine in Kitimat and owned a farm in Delta, British Columbia. His farm loss claims for 1987–89 had been audited and denied on the basis they were personal and not business losses.[557] A check of the CRA's computers in November

[557] For facts, see *Ling*, *supra* note 555. (Disclosure: I worked with the CRA auditor James Thatcher in 2019–2022.)

1994 revealed that Dr. Ling had claimed farming losses for 1990–93. Thatcher advised Dr. Ling that an audit would be conducted.

On June 5, 1995, Thatcher and Arvind Pacheco of the CRA met with Dr. Ling's accountant, where they examined Ling's records. They determined that his Medical Service Plan receipts were deposited into his accounts twice a month but other deposits could not be identified. On June 7, 1995, Thatcher and Pacheco arrived at Dr. Ling's office at the Kitimat General Hospital and requested to review two receipt books. These records were compared with bank deposits in Dr. Ling's accounts. They deduced that Dr. Ling was not reporting all his income.

Another meeting was held at Dr. Ling's farm in August, and by mid-September additional information was obtained. On December 18, 1995, Dr. Ling attended the CRA's office in downtown Vancouver, where he met with auditors for about three hours. During the meeting, Ling admitted he mistakenly failed to report certain amounts of income. At no point was Ling advised of his constitutional rights. Following another meeting on December 29, 1995, additional documents were obtained from various brokerage firms and chartered banks, with Ling's permission.

After December 18, 1995, and before January 18, 1996, Pacheco met with his group head, Mr. Fleming, and Mr. Richard Olney of Special Investigations. The outcome of that meeting was a referral to Special Investigations on January 18, 1996.

Special Investigations served requirements on four banks and on Dr. Ling's accountant. On February 28, 1995, Onley and Fleming met Dr. Ling and cautioned him as to his constitutional rights at the outset of this meeting: (1) he did not have to make any statements, (2) any statements could be used against him as evidence and (3) he had a right to retain counsel. Dr. Ling exercised these rights and refused to speak to Onley and Fleming.

The Crown charged Dr. Ling with six counts of committing tax offences. He was tried before the Provincial Court of British

Columbia in July 1997. Ling sought a stay and, if not, an exclusion of evidence obtained by the auditors, based on an infringement of his *Charter* rights. Provincial Court Judge Graham denied the motion. He held the criminal investigation did not commence after the meeting of December 18, 1995, until the Group Head told the auditor to refer the file to Special Investigations. Dr. Ling was convicted on all six counts.

On appeal, the British Columbia Supreme Court reversed the convictions on the basis the predominant purpose of the audit shifted to criminal enforcement from an administrative action immediately after the meeting of December 18, 1995. The Court disagreed with the finding at trial that the investigation had not commenced after that meeting merely because CRA auditor Thatcher was of the view it was premature to refer the file to Special Investigations until he could complete the audit. The Court ordered a new trial on all counts, with special attention paid to apply *Charter* principles to all evidence obtained after the meeting of December 18, 1995.

Dr. Ling appealed on the basis that all evidence should be subject to *Charter* principles, but the British Columbia Court of Appeal dismissed the appeal. Ling appealed to the Supreme Court.

The constitutional challenge by Mr. Jarvis and Dr. Ling under the *Charter* was not against the Minister's power to audit taxpayers or to compel taxpayers to produce documentary evidence for the purpose of administering or enforcing compliance with the ITA. Such a challenge would fail, given Justice Wilson's decision in *McKinlay Transport.* Instead, the attack is directed at excluding from a criminal trial the evidence gathered during an administrative audit of the taxpayers, and under the requirement letters. The position is that the Minister's officials breached the taxpayers' rights in ss. 7 and 8 of the *Charter* and the evidence obtained should be excluded under the *Charter* from admission at any trial concerning a tax offence.

Justices Major and Iacobucci in *Jarvis* posed and answered three questions. First, is there a distinction between the CRA's audit and criminal investigative functions under the ITA? Second, if there is, when does the CRA exercise its audit function, and when does it exercise its investigative function? Third, what are the legal consequences for the taxpayer when the CRA exercises its investigative function?[558] They answered each question from the perspective of the role that income taxation has in our democracy for the government and the individual.

Their decision seeks to balance the regulatory needs associated with ensuring an efficient and practical system for taxing income with fundamental principles of justice as associated with ensuring that the state does not abuse individual rights and freedoms. Justices Major and Iacobucci also provided an overview of Canada's self-assessment and self-reporting income tax system. They stated, "Governments, undisputedly, require revenue to finance their operations and to implement social programmes," and cited a number of decisions that considered the matter, including Justice Wilson's 1990 decision in *McKinlay Transport.*

Major and Iacobucci sought to achieve a balance through two holdings. First, the Minister's authority to ensure that taxpayers comply with Canada's income tax law obligates taxpayers to do so honestly, including when under audit or when required to provide information by demand letter. Second, the Minister's authority to compel taxpayers to provide information ends when the *predominant purpose* of the Minister's inquiry concerns investigating a penal liability articulated in s. 239 of the ITA.

Also, Justices Major and Iacobucci found that the existence of the state pitted against a taxpayer in a penal liability sense is a contextual determination where no one factor is necessarily determinative, as the totality of the circumstances must be assessed.

[558] *Jarvis, supra* note 554, SCC para. 1, p. 765.

The factors to consider were listed.[559] They summarized the principles as follows:

> In summary, wherever the predominate purpose of an inquiry or question is the determination of penal liability, criminal investigatory techniques must be used. As a corollary, all *Charter* protections that are relevant in the criminal context must apply.
>
> ...
>
> By way of summary, the following principles emerge:
>
> 1. Although the ITA is a regulatory statute, a distinction can be drawn between the audit and investigative powers that it grants to the Minister.
> 2. When, in light of all relevant circumstances, it is apparent that CCRA officials are not engaged in the verification of tax liability, but are engaged in the determination of penal liability under s. 239, the adversarial relationship

[559] *Ibid.*, SCC para. 94, pp. 806–07. The listed factors are as follows:

(a) Did the authorities have reasonable grounds to lay charges? Does it appear from the record that a decision to proceed with a criminal investigation could have been made [emphasis added by Court]?

(b) Was the general conduct of the authorities such that it was consistent with the pursuit of a criminal investigation?

(c) Had the auditor transferred his or her files and material to the investigators?

(d) Was the conduct of the auditor such that he or she was effectively acting as an agent for the investigators?

(e) Does it appear that the investigators intended to use the auditor as the agent in the collection of evidence?

(f) Is the evidence sought relevant to taxpayer liability generally? Or, as is their case with evidence as to the taxpayer's *mens rea*, is the evidence relevant only to the taxpayer's penal liability?

(g) Are there any other circumstances or factors that can lead the trial judge to the conclusion that the compliance audit had in reality become a criminal investigation?

These factors can be applied to federal and provincial departments and agencies in different enforcement settings.

between the state and the individual exists. As a result, *Charter* protections are engaged.

3. When this is the case, investigators must provide the taxpayer with a proper warning. The powers of compulsion in ss. 231.1(1) and 231.2(1) are not available, and search warrants are required in order to further the investigation.[560]

Application to Mr. Jarvis:

In summary, there was nothing in the record established that Goy-Edwards obtained taxpayer information for the purpose of advancing a criminal investigation. She did not use misleading tactics to obtain information under the civil audit power and requirement authority for the purpose of advancing an investigation of a penal liability. Goy-Edwards and Chang had only minimal contact once the file was transferred to Special Investigations.

It was not improper for Goy-Edwards to bring Moriarity to the meeting at Mr. Jarvis' farm on April 11. He could provide a second opinion as to whether the matter should be referred to Special Investigations. Goy-Edwards should not have described him as an assistant, "but this did not change the fact the referral to Special Investigations was the auditor's determination."[561]

The record established that the CRA obtained little new information at the meeting with Jarvis on April 11. Goy-Edwards sought confirmation of her suspicion that tax evasion had occurred, but the objective was to determine whether to refer the file. Much of the information relied on to obtain the warrants was in the CRA's possession before April 11.[562] The searches were valid, and the evidence obtained was admissible at a new trial. But the banking records that Special Investigations obtained under the requirement

---

[560] *Ibid.*, SCC paras. 98–99. pp. 809–10.

[561] *Ibid.*, SCC para. 102, p. 811. "So long as there has been no crystallization of the adversarial relationship, there is, in our view, nothing wrong with an auditor seeking the counsel of another before completing the transfer paperwork."

[562] *Ibid.*, SCC paras. 100–05, pp. 811–12.

letters were to be excluded because it could not rely on the civil requirement power to advance an investigation into a penal liability. (Chief Justice McLachlin and Justices L'Heureux-Dubé, Gonthier, Bastarache, Binnie, Arbour and LeBel concurred.)

Application to Dr. Ling:

In *Ling*, the Supreme Court applied the principles set out in *Jarvis*. The issue was whether Dr. Ling could claim immunity in respect of the information compelled by the auditors during the administrative audit.

Justices Major and Iacobucci answered as follows: (1) the CRA did not have reasonable grounds to lay charges before December 18, 1995; (2) it did not appear prior to the December 18 meeting that a decision to proceed with a criminal investigation could have been made; (3) the general conduct of the tax authorities was not such that it had decided the taxpayer was under investigation for s. 239 offences; (4) the decision to proceed with a criminal investigation was made after December 18, 1995; (5) the CRA auditors never transferred their files and materials to the investigators until January 18, 1996; (6) the conduct of the auditors was not such that they were effectively acting as agents for the investigators; and (7) it does not appear that the investigators intended to use the auditors as their agent in the collection of evidence.[563]

Consequently, the information the CRA civil auditors gathered up to and including their meeting with Dr. Ling at the CRA's Vancouver office on December 18, 1995, was admissible evidence at trial. Information CRA criminal law investigators gathered pursuant to the requirement letter of December 29, 1995, and evidence derived therefrom was inadmissible under subs. 24(2) of the *Charter*. (Chief Justice McLachlin and Justices L'Heureux-Dubé, Gonthier, Bastarache, Binnie, Arbour and LeBel concurred.)

The next two decisions concern the GAAR and the avoidance of tax by acting on clever advice rather than evading tax. There is

---

[563] *Ling*, *supra* note 555, SCC para. 31, p. 827.

no real downside other than paying the tax and interest, and possible reputational risk if the public becomes hostile to the result. The decisions are extremely important in the context of the avoidance of income tax.

Canada Trustco (2005);[564] *Mathew (2005)*[565]

A significant incongruity exists between the Supreme Court's decisions in *Canada Trustco* and *Mathew*. It held in *Canada Trustco* that the GAAR did not apply to deny the deduction of CCA lacking in commercial substance and reality. But the Court held in *Mathew* the GAAR applied to deny the deduction of a real commercial loss acquired from unrelated taxpayers. The reason for this incongruity is obscured by the difficulty in understanding the facts in *Canada Trustco* in commercial, legal and income tax terms. The transactions require a dogged perseverance to master, and if that is somehow done, the task remains of placing them in their commercial, legal and tax contexts.

The plethora of facts in *Canada Trustco* obscure a simple detail: no commercial financing was advanced on a purported capital (financing) lease despite commercial financing being the *sin qua non* of such a lease. This is important to note at the outset for two reasons.

First, at trial, Justice Campbell Miller found that the "normative comparable" in respect of the leasing arrangement before the

---

[564] *Canada Trustco Mortgage Co. v. The Queen*, 2005 SCC 54, [2005] 2 SCR 601, dismissing the Crown's appeal from 2004 FCA 67, 2004 DTC 6119, [2004] 2 CTC 276 (FCA), affirming the Tax Court, which allowed the taxpayer's appeal, 2003 TCC 215, 2003 DTC 587, [2003] 4 CTC 2009 (TCC). *Canada Trustco Mortgage Co. v. Canada* – SCC Cases (scc-csc.ca). The Tax Court decision is at *Canada Trustco Mortgage Company v. The Queen* - Tax Court of Canada (tcc-cci.gc.ca).

[565] *Mathew v. The Queen*, 2005 SCC 55, [2005] 2 SCR 643, affirming (*sub nom. Kaulius*), 2003 FCA 371, 2003 DTC 5644, [2004] 1 CTC 115 (FCA), affirming the Tax Court, which dismissed the taxpayer's appeal, 2002 DTC 1637, [2003] 1 CTC 2045 (TCC). *Mathew v. Canada* – SCC Cases (scc-csc.ca). The Federal Court of Appeal decision is at *Kaulius v. Canada* – Federal Court of Appeal (fca-caf.gc.ca).

Tax Court was "the *ordinary* sale-leaseback of exempt property" [emphasis added]. Such a lease "converts the seller's capital asset into cash, while enabling the seller to retain operational control over the assets, thanks to the lease." That type of lease is a "method of affording business the possibility of financing at potentially more favourable rates than traditional lenders." Miller thus treated the Canada Trustco sale-leaseback transaction as an ordinary sale-leaseback of "exempt property"[566] that falls within the scope of the policy of affording business favourable financing rates, and that is "why such sale-leasebacks are not subjected to GAAR."[567]

Second, the Supreme Court's *Canada Trustco* decision also treats a sale-leaseback arrangement concerning exempt property that provides no commercial financing as an ordinary sale-leaseback transaction. This holding helps deflect in a way that puts the cart before the horse, so to speak. It places the emphasis on the purpose for an exception in the exempt property definition for highway trailers from rules meant to limit in certain circumstances the deduction of accelerated CCA amounts. The so-called *horse* that comes before that cart is whether the taxpayer incurred an actual commercial cost. Because if it did not, how does allowing any CCA deduction, let alone accelerated CCA, satisfy the basic test that applies to all expenses—incurred for the purpose of gaining or producing income from a source? How can a cost that is not incurred commercially magically satisfy that test? The answer is to make a sale-leaseback arrangement that has no commercial financing an *ordinary* transaction.

In 1996, Canada Trustco took $25 million of its own funds and borrowed about $97 million from the Royal Bank on a non-recourse basis. It then acquired certain transport trailers from an American company, Transamerica Leasing Incorporated (Transamerica), which was already leasing the trailers to others in the United States.

---

566 "Exempt property" is defined by *Income Tax Regulation* 1100(1.13) and includes "trailers" designed to haul freight.

567 *Canada Trustco, supra* note 564, TCC para. 82.

The Supreme Court indicated that Canada Trustco acquired "absolute ownership" of those trailers for $120 million on December 17, 1996. That same day, for "administrative convenience," Canada Trustco appointed Transamerica "trustee and agent" to hold in its name for Canada Trustco "title, certificate of ownership, registration and like documentation in respect of the trailers." This should mean that Transamerica would be identified as that owner, not Canada Trustco, if anyone searched for the name of the registered owner of the transport trailers (e.g., the police or border officials).[568]

Next, Canada Trustco leased the trailers to a company incorporated in England. The trailers then circled back to Transamerica under a sublease and continued to be leased to the original lessees.

Transamerica took the $120 million of funds it received from Canada Trustco and immediately paid $116.4 million (after deducting a $3.6 million facilitation fee) into bank accounts for the benefit of Canada Trustco and its lender. The payment was ostensibly a pre-payment of lease payments. In commercial terms, the result was that Transamerica did not realize equity from the sale-leaseback transaction in respect of its trailers. It was in it for the facilitation fee.

The first $97.35 million of Transamerica's $116.4 million payment was placed on deposit for the benefit of the Royal Bank. That deposit caused the loan the Royal Bank made to Canada Trustco (about $97 million) to disappear from both of their balance sheets. The commercial terminology for this financial engineering is "defeasement."

A defeased loan is not recognized for commercial or regulatory purposes although it is suggested by many that such a loan must be recognized for tax purposes because of its "legal substance." Ah yes, the debt existed in legal terms because it technically had not

[568] *Ibid.*, SCC, Parts III and IV (Purchase and Sale of Trailers) of Appendix.

been repaid; its repayment sat in an offshore account, waiting for the time repayment came due under the debt's legal form.

Further, CT Financial Services—the parent corporation of Canada Trustco—stated in its Annual Financial Report that Canada Trustco's investment portfolio was being *reduced* and *not increased* as might otherwise be suggested by its $120 million trailer purchase.

> … Canada Trust also holds a portfolio of loans and leases to government agencies and large companies. Canada Trust does not intend to make any significant increase in this class of investment [loans and leases to governments and large companies] and since 1995, it has gradually reduced the size of the existing portfolio …[569]

Relevancy: This suggests that Canada Trustco did not intend to acquire any significant interest in the trailers on commercial terms for the purpose of entering into capital (financing) leases. Agreed Facts 5 and 6 in the Tax Court decision provide that Canada Trustco's Senior Credit Committee and Executive Committee approved of the 1996 transactions.[570] Appendix A to the Tax Court decision sets out the tax and accounting results in financial terms.[571]

The remaining portion of Transamerica's payment of $116.4 million, about $20 million, was placed in the Isle of Jersey with the Royal Bank of Canada Trust Company. As trustee, it purchased an Ontario savings bond with the funds for the benefit of Canada Trustco. By locating the bond in a tax haven in 1996, it presumably earned interest, free of taxation. Over time, the bond grew to a pre-determined amount—$33.5 million in December 2005. The bond was pledged as security to Canada Trustco on the basis

[569] *Ibid.*, TCC para. 4 (Agreed Facts: A. Introduction, number 3).
[570] *Ibid.*, TCC para. 4 (Agreed Facts: B. Approval to enter into said transactions, number 5).
[571] *Ibid.*, TCC at 2003 DTC p. 590 (see pp. 608–10 for appendixes), [2003] 4 CTC pp. 2013–14. (see pp. 2046–47 for appendixes).

Transamerica would use it to pay Canada Trustco to reacquire the trailers or in respect of the lease's termination value.

The result is Canada Trustco's commercial return gambit came out of Canada's treasury. Similar "sale in, lease out" and "lease in, lease out" tax avoidance schemes involving other commercial actors circulated the globe at the time, including targeting the American and British treasuries.

In the United States alone, over $35 billion of artificial deductions were claimed under the suspect leasing schemes. Congress shut the schemes down with amendments effective in March 2004. The American judiciary then disallowed pre-existing schemes in case after case, relying on judicial guidelines dating to the 1930s, while the British House of Lords (judicial branch) allowed the schemes in a 2004 decision.[572]

Canada Trustco claimed it incurred capital cost in respect of the trailers equal to about $120 million. (Class 10 property is eligible for a 30 percent CCA rate, computed annually on a declining balance basis.) The acquisition of $120 million of trailers for the purpose of gaining or producing income is said to be the legal substance of the transactions.

However, the above is not how the Supreme Court summarized the facts in its opinion. It can be said that the Court's summary fails to note that the Canada Trustco defeased borrowing from the Royal Bank was on neither company's balance sheet. Nor does the summary indicate that the transactions are not a commercial financing sale-leaseback arrangement. The summary never notes that Transamerica was not paid an amount that would reflect its realizing equity it had in the trailers (see footnote

[572] Robert W. Wood, "What *Wells Fargo* Brings to the SILO/LILO Debate," *Tax Notes [Tax Analysts]*, June 27, 2011, pp. 1389–93. Wells Fargo claimed $112 million of deductions. For example, see *Wells Fargo & Co. v. United States*, 641 F.3d 1319 (Fed. Cir., 2011). The British judiciary allowed the schemes. See *Barclays Mercantile Business Finance Ltd. v. Mawson (Her Majesty's Inspector of Taxes)*, [2004] UKHL 51, [2004] BTC 414 (HL), which dismissed the Crown's appeal from [2003] BTC 81 (CA), which reversed [2002] BTC 388 (High Court).

for the Court's summary).[573] Nor does the summary indicate that Transamerica received a fee of less than $4 million to facilitate Canada Trustco avoiding tax otherwise owing.

In the Tax Court, Canada Trustco described the regulatory effect of its borrowing $97 million:

> Mr. Lough described the benefit of the financial arrangement as improving the economics of the transaction, *by allowing the netting of the non-recourse loan against the total value of the lease for purposes of financial reporting on the balance sheet which reduced the amount of capital the Appellant was required by regulatory*

[573] *Canada Trustco, supra* note 564. The SCC stated (paras. 2–3):

The respondent, Canada Trustco Mortgage Company ("CTMC"), carries on business as a mortgage lender. As part of its business operations, CTMC enjoyed large revenues from leased assets. In 1996 it purchased a number of trailers which it then circuitously leased back to the vendor, in order to offset revenue from its leased assets by claiming considerable capital cost allowance ("CCA") on the trailers in the amount of $31,196,700 against $51,787,114 for the 1997 taxation year. The essence of the transaction is explained in the memorandum of Michael Logan, CTMC's officer in charge of the recommendation to proceed: 'The transaction provides very attractive returns generating CCA deductions which can be used to shelter other taxable lease income generated by Canada Trust.' This arrangement allowed CTMC to defer paying taxes on the amount of profits reduced by the CCA deductions which would be subject to recapture into income when the trailers were disposed of at a future date, and presumably in excess of the amount claimed as CCA.

The details of the transaction are complex and described in greater detail in the Appendix. Briefly stated, on December 17, 1996, the respondent, with the use of its own money and a loan of approximately $100 million from the Royal Bank of Canada ("RBC"), purchased trailers from Transamerica Leasing Inc. ("TLI") at fair market value of $120 million. CTMC leased the trailers to Maple Assets Investments Limited ("MAIL") who in turn subleased them to TLL, the original owner. TLI then prepaid all amounts due to MAIL under the sublease. MAIL placed on deposit an amount equal to the loan for purposes of making the lease payments and a bond was pledged as security to guarantee a purchase option payment to CTMC at the end of the lease. These transactions allowed CMTC to substantially minimize its financial risk. They were also accompanied by financial arrangements with various parties, not relevant to this appeal.

> *authorities to hold, and also by relying on leveraged lease accounting to draw income to the early part of the lease* [emphasis added].[574]

As noted, the netting means in commercial terms that the $97 million defeased loan did not exist for accounting, commercial, economic or bank regulatory purposes. But the Tax Court merely noted that the netting had a positive effect on Canada Trustco's ability to satisfy bank regulators in respect of its capital reserve requirements:

> The communications [between the Vice-President of Taxation for TD Bank Financial Group, and the Canada Customs and Revenue Agency] talk in terms of the positive impact on TAC [Total Asset to Capital] and BIS [Bank for International Settlement] requirements of OSFI [Office of the Superintendent of Financial Institutions for Canada].[575]

Similarly, in the Supreme Court, Part XII of the decision's Appendix states that the "use of non-recourse debt [The Royal Bank had no recourse against Canada Trustco] significantly improved ... [Canada Trustco's] management of regulatory requirements." But the bottom line is the Royal Bank did not need recourse against Canada Trustco because it was repaid its $97 million loan in commercial terms. This is why the loan was defeased, and it should come as no surprise to anyone that a loan to Canada Trustco that had been immediately repaid in commercial terms under the tax avoidance plan did not affect its management of regulatory requirements.

Capital reserve requirements are what regulators require banks to satisfy to protect the public from bank failures. They limit the amount that the banks can loan and upon which they can earn interest income. This includes mortgages, commercial loans and consumer loans to individuals. But Canada Trustco's scheme had

[574] *Ibid.*, TCC para. 6 (TCC at 2003 DTC p. 592, [2003] 4 CTC p. 2018.
[575] *Ibid.*, TCC at the decision's footnote 4 (2003 DTC p. 593, [2003] 4 CTC p. 2020).

no adverse effect on its ability to make loans, as it did not in commercial or regulatory terms owe one red cent to the Royal Bank concurrent with defeasement.

Justice Major and Chief Justice McLachlin found in *Canada Trustco* that there are two steps when considering under the GAAR whether the scheme abused the tax provisions. Step 1 is to consider the object, spirit and purpose of the provisions in issue. To do so, the "textual, contextual and purposive" interpretive approach is to be used to interpret the provisions. Step 2 is to examine the factual context to determine if an avoidance transaction frustrates the object, spirit and purpose of those provisions.[576]

The Supreme Court also referred to transactions being an abuse if they are "wholly dissimilar to the relationships or transactions that are contemplated by the provisions":

> Abusive tax avoidance may be found where the relationships and transactions as expressed in the relevant documentation lack a proper basis relative to the object, spirit or purpose of the provisions that are purported to confer the tax benefit, or where they are *wholly dissimilar to the relationships or transactions that are contemplated by the provisions* [emphasis added].[577]

Only if the Supreme Court considered the Canada Trustco sale-leaseback arrangement wholly dissimilar to the transactions contemplated by the provisions would it offend the tax law under the GAAR. Given this framing of the question, it is apt to ask what represents an abuse under the GAAR if it does not include a sale-leaseback arrangement that

- provides no commercial proceeds to the vendor (and no commercial financing) other than the payment of an approximate $3.6 million facilitation fee to the vendor, and

[576] *Ibid.*, SCC para. 60.

[577] *Ibid.*

- is done *solely* by a taxpayer (Canada Trustco) to obtain $120 million of CCA tax deductions in return for paying the vendor a fee of less than $4 million, combined with a $97 million Royal Bank loan that was commercially repaid by the vendor of the trailers from the start; coupled with a $20 million bond located in a tax haven accruing to $33.5 million in 2005, payable to Canada Trustco, nine years later.

How can such an arrangement not be an abuse of the CCA regime in the narrow sense, and the ITA as a whole in the broader sense, to ensure that the computation of a taxpayer's commercial profit is accurate for income tax assessment?

The Supreme Court's answer in *Canada Trustco* was as follows (para. 41): "[C]ourts cannot search for an overriding policy of the Act that is not based on a unified, textual, contextual and purposive interpretation *of the specific provisions in issue*" [emphasis added]. These are telling words because, by focusing a search for an "overriding" policy on specific provisions in issue, the Supreme Court placed a significant judicially created constraint on the application of the GAAR.

As previously discussed, Justice Abbott in his 1958 opinion in *British Columbia Electric Railway Co.* held that all business outlays, whether expenses or capital amounts, are deductible only to the extent that they are incurred for the purpose of gaining or producing income. At that time, he also noted that it can be presumed that the outlays incurred by a business satisfy this purpose test. But this is a presumption only. The outlays could be personal in nature, or for that matter may have been incurred solely for the purpose of avoiding income tax rather than for the purpose of gaining or producing income from a source of income.

But the Supreme Court found that "Parliament intends taxpayers to take full advantage of the provisions of the Act that confer tax benefits … [and it] did not intend the GAAR to undermine this basic tenet of tax law."[578] The tax benefits being referred to in the case are nothing more than CCA, which is *not a tax benefit* unless it

[578] *Ibid.*, SCC para. 61.

is accelerated *or not paid for out of the taxpayer's pocket such as where it is artificial in nature.* There is simply no discussion of the point that deduction of cost from gross revenue goes hand in hand with computing "profit" from a business source and that profit is understated, or a loss is overstated, in commercial terms to the extent an artificial cost is allowed to be deducted in computing that profit (or loss).

The result was the Supreme Court never questioned why the CCA deducted by Canada Trustco might be described as effecting "tax benefits" under the structure, and it found that the GAAR assumes the conferment of a tax benefit under the plain language of a provision is not abusive and a reverse onus exists in which the Crown must prove otherwise:

> The GAAR may be applied to deny a tax benefit only after it is determined that it was not reasonable to consider the tax benefit to be within the object, spirit or purpose of the provisions relied upon by the taxpayer. The negative language in which s. 245(4) is cast indicates that the starting point for the analysis is the assumption that a tax benefit that would be conferred by the plain words of the Act is not abusive. This means that a finding of abuse is only warranted where the opposite conclusion – that the avoidance transaction was consistent with the object, spirit or purpose of the provisions of the Act that are relied on by the taxpayer – cannot be reasonably entertained. In other words, the abusive nature of the transaction must be clear.[579]

Although the Supreme Court found that the "central inquiry is focused on whether the transaction was consistent with the purpose" of the CCA provisions in issue, it found that the text, context and object of the legislation all supported Canada Trustco's deductions:

> Textually, the CCA provisions use "cost" in the well-established sense of the amount paid to acquire the assets.

[579] *Ibid.*, SCC para. 62.

> Contextually, other provisions of the Act support this interpretation. Finally, the purpose of the CCA provisions of the Act, as applied to sale-leaseback transactions, was, as found by the Tax Court judge, to permit deduction of CCA based on the cost of the assets acquired. This purpose emerges clearly from the scheme of the CCA provisions within the Act as a whole. The appellant's argument was not that the purpose of these provisions was unclear, but rather that the GAAR ought to override their accepted purpose and effect, for reasons external to the provisions themselves.[580]

To the Supreme Court, Canada Trustco had "paid" for the trailers, and the CCA provisions in issue do not refer to "economic risk." The GAAR was not intended to apply to such a transaction.

> The applicable CCA provisions of the Act do not refer to economic risk. They refer only to "cost." Where Parliament wanted to introduce economic risk into the meaning of cost related to CCA provisions, it did so expressly, as, for instance, in s. 13(7.1) and (7.2) of the Act, which makes adjustments to the cost of depreciable property when a taxpayer receives government assistance. "Cost" in the context of CCA is a well-understood legal concept. It has been carefully defined by the Act and the jurisprudence. Like the Tax Court judge, we see nothing in the GAAR or the object of the CCA provisions that permits us to rewrite them to interpret "cost" to mean "amount economically at risk" in the applicable provisions.[581]

For the Supreme Court, finding otherwise would "invite inconsistent results." The result would "vary with the degree of risk in each case." Note how the Court is suggesting potential inconsistent results for other taxpayers when, in the case before it, Canada

[580] *Ibid.*, SCC para. 74.

[581] *Ibid.*, SCC para. 75. See paras. 72–74 for "paid."

Trustco had no commercial risk except that the Minister might deny its tax benefits under the GAAR. But doing so "would offend the goal of the Act to provide sufficient certainty and predictability to permit taxpayers to intelligently order their affairs. For all these reasons, we agree with the Tax Court judge's conclusion that the cost was $120 million, not zero as argued by the appellant."[582]

The *Canada Trustco* so-called *ordinary* sale-leaseback arrangement occurred in late 1996, five years *before* the 2001 Enron accounting scandal in the United States. It concerned structured transactions, some of which dated to 1995 and were the proverbial canary singing loudly in a mine with noxious gas; the mine vein being targeted at least initially was the treasuries of western democracies. What is not well known about the Enron scandal is that senior management realized that tax avoidance schemes targeting western democracies could be used to create long-term "tax benefits" that could be converted into short-term "accounting income." The *U.S. Congressional Joint Committee on Taxation* put the matter this way in its February 2003 Report:

> As Enron's management came to realize that tax-motivated transactions could generate financial accounting benefits, Enron looked to its tax department to devise large transactions that would increase its financial accounting income. Enron came to view the role of its tax department as more than managing its Federal income tax liabilities. Rather, Enron's tax department became a source of financial statement earnings, thereby making it a profit center for the company. With an emphasis on short-term profitability and cash flow, Enron used various techniques to generate current financial statement net income and increase cash flows. Enron also used techniques with respect to its tax planning by engaging in 12 large structured transactions during the period 1995 until it filed for bankruptcy. At their core, Enron's structured

[582] *Ibid.*

> transactions were designed to permit Enron to take the position that its long-term tax benefits could be converted to current or short-term financial statement net income. In most of the structured transactions discussed in this Report, the origin of the financial accounting benefits was their reduction in Federal income tax that the transaction was anticipated to provide either currently or in the future.[583]

With respect to the complexity of the transactions, the following was stated:

> Enron had the incentive and the ability to engage in unusually complicated transactions in order to preclude meaningful review.[584]

With respect to Enron's relationship with the Internal Revenue Service:

> Corporations like Enron have an inherent advantage over the IRS. Enron relied on advice from sophisticated and experienced lawyers, investment bankers, and accountants. Assertions of attorney-client privilege hinders the ability of the IRS to obtain many of the most instructive documents, which impedes the IRS's ability to audit the transaction. Enron's activities shows [sic] that the IRS cannot minimize the importance of loss companies on examination because to do so would ignore a breeding ground for tax-motivated transactions that also could be used by taxpaying companies.[585]

With respect to Enron's purported business purposes for the transactions, the role of accommodating parties, the complexity of

---

[583] *Report of Investigation of Enron Corporation and Related Entities Regarding Federal Tax and Compensation Issues, and Policy Recommendations*, Prepared at the Request of Senator Max Baucus and Senator Charles Grassley, U.S. Senate Committee of Finance, February 2003, Volume 1: Report, Staff of the Joint Committee on Taxation, p. 8.
[584] *Ibid.*, p. 16.
[585] *Ibid.*

the structures and the related corporate cost-benefit risk equation associated with engaging in the transactions solely for tax purposes, the Report stated:

> Enron's aggressive interpretation of business purpose, the cooperation of accommodation parties, the protections provided by tax opinions, the complex design of transactions, advantages over the IRS—all were factors that contributed to Enron's ability to engage in tax-motivated transactions. Until the costs of participating in tax-motivated transactions are substantially increased, corporations such as Enron will continue to engage in transactions that violate the letter or the spirit of the law.[586]

The United States Senate Committee's mammoth 2003 Report was preceded in December 2002 by a staff report of the U.S. Senate Permanent Subcommittee on Investigations, which reported on four structured transactions, one of which concerned Enron's tax avoidance dealings in Canada.[587] All the structures were funded and facilitated by U.S. financial institutions.

Well before the *Canada Trustco* decision in 2005, tax avoidance that has no commercial reality (or substance) had become ordinary throughout the industrial world. Tax divisions of large corporations became sources of shareholder value realized through tax avoidance targeting the treasuries to which taxpayers pay their taxes. This included so-called *ordinary* sale-leaseback transactions.

What got Enron into real legal trouble was using artificial amounts to dupe stock market investors into thinking real commercial income was earned, which was a fantasy built on the non-commerciality of the so-called *tax benefits*. The massive scandal resulted in one of the world's largest accounting firms, Arthur Anderson

---

[586] *Ibid.*

[587] *U.S. Senate Permanent Subcommittee on Investigations Staff Report on Fishtail, Bacchus, Sundance, and Slapshot: For Enron Transactions Funded by U.S. Financial Institutions*, December 11, 2002, pp. 1–36.

LLP, collapsing before a jury convicted it of criminal conduct. In January 2005, the U.S. Supreme Court reversed this conviction (some actors within the firm destroyed massive amounts of documents), based on the trial judge's faulty jury instructions.[588]

By 2008, world financial markets were in a state of collapse, and major financial institutions teetered on the brink of insolvency only to be propped up with taxpayer funds. Underlying this collapse was regulatory failure and risk within opaque financial instruments, which in that case were derivatives.

The result in *Canada Trustco* should be compared to the Court's denial under the same GAAR of the tax avoidance result in *Mathew*.[589] If *Canada Trustco* reveals the alchemy of paper becoming gold, the elixir of tax avoidance was no panacea for a bunch of Canadian tax lawyers in *Mathew*.

In *Mathew*, the basis for finding an abuse of the tax law under the GAAR was that there is a scheme in that law meant to deny the trading and selling of losses by one taxpayer to an unrelated person. This had occurred, and a provision was misused to obtain the result. While one can understand why the GAAR should apply to the sale of a commercial loss in such a case, the difficulty is that the same Supreme Court failed to detect a scheme in the tax law that says only commercial costs can be deducted to compute commercial income—not artificial amounts.

The Supreme Court acknowledged in *Canada Trustco* that the explanatory notes that accompanied the introduction of the GAAR indicate the ITA is "intended to apply to transactions with real economic substance." But while those notes refer to "economic substance," the Court stated that the tax abuse rule in subs. 245(4) "does not consider a transaction to result in abusive tax avoidance merely because an economic or commercial purpose is not evident."

---

[588] *Arthur Anderson LLP v. United States*, 544 US 696 (2005).

[589] *Mathew*, *supra* note 565.

Instead, the "central inquiry is focused on whether the transaction was consistent with the purpose of the provisions … that are relied on by the taxpayer, when those provisions are properly interpreted in light of their context." Were they frustrated? The Court answered, *No*.[590]

Given this, it may (or may not) come as a complete surprise that 40 years earlier, the Supreme Court denied in *Harris* the artificial CCA deductions created under a far less complicated lease-financing scheme that a doctor entered into in respect of a Toronto gas station.[591] Justice John Cartwright, for a unanimous Supreme Court, applied the law of perpetuities to *void* the option to acquire the property in Dr. Harris' 200-year lease (which law never applied in *Canada Trustco*). He also stated that if it had been necessary, "I would have had no hesitation in holding that it was a deduction in respect of an expense incurred in respect of a transaction that if allowed would artificially reduce the income of the appellant and that consequently its allowance was forbidden by the terms of s. 137(1)." (Justices Abbott, Judson, Hall and Spence concurred.) Parliament repealed the successor to that

[590] *Canada Trustco, supra* note 564, paras. 56–57.

[591] *Harris (Dr. Louis J) v. MNR*, [1966] SCR 489, dismissing the taxpayer's appeal from (1964), [1965] 2 Ex. CR 653, 64 DTC 5332, [1964] CTC 562, dismissing the taxpayer's appeal from 63 DTC 160, (1963) 31 Tax ABC 113 (TAB). Dr. Harris had an option exercisable in two hundred years to acquire the service station for $19,500. In *Harris*, the terms of the lease were structured to rely on a CCA provision to create the tax avoidance result. At that time, subs. 18(1) of the 1952 ITA provided that a lessee of property (Dr. Harris), with an option to purchase the property (true), incurred a capital cost for depreciation purposes equal to the rent payable over the term of the lease ($3,100.08 a year x 200-year term) plus the option price ($19,500). Under that rule, the capital cost of Dr. Harris' leasehold interest in the service station became a fantastically high $639,516 for a property valued at less than $40,000. The CCA for this capital cost in 1960 was $30,425, and similar claims could be expected to occur indefinitely until a fictional $639,516 of capital cost was fully depreciated. *Harris v. Minister of National Revenue* – SCC Cases (scc-csc.ca). The Exchequer Court decision is at *Harris v. Minister of National Revenue* – Office of the Commissioner for Federal Judicial Affairs Canada (fja-cmf.gc.ca).

anti-avoidance rule, regarding artificial reductions of income, when enacting the GAAR.

Canada Trustco does not cite or discuss its decision in *Harris* or the above-referenced artificial reductions rule considered in that case, or the explanatory note regarding its analogous successor's repeal on the enactment of the GAAR in 1988. Yet, the Supreme Court had before it in *Canada Trustco* artificial deductions under a lease-financing arrangement. That 1988 note makes clear that the GAAR "is intended to encompass all types of abusive and artificial tax avoidance schemes including the types to which existing subsection 245(1) [Undue or Artificial Reductions of Income] already applies."[592]

In the 40-year interval, the main difference has nothing to do with the statutory law. It concerns the judiciary accepting that the legal form of a *no commercial financing* sale-leaseback transaction had become an ordinary transaction for income tax purposes despite the GAAR.

Justice John Major retired in late 2005. He was replaced by Justice Marshall Rothstein.

[592] Canada, Department of Finance, Technical Note to a Bill Amending the *Income Tax Act* and Related Statutes, November 1988 (The Honourable Michael Wilson, Minister of Finance). The note to the repeal of former subs. 245(1), Undue or Artificial Reductions to Income, states: "New section 245 [the GAAR] replaces existing subsection 245(1), which only applies to transactions resulting in deductions relevant in computing income. The wording of the new provisions is intended to encompass all types of abuses and artificial tax avoidance schemes including the types to which existing subsection 245(1) applies." For note, see David Sherman's *Department of Finance Technical Notes*, Thomson Reuters.

MARSHALL ROTHSTEIN: AN AFFINITY FOR INCOME TAX CASES

Conservative Prime Minister Stephen Harper elevated Marshall Rothstein to the Supreme Court in 2006 from the Federal Court of Appeal, replacing Justice John Major. Rothstein had been a civil litigator, and lecturer of law, in his native Manitoba prior to his appointment to the Federal Court in 1992. Liberal Prime Minister Jean Chretien elevated him to the Federal Court of Appeal in 1999.

An expert in transportation and regulatory law, Justice Rothstein appears to have acquired an affinity for deciding contentious income tax disputes at the Federal Court and the Supreme Court. His income tax decisions were precedent-setting as for the taxpayer so as for the Crown.

Of the judges selected, Marshall Rothstein is the most neutral in terms of approach to income tax and its avoidance, although he distinctly favoured taxpayers over the Crown. But he heard 15 income tax cases, only 7 of which concerned tax avoidance. Without Rothstein, it appears that the Supreme Court would have granted leave to appeal in fewer income tax disputes than it did from his arrival in 2006 to his retirement in 2015. Even then, the Court decided fewer income tax cases during the decade than it decided in Canada's centennial year, 1967.

Justice Rothstein has expressed the view that as a judge it is "inappropriate" to consider the terms "abuse" and "misuse" in the GAAR "as implying moral opprobrium regarding the actions of a taxpayer to minimize tax liability utilizing the provisions of the *Income Tax Act* in a creative way."[593] As a private citizen, he has opined that moral concerns have "no place in a GAAR analysis":

> Moral concerns arise in evasion and other criminal cases. They may also arise where gross negligence or willful blindness are factors, as was the case in *Guindon*. [Footnote below.]

[593] *Copthorne Holdings*, *infra* note 627, para. 65.

> But they have no place in a GAAR analysis where a taxpayer, albeit without success, relies on certain transactions and an interpretation of the Act to achieve a result without deception and with technical compliance with the Act.[594]

The extent to which other Canadians agree with the above sentiment is a separate matter. Justice Rothstein's first income tax avoidance opinion as a Supreme Court judge involved a tax shelter.

Allan McLarty (2008)

Rothstein emphasized in a 7–2 split for the Supreme Court in *McLarty*: "[The] role of the court is solely to adjudicate disputes between the Minister and the taxpayer … [and it] is not a protector of government revenue."[595]

Allan McLarty, a Calgary lawyer, purchased in 1992 an interest in seismic data for $15,000 in cash and $85,000 under a limited-recourse promissory note for a total of $100,000. He deducted Canadian exploration expenses of $100,000 in computing his income, thereby sheltering his other income from tax.

The tax-shelter industry often bases sales of tax-shelter property to potential participants on their financing the cost of an acquisition with limited-recourse debt to cash multiples of three to six times; the math is straightforward. For instance, if a taxpayer acquires a tax shelter property for $100,000, at a debt to cash multiple of four, the taxpayer borrows $80,000 on a limited-recourse basis and pays

---

594 Marshall Rothstein, "A Judge's Perspective on the General Anti-Avoidance Rule," pp. 551–573 (at pp. 572–73), in Brian J. Arnold (Editor), *The General Anti-Avoidance Rule*, *supra* note 299. Rothstein J. also wrote the majority opinion in *Guindon v. The Queen*, 2015 SCC 41, [2015] 3 SCR 3, which is not profiled. The Supreme Court held that the third-party penalty rules impose civil rather than criminal penalties on persons that knowingly, or with culpable conduct, make or participate in the making of a false statement for income tax purposes. (Disclosure: I was the lead drafter of those rules.) *Guindon v. Canada* – SCC Cases (lexum.com).

595 *The Queen v. Allan McLarty*, 2008 SCC 26, [2008] 2 SCR 79, para. 75. *Canada v. McLarty* – SCC Cases (scc-csc.ca).

the promoter $20,000 in cash. The promoter arranges for the limited-recourse debt. The enticement for the taxpayer is that the tax savings exceed the amount that the taxpayer is personally obligated to ensure is paid.

If the promoter is selling a $100,000 deduction to a taxpayer whose marginal tax rate is 50 percent, the deduction is worth $50,000 (i.e., $100,000 x 50%) less the $20,000 cash paid to the promoter. The net $30,000 is otherwise payable as tax to the federal and provincial treasuries. This result is in effect guaranteed to the taxpayer regardless of whether the tax shelter property earns one cent, subject to the CRA's denying the benefit and the judiciary's determining there is non-compliance with the ITA.

On December 1, 1994, Liberal Finance Minister Paul Martin and National Revenue Minister David Anderson issued a six-page joint announcement. Martin proposed new rules "to protect the tax base." The proposals included a rule under which the cost of a tax-shelter property financed with limited-recourse debt is recognized for tax purposes only to the extent the principal is repaid. Anderson announced that Revenue Canada "will increase its review and audit of tax shelters … to ensure that they meet the current requirements of the tax law."[596]

How was such a tax avoidance result possible under the pre-existing tax law? Justice Rothstein's decision in *McLarty* provides the Supreme Court's answer to that question.

---

[596] Canada, News Release 94–112 (December 1, 1994), "Measures Limiting the Use of Tax Shelters Announced." (Disclosure: I was the Finance Canada contact person on that release.) *The Financial Post* reported the joint announcement as its lead story on p. 1 the next day. It noted that Minister Anderson indicated that the proposals were meant to "improve the fairness in the tax system." Jill Vardy, "Tax Shelter Crackdown," *Financial Post*, December 2, 1994, p. 1. The Federal Court of Appeal cited the 1994 News Release on the purpose of the "tax shelter" registration rules in *Krumm v. The Queen*, 2021 FCA 78, para. 18. The Federal Court of Appeal's decision is at *Krumm v. Canada* – Federal Court of Appeal (fca-caf.gc.ca).

Allan McLarty was not personally liable to make good on the $85,000 debt used to acquire his $100,000 interest in the seismic data. That detail is the focus of the tax dispute. McLarty was not personally liable for any portion of the $85,000 debt because the terms of the promissory note limited its repayment to a percentage of potential revenues and proceeds from licensing, cash flow and sale proceeds arising from McLarty's interest in the seismic data.

The Minister's auditors in Calgary maintained that $85,000 of the $100,000 of Canadian exploration expenses could not be deducted. In doing so, they relied on precedent including the Supreme Court's unanimous 1980 decision in *Mandel*.[597] In that case, the Court dismissed orally the taxpayer's appeal of a Federal Court of Appeal finding that a film tax shelter acquired by a limited partnership for $577,892 had a tax cost of $155,000, the portion the partners funded in cash. The difference was a contingent liability repayable only out of film revenues, if any.

In *McLarty*, the lender (1) received 60 percent of any licensing revenues payable in reduction of the debt; (2) would be paid 60 percent of any cash received for selling the data in reduction of the debt; and (3) [the key term in issue] could, if all or part the debt was unpaid by December 31, 1999, appoint a trustee to sell for cash McLarty's undivided 20 percent participating interest in the seismic data.[598] Is this a *bona fide* default provision given the arrangement, when considered as a whole?

Justice Rothstein, for the majority, held that McLarty's $85,000 promissory note was not a contingent liability, and therefore the $100,000 was deductible as Canadian exploration expenses even though the seismic data later sold for $17,600. There remained $93,242 owing on the note by the end of 2001. Consequently,

---

[597] *Lawrence H. Mandel v. The Queen*, [1980] 1 SCR 318, affirming 78 DTC 6518, [1978] CTC 780 (FCA). Justice Martland delivered the oral reasons for himself and Justices Dickson, Estey, McIntyre and Chouinard. https://decisions.scc-csc.ca/scc-csc/scc-csc/en/item/5649/index.do.

[598] *McLarty*, *supra* note 595, para. 86.

McLarty's $15,000 cash payment was all he personally paid to claim $100,000 of fully deductible expenses for tax purposes. (Chief Justice McLachlin and Justices Binnie, LeBel, Deschamps, Fish and Charron concurred; Justices Bastarache and Abella dissented.)

This is the type of fiscal alchemy that undermines the general public's faith in government and politicians. The majority in *McLarty* appears to have been sensitive to the result. As noted, they stated that the Supreme Court is "is not a protector of government revenue." But, based on the oral hearing, it appears the majority was so concerned by 2008 about possible adverse commercial law implications for limited recourse debt if it found McLarty's liability to be a contingent liability, that it distinguished its 1980 precedent in *Mandel*.[599]

The distinction drawn to make the liability absolute instead of contingent was done in a wholly tax avoidance context; it was based on McLarty's lender's having a right at a time specified in the note to sell his interest in the seismic data if there were shortfalls in repayment out of revenues and cash flow.[600] There is no apparent *bona fide* commercial purpose for the acquisition of the data, the debt or its default right, other than tax avoidance, which the Court had made through its earlier precedent the only purpose a taxpayer needs. Recall, Wilson stated in *Stubart Investments* that there needs

---

[599] See the comments of Justices Rothstein and LeBel at the oral hearing in respect of the concern of possible adverse results under commercial law principles: Transcript of oral hearing in *Her Majesty the Queen v. Allan McLarty* (docket file 31516), pp. 11–12. I obtained a copy of the transcript from the Supreme Court of Canada, which was prepared by A.S.A.P. Reporting Services Inc. Also, in addition to distinguishing *Mandel*, Rothstein J. also found that the Federal Court of Appeal's 1999 decision in *Global Communications Ltd. v. The Queen*, 99 DTC 5377, which found that the limited recourse loan in a similarly sophisticated seismic data tax shelter was contingent, was bad law.

[600] *McLarty*, *supra* note 595. The majority noted that the Federal Court of Appeal applied the distinction when finding the limited-recourse debt was not a contingent liability.

to be "no business purpose other than a tax purpose."[601] This is judge-made law.

Rothstein did note that the Minister maintained that the taxpayer and vendor never dealt with each other at arm's length and claimed the value of the data had been inflated. But the Supreme Court held that the vendor and McLarty dealt with each other at arm's length. The Court reversed the Federal Court of Appeal on this point, which would have sent the dispute back to the Tax Court to determine the value of the tax shelter property.[602]

In dissent, Justices Bastarache and Abella applied the Supreme Court's 1980 decision in *Mandel*.[603] The liability was contingent and not absolute because the sale of the data, and therefore the amount of the liability, "depend on revenue generation uncertain and, accordingly, contingent … [which] means that Mr. McLarty's obligation to resell the venture data is also contingent, because it too depends on whether sufficient revenues have been generated to cover the face value of the promissory note."[604] In response to the dissent, Rothstein stated: "With respect, I think my colleagues, like the Minister, are conflating the issue of whether the security is sufficient to repay the full

---

[601] *Stubart Investments*, *supra* note 386, p. 540.

[602] *McLarty*, *supra* note 595. The Supreme Court unanimously held that the vendor and taxpayer dealt at arm's length, reversing the Federal Court of Appeal which had reversed the Tax Court on that matter. The majority (the Justices in dissent did not articulate their reasoning for why the transaction was arm's length) stated (para. 34):

> What is at the root of the Minister's difficulty in this case is that the Minister believes the price of the asset McLarty acquired was overvalued and that the data, as the only collateral security, was insufficient to cover repayment of the note. In fact, in January 2006, McLarty's 1.57% interest in the seismic data was sold through an independent receiver for approximately $17,600 of which 60% or only about $10,500 was used to repay the note. There are remedies for the Minister where assets are overvalued solely to obtain a tax advantage. Trying to characterize the loan portion of the purchase price as contingent in this case was not one of them.

[603] *Ibid.*, para. 85.

[604] *Ibid.*, para. 89.

value of the note and implicitly, that the seismic data was overvalued, with the issue of whether the liability is absolute or contingent."[605]

Justice Rothstein also issued opinions in the Supreme Court's third and fourth GAAR decisions. The first is his minority dissent in *Lipson* on January 8, 2009, toward the end of the 2007–2009 crisis in global financial markets. His second is the Court's unanimous holding that applied the GAAR in *Copthorne Holdings* in December 2011. The opinions suggest Rothstein's approach to GAAR changed in those three years.

Earl Lipson (2009)

The Supreme Court's decision in *Lipson* is fascinating on several levels. Some of the Supreme Court and lower-court judges who had decided for and against the taxpayer in *Singleton* were back for a rematch in *Lipson*, this time under the GAAR—Rothstein was one of those judges. The decision was made by a fractured seven-member Supreme Court panel deciding whether the GAAR applied.[606]

The *Lipson* dispute concerned a series of transactions in which a high-income husband and his wife sought to finance the 1994 purchase of a home in Toronto costing $750,000. They undertook the transactions to create deductible interest amounts.[607]

---

[605] *Ibid.*, para. 41.

[606] *Earl Lipson et al. v. The Queen*, 2009 SCC 1, [2009] 1 SCR 3, dismissing the taxpayers' appeal from 2007 FCA 113, 2007 DTC 5172, [2007] 3 CTC 110, affirming 2006 TCC 148, 2006 DTC 2687, [2006] 3 CTC 2494. *Lipson v. Canada* – SCC Cases (scc-csc.ca).

[607] *Ibid.* Under the plan, Mrs. Lipson borrowed $562,000 from a bank to finance the purchase from Mr. Lipson of shares of a family company (Mr. Lipson would have used the funds to buy their home). Mrs. Lipson could not afford to pay the interest owing on her bank loan, and she and her husband obtained a $562,000 mortgage the proceeds of which were used to repay Mrs. Lipson's bank loan used to acquire the shares. Since her original loan was to acquire shares, the amount of the mortgage used to repay that loan was deemed by subs. 20(3) to be used for the same purpose as the original loan (to acquire shares), making the interest deductible to Mrs. Lipson in respect of her shares. The interest deductions resulted in annual losses on her shares, which were attributed to Mr. Lipson

A 7–2 Supreme Court majority had blessed a similar plan eight years earlier in *Singleton*.

In *Singleton*, Rothstein issued the majority opinion in 1999 for the Federal Court of Appeal, which allowed Singleton's appeal reversing Chief Justice Bowman of the Tax Court. In the context of doing so, Rothstein treated Singleton's withdrawal of capital from his law partnership to finance a purchase of the home as a separate transaction from his borrowing to replenish his capital in the law partnership. He held the taxpayer could deduct the interest on the loan used to replenish the capital.[608] Major led a Supreme Court majority in dismissing the Crown's appeal. But Justice Louis Lebel dissented, holding the *Singleton* case fell squarely into the *obiter* of Dickson in *Bronfman Trust* that such a scheme would appear to be disallowed as a formality or tax sham.

In *Lipson*, Justice LeBel's majority opinion denied Mr. Lipson's loss claimed under a tax avoidance plan that had significant technical differences from the plan in *Singleton*. Like *Singleton*, it relied on the interest deduction provision (which the Court applied differently in *Bronfman Trust* and *Singleton*). Unlike *Singleton*, the Lipson plan turned the income attribution rules meant to counter family income splitting, against the Minister, by attributing to Mr. Lipson from Mrs. Lipson a loss resulting from the interest deductions, to reduce his net income for tax purposes.

In the Tax Court, Chief Justice Bowman, who had denied at trial the planning in *Singleton*, applied the GAAR in the *Lipson* case. He did so on the basis the planning was an abuse of the provision allowing interest deductibility when financing the acquisition of property for the purpose of gaining or producing income.

---

under the attribution rules in s. 74.1 because, when he transferred the shares to her, he did not elect out of a rollover of the shares at his cost under s. 73.

[608] Marshall Rothstein commented on his Federal Court of Appeal decision in *Singleton* at Marshall Rothstein, "A Judge's Perspective on the General Anti-Avoidance Rule," pp. 551–73, p. 554, in Brian J. Arnold (Editor), *The General Anti-Avoidance Rule, supra* note 299.

He considered the various transactions as a series and held that its "overall purpose, as well as the use to which each individual provision was put, was to make deductible, the interest on money used to buy a personal residence."[609]

The Federal Court of Appeal dismissed the appeal. Justice Marc Noël found that Bowman could consider the transactions as a series and apply the GAAR on the basis the result was not within the "object, spirit, or purpose" of the interest deductibility rule.

It is significant that the Tax Court and Federal Court of Appeal reasoning had adverse consequences for numerous high-income families across Canada who had employed the Singleton shuffle tax-avoidance plan, which did not rely on the attribution rules. Their reasoning for why there was an abuse under the GAAR had just knocked out the tax avoidance plan the Supreme Court had blessed eight years earlier in *Singleton* in a non-GAAR context. If the *Lipson* planning was an abuse of interest deductibility under the GAAR, so was the Singleton shuffle.

On May 3, 2008, Jamie Golombek reported for the *National Post* that a "capacity crowd" had attended the Supreme Court's hearing of oral arguments in the *Lipson* case. A tax professional with the *Canadian Imperial Bank of Commerce*, Golombek reported that the Court technically permitted the interest deductions under the Singleton shuffle. He then noted that the Crown "seems to be focusing on how the Lipsons handled the transfer of the shares" under the income-splitting attribution rules.[610]

In *Lipson*, LeBel found, for the majority, that tax avoidance permitted under the *Duke of Westminster* principle has never been absolute, and that GAAR limits such planning. LeBel also found that the Crown failed to establish an abuse of the interest deductibility provision. He cited *Ludco Enterprises* as finding that the purpose of the

---

[609] *Earl Lipson, supra* note 606, TCC para. 23. *Lipson v. The Queen* – Tax Court of Canada (tcc-cci.gc.ca).

[610] Jamie Golombek, "Supreme Court to Sort It Out: Interest Deductibility," *National Post*, May 3, 2008, FW6.

rule is to incent an accumulation of capital to produce "income," or "taxable income" per *Shell Canada*.[611]

Both *Ludco Enterprises* and *Shell Canada* were blatant tax avoidance schemes denied by the Federal Court of Appeal, which the Supreme Court reversed. Tax on income that would otherwise be taxable was avoided in both cases. This suggests the Court constrained the purpose test in the interest deductibility rule in a manner that allowed taxpayers to use it to avoid tax.

But Justice LeBel held, for the majority, that the transactions attribute "the interest deduction under s. 74.1(1) [to Mr. Lipson] and this attribution frustrates the object, spirit and purpose of that provision."[612] As such, the GAAR applied to deny the tax benefit. (Justices Morris Fish, Rosalie Abella and Louise Charron concurred.)

In this way, the majority weaved around the interest non-deductibility issue on homes by applying the GAAR on the basis the taxpayers abused the attribution rules. This had a significant practical result. While Mr. Lipson was denied the deduction of the losses, Mrs. Lipson was entitled to deduct the interest in computing her income from the shares she acquired from Mr. Lipson because there was no abuse of the interest deductibility rule.

This, in turn, meant the GAAR did not impede high-income Canadians from exploiting the Singleton shuffle on a go-forward basis—to turn their mortgage interest into tax deductions.

Justice Binnie, in dissent, found the GAAR did not apply; "the spousal 'twist' added to *Singleton* should not cause the entire series

---

[611] *Earl Lipson, supra* note 606, SCC para. 29. LeBel J. stated: "The purpose of this provision is to 'create an incentive to accumulate capital with the potential to produce income' (*Ludco Enterprises* …, at para. 63), or to 'encourage the accumulation of capital which would produce taxable income' (*Shell Canada* …, at para. 57)." He also stated (para. 41): "Mrs. Lipson financed the purchase of income-producing property with debt, whereas Mr. Lipson financed the purchase of the residence with equity. To this point, the transactions were unimpeachable."

[612] *Ibid.*, para. 48.

of transactions to be characterized as abusive." (Justice Deschamps concurred.[613]) In doing so, he called the GAAR "a weapon that, unless contained by the jurisprudence, could have a widespread, serious and unpredictable effect on legitimate tax planning."[614] That so-called *weapon* is a law duly enacted by Parliament to address what Brian Arnold and James Wilson said is "a lack of adequate judicial limits on acceptable tax avoidance activity."[615]

Stepping into this dispute is Justice Rothstein's minority dissent that itself is unusual. He began by noting he had read the opinions of LeBel and Binnie. He agreed with Binnie that the GAAR did not apply but disagreed with Binnie's reasons. Since the GAAR is in fact a "provision of last resort,"[616] the Minister can apply it only "when he has no other recourse." Rothstein held, in dissent, that this was not the case; a special anti-avoidance rule within the attribution rules applied to deny the attribution of Mrs. Lipson's loss to Mr. Lipson. The GAAR did not apply, given the special anti-avoidance rule should have been applied.

In *obiter*, Justice LeBel, for the majority, indicated that the approach Justices Binnie and Deschamps took, in dissent, "essentially guts the GAAR and reads it out of the ITA."[617] In the case of Justice Rothstein's dissent, LeBel noted that Rothstein agreed the transactions ran afoul of the tax law but should be denied under a special anti-avoidance rule that the taxpayer and the Crown agreed did not apply. As such, it was not open to the Supreme Court to consider that anti-avoidance rule.

The Supreme Court's decision in *Lipson* suggests a deep internal split in the Court about when, and if, the Minister can apply

---

[613] *Ibid.*, para. 59.

[614] *Ibid.*, para. 55.

[615] Brian J. Arnold and James R. Wilson, "The General Anti-Avoidance Rule–Part 1," (1988), 36:4 *Canadian Tax Journal* 829. At p. 848, Arnold and Wilson cite the Honourable Michael Wilson's 1987 *White Paper on Tax Reform*, Canada, Department of Finance (June 18, 1987), p. 129.

[616] *Earl Lipson*, *supra* note 606, SCC paras. 104–06.

[617] *Ibid.*, para. 52.

the GAAR to deny a tax avoidance scheme available to very few taxpayers. It also suggests the Court recognized that if it upheld the reasons of the Tax Court and Federal Court of Appeal, all those taxpayers who undertook the Singleton shuffle also could be reassessed under the GAAR and denied their interest deductions. This also appears to be the reason why the Court granted the taxpayer leave to appeal. The Court left the Singleton shuffle intact for taxpayers having the capital necessary to undertake, as Justice Judson once said, "shuffles with the cheques."[618]

Justice Rothstein's next two opinions involve a concurring minority opinion and a concurring dissent. The second decision suggests the Supreme Court has interpreted the Indigenous tax exemption for property located on a reserve too broadly in respect of income.

Bastien Estate (2011);[619] *Dubé (2011)*[620]

To understand what the Supreme Court did to the Indigenous exemption from tax for property situated on a reserve, one should focus on the facts. The Court's approach raises significant policy questions few seem willing to ask. More on that after considering the facts and approach taken in *Bastien Estate* and the way the majority applied that approach in *Dubé*.

In *Bastien Estate*, the late Rolland Bastien was exempt from tax on his personal property situated on a reserve. He had carried on a moccasin-manufacturing business with success, and it produced tax-exempt income. In this context, he claimed an exemption from interest income earned from term deposits made to an on-reserve institution that was part of a large credit union doing business in Quebec. The lower courts denied the exemption because the credit

---

[618] For quote, see *Smythe* as cited at *supra* note 265.

[619] *Bastien Estate v. The Queen*, 2011 SCC 38, [2011] 2 SCR 710. *Bastien Estate v. Canada* – SCC Cases (scc-csc.ca).

[620] *Dubé v. The Queen*, 2011 SCC 39, [2011] 2 SCR 764. *Dubé v. Canada* – SCC Cases (scc-csc.ca).

union generated its income in the mainstream of commercial activity in Quebec rather than on the reserve.

Justice Thomas Cromwell, for the majority, found that where the credit union earned its income was irrelevant to the question of whether the interest it paid to Mr. Bastien was tax exempt. But when doing so, Cromwell applied in his own way the two-step analysis Justice Charles Gonthier undertook in respect of the exemption for a unanimous Supreme Court in its 1992 *Williams* decision.[621]

In *Williams*, Gonthier noted that the purpose of the exemption is "to preserve the entitlements of Indians to their reserve lands and to ensure that the use of their property on their reserve lands was not eroded by the ability of governments to tax, or creditors to seize. The corollary of this conclusion was that the purpose of the sections was not to confer a general economic benefit upon the Indians." He cited Justice La Forest for the position that the purpose of the exemption "is not to remedy the economically disadvantaged position of Indians by ensuring that Indians may acquire, hold, and deal with property in the commercial mainstream on different terms than their fellow citizens."[622]

In effect, Cromwell and the majority read down the commercial mainstream aspect of the *Williams* decision. He found that the key factors relevant were as follows: (1) the debtor credit union had its branch residing on the reserve; (2) the creditor Mr. Bastien resided on the reserve; (3) the interest was paid and received on the reserve; and (4) in law, the contracts between the credit union and Mr. Bastien were on the reserve. (Chief Justice McLachlin and Justices Binnie, Fish and Charron concurred.)

But reading down the commercial mainstream factor can, depending on the case, create special rights for Indigenous Canadians operating in the commercial mainstream. As noted, however, Mr. Bastien lived on the reserve and generated his income

[621] *Glen Williams v. The Queen*, [1992] 1 SCR 877. https://scc-csc.lexum.com/scc-csc/scc-csc/en/item/866/index.do.
[622] *Ibid.*

from an on-reserve business. Given this, it is understandable the majority held that his interest income was exempt from tax under the exemption.

Justices Deschamps and Rothstein reached the same result in *Bastien Estate* for different reasons. They noted the place where the interest was paid was not relevant because the taxing provision did not care from where the interest was paid. But Bastien's residency on the reserve was relevant, as it would help benefit the economy of the reserve if he lived and spent his money on the reserve. It was also relevant that the credit union resided on the reserve, that Bastien earned the capital from on-reserve activity and that he invested it in contracts signed and located on the reserve. They also agreed with the majority that it did not matter whether the activity that generated the capital arose in the context of a traditional Indigenous way of life.

However, Deschamps and Rothstein rejected the majority's approach when weighing the different connections that could, in certain cases, give too much weight for tenuous connections to the reserve. The problem was the majority gave significant weight "to connecting factors that can be easily manipulated." In the case, that was "the effect of the importance [the majority] attached to the contractual aspects of the investment contract rather than to the property's concrete and discernible connections with the reserve."[623] The majority approach was also inconsistent with the purpose of the exemption.

The *Dubé* decision is the first Supreme Court decision concerning the exemption to draw a dissent. Mr. Alexandre Dubé, who "is an Attikamek Indian and has been a member of the Obedjiwan Reserve since birth," owned real property off reserve and operated a business transporting on-reserve Indigenous Canadians to medical treatment in Roberval, Quebec.[624] Crucially, Mr. Dubé did not have his principal residence on that reserve; he had a secondary

[623] *Dubé*, *supra* note 620, para. 102.
[624] *Ibid.*, paras. 5 and 31.

residence on the reserve. Also, he invested his capital at a financial institution located at another reserve.[625]

Mr. Dubé claimed a tax exemption under the *Indian Act* on the resulting income from his on-reserve invested capital. This sounds a lot like some other successful Canadians who attempt to avoid tax on their property income by locating capital offshore in a tax haven. Nevertheless, Justice Cromwell led a 5–2 Supreme Court majority to allow the taxpayer's appeal. He gave considerable weight to the fact Dubé invested the capital at an on-reserve financial institution, and little weight to Dubé's having his principal residence off the reserve and that his capital was at another reserve.

Justices Deschamps and Rothstein dissented. They did so after noting "[that] Mr. Dubé did not reside on the reserve, that he was unable to explain where large deposits made at the Caisse populaire Desjardins de PointeBleue came from and that the judge was unable to establish a connection between the deposited capital and the transportation company operated by Mr. Dubé." To allow an exemption from income tax "in such circumstances would be tantamount to turning the reserve into a tax haven for Indians engaged in unspecified for-profit activities off the reserve."[626]

Is s. 87 of the *Indian Act* intended to allow a reserve to be turned into a domestic tax haven for Indigenous persons to earn tax-free returns on capital even though they do not have a principal residence on the reserve? What public policy purpose does this serve other than the self-interest of the person benefiting from such an exemption in such circumstances?

Can an off-reserve superior court judge or a professional athlete who is a status Indian with an on-reserve second residence pull off such a maneuver? This is the type of tough question that someone needs to ask, but for which few if any are prepared to ask. Chief

[625] *Ibid.*, para. 14.
[626] *Ibid.*, paras. 39–40.

Justice Dickson framed the interpretive question in *Nowegijick*, based on whether the wording can be *reasonably* interpreted in favour of an exemption.

The Supreme Court's majority decision in *Dubé* is consistent with the Court's extensive *Charter*-era tax avoidance precedent—the Court has treated Canadians with investment capital extremely well when it comes to avoiding income tax. Whether that capital is located in offshore tax havens or on a reserve, this is the type of treatment that can spawn deep divisions within a society.

The next decision is the Supreme Court's fourth decision under the GAAR.

Copthorne Holdings (2011)

Less than three years after *Lipson*, Justice Rothstein led a unanimous Supreme Court in applying the GAAR in *Copthorne Holdings*.[627] The taxpayer sought to shift $67 million of corporate surplus earned in Canada to non-resident shareholders, without paying non-resident withholding taxes.

The *Copthorne Holdings* scheme is complicated—too complicated to discuss in any detail, but its nuts and bolts concern a plan to double Copthorne Holding's cross-border corporate paid-up capital (PUC). Such capital normally can be distributed tax free to shareholders because it represents the amount of capital shareholders paid to the corporation for issued shares. This plan avoided a PUC reduction rule that otherwise applies on a vertical amalgamation; the rule is meant to ensure that an amalgamated corporation does not overstate its PUC. Rothstein applied the GAAR holding the following:

> I agree with the Tax Court's finding that the taxpayer's "double counting" of PUC was abusive in this case, where the taxpayer structured the transactions so as to

[627] *Copthorne Holdings Ltd. v. The Queen*, 2011 SCC 63, [2011] 3 SCR 721. *Copthorne Holdings Ltd. v. Canada* – SCC Cases (scc-csc.ca).

> "artificially" preserve the PUC in a way that frustrated the purpose of s. 87(3) governing the treatment of PUC upon vertical amalgamation.[628]

Before doing so, Rothstein put the GAAR into the context of being an interpretive rule that determines the "object, spirit or purpose" of the provisions in which the transactions are in "strict compliance" with the legislative text, with the GAAR being a provision of "last resort."[629] This type of terminology is found in earlier GAAR decisions. But if parsed, what it says is the Supreme Court believes that the British *Duke of Westminster* principle deserves so much judicial deference that Parliamentary action to undermine it must be applied by the Minister and the judiciary only as a last resort. One wonders what Patrick Kerwin, Douglas Abbott, Ronald Martland, Wilfred Judson and John Cartwright might say about this if they were alive.

It is highly questionable that Parliament intended the GAAR to be a rule of interpretation; it is certainly not written as such. It is a substantive rule meant to deny abusive tax avoidance arrangements that survive a textual, contextual and purposive interpretation of the provisions in issue, and the ITA read as a whole. To date, the Supreme Court has essentially used the plain-meaning approach in non-GAAR cases, which is highly questionable. In GAAR cases, while the Supreme Court reverts to the true textual, contextual and

---

[628] *Ibid.*, para. 127.

[629] *Ibid.*, para. 66. Rothstein J. stated (para. 66):

> The GAAR is a legal mechanism whereby Parliament has conferred on the court the unusual duty of going behind the words of the legislation to determine the object, spirit or purpose of the provision or provisions relied upon by the taxpayer. While the taxpayer's transactions will be in strict compliance with the text of the relevant provisions relied upon, they may not necessarily be in accord with their object, spirit or purpose. In such cases, the GAAR may be invoked by the Minister. The GAAR does create some uncertainty for taxpayers. Courts, however, must remember that s. 245 was enacted 'as a provision of last resort' (*Trustco*, at para. 21).

purposive approach (which factors in the object and spirit), that is doing what it should be doing in non-GAAR and GAAR cases.

The Supreme Court also gives little weight to abusing the policies reflected in the ITA read as a whole, in the absence of an abuse of a particular provision. For example, the ITA is meant to impose tax on business profit computed under best commercial principles, which does not include allowing offsets for artificial amounts. The shift in the 1948 ITA away from ministerial discretion to constrain tax avoidance did not contemplate allowing artificial deductions and was accompanied by an anti-avoidance rule that denied them. Yet, the transactions in *Canada Trustco* survived the GAAR.

Despite these observations, Justice Rothstein's decision in *Copthorne Holdings* breathed new life into a dying patient, and some argue it has notably improved the Crown's success rate in GAAR disputes. More on that in Part VI.

Rothstein in the next decision overturned Dickson's unanimous 1977 decision in *Moldowan*.[630]

John H. Craig (2012)

John Craig is a prominent Bay Street corporate-commercial lawyer. He also raced horses, incurring substantial losses exceeding $200,000 in each of 2001 and 2002.

Perhaps the most unusual aspect of the *Craig* decision is that a unanimous Federal Court of Appeal decided it had the authority to overturn Chief Justice Dickson's decision for the Supreme Court in *Moldowan*. As mentioned, tax practitioners had been complaining about the *Moldowan* decision since 1977; the literature is filled with articles against Dickson's reasonable expectation-of-profit test. Yet, the Supreme Court's 2002 decisions in *Stewart*,[631] and *Walls*,[632] are infused with judge-made law, which holdings say an ancillary intent to earn profit is somehow a source of income in a tax shelter

[630] *Moldowan*, *supra* note 349.

[631] *Stewart*, *supra* note 518.

[632] *Walls*, *supra* note 519.

context in which the taxpayer expects or intends annual losses only, plus maybe capital gains.

Rothstein, for a unanimous Supreme Court in *Craig*, overturned *Moldowan*.[633] He gave three reasons for doing so, after noting the Court of Appeal went beyond its jurisdiction by overturning *Moldowan*.

First, Rothstein determined that Dickson's decision should be reviewed because by "requiring that the second exception [the combination test] apply only where the other source of income was subordinate to the farming source of income, *Moldowan* collapsed the second exception into the first."[634]

Second, "there has been significant judicial, academic and other criticism of *Moldowan* from its issuance in 1977."[635]

Third, relying on Justice McLachlin's unanimous 1999 decision in *Shell Canada*,[636] the purpose of the restricted farm loss rules should be read down:

> [T]his Court has held on a number of occasions that unexpressed legislative intention under the guise of purposive interpretation is to be avoided (*Shell*, at para. 43). There is no doubt that s. 31(1) is, as Dickson J. recognized, an awkwardly worded and intractable section and the source of much debate. Nonetheless, the section is clear that two distinct exceptions to the loss deduction limitation can be identified. A judge-made rule that reads one of the exceptions out of the provision is not consistent with the words used by Parliament.[637]

---

[633] *The Queen v. John H. Craig*, 2012 SCC 43, [2012] 2 SCR 489. *Canada v. Craig* – SCC Cases (scc-csc.ca).

[634] *Ibid.*, para. 28.

[635] *Ibid.*, para. 29.

[636] *Shell Canada Ltd. v. The Queen*, [1999] 3 SCR 622, allowing the taxpayer's appeal from 98 DTC 6177, [1998] 2 CTC 207 (FCA), which reversed in part 97 DTC 395, [1997] 3 CTC 2238 (TCC)). *Shell Canada Ltd. v. Canada* – SCC Cases (scc-csc.ca).

[637] *Ibid.*, para. 30.

After doing so, Rothstein held, relying on the Supreme Court's 2002 decision in *Stewart*, that there is nothing in the restricted farm loss rules that farming must be the taxpayer's predominant source of income under the combination exception:

> I see nothing in the words or context in s. 31(1) to support the proposition that farming must be the predominant source of income when viewed in combination with another source, in order to avoid the loss deduction limitation of the section. It is also not possible to relegate s. 31(1) to applying only to "hobby" or "gentleman" farmers because, for a loss to be deductible at all, farming must be a source of income. A taxpayer who is engaged in farming in a non-commercial manner, with no profit or intention to profit, does not have a source of income from farming and therefore no loss for income tax purposes, limited or not (*Stewart v. Canada*, 2002 SCC 46, [2002] 2 S.C.R. 645, at paras. 51–54).[638]

While the phrase "chief source" is in the section, based on the Tax Court's determination that Craig's chief source of income was farming in combination with practicing law, he could deduct the farming losses from his income from practicing law. (Justices Louis LeBel, Marie Deschamps, Rosalie Abella, Thomas Cromwell, Michael Moldaver and Andromache Karakatsanis concurred.)

Or one might argue consistency demands that the Supreme Court not risk reaching unintended legislative intent with respect to the phrase "chief source" by reading down the "context" and "purpose" in which that phrase was used under a supposed textual, contextual and purposive interpretive approach. It is simply not true to say, as the Supreme Court stated in *Craig*, that Dickson's interpretation of the test "reads one of the exceptions out of the provision." Rather, his interpretation supported farmers who had to go off farm to supplement their farming source of

[638] *Ibid.*, para. 39.

income while restricting the ability of executives and professionals to go on farm to shelter from tax their income earned from a source in the big city with farming losses computed under the cash method tax preference all the while living on a rural estate or racing horses.

After the decision, Conservative Finance Minister James F. Flaherty recommended in his 2013 Budget that Parliament "restore the intended policy" by codifying "the chief source of income test," the "purpose" of which "is consistent with" Chief Justice Dickson's interpretation in *Moldowan.*[639]

Justice Rothstein also delivered the Supreme Court's 2012 decision in *GlaxoSmithKline*, which concerns transfer pricing.[640]

GlaxoSmithKline (2012)

GlaxoSmithKline paid a non-arm's length offshore supplier located in Switzerland $1,500 per kilogram for ranitidine, used in Canada to make the medicine Zantac. It had a separate licence agreement with another non-arm's length offshore corporation that allowed GlaxoSmithKline to use the patent to manufacture Zantac and to use the trademark.

In comparison, by 1990, two Canadian generic drug companies making and selling products that competed with Zantac were paying between $194 and $304 per kilogram for ranitidine. The Minister attacked GlaxoSmithKline's non-arm's length supply agreement on the basis that it was shifting otherwise taxable income offshore by deducting the supply payments for manufacturing Zantac.

The Tax Court essentially upheld the Minister's reassessment of *GlaxoSmithKline*. A key finding was that based on the Supreme

---

[639] Canada, Department of Finance, *2013 Budget Plan*, "Restricted Farm Losses," March 21, 2013, pp. 362–63 (The Honourable James M. Flaherty, Minister of Finance); SC, 2013, c. 40, s. 20.

[640] *The Queen v. GlaxoSmithKline Inc.*, 2012 SCC 52, [2012] 3 SCR 3. *Canada v. GlaxoSmithKline Inc.* – SCC Cases (scc-csc.ca).

Court's 2001 decision in *Singleton*, the supply agreement and the licence agreement were to be treated as separate agreements.

But the Federal Court of Appeal disagreed and held that the Tax Court should have considered the non-arm's length licence agreement when determining what is reasonable under the supply contract in a transfer pricing context under the applicable provision (then subs. 69(2)).

The word "reasonable" was relevant when interpreting both para. 20(1)(*c*) in *Singleton,*[641] and subs. 69(2) in *GlaxoSmithKline*. While the Supreme Court refused to consider the two contracts together in *Singleton*, the Federal Court of Appeal conjured a "reasonable businessperson test" to distinguish *Singleton*; the licence agreement was found to be central to *GlaxoSmithKline*'s "business reality."

One can only marvel at the judicial inconsistency and how "business reality" suddenly becomes central to deciding a tax avoidance case, when it assists the taxpayer. The Federal Court of Appeal ordered the matter back to the Tax Court to determine the "reasonable amount" payable under the licence agreement. The Crown appealed.

Osler's Al Meghji was lead counsel for the taxpayer. Canada's top income tax litigator during the first two decades of the 21st century, once again he was successful before the Supreme Court seven years after successfully litigating *Canada Trustco* under the GAAR in 2005. At Osler, Meghji has surrounded himself with a team of leading tax professionals.

Justice Rothstein dismissed the Crown's appeal and provided lengthy reasons on how transfer pricing cases should be determined. (Chief Justice McLachlin and Justices Deschamps, Abella,

---

[641] In *Singleton, supra* note 546, the provision in issue, subs. 20(1), opens the various deductibility provisions in respect of a business or property source of income with words that limit the deduction to amounts "wholly applicable to that source or such part of the following amounts as may reasonably be regarded as applicable" to the source of income. This includes deducting interest under para. 20(1)(*c*), which limits the interest deduction to no more than the "reasonable amount."

Cromwell, Moldaver and Karakatsanis concurred.) With respect to why the Supreme Court's approach in *Singleton* did not apply, Rothstein, for a unanimous Supreme Court, stated:

> With respect, the approach of the Tax Court judge and the argument of the Minister ignore the difference between s. 20(1)(c)(i) and s. 69(2). Nothing in s. 20(1)(c)(i) entitles a court to search for anything other than the use to which the borrowed funds are put. The factual determination is simply whether the use of borrowed funds was for the purpose of earning income.[642]

What about the purpose test in s. 20(1)(c)(i)? It seems to have gone missing in action. We know the above is judge-made law because Major in *Singleton* interpreted the interest deductibility provision in s. 20(1)(*c*) differently from the way Dickson did in *Bronfman Trust.* Major applied the plain-meaning interpretive approach, and Dickson emphasized commercial substance and reality and then discerned that the borrowing was not done for a *bona fide* income-earning purpose.

Although Rothstein, for the Supreme Court, looked to "business reality" in *GlaxoSmithKline,* as in Iacobucci's decision in *Tennant,* the result favoured the taxpayer. The question that remains is whether the Court is prepared to emphasize commercial substance and reality over legal form in a non-GAAR context when to do so would deny tax avoidance.

There is a significant practical difference between the approaches taken by the Tax Court in *GlaxoSmithKline* and that of the Federal Court of Appeal and the Supreme Court. Under the Tax Court approach, the amounts subject to being non-deductible payments meant the Canadian corporation's taxable income increased by those amounts. The combined federal and provincial tax rate was about 40 percent.

---

[642] *GlaxoSmithKline, supra* note 640, para. 34.

Under the Federal Court of Appeal and Supreme Court's approach, the taxpayer and Minister were left to re-calculate the "reasonable amount" payable under a non-arm's length supply agreement with reference to the licence agreement. This would increase the deduction against taxable income; no domestic corporate tax applied to it. Rather, the unreasonable amount was subject to a 10 percent tax on royalties arising in Canada and paid to a person residing in Switzerland. This tax rate would have been nil if the royalty that arose in Canada had been paid on a patent beneficially owned by a resident of Switzerland.[643] It is unclear whether the Supreme Court realized that its decision gave a road map for avoiding withholding tax in addition to domestic income tax; that is, by locating ownership of the patent in Switzerland.

Brian Arnold made two key points in his review of *GlaxoSmithKline*. First, the original royalty rate set under the licence agreement was too low at 6 percent to avoid the 40 percent domestic corporate tax rate on corporate profits. Second, when caught avoiding that domestic tax by overstating the price of the drug under the supply agreement, the approach of the Federal Court of Appeal and Supreme Court allowed the taxpayer to benefit from its own underpricing of the royalty. That is, the practical result was to allow the taxpayer to increase its 10 percent tax and drop its 40 percent tax, netting the difference in the process. Arnold concluded the decision "does not make sense to me." In passing, he noted the Court's decision in *Singleton* is wrongly decided because the interest deductibility rule in para. 20(1)(*c*) requires the Court to determine the purpose to which the funds were used, not just how they were used.[644]

---

[643] See Article 12 of the *Convention between Canada and Switzerland for the Avoidance of Double Taxation with Respect to Taxes on Income and on Capital* (signed May 5, 1997, and the Protocol signed on October 22, 2010). The nil amounts are in article 12(3). "Royalty" is defined in article 12(4) to include a right to use intangible property such as copyright, patents and trademarks. The Treaty is at https://www.canada.ca/en/department-finance/programs/tax-policy/tax-treaties/country/switzerland-convention-consolidated-1997-2010.html.

[644] Brian J. Arnold, *The Arnold Report*, "The Supreme Court, Transfer Pricing, and Drugs," Posting 40, November 19, 2012, Canadian Tax Foundation.

The last decision of Justice Rothstein profiled dates to late September 2013; it concerns a tax avoidance plan undertaken by a credit union in British Columbia.

Envision Credit Union (2013)

On January 1, 2001, the Delta Credit Union and First Heritage Savings Credit Union amalgamated for commercial reasons to form the Envision Credit Union (Envision) under the *Credit Union Incorporation Act* of British Columbia. The amalgamation also sought to create significant tax benefits.[645]

Section 87 of the ITA provides rules that apply to a "qualifying amalgamation," which rules provide for a tax-deferred rollover of the tax attributes of the amalgamating corporations into the new amalgamated corporation. The wrinkle in the case is that the tax plan sought to undertake something called a "busted amalgamation," which in general terms means the parties did not want to undertake a tax-deferred amalgamation. To do so, the amalgamation was structured not to apply to certain surplus real estate, which at amalgamation was conveyed to a subsidiary corporation.

By trying to bust the amalgamation rollover rule, the parties sought to create significant tax attributes for Envision to use on a go-forward basis to reduce income tax. First, Envision claimed a capital cost increase of its depreciable property to $51 million from $20 million when amalgamating the credit unions' CCA pools, which it would use to deduct CCA on the same old depreciated assets. The desired tax avoidance result is like that in the very first case considered in *Bench Strength—Pioneer Laundry* (1938). The two decisions span a period of 75 years in the Canadian income tax system.

The second tax benefit sought was to create a new preferred-rate amount (PRA). Envision sought to reset its PRA to nil instead of the amalgamating credit unions' prior combined PRA of

645 *Envision Credit Union v. The Queen*, 2013 SCC 48, [2013] 3 SCR 191. *Envision Credit Union v. Canada* - SCC Cases (scc-csc.ca).

$72,341,531.[646] Conservative Finance Minister James M. Flaherty, in his 2013 Budget, announced the phase-out of the PRA tax preference during the 2013–2016 period, which Parliament enacted. At the time, the PRA preference was described as follows: "The amount of taxable income eligible for the additional deduction is subject to a limit based on the credit union's cumulative taxable income that was taxed at the preferential rate (including as a result of the additional deduction) and the amount of their deposits and member shares."[647] As mentioned, Envision sought to reset its PRA as if it had not previously benefited from the tax preference.

Envision Credit Union was unsuccessful in the Tax Court and Federal Court of Appeal on its claims for the 2002–04 tax years. The courts differed in their reasoning. The Tax Court held that while the amalgamation was not a "qualifying amalgamation," past company-law precedent concerning mergers applied to effect a roll-over of the merging credit inions' tax attributes. The Federal Court of Appeal held that a "qualifying amalgamation" had occurred because the real estate passed to Envision on the amalgamation (on its way to its subsidiary), and it also agreed with the Tax Court that company law effected the same result. The Supreme Court granted Envision leave to appeal.

Justice Rothstein opened his majority decision with the following two sentences: "Every taxpayer is entitled to order his or her affairs so that the tax payable is less than it otherwise would be. Taxpayers often engage in tax planning to achieve that result." But Rothstein then indicated that any such planning is subject to the rules of the ITA and other statutes.

In his decision, Rothstein focused on s. 23 of the *Credit Union Incorporation Act* requiring the amalgamated credit union being

[646] For reasons within the technical details related to claiming a PRA, the difference did not change the tax rate Envision Credit Union paid on its 2001 income.
[647] Canada, Department of Finance, *2013 Budget Plan*, "Phasing out the Additional Deduction for Credit Unions," March 21, 2013, p. 152 (The Honourable James M. Flaherty, Minister of Finance).

"seized" and "possessed" of all of the property of each of its amalgamating credit unions. The parties to the amalgamation could not contract out of the provision. Rothstein also held that Evasion's "seizure" of property was not by conveyance to it but similar to a corporation changing its name. On amalgamation, the original corporations became one legal entity. The result was a "qualifying amalgamation" under the ITA, and it resulted in a rollover of the tax attributes of the amalgamating corporations to Envision.

Envision also questioned whether the amalgamation agreement may have been invalid if it could not structure its affairs to ensure the surplus real estate did not become its property. Rothstein rejected this suggestion; while there might be practical problems in invalidating an amalgamation that occurred 10 years before, "I would not give effect to that argument. Tax consequences which flow from the application of tax law cannot be tailored to avoid negative corporate law consequences."[648] He next went through the amalgamation agreement and found that practical consequences did not arise in the case. (Chief Justice McLachlin and Justices LeBel, Moldaver, Karakatsanis and Wagner concurred.)

Justice Thomas Cromwell issued a separate minority opinion. He agreed that Envision's "seizure" of all the assets was not by conveyance to it, but this was all that was necessary to decide the case. Cromwell did not agree that it was necessary, and indicated it was undesirable, to hold that the parties to an amalgamation cannot contract out of s. 23 of the *Credit Union Incorporation Act*.

Justice Marshall Rothstein retired in August 2015. He was replaced by Justice Russell Brown.

---

[648] *Envision Credit Union*, *supra* note 645, para. 42.

BEVERLEY MCLACHLIN: THE RULE OF LAW AND "CONSCIOUS OBJECTIVITY"

Chief Justice Beverley McLachlin is not selected despite the fact a convincing argument can be made for her inclusion. She has the quantitative numbers, having decided 58 income tax cases of which 18 concerned tax avoidance. McLachlin also wrote the opinion for the taxpayer in some key tax avoidance cases decided in the 1990s before she became the chief justice.

From rural Alberta, Beverley McLachlin led her law school class at the University of Alberta. After graduating, she practised law as a civil litigator in Alberta and British Columbia for several years and later taught law at the University of British Columbia. Chief Justice McLachlin began her judicial career in 1981 with the County Court of Vancouver and quickly rose up the judicial hierarchy. Conservative Prime Minister Brian Mulroney appointed McLachlin to the Supreme Court in 1989, replacing Justice William McIntyre. Liberal Prime Minister Jean Chretien elevated McLachlin in 2000. She is the first woman to be chief justice.

Academics Ian Greene and Peter McCormick wrote about McLachlin's influence in their 2019 book *Beverley McLachlin, The Legacy of a Chief Justice.* They stated her judicial touchstones are "the rule of law, a thorough, impartial and sympathetic canvassing of submissions by the parties—what she has referred to as 'conscious objectivity'—and reliance on sound evidence."[649]

McLachlin was pro-taxpayer in her decisions, especially in tax avoidance cases. There is also an intriguing deviation in her statistics concerning tax avoidance, which is expanded upon in Part V. The most significant of Chief Justice McLachlin's income tax opinions include her: 1997 opinion in *Hickman Motors*;[650] 1999

[649] Ian Greene and Peter McCormick, *Beverley McLachlin: The Legacy of a Supreme Court Chief Justice* (Toronto: James Lorimar & Company, 2019), p. 47.

[650] *Hickman Motors, supra* note 512. *Hickman Motors Ltd. v. Canada* – SCC Cases (scc-csc.ca).

unanimous decision in *Shell Canada*,[651] and unanimous co-opinions with Justice Major in the previously considered 2005 GAAR cases *Canada Trustco* and *Mathew*.[652]

In 1997, McLachlin provided an inkling in her *Hickman Motors* opinion of what the Supreme Court would do in income tax avoidance cases in general, and more specifically to the source of income concept in *Ludco Enterprises* (2001) and *Stewart* and *Walls* (2002).

Hickman Motors (1997)

The Hickman name is well known throughout Newfoundland and Labrador. Hickman Motors Limited operated a profitable General Motors dealership in St. John's in the early 1980s and was but one company within a wider group of associated corporations.

The beginnings of the Hickman group date to the early 20th century. Albert Edger Hickman, who was born in 1875, was a successful businessman and politician by then.[653] He was the leader of the Newfoundland Liberal Party in the 1920s and briefly the Prime Minister of Newfoundland after it had gained independence from the United Kingdom.[654]

The *Hickman Motors* income tax case was an outcome of the deep recession that gripped Canada *circa* 1981 during which the Hickman group faced financial difficulties. Although the group's consolidated financial statements showed a profit, one company within the group was incurring large losses—Hickman Equipment Ltd., which lost $1.8 million. Most of the companies within the group guaranteed Hickman Equipment's line of credit and A. E. Hickman Ltd. provided a guarantee to John Deere Ltd. in respect of the group's John Deere franchises.

---

[651] *Shell Canada*, *supra* note 636. *Shell Canada Ltd. v. Canada* – SCC Cases (scc-csc.ca).
[652] *Canada Trustco*, *supra* note 564; *Mathew*, *supra* note 565.
[653] See Robert D. Pitt, *The Canadian Encyclopedia (Historica)*, online, "Hickman, Albert Edgar." Albert Edgar Hickman | The Canadian Encyclopedia. Accessed February 2023.
[654] *Ibid.*

After a reorganization, Hickman Motors acquired $876,859 of business loss carryovers on the winding-up of Hickman Equipment. It also deducted CCA of about $2.1 million in respect of the heavy equipment it acquired from Hickman Equipment, which it owned for five days over the holidays beginning in late December 1984.

The Minister allowed the business loss carryovers rolled up to Hickman Motors but denied the approximate $2.1 million in CCA deductions it claimed for its 1984 taxation year. For this position, the Minister relied on a regulation, which excludes from depreciable property any property "not acquired by the taxpayer for the purpose of gaining or producing income." Hickman Motors acquired the equipment on December 28, 1984, and transferred it to a newly created sister corporation on January 2, 1985. There was little or no evidence that it carried on an equipment rental business that earned revenue during the five-day period.

The lower courts denied Hickman Motors its $2.1 million CCA deduction on the basis it did not acquire the property for the purpose of gaining or producing income. The Federal Court of Appeal noted that Hickman Motors failed to report any income for tax purposes from the equipment and held Hickman Motors had no reasonable expectation of profit from the activity, as required under the Supreme Court's 1977 decision in *Moldowan*.

The Supreme Court reversed the Federal Court of Appeal in a 3–1–3 judgment in which Justice L'Heureux-Dubé provided the swing opinion. Justice Iacobucci led the dissenting three. *Hickman Motors* is the second significant income tax case profiled in which Iacobucci and Major differ in outcome; Major concurred with McLachlin's opinion. They were each other's closest comparable in income tax disputes prior to McLachlin's becoming the chief justice.

Justice McLachlin found that Hickman Motors carried on the equipment business for the five-day period, and it was a source of income from which it could deduct the $2.1 million of CCA. She applied regulation 1102(14) on the basis that it deemed Hickman

Motors to be carrying on the equipment business that Hickman Equipment carried on before its winding up.

Regulation 1102(14) deems the depreciable property of a subsidiary corporation to be of the same prescribed class to the parent corporation on the winding up. This ensures the parent corporation is subject to recapture on excess CCA claims made by the subsidiary if the property is disposed of, and it entitles the parent to deduct CCA if the property is used for the purpose of earning income. McLachlin found this meant Hickman Motors was deemed to carry on the subsidiary's business despite a lack of supporting evidence that it carried on the business. She rested her opinion on the *Duke of Westminster* principle and Wilson's minority opinion in *Stubart Investments* that a transaction needs no business purpose other than the tax purpose. (Justices La Forest and Major concurred.)

Justice Iacobucci, in dissent, found that the winding-up rule created no right for Hickman Motors to deduct the CCA in respect of the acquired equipment. The five-day period had to involve a separate business that met the source requirement. The lower courts found that while Hickman Motors carried on a car dealership business, it never continued to carry on the equipment rental business of its subsidiary. Further, there was no evidence to establish that any revenue was received in respect of renting the equipment. (Justices Sopinka and Cory concurred.)

Justice L'Heureux-Dubé's opinion is the longest, allowing the deduction. Numerous cases were cited over the course of the opinion. She rejected the application of the "reasonable expectation of profit" test in determining whether CCA is deductible, reserving the test for cases in which the issue is whether activity is a business or hobby. While L'Heureux-Dubé agreed with Iacobucci that the winding-up rule created no right to deduct CCA (making her and Iacobucci's dissent the majority position on that narrow aspect of the case), she took direct issue with several aspects of his dissent.

L'Heureux-Dubé found that since a corporation claimed the CCA, the presumption was in respect of a source of income. Based on this, she shifted the onus to the Minister to rebut the presumption and held the Minister had not done so. As for the regulation, it did not require revenue during a specific minimum period, albeit she prorated about $20,000 from general revenues earned by Hickman Motors to the five-day period.

In *Hickman Motors*, McLachlin and Major made it clear that they would apply the *Duke of Westminster* principle in future non-GAAR income tax cases coupled with the Supreme Court's *Charter*-era judicial guideline that a tax avoidance transaction needs no business purpose other than the tax purpose.

It was about to get much worse for the Crown in tax avoidance disputes.

Shell Canada (1999)

Shell Canada concerns a blatant cross-border tax avoidance arbitrage involving the taxpayer's need to borrow American currency for use in its business; step-transactions denominated in New Zealand currency were inserted into the series. Although the tax avoidance plan was complex, it effected a simple result: the arbitrage step-transactions converted non-deductible loan principal into deductible interest, thus avoiding tax.

These interest deductions lowered Shell Canada's income for tax purposes annually over the course of the plan; when it ended, the arbitrage transactions resulted in realized taxable capital gains. This resulted in two tax benefits. First, while the converted principal became taxable capital gains, it was several years after the non-deductible principal that had been converted into interest first became deductible. This created a valuable tax deferral. The second benefit was that the offsetting capital gains were not fully taxable unlike the arbitrage interest deductions that were fully deducted.

Justice McLachlin found for a unanimous Supreme Court that the transactions complied with the ITA in a non-GAAR context. When doing so, McLachlin expressed a judicial policy that judges should not search for the object or spirit of the statutory income tax law, as judges have a duty to apply a supposed "unambiguous" tax provision. That is the judicial policy Justice Wilson followed in *Mattabi Mines*.

McLachlin rested her holding in *Shell Canada* on "this Court's tax jurisprudence that a searching inquiry for either the 'economic realities' of a particular transaction or the general object and spirit of the provision at issue can never supplant a court's duty to apply an unambiguous provision of the Act to a taxpayer's transaction."[655] The plain-meaning approach applied to allow the tax avoidance result. Citations included Iacobucci's unanimous 1994 holding in *Antosko*, which McLachlin noted Major applied the next year in *Friesen*. (Justices L'Heureux-Dubé, Gonthier, Iacobucci, Major, Bastarache and Binnie concurred.)

What is left unexplained is that if the interest deductibility provision is so unambiguous, why has the Supreme Court considered several cases on its meaning? The lack of ambiguity was reached after reading down the Court's prior precedent. Specifically, McLachlin narrowed down Dickson's 1987 holding in *Bronfman Trust*. She paid lip service to the Supreme Court's being sensitive to "economic realities" and then held that the Court cannot recharacterize a taxpayer's "*bona fide* legal relationships."

> This Court has repeatedly held that courts must be sensitive to the economic realities of a particular transaction, rather than being bound to what first appears to be its legal form: *Bronfman Trust*, *supra*, at pp. 52-53, *per* Dickson C.J.; *Tennant*, *supra*, at para. 26, *per* Iacobucci J. But there are at least two *caveats* to this rule.
>
> First, this Court has never held that the economic realities of a situation can be used to recharacterize a taxpayer's *bona fide* legal relationships. To the contrary, we have held that, absent a specific provision of the Act

[655] *Shell Canada*, *supra* note 636. *Shell Canada Ltd. v. Canada* – SCC Cases (scc-csc.ca).

> to the contrary or a finding that they are a sham, the taxpayer's legal relationships must be respected in tax cases. Recharacterization is only permissible if the label attached by the taxpayer to the particular transaction does not properly reflect its actual legal effect: *Continental Bank Leasing Corp. v. Canada*, [1998] 2 S.C.R. 298, at para. 21, *per* Bastarache J.
>
> Second, it is well established in this Court's tax jurisprudence that a searching inquiry for either the "economic realities" of a particular transaction or the general object and spirit of the provision at issue can never supplant a court's duty to apply an unambiguous provision of the Act to a taxpayer's transaction. Where the provision at issue is clear and unambiguous, its terms must simply be applied: *Continental Bank*, *supra*, at para. 51, *per* Bastarache J.; *Tennant*, *supra*, at para. 16, *per* Iacobucci J.; *Canada v. Antosko*, [1994] 2 S.C.R. 312, at pp. 326–27 and 330, *per* Iacobucci J.; *Friesen v. Canada*, [1995] 3 S.C.R. 103, at para. 11, *per* Major J.; *Alberta (Treasury Branches) v. M.N.R.*, [1996] 1 S.C.R. 963, at para. 15, *per* Cory J.[656]

McLachlin added: "[A]bsent a specific provision of the Act to the contrary, it is not the courts' role to prevent taxpayers from relying on the sophisticated structure of their transactions, arranged in such a way that the particular provisions of the Act are met, on the basis that it would be inequitable to those taxpayers who have not chosen to structure their transactions that way."[657]

As such, Justice Beverley McLachlin's judicial-policy approach to sophisticated tax avoidance planning in 1999 was the exact opposite of what Brian Dickson expressed in 1987 when deciding *Bronfman Trust*. Who if either was the activist?

---

[656] *Ibid.*, SCC paras. 39–40.

[657] *Ibid.*, para. 45.

Two years after *Shell Canada*, the Supreme Court essentially struck down its *Bronfman Trust* precedent in *Singleton* and *Ludco Enterprises*.

Ten years after *Shell Canada*, the Supreme Court saw no need to cite either *Bronfman Trust* or Dickson's *obiter* concerning a manipulating sequence of events that effected a patina of compliance in an interest deductibility context. Rather, in its 2009 *Lipson* GAAR decision, not one of the Court's seven judges in the majority and dissenting opinions could muster up a finding that the taxpayers were abusing the interest deductibility rules by using the Court's Singleton shuffle precedent to deduct interest on a personal residence. That left only those who misused the attribution rules as effecting an abuse.

Chief Justice McLachlin was not selected because it was a close call between her and Major whose co-writing of *Jarvis* and *Ling* tipped the balance to him. But why wasn't McLachlin selected instead of Dickson as the hypothetical chief justice, given the extent to which his leading precedent has been distinguished, read down, confined and outright overturned? In comparison, McLachlin's influence appears to be more significant—especially in the context of tax avoidance.

The selection of a hypothetical chief justice factors in the future and is not based solely on the past. The dispute between Chief Justices McLachlin and Dickson over which judicial policy approach to take when deciding income tax avoidance cases has been ongoing since the enactment of a national income tax in the United Kingdom in the early 19th century. The approach the judiciary takes has ebbed and flowed over the decades as times have changed.

The times changed with the global crisis in financial markets *circa* 2007–2009, resulting in a slow shift in Canada toward the views of Dickson in judicial policy terms in income taxation and its avoidance. In this shift, his judicial policy approach will be, it is predicted, more significant than McLachlin's until at least 2040.

Chief Justice Beverley McLachlin retired in December 2017. She was replaced as a member of the Supreme Court by Justice Sheilah Martin.

The next Part of *Bench Strength* provides statistics for the chosen nine justices and Chief Justices Cartwright and McLachlin. Readers can compare the results in income tax disputes to get a math-based sense of each justice's approach to income taxation.

PART V

Statistical Results: The Judges and the Supreme Court

PART V PROVIDES TWO sets of statistics in respect of the Supreme Court's income tax decisions from 1920 to 2019 inclusive. The data comes from 399 federal and provincial income tax cases in which 441 issues (disputes) were identified as being decided by the Court during those one hundred years.[658]

[658] The data base has variables that include: (1) identification of the appellant (i.e., the taxpayer or Crown); (2) the type of income tax dispute (income-revenue, expenses-tax preferences and other such as administrative or constitutional law); (3) whether a decision classified under the first two types of disputes concerned tax avoidance; (4) the type of tax avoidance (i.e., artificial tax attributes, diversions of income and acquisitions of losses, and conversions into tax-preferred amounts such as capital gains); (5) each judge's vote in the dispute; and (6) the dispute's outcome. It also identifies reversals and dissents case by case, judge by judge and issue by issue. I inputted the data and, to determine judges who are not identified in the published reports, researched the Supreme Court's case files. A discrepancy was noted for the decision *MNR v. John Colford Contracting Co. Limited,* [1962] SCR viii, [1962] CTC 546, 62 DTC 1338. *Canada Tax Cases* refers to the five members assigned to the panel, but only four—Taschereau, Fauteux, Ritchie and Abbott, JJ.—were present for the decision according to the judgment book. Martland J. is the fifth judge, and he has not been treated

Table V1 provides the first set of statistics with results for the judges selected to the hypothetical panel of nine and the two alternates. The results are for income tax cases in general and the tax avoidance subset. General comments are made about the statistics presented in table format.

Table V2 provides the second set of statistics with general results for the decisions of the Supreme Court as an institution with respect to its deciding income tax and tax avoidance disputes over one hundred years. The statistics compare results for the pre-*Charter* and *Charter* eras.

---

as participating in the decision for statistical purposes, given the discrepancy. The Annex provides a list of the cases classified as income tax avoidance and *infra* notes 659 and 747 discuss why some cases were not classified as concerning income tax avoidance.

RESULTS OF EACH SELECTED JUDGE'S APPROACH TO INCOME TAX

The statistics in Table V1 highlights the extent to which the results differ for the judges in the pre-*Charter* and *Charter* eras.

The first column to the left in Table V1 identifies each judge, including the two not selected. The first three columns to the right of each judge provide (1) the number of income tax cases the judge participated in, (2) the percentage of those cases the judge decided for the taxpayer (including by dissent) and (3) the percentage the judge decided for the Crown (including by dissent). To the right of those columns are three more columns that identify (1) the subset number of income tax avoidance cases the judge participated in, (2) the percentage of those cases the judge decided for the taxpayer (including by dissent) and (3) the percentage the judge decided for the Crown (including by dissent).

Table V1: Statistical Results (Supreme Court Judges in an Income Tax Context)

Per Justice	Income Tax Cases	For Taxpayer	For Crown	Tax Avoidance Cases	For Taxpayer	For Crown
Pre-Charter Era						
Kerwin	77	19%	81%	25	8%	92%
Abbott	112	13%	87%	45	13%	87%
Martland	123	22%	78%	45	11%	89%
Judson	125	18%	82%	50	10%	90%
Cartwright	95	38%	62%	29	17%	83%
Both Eras						
Dickson	45	38%	62%	14	36%	64%
Charter Era						
Wilson	20	55%	45%	4	75%	25%
Iacobucci	43	65%	35%	16	81%	19%
Major	43	60%	40%	16	88%	12%
Rothstein	15	60%	40%	7	57%	43%
McLachlin	58	66%	34%	18	78%	22%

**Percentages round to nearest full percent*

The extent to which the judges' percentages for the taxpayer or Crown deviate in the pre-*Charter* era versus the *Charter* era (or *vice versa*) raises a number of questions, most of which are beyond the scope of answering in detail in *Bench Strength*. But general observations are provided below.

For some readers, perhaps the most noticeable aspect of the statistics is the extent to which the judges in the pre-*Charter* era could be said to be pro-Crown and against income tax avoidance. For each judge, the percentage of his decisions for the Crown goes up when the matter concerns tax avoidance (except for Abbott, whose percentage for the Crown is 87 percent regardless). This includes Chief Justice John Cartwright, and the increased percentages against tax avoidance can be explained in part by these judges living their lives when the culture emphasized duties—not rights.

Chief Justice Patrick Kerwin and Justices Douglas Abbott, Ronald Martland and Wilfred Judson have similar statistics spread over a very high number of cases. The percentage of their decisions for the Crown is 78–87 percent in all cases and 87–92 percent in tax avoidance cases. Kerwin is the key influencer of the direction the Supreme Court took to income tax and its avoidance from 1938 to the late 1950s, but it was Abbott, Martland and Judson, who carried that legacy forward as a powerful core block from 1958 into the 1970s.

When interpreting the statutory law, the pre-*Charter* judges considered the context in which the text existed and its purpose. They and their contemporaries did so with knowledge of and with a temporal connection to Parliament's decision to modernize Canada's statutory income tax law in 1948. Finance Minister Douglas Abbott brought detailed knowledge about the policy and politics underlying this modernization to the Supreme Court in 1954.

The statistics of Chief Justices Brian Dickson and John Cartwright are identical across all income tax disputes, but Dickson's statistics are not as intense for the Crown in tax avoidance, although he decided far fewer cases. While he favoured the

Crown in 64 percent of income tax avoidance cases compared to Cartwright's 83 percent, there is an anomaly in Dickson's results. He decided for the Crown in 9 of 14 income tax avoidance cases, but all 9 decisions for the Crown were before the enactment of the *Charter*. Dickson decided 2 of 2 tax avoidance cases for the taxpayer after April 1982—*George Golden et al.* in 1986 and *McClurg* in 1990.[659] But two cases are insufficient to draw any conclusions.

For other readers, perhaps the most notable aspect of the statistics is the extent to which the judges in the *Charter* era were pro-taxpayer especially in tax avoidance cases. Their percentage for the taxpayer and against the Crown goes up significantly in tax avoidance cases (except for Justice Rothstein). This is surprising if one fails to appreciate at least three things.

First, the selected *Charter*-era judges had a temporal connection to Parliament's decision along with a substantial majority of the provinces to change Canada's constitution and enact the *Charter* in April 1982. This gave significant legal recognition to a cultural and legal shift that emphasizes rights over societal obligations. Contemporaneously, the economy shifted to *laissez-faire*.

Second, the *Charter* era were appointed to the Supreme Court long after the modernization of the statutory income tax law

[659] Chief Justice Dickson's 1974 and 1987 decisions in *Angle* and *Bronfman Trust* were not classified as tax avoidance cases. *Angle* is a collection case, and such cases were not classified as tax avoidance. The exclusion of *Bronfman Trust* from the tax avoidance decisions was a close call, given that the trust did not have a *bona fide* purpose of earning income from the borrowed funds, but it is likely most tax practitioners would not consider the case to concern tax avoidance. The following four decisions concerning interest deductions were classified as tax avoidance: Justice McLachlin's 1999 decision in *Shell Canada*, Justice Major's 2001 decision in *Singleton,* Justice Iacobucci's 2001 decision in *Ludco Enterprises* and Justice LeBel's 2009 GAAR decision in *Lipson*. But an interest deduction case not classified as tax avoidance was Justice Deschamps' 2005 decision in favour of Quebec Revenue in *Moufarrège*, *infra* note 670, wherein about 65 percent of the borrowed funds ($300,000) were used to acquire shares of a Quebec-based corporation and 35 percent ($155,000) were used to acquire four condominiums in Vancouver, which may have been tax-shelter property. For the list of cases classified as tax avoidance, see the Annex.

in 1948. They were not there, so to speak, when a delicate balance was struck that resulted in Parliament's removing almost all of the statutory rules that granted the Minister of National Revenue the discretion to constrain tax avoidance.

Under this modernization, relief for commercial interests was balanced by (1) the underlying commercial purposes reflected in the modernized law, including the "for the purpose of gaining or producing income" test, and its connection to the existence of a source of income from a business or property; and (2) granting the Minister broad powers to obtain information from, and on, taxpayers as well as to collect taxes owing. The Supreme Court lost its temporal connection to that balance in the *Charter* era.

Third, the *Charter*-era judges have taken the plain-meaning interpretive approach to the text of the statutory income tax law, which meant they intended to read down the legislation's context and purpose. They followed that interpretive approach with predictable results. Commercial interests sought this approach, and their legal and accounting tax representatives predicated its justification on minimizing uncertainty in tax planning. A judge who follows a textual approach knows full well that the results are likely to defy commercial reality, which skews results in favour of tax avoiders.

Justice Bertha Wilson's statistics should be considered in light of her not being able to swing two pre-*Charter* holdovers to her strict interpretive approach—Chief Justice Brian Dickson and Justice Willard Estey. The clarity and confidence with which she articulated that approach in her decisions may have led later judges, tax practitioners and academics to assume that she was correct when she held in 1984 that the *Duke of Westminster* principle applied in *Stubart Investments* despite the Supreme Court's never expressly applying it in a majority income tax decision, and the British Privy Council's oversight of the Court ending 35 years earlier.

Justices Frank Iacobucci and John Major and Chief Justice Beverley McLachlin formed a powerful core block in income tax cases in the 1990s and early 2000s. They emphasized taxpayer rights and allowed tax avoidance results that defy commercial substance and reality. In doing so, they continually cited Justice Wilson and their own decisions. Justices Iacobucci's and Major's statistics are similar, and it is noteworthy that their percentages favouring taxpayers increase significantly in cases involving tax avoidance. Iacobucci's percentage for the taxpayer is 65 percent in all cases and increasing to 81 percent in tax avoidance cases; Major's percentage for the taxpayer is 60 percent in all cases and increasing to 88 percent in tax avoidance cases.

In the case of Justice Marshall Rothstein, his percentage for taxpayers at 60 percent goes down slightly in tax avoidance cases to 57 percent. But Rothstein also participated in fewer income tax cases than any other selected judge. While he favoured the taxpayer, his statistics are, along with Chief Justice Brian Dickson, the most balanced. Rothstein was about as pro-taxpayer as Dickson was pro-Crown.

Chief Justice Beverley McLachlin's closest comparable in tax avoidance is not easily discerned because her approach appears to have shifted after she became chief justice in January 2000. Prior to 2000, McLachlin favoured taxpayers by a wide margin—especially in tax avoidance cases. From 1990 to 1999 inclusive, she decided 81 percent of income tax cases for the taxpayer and 89 percent of tax avoidance cases for the taxpayer. From 2000 to 2017 inclusive, McLachlin decided 52 percent of income tax cases for the taxpayer and 67 percent of tax avoidance cases for the taxpayer.

McLachlin's statistics are thus deceptive in the sense something appears to have changed in her approach to income tax from January 1, 2000, to December 14, 2017. After she became chief justice in 2000, the Supreme Court drew significant criticism in 2001 from Professor Brian Arnold in the tax literature about its approach to tax avoidance.[660] Constitutional Law Professor Robert Martin discussed and cited Arnold's criticism in his controversial

[660] Arnold, "Reflections on the Relationship between Statutory Interpretation and Tax Avoidance," *supra* note 3.

2003 book *The Most Dangerous Branch: How the Supreme Court Has Undermined Our Law and Democracy.*[661]

Martin thus gave Arnold's criticism a much higher profile in academia than might otherwise have occurred, and it is reported that McLachlin "hates it when people criticize the court" and cares about "what people say" about her.[662] This should not come as a surprise, but did the criticism cause her to begin to distance herself from the precedent she helped create during the 1990s? *Perhaps.*

The Supreme Court decided 15 income tax avoidance cases while McLachlin was the chief justice, less than one per year. But six of those decisions had occurred in the three years before 2003 when Martin's book was published, meaning the Court heard only nine income tax avoidance cases during the next 15 years under her leadership. Notably, Chief Justice McLachlin wrote only four income tax opinions over the 18-year period between January 2000 to her retirement in late December 2017. Further, three of her four post-1999 opinions were co-written: two with Justice Major in the 2005 GAAR cases *Canada Trustco* and *Mathew*, and one with Justice Louis LeBel in *Redeemer Foundation,*[663] in 2008. The Crown was successful in two of those three decisions.

The fourth opinion was McLachlin's 2011 dissent for the Crown in *Canada Trustco #2,*[664] which concerned a tax-debtor lawyer in British Columbia who avoided paying his tax liability by making deposits by cheque from his law firm trust account to a joint account he had with his wife at Canada Trustco. In the dispute, the Minister issued a requirement to Canada Trustco that it pay the Receiver General for Canada the deposits as the tax-debtor lawyer made

---

[661] Robert Martin, *The Most Dangerous Branch: How the Supreme Court Has Undermined Our Law and Democracy* (Montreal-Kingston: McGill-Queen's University Press, 2003), p. 29.

[662] Slayton, *Mighty Judgment, supra* note 160, pp. 160 and xxi.

[663] *Redeemer Foundation v. MNR*, [2008] 2 SCR 643, 2008 SCC 46. *Redeemer Foundation v. Canada (National Revenue)* – SCC Cases (scc-csc.ca).

[664] *Canada Trustco Mortgage Co. v. The Queen*, [2011] 2 SCR 635, 2011 SCC 36. *Canada Trustco Mortgage Co. v. Canada* – SCC Cases (scc-csc.ca).

them into the joint account. It refused to do so and was successful in the Supreme Court, with Justice Marie Deschamps' issuing the majority opinion interpreting the *Bills of Exchange Act* and allowing Canada Trustco's appeal. (Justices Ian Binnie, Marshall Rothstein and Thomas Cromwell concurred.)

McLachlin, in dissent, interpreted the *Bill of Exchange Act* in light of the requirement provision. She refused to give that income tax provision a narrow meaning:

> The scope of the operation of s. 244(1) is not narrowly confined, but exists wherever the tax debtor is in a position at law to enforce payment from the party served with the requirement to pay. To adopt a more restrictive view of its content would be to undermine the proper functioning of the power the provision grants the Minister.[665]

(Justices Morris Fish and Rosalie Abella concurred.)

The next set of statistics consider the approach the Supreme Court took as an institution to income tax and its avoidance in the pre-*Charter* and *Charter* eras.

---

[665] *Ibid.*, para. 65.

COMPARING THE RESULTS IN INCOME TAX DISPUTES (PRE-CHARTER V. CHARTER ERAS)

Table V2 highlights the extent to which the Supreme Court's shift to emphasizing the legal form of a taxpayer's transactions and applying the plain-meaning interpretive approach affected the results in income tax. Unlike in Table V1, these statistics are computed on a dispute-by-dispute basis thereby identifying results where cases have more than one dispute.[666]

A word of caution is in order because statistics can be deceiving and should be approached carefully without jumping to conclusions. Table V2 provides an example of this because the statistics reflect the whole 1920–2019 period and its two subsets. Considering the statistical results for the whole period blurs the distinct results for the pre-*Charter* era versus the *Charter* era.[667]

Table V2 is meant to supplement the previous analysis of the selected judges' income tax decisions and to provide a general sense of the extent to which the statistical results appear to be consistent with the general theme of this undertaking—the extent to which the Supreme Court and its judges approached the statutory income tax law differently before and after the enactment of the *Charter*. But this does not prove the *Charter* caused the change. The *Charter* was used as a break point in the data because the

[666] Several cases before and after the enactment of the *Charter* in 1982 concern decisions on two or more tax issues. For example, *Premium Iron Ores* (1966), *supra* note 98, has two significant issues, both won by the taxpayer. While they were treated as one case when computing the statistics for the judges (the dispute that drew a dissent from Justices Ritchie and Abbott), the results for both issues are reflected in the statistics for the Supreme Court over the 1920-2019 period.

[667] The pre-*Charter* and *Charter* eras have subperiods that are not reflected in Table V2. The pre-*Charter* period could be subdivided—for example, into (1) the period before the enactment of the 1948 Act and (2) the period from 1949 to the enactment of the *Charter* in 1982. The *Charter* era could be subdivided between the periods before and after the global financial crisis of 2007–2009. Other subdivisions within periods could also be tested. Undertaking such analysis is beyond the purpose of this part.

Table V2: Statistical Results of the Supreme Court Income Tax Decisions from 1920 to 2019* (Based on Income Tax Disputes)

	Pre-Charter Era, 1920–April 17, 1982	**Charter Era, April 18, 1982–December 31, 2019**	**Total 1920–2019**
From Total Cases	**299**	**100**	**399**
Total of All Disputes	**332**	**109**	**441**
For *Taxpayer* (All)	28%	56%	35%
For *Crown* (All)	72%	44%	65%
Tax Avoidance (TA) Disputes Only	**109**	**33**	**142**
For *Taxpayer* (TA)	17%	73%	30%
For *Crown* (TA)	83%	27%	70%

**Percentages rounded to nearest percent. The above table excludes municipal income tax cases decided by the Supreme Court. Municipal income tax in the Maritime Provinces predates Canada's Confederation in 1867, which tax ended during the Second World War.*

timing of its enactment occurred when a number of previously discussed economic, cultural and legal events coalesced historically.

Before the enactment of the *Charter*, taxpayers were successful in only 28 percent of all income tax cases and in 17 percent of all income tax avoidance disputes, while the Crown was successful in 72 percent of all income tax disputes and in 83 percent of tax avoidance disputes. The Crown's success rate thus went up significantly if the dispute concerned tax avoidance.

After the enactment of the *Charter*, taxpayers were successful in 56 percent of all income tax disputes and in 73 percent of all income tax avoidance disputes, while the Crown was successful in 44 percent of all disputes and in only 27 percent of tax avoidance disputes. The taxpayer success rate thus went up significantly if the dispute concerned tax avoidance.

The above statistics are what might be expected for a Supreme Court whose judges emphasized the commercial substance and reality of a taxpayer's transactions in the pre-*Charter* era and the object and spirit of the statutory law especially in tax avoidance cases. The same can be said for judges who emphasized the legal form of a taxpayer's transactions and applied the plain-meaning approach in the *Charter* era. The approach taken can be expected to lead to a result in tax avoidance cases. In this sense, the approach the Court and its judges took is result driven. Nevertheless, this does not explain why the Court and its judges followed the chosen approach.

We know that Justice Bertha Wilson followed the *Duke of Westminster's* strict approach because for her the context of business requires certainty; to deliver it to business, she read down the context and purpose of the text in the statutory income law. This is what business demanded and what the Supreme Court delivered through the judges that followed Wilson.

In the process, myths were created about the Canadian judiciary's previously adhering to the *Duke of Westminster* principle and its strict interpretive approach in income tax avoidance cases. The lower-court decisions that followed the precedent were invariably reversed or not heard by the Supreme Court. But taxpayers who had *bona fide* intent or purpose did succeed occasionally before the Court despite the matter concerning tax avoidance (e.g., *James Cameron*), or the matter concerning an overarching legal principle such as the *Salomon* principle (e.g., *Army & Navy Department Store (Western) Ltd.*) or the meaning of corporate control (e.g., *Dworkin Furs et al.*).

Table VI also shows that the Supreme Court has decided 25 percent of all income tax cases after the enactment of the *Charter* despite the period spanning about 38 percent of those one hundred years.

Where does the Supreme Court go in income tax in the future? The final part considers that subject as part of providing a big picture conclusion to what you have read.

PART VI

Concluding Reflections

CANADIAN POLITICIANS THROUGH ELECTED governments have chosen, since 1940, to make progressive income tax the primary source of federal revenues, shifting from regressive taxes such as sales taxes, excise taxes and tariffs.

Initially, corporations and individuals shared the income tax burden, but over time, it shifted to personal income tax. The main shift to personal income tax occurred before the enactment of the *Charter* in 1982 and the Supreme Court's 1984 income tax decisions in *Stubart Investments* and *James Richardson & Sons*. The percentage of corporate income tax fell as a percentage of all income taxes from 47 percent in fiscal 1949–50 to 40 percent in fiscal 1964–65, to 28 percent in fiscal 1980–81, to 23 percent by fiscal 2017–18, with corporate tax projected in Budget 2019 to be 20 percent of all income taxes for fiscals 2021–22, 2022–23 and 2023–24—with the percentage of personal tax increasing by a similar amount [The Covid pandemic upended the government's post-2019 projections and the downward trend initially revered, which is discussed in the epilogue.].[668]

[668] Percentages were computed from Budget documents and tables. The three main categories of income taxes are personal and corporate taxes plus

The profiled *Charter*-era disputes hint at this shift to personal income tax. Of the post-1982 cases profiled, 19 concern personal income tax,[669] while 14 additional personal income tax disputes were not profiled.[670] These 33 personal income tax cases—which do not include administrative, collection and criminal law income tax cases involving individuals—represent almost one-third of the

---

non-resident withholding taxes collected on certain incomes paid to offshore persons, such as interest, rents, dividends, royalties and management fees. For fiscal 1949–50, excess profits taxes were included in the income tax base and treated as corporate taxes. See House of Commons Debates for fiscal 1949–50 (March 28, 1950) and for 1964–65 (June 1, 1967). For fiscal 1980–81, see the 1981 Budget Papers (November 12, 1981, Table 2.2, p. 11); for fiscal 2014–15, the 2016 Budget Papers (March 22, 2016, Table A1.3, p. 235). The remainder of the percentages were computed from Table A2.5 in the 2019 Budget Plan (p. 285).

[669] The 19 personal income tax cases are as follows: (1) *Nowegijick, supra* note 354; (2) *Savage, supra* note 360; (3) *George Golden, supra* note 438; (4) *Bronfman Trust, supra* note 366; (5) *McClurg, supra* note 370; (6) *Symes, supra* note 93; (7) *Antosko, supra* note 471; (8) *Friesen, supra* note 536; (9) *Tennant, supra* note 480; (10) *Neuman, supra* note 499; (11) *Stewart, supra* note 518; (12) *Walls, supra* note 519; (13) *Singleton, supra* note 546; (14) *Mathew, supra* note 565; (15) *McLarty, supra* note 595; (16) *Earl Lipson, supra* note 606; (17) *Bastien Estate, supra* note 619; (18) *Dubé, supra* note 620; and (19) *Craig, supra* note 633.

[670] The 14 non-profiled personal income tax cases are as follows: (1) *Fries v. The Queen*, [1990] 2 SCR 1322, *Canada v. Fries* – SCC Cases (scc-csc.ca); (2) *Williams, supra* note 621; (3) *Friedberg, supra* note 457; (4) *Gagnon v. The Queen*, [1986] 1 SCR 264, *Gagnon v. The Queen* – SCC Cases (scc-csc.ca); (5) *Thibaudeau, supra* note 474; (6) *Swartz v. The Queen*, [1996] 1 SCR 254, *Schwartz v. Canada* – SCC Cases (scc-csc.ca); (7) *Swantje v. The Queen*, [1996] 1 SCR 73, *Swantje v. Canada* – SCC Cases (scc-csc.ca); (8) *Hall v. Deputy Minister of Revenue (Quebec)*, [1998] 1 SCR 220, *Hall v. Quebec (Deputy Minister of Revenue)* – SCC Cases (scc-csc.ca); (9) *Backman v. The Queen*, [2001] 1 SCR 367, 2001 SCC 10, *Backman v. Canada* – SCC Cases (scc-csc.ca); (10) *Gifford v. The Queen*, [2004] 1 SCR 411, 2004 SCC 15, *Gifford v. Canada* – SCC Cases (scc-csc.ca); (11) *Tsiaprailis v. The Queen*, [2005] 1 SCR 113, 2005 SCC 8, *Tsiaprailis v. Canada* – SCC Cases (scc-csc.ca); (12) *Deputy Minister of Revenue (Quebec) v. Moufarrège*, [2005] 2 SCR 598, 2005 SCC 53, *Moufarrège v. Quebec (Deputy Minister of Revenue)* – SCC Cases (scc-csc.ca); (13) *Dunne v. Quebec (Deputy Minister)*, [2007] 1 SCR 853, 2007 SCC 19, *Dunne v. Quebec (Deputy Minister of Revenue)* – SCC Cases (scc-csc.ca); and (14) *Fundy Settlement v. The Queen*, [2012] 1 SCR 520, 2012 SCC 14, *Fundy Settlement v. Canada* – SCC Cases (scc-csc.ca).

one hundred income tax cases the Supreme Court has decided over the period of April 18, 1982–December 31, 2019. On average, the Court decided fewer than three cases per year during this period.

This shift has not been subject to significant public scrutiny, although Eric Reguly of the *Globe and Mail* has on occasion discussed the declining share of taxes paid by corporations in his column. In 2017, he suggested an "ugly side of globalization is relentless corporate tax competition."[671] As noted, the shift began well before 1982 and continues as part of a broader worldwide phenomenon.

There are several reasons underlying the shift to personal income tax, but considering them is beyond the scope of *Bench Strength.* One thing relevant about the shift in this context is that successful corporations and their owners can take a sophisticated approach to taxation—for example, organizing themselves into like-minded associations representing large or small businesses, funding think tanks, or hiring tax professionals to plan and lobbyists to help persuade politicians and governments to see things their way.

Throughout history, people have organized to shift the burden of taxation to others, if not outright avoid or evade it. Some economic think-tanks on the right explain in policy terms why certain forms of taxes are more efficient in economic terms, while other think-tanks on the left explain in policy terms why one form of tax is fairer than another form. This discourse often distills to why consumption taxes such as the Goods and Services Tax are more efficient and should replace income taxes versus why income taxes are a fairer form of taxation in terms of equity among taxpayers and should replace consumption taxes.

In this discourse, average-income individuals and their families are on their own. But as income goes up, high-income and wealthy individuals tend to be exposed to paying a disproportionate amount

[671] Eric Reguly, "Corporate Tax Rates Are Getting Ridiculously Low. Guess Who Will Pay More?," *Globe and Mail*, February 1, 2017.

of personal income tax compared to others. They also tend to own private corporations and set up family trusts, obtaining significant tax benefits in the process, which many elected politicians are loath to reduce or end. You hear noise about this, but you do not hear a whole lot about effective action. How the income of these individuals and their corporations and trusts are taxed is fundamental to ensuring a prosperous country, and it needs to be done in a balanced manner. The answer cannot be to impair our collective standard of living by imposing too onerous tax rates on success or by shifting taxes to those who can least afford them, and expect a positive economic *and* democratic outcome.

Some high-income and wealthy individuals may feel hard done by; their individual success may be viewed by many as a golden goose to pluck. They can pay for tax avoidance advice or suspect tax shelters thereby attempting to shift the burden of corporate and personal tax to individuals down the taxable income table, who do not or cannot afford to pay for tax avoidance advice or cannot afford to risk failed planning under the tax law. The extent to which this shift is allowed to occur often turns on the interpretive approach taken, as has been detailed by profiling the most influential judges and their opinions in *Bench Strength*.

As an institution, the Supreme Court has taken an active role in the way in which Canada's judiciary interprets and applies the statutory income tax law. It began to do so at least by the time Patrick Kerwin issued his 1938 swing opinion in *Pioneer Laundry*. Whether it was the Irish in him, or that he considered the spirit of the statutory law and not just its black letters, Chief Justice Kerwin did not follow the British tax avoidance precedent. His rejection of the 1935 *Duke of Westminster* principle as being applicable in interpreting Canada's statutory income tax law in a tax avoidance context held for almost 50 years. This is despite the Supreme Court never again stating that the *Duke of Westminster* principle is inapplicable in a Canadian income tax avoidance dispute after the Judicial Committee of the Privy Council in 1939 overturned the Court's decision in *Pioneer Laundry*.

The country survived the Second World War intact. In 1949–50, Canada, its taxpayers, tax professionals, the Department of National Revenue and a Supreme Court finally free of Privy Council oversight began to chart a new way forward under the modernized *Income Tax Act*. Taxpayers were granted new rights, including the right to use best commercial principles to compute business income as modified by statutory law. The Minister's discretionary power to constrain tax avoidance was essentially ended in a context where the "for the purpose of gaining or producing income" test was added, along with broad powers related to auditing taxpayers and collecting unpaid taxes.

This change in Canadian income taxation occurred just as the post-war economy began to boom and the Supreme Court heard an expanding caseload of income tax disputes. The Court's then-message to Canadians was as follows: pay your income tax and don't avoid it. Kerwin had led this approach and became the Court's chief justice in 1954.

At that very moment, Liberal Finance Minister Douglas Abbott left the cabinet room on Parliament Hill and walked the short distance west along Wellington Street to the Supreme Court Building. He brought to the Court a wealth of knowledge about the politics and policy behind the modernized income tax law. He had lived and breathed that policy and politics for more than a decade—first, assisting Finance Minister J.L. Ilsley and then on his own as the minister responsible for ensuring Parliament passed the *Income Tax Act*, 1948. The situation is unprecedented in the Court's as well as Canada's history.

Justice Abbott may have taken some flak for his move to the Supreme Court; politics are like that. Legal academics also panned the appointment of a leading politician more than a decade removed from practising law. But no one should discount his contribution to Canada's income tax system as a politician or a judge and thus miss the big picture.

Abbott was the one to establish the methodology for applying the modern "for the purpose of gaining or producing income" test.

He did likewise for establishing the methodology for a trading business when it computes its gross income by deducting the cost of inventory. The related principles are fundamental to computing a taxpayer's income (or loss) from a business or property source. In less than 20 years, Abbott heard more than one hundred income tax cases, averaging more than five cases a year.

In 1958, Ronald Martland and Wilfred Judson joined the Supreme Court and became judicial forces of increasing influence in income tax over the next two decades. Justice Martland was the more neutral of the two. You can see it in his 1962 decision in *Irrigation Industries*, which sought to treat share sales differently under the adventure in the nature of trade case law, and in the way in which he sought a middle ground between Justice Judson's 1974 majority opinion in *Jack Appleby* and Justice Pigeon's dissent.

It was Judson, who led the Supreme Court in emphasizing commercial substance over legal form in income tax. His precedent-setting decisions ranged from the adventure case law to corporate surplus-stripping schemes and the meaning of "legal control" of a corporation. He brought a mindset that sought to inform income tax decisions with elements of the law of equity and trusts. This includes his 1969 holdings in *Smythe* and *Craddock*, which did not recognize the surplus received from legal sales of shares as tax-exempt capital gains in a context where the sales had no *bona fide* commercial purpose.

The situation had evolved so much by 1983 that E.A. Driedger could confidently stipulate in *Construction of Statutes* (2nd ed.) that there is only one way to interpret a statute in Canada—to apply an approach that gives due consideration to the text, context and object of the provisions in issue.

But Canada's economic boom ended during the disorienting 1970s. Unemployment rates and inflation soared out of control. Confidence in the old ways waivered. The culture had moved on from the hard years of the Great Depression and Second World War and was shifting to emphasizing individual rights and freedoms and away from a duty-bound era. All of this coalesced by the early 1980s, and the old ways of doing things gave way to a newer approach—not necessarily a better approach in important ways.

In income taxation, the shift was toward taxpayer rights and away from taxpayer obligations. When this shift occurred, in order to ensure it took hold, it needed to emphasize a strict or plain-meaning approach. Justice Bertha Wilson from the corporate-commercial tax law firm Osler led this shift, beginning with her minority 1984 opinion in *Stubart Investments*. Concurrently, she and the Supreme Court in *James Richardson & Sons* constrained the Minister of National Revenue's ability to undertake so-called *fishing expeditions* for information on unnamed taxpayers. The times they were a-changin'.[672]

Wilson's approach to the statutory income tax—the plain-meaning approach because business requires certainty—may never have taken firm hold but for another event affecting the Supreme Court by the early 1990s. That factor was pressure from activists seeking to effect law reform by instilling their social values and *Charter* values into statutory interpretation. Ian Bushnell of the University of Windsor Law School advanced this leftist agenda in late 1992 with the publication of *The Captive Court*. In doing so, he carved out a plain-meaning safe harbour for commercial and tax law.

Justice Frank Iacobucci, who had been a leading corporate-commercial law academic at the University of Toronto Law School, provided the reasons that helped protect the ITA from that activist agenda. He turned to Bertha Wilson's plain-meaning approach in *Mattabi Mines*, which would be applied if the text of the statutory law is determined to be "unambiguous"; a cementing into the case law of her distinctly different approach. In doing so, Iacobucci led the Supreme Court in a new direction in income tax throughout the 1990s and early 2000s. In case after case, he emphasized legal

[672] The Canadian judiciary's post-1982 narrowing of the Minister of National Revenue's audit and collection powers has been touched on in *Bench Strength*, and it has continued despite the Supreme Court's 1990 decision in *McKinlay Transport*, *supra* note 452, to pull back from its *James Richardson & Sons* (*supra* note 425) precedent.

form and applied a plain-meaning approach that read down, confined and distinguished the old precedent that emphasized commercial substance and the object and spirit of the statutory law.

Justice John Major was normally in agreement with Justice Iacobucci on the way forward, as was Chief Justice Beverley McLachlin. They formed a powerful cohesive block similar to that formed by Justices Abbott, Judson and Martland in the late 1950s and 1960s. The blocks did not form on all cases, but they did form as an overall pattern.

Together Justices Iacobucci, Major and McLachlin weakened the standards associated with long-standing intent and purpose tests fundamental to the computation of income (loss) from a source under the ITA. The results in tax avoidance disputes were consistent with Justice Wilson's view that there need be no business purpose for a transaction other than the tax purpose, which accepts that a taxpayer's main and even sole purpose for a transaction may be to avoid income tax.

To use a phrase Justice Estey employed in *Stubart Investments*, the above post-1982 judicial construct stands "in sharp contrast" to the wording of par. 18(1)(a) of the ITA, which denies deductibility when the following purpose test is not met: "no outlay or expense except to the extent that it was made or incurred by the taxpayer for the purpose of gaining or producing income from a business or property."

Chief Justice Brian Dickson's tenure on the Supreme Court spanned the pre-*Charter* and *Charter* eras. Perhaps more than anyone else, it is his precedent-making 1977 and 1987 decisions in *Moldowan* and *Bronfman Trust* that had to be read down, confined and outright overturned. This is not a surprise because his judicial philosophy in deciding income tax disputes was the opposite of those who read down, confined and overruled that precedent. Dickson looked to commercial substance and *bona fide* purposes as a basis for constraining income tax avoidance and its pernicious effect over the long term on the legitimacy of the income tax system.

On April 27, 1997, Justice Rosalie Abella of the Supreme Court in a non-tax context stated in a speech: "Almost every time judges interpret, they make law, and, implicitly weigh competing values."[673] Her speech was titled "The Media and the Courts" and was hosted by The Empire Club at The Canadian Club in downtown Toronto. It does not appear that anyone in the media at that event realized or questioned why the Court had changed its approach to income tax. A majority of its judges had made a judicial "policy" decision to emphasize legal form and to use the plain-meaning approach when interpreting the ITA without meaningful regard to commercial substance and reality in case after case as detailed earlier, and to pay lip service to the unifying textual, contextual and purposive interpretative approach in income tax cases.

By the early 2000s, the Enron scandal hit the public consciousness on front pages of newspapers and in other media in the United States and Canada. The company had converted opaque tax avoidance plans into schemes to advance its stock price in markets for securities by duping investors. The scandal took down one of the largest accounting firms in the world.

The Supreme Court in its 2005 *Canada Trustco* decision blessed a sale-leaseback tax avoidance scheme that circulated the western democracies; artificial CCA deductions were allowed despite Parliament's having enacted the GAAR. Chief Justice McLachlin and Justice Major held that the artificial CCA deductions were not abusive tax benefits under the GAAR, based on the transaction being an *ordinary* sale-leaseback transaction. In comparison, they denied in *Mathew* the deduction of a real commercial loss under the GAAR, which had been purchased on an arm's length basis. This meant that the Court discerned an abuse of the ITA in the case of the deduction of a

---

[673] Abella J., "The Media and the Courts," Julia Hannaford and Edward Badovinac (Editors), The Empire Club of Canada Speeches 1996–97 (Toronto: The Empire Club Foundation, 1997), pp. 546–57, posted at *The Media and the Courts: The Empire Club Addresses* (accessed February 6, 2023).

real commercial loss but failed to do so in the case of deducting artificial CCA.

Moreover, by March 2004, large corporations in the United States, many of them financial institutions, had claimed more than $35 billion of artificial deductions under similar leasing schemes that had targeted the U.S. treasury. In London, the British House of Lords in its 2004 *Barclays Mercantile Finance* decision allowed a copycat sale-leaseback tax avoidance scheme to succeed.[674] Unlike the Supreme Court of Canada, the House of Lords had an excuse—the United Kingdom had no GAAR.

Lee Sheppard, a well-known U.S. commentator and editor for American tax publications, began writing about the schemes in late 1998. She wrote specifically about the House of Lords 2004 *Barclays Mercantile Finance* decision for *Tax Analysts* in December 2004. Sheppard described how narrowly the Lords interpreted the British CCA regime despite purportedly applying a purposive interpretive approach and, what was even more unbelievable to her, considered the funds were incurred to acquire depreciable property despite remaining in the control of the bank that advanced the defeased loan. Sheppard concluded that the "obvious lesson" is "[b]uild your tax shelter into your business, and make your business look more complicated than it is."[675] In other words, camouflage the artificiality inside a real business under a mountain of legal paperwork.

Canada's Supreme Court had denied a taxpayer artificial CCA deductions under a far less complicated leasing scheme 40 years

[674] *Barclays Mercantile Finance*, *supra* note 572.

[675] Lee A. Sheppard, "News Analysis: The Private Law of Deferred Subscription Agreements," at "Across the Pond," *Tax Analysts*, December 15, 2004, pp. 5–9. Sheppard noted that the transactions under consideration in *Barclays Mercantile Finance* concerned a builder of a pipeline that financed its construction with funds from a syndicate of banks other than Barclays, "which debt it still owed despite the purported sale [of the pipeline] to Barclays." For her 1998 article, see "News Analysis: Lease In, Lease Out: Safe Harbor Leasing Revisited," *Tax Analysts*, December 8, 1998. SILOs are "Sales In, Lease Out" and LILOs are "Lease In, Lease Out." *Canada Trustco* and *Barclays Mercantile Finance* concern SILOs.

earlier in *Harris*.[676] In 1966, the Court did so with reference to the artificial income reduction anti-avoidance rule the GAAR replaced. Fifty years later, the Court in *Canada Trustco* treated the GAAR as if it were a rule of statutory interpretation, taking the approach (without citing it) the House of Lords took the prior year in a non-GAAR context in *Barclays Mercantile Finance*.

In comparison, the American judiciary shot the schemes down, using judicial guidelines dating to the 1930s.[677] Sheppard indicated in 2004 that one lesson for American tax shelter promoters would be to sell such schemes in Britain; the same could be said for selling them in Canada.

World financial markets were in a state of crisis by 2007–2009. To blame were the Western governments' deference to self-interested commercial actors on Wall Street and in London, who were allowed to self-regulate their derivatives trading in world financial markets. The economic and political currents are still playing out across the Western democracies.

Despite it all, a Supreme Court majority in its 2008 *McLarty* decision deferred to commercial interests in a tax shelter dispute when holding that the limited-recourse debt was not a contingent liability because it had a default clause, distinguishing it from the 1980 precedent in *Mandel*. The Court advised that it "is not a protector of government revenue" in a context in which the Court has accepted since 1984 that there need be no business purpose to a transaction other than the tax purpose despite the wording of par. 18(1)(a) of the ITA.

Next, the Supreme Court split in its 2009 *Lipson* decision about when, and if, the Minister of National Revenue could ever invoke the GAAR to deny tax avoidance schemes. The scheme sought to turn otherwise non-deductible personal interest, on the purchase

---

[676] *Harris*, *supra* note 591.

[677] For example, see Jerald David August, "Court of Claims Strikes Down Wells Fargo's Silos Tax Shelters," *Lexology*, January 20, 2010 (accessed April 1, 2021); and more recently, Dan Smith, "Tax Court Holds Against Taxpayer in LILO/SILO Case *John Hancock*," Sherman & Sterling LLP (accessed April 1, 2021).

of a home, into deductible interest. The Court had blessed a similar scheme eight years earlier in *Singleton* (the Singleton shuffle). This time, it was like a deer caught in the headlights when staring wide-eyed into the GAAR potentially denying all those high-income taxpayers their interest deductions it had allowed eight years earlier. The only thing the majority and dissenting judges agreed on was that there was no abuse of the interest deductibility rule. It was not the Court's finest hour. The media failed to grasp or even realize what had just occurred in terms of how different classes of taxpayers are treated.

Justice Marshall Rothstein was the one Supreme Court judge who by 2009 wanted to hear income tax disputes. All taxpayers should thank him for his interest. He came to the disputes a non-tax professional armed with a quick mind and an affinity for the nature of the disputes before him. There appears to be a subtle shift to the Crown in his decisions over time, but that should not be overstated even if true. Within three years, he went from (1) writing the majority opinion for the taxpayer in *McLarty* to (2) dissenting on applying the GAAR in *Lipson* to (3) writing the unanimous opinion applying the GAAR in *Copthorne Holdings*. Something had changed, and it wasn't the statutory tax law.

After the global financial crisis subsided in 2009, the Supreme Court appears to have embarked on a slow shift toward commercial substance and reality in its approach to income taxation. The shift may have been more pronounced except for two reasons. First, the Court no longer hears the 5–15 income tax cases it normally heard annually between 1950 and 1980. Second, the Court faces a wall of recent precedent based on the plain-meaning approach. It sought to cut the Court off from applying its earlier extensive commercial substance precedent.

Why? Apparently Canadian commercial interests would suffer unfair burdens if the Supreme Court does not extend them certainty and predictability in tax when planning transactions. Meanwhile, American commercial interests seem to survive quite well despite the American courts' using judicial principles since at least the Great Depression that constrain abusive tax avoidance.

In income taxation, there tends to be a lot of chatter from some tax professionals about the rule of law being undermined by provisions such as the GAAR. The rule of law was also referred to when discussing Chief Justice Beverley McLachlin's influences. It is a bedrock principle underlying Canada's parliamentary democracy and its constitution. Some argue the GAAR causes uncertainty and renders the law unpredictable, which is inconsistent with the rule of law.

In *Reference re Succession of Quebec*, a unanimous Supreme Court in 1998 opined that the consent of the governed cannot exist without the rule of law. But for that law to be accorded legitimacy, it would be a grave mistake to equate legitimacy with the sovereign will or majority rule alone to the exclusion of other constitutional values. The full statement is as follows:

> The consent of the governed is a value that is basic to our understanding of a free and democratic society. Yet democracy in any real sense of the word cannot exist without the rule of law. It is the law that creates the framework within which the "sovereign will" is to be ascertained and implemented. To be accorded legitimacy, democratic institutions must rest, ultimately, on a legal foundation. That is, they must allow for the participation of, and accountability to, the people, through public institutions created under the Constitution. Equally, however, a system of government cannot survive through adherence to the law alone. A political system must also possess legitimacy, and in our political culture, that requires an interaction between the rule of law and the democratic principle. The system must be capable of reflecting the aspirations of the people. But there is more. Our law's claim to legitimacy also rests on an appeal to moral values, many of which are imbedded in our constitutional structure. It would be a grave mistake to equate

> legitimacy with the "sovereign will" or majority rule alone, to the exclusion of other constitutional values.[678]

The Supreme Court stated the above at a time when it was allowing one tax avoidance scheme after another by emphasizing a transaction's legal form and applying the plain-meaning interpretive approach to the statutory income tax law. Yet tax revenue, lots of revenue, is required to put the stated values in action in a reasonably organized manner.

Raising that money depends on the consent of the governed, which in turn rests in large part on the legitimacy they extend to the laws enacted to raise that money. This legitimacy cannot co-exist with an income tax system in the 21st century, in which the text of the statutory law is being read based on its literal, plain or strict meaning without due consideration being given to the context in which that test exists and its purpose.

Describing a textual interpretive approach as the textual, contextual and purposive (TCP) approach—when an essentially textual approach is used—undermines the legitimacy of the income tax system. It suggests the judiciary is doing something that it is not doing and reveals the extent to which the judiciary has narrowed down the GAAR to a rule of interpretation.

Yet Professor David Duff suggests the first interpretive merry-go-round is "rightly constrained by the text of the applicable provisions."[679] He argues that "the TCP approach [in tax cases] is constrained by the text of the relevant provisions in a way that the GAAR is not—consistent with the rule-of-law principles of legislative supremacy and legal certainty, the latter of which is

---

[678] *Reference re Secession of Quebec*, [1998] 2 SCR 217 (para. 67).

[679] David Duff, "The Interpretive Exercise under the General Anti-Avoidance Rule," pp. 383–406 (p. 384), in Brian J. Arnold (Editor), *The General Anti-Avoidance Rule, supra* note 299. Arnold also considers and questions Duff's argument at: *The Arnold Report*, "The Role of Purpose in the Textual, Contextual and Purposive Approach to Statutory Interpretation—IV," Posting 205, June 9, 2021, Canadian Tax Foundation.

legitimately superseded by an anti-abuse principle in the context of the GAAR."[680]

Given this, some effort should be made to discern when a "last resort" engages. Is it where an abuse may exist despite the TCP approach being applied to provisions without reading down their context or purpose. Or should it be applied under the GAAR only after applying a plain-meaning approach?

Since the Supreme Court had not firmly decided to apply the plain-meaning approach by the time the GAAR was enacted, it is not true to say that applying the GAAR as a last resort was meant only after the Court applied the plain-meaning approach. Further, applying the TCP approach as a last resort to discern the purpose, object and spirit of statutory income tax law under the GAAR fails to account for the underlying history that reveals the Court emphasized the commercial substance and reality of a taxpayer's transactions, in light of the object and spirit of the text in issue, beginning at least by the early 1950s. Rather, reading the TCP approach down to a plain-meaning approach in non-GAAR cases seems to legitimize the Court's switch in the 1990s to emphasizing the legal form of transactions and applying the plain-meaning approach when interpreting income tax provisions, which was and remains contentious.

It could hardly be supposed that Parliament meant the GAAR to be a rule of statutory interpretation. First, the GAAR is in Part XVI of the ITA, which concerns tax avoidance, and not Part XVII, which concerns interpretation. Second, the GAAR provides a set of substantive rules that apply to facts that establish a "tax benefit" and an "avoidance transaction." It then asks whether the avoidance transaction is a "misuse" of a provision of the ITA (or a regulation or tax treaty) or an "abuse" of those provisions "read as a whole."

As a *last resort*, the GAAR is present to address misuses and abuses that would otherwise survive interpreting the ITA using the

[680] *Ibid.*, p 406.

true textual, contextual and purposive approach. This is not to say that a rule of interpretation could not be added to the GAAR; for instance, a rule could be added to instruct the judiciary to apply an "economic substance" test when determining whether there is a misuse or abuse, which to date the Supreme Court has not done despite the explanatory notes suggesting it is intended.

It should also be emphasized in this context that just because some may argue that avoiding significant amounts of income tax otherwise payable is not immoral does not mean that average Canadians agree. Assaf Likhovski noted in the *Cardozo Law Review* when contextualizing the 1935 American *Gregory* and British *Duke of Westminster* decisions, that tax avoidance had become a discussion point in the American professional literature by the late 1920s and early 1930s, including law reviews and tax planning guides.[681] The objective was to render the activity amoral and distinguish it from criminal tax evasion thus cloaking it with an air of social acceptability.[682] The main audience was American tax professionals, their wealthy clients and the judiciary. This was not and is not the American or Canadian public writ large.

This discourse was and continues to occur within a narrow group, much like legal academics writing about the *Charter* for each other and the judiciary. Millions of taxpayers know nothing about this discourse. The general public is an entirely different audience, and don't be surprised that it might express concern in moral terms about aggressive tax avoidance behaviour.

These currents were spilling over into Canada by the 1930s when Chief Justice Kerwin decided *Pioneer Laundry*, which the Privy Council reversed, and they continue to play out in the 21st century

---

[681] Likhovski, "The Duke and the Lady: Helvering v. Gregory and the History of Tax Avoidance Adjudication," *supra* note 51, pp. 991–1002. See *M.D. Donald Ltd.*, *supra* note 24 (and the discussion in that note) for a Supreme Court decision on the "ambiguous" meaning of the word "evade" in the context of intent to enter a transaction and its substance and legal form.

[682] *Ibid.*

in the context of the legitimacy the public confers on the statutory income tax law. That is the legitimacy that is of most concern.

Judges should be circumspect when responding to questions posed by tax professionals about the "role of 'morality' in deciding a case." In 2013, three judges—one from the Supreme Court, one from the Federal Court of Appeal, and one from the Tax Court—were posed this question at the *Canadian Tax Foundation's* 2013 Tax Conference. Leading tax editor David Sherman reported in *GST & HST Times:* "Each judge assured the audience that morality plays no part in determining how the law applies." These questions can be perceived as establishing a litmus test that the judge either passes or fails for tax professionals when answering. While Sherman noted the audience was "assured" by the three answers, average taxpayers may not be so "assured."[683]

More generally, what is not needed is political virtue messaging on taxation as Canada emerges from a world pandemic deeply in debt. The type of debt that, under sustained high interest rates, a stagnant economy or continued tepid productivity growth, could destroy the aspirations of younger Canadians and generations to come. Yet one has little or no confidence that the hard reality of what this means is appreciated or understood by politicians.

Let us be clear. Walk the talk. Decide to lower taxes (and cut spending) or raise taxes (while cutting spending) in a balanced way that considers economic efficiencies and an ability to pay. Here is an idea: carve back all the special tax preferences and spending measures handed out like trick-or-treat candy to preferred groups on the right and left who have the ear of politicians, most of whom fear politically going against their respective bases' demands.[684]

---

[683] David Sherman, "What's New in GST and HST?," *GST & HST Times*, Supplement to Canada GST Service Release No. 228C—November 2013 (Carswell).

[684] That is not to say that there should be no tax preferences, but they should be limited in number and directed at achieving broadly supported and narrowly targeted cultural, economic and social objectives in an efficient manner, with measurable objectives.

Instead, politicians do what Mackenzie King did in 1930 and 1936—extend tax preferences to special interest groups. Not what R.B. Bennett did in 1934–35 when he sought to ensure a powerful sector of the economy actually paid tax close to the intended rate. The sector, horrified by that possibility, turned with success to King for relief. Canadian taxpayers deserve better.

Two pre-election events that occurred between May and mid-July 2021 encapsulate major deficiencies in the Canadian income tax system for which blame should be widely shared. While these deficiencies do not rest at the feet of the Supreme Court, they need to be mentioned to put matters into context.

The first event was hearings the House of Commons' Standing Committee on Finance convened in May and June 2021 on the CRA's actions to counter tax evasion and avoidance. The second concerned Parliament's passage of Bill C-208, an opposition Conservative member's bill that further opened the floodgates on tax avoidance schemes that convert a private corporation's surplus into tax-exempt or tax-preferred amounts such as capital gains. In Committee, parliamentarians express concern about tax evasion and avoidance; at the same time, parliamentarians are further opening the floodgates to allow tax avoidance. It simply makes no sense.

Brian Arnold discussed the House of Commons' hearings on tax evasion and avoidance, including the testimony of witnesses from the private sector and the CRA in his article "The Wealthy and the Tax System," posted to *The Arnold Report* at the *Canadian Tax Foundation* on July 19, 2021. He was struck by the "appalling lack of basic knowledge about the tax system by MPs from all parties on the Committee." It was so bad that Arnold offered to design and teach, for free, a basic tax course to MPs.

But Arnold's main point was "that the favourable treatment of the wealthy in our tax system is not a new phenomenon." He also noted that "wealthy individuals who enter into aggressive tax avoidance schemes know that, if the schemes are successful, they will not be paying their fair share—they simply do not care."

Who is "wealthy" is a pertinent question. Arnold noted that politicians were referring to families with $10 million–$20 million of wealth as being "wealthy" or "ultra-rich." What he did not mention is that many of these families qualify for any number of tax preferences available to "small business." This is because significant preferences are extended to corporations controlled by a family so long as the total *corporate* taxable capital, *not value that is often a multiple of capital*, remains below $15 million on an associated corporation basis [raised to $50 million in the 2022 Budget; more on that in the epilogue]. If corporate "taxable capital employed in Canada," as defined in the ITA, remains below $15 million, a family is *good to go*, so to speak, which does not even include significant after-tax corporate earnings moved to a family trust, including through tax avoidance schemes.

The tax system thus has a built-in tax incentive encouraging owner-managers of successful Canadian private corporations to remain a so-called *small business* and to undertake extensive tax planning to ensure this remains the case. It makes no sense in economic or tax policy terms. Yet Parliament has granted and enhanced preferences for small business periodically at the behest of lobbying groups, paying little or no attention to just what is a small business corporation. At the first sign of any pushback, these lobby groups speak to a friendly media outlet or politicians about mom-pop operations or farmers trying to make ends meet earning modest amounts of income; they never trot out the small business corporations earning hundreds of thousands of dollars or more a year.

The second event concerns what happens to those millions of dollars of after-corporate tax surpluses inside many of those successful private corporations. The ITA contemplates that these surpluses will be taxed on distribution as dividends. In fact, corporate income tax rates are set significantly lower than personal income tax rates to encourage corporate businesses to invest in the economy on the understanding that the distributions will be integrated with the personal income taxes when taxed as dividends. To limit double tax, individual recipients are extended dividend tax credits that offset personal taxes by corporate tax on the earnings.

Nevertheless, the income tax bill on those surpluses can be cut almost in half, or eliminated in some cases, simply by converting the surplus into tax-preferred taxable capital gains or tax-exempt amounts. In fact, four such cases have been discussed at length in *Bench Strength*: Chief Justice Kerwin's majority 1942 decision in *Emily Merritt*,[685] Justice Judson's 1969 decisions in *Smythe*,[686] and *Craddock*,[687] and Justice Rothstein's 2011 decision in *Copthorne Holdings*.[688] The first three discussions also mentioned politicians who cared about, and understood, the issue in tax policy terms: Prime Minister R.B. Bennett, Finance Ministers Douglas Abbott and Walter Gordon and National Revenue Minister E.J. Benson. Each was a lawyer or accountant knowledgeable about the income tax system. At least one did not—Prime Minister Mackenzie King.

For several years, tax practitioners, tax academics and others have sought a major tax reform undertaking, which never gets political traction. Their assumption seems to be that any outcome would go the way that those who recommend such an undertaking think it should go, or possibly the outcome could not be any worse than the current situation. Experience suggests that those who have wealth and their representatives would seek to ensure that any reform would be minimal in effect on them.

So, it was in that context that Arnold posted his article shortly after the second event occurred in Ottawa concerning corporate surplus stripping, passage of opposition Conservative Bill C-208 and its opening of the tax avoidance floodgates even further. Of course, the bill was couched in terms of providing relief for farmers and small business, without any sense of the extent to which

[685] *Emily Merritt*, *supra* note 21.
[686] *Smythe*, *supra* note 248.
[687] *Craddock*, *supra* note 249.
[688] *Copthorne Holdings*, *supra* note 627.

those taxpayers and others who could benefit were in fact also high-income and/or wealthy. It simply did not matter.

Allan Lanthier, a retired leading tax professional, wrote about the unfolding disaster for the *Financial Post* on June 29, 2021.[689] The story was followed the next day by a press release written by someone who did not want to respect the meaning of "Royal Assent."[690] The government planned to delay the new law until January 1, 2022, and clarify it to prevent avoidance.

Lanthier had moderated for the *Canadian Tax Foundation* a panel on corporate surplus stripping in 2017 after the Department of Finance released its paper on the taxation of private corporations.[691] The third element in that paper concerned corporate surplus stripping, which did not gain wide public comment in media, lost in the uproar over the first two proposals: "Income Sprinkling" and "Holding Passive Investments Inside Private Corporations."

Corporate surplus stripping concerns an abuse of Canada's income tax system that dates to the early years of the *Income War Tax Act*. It and the ITA include numerous anti-avoidance rules to counter such activity by way of (1) the shareholder taxable benefit and shareholder loan rules in s. 15; (2) various deemed dividend rules in s. 84; (3) the deemed dividend rules in ss. 84.1, 212.1 and 212.2; (4) the benefit rule in s. 246; and (5) the GAAR in s. 245.

---

[689] Allan Lanthier, "New Legislation Puts High-Income Tax Avoidance on Steroids," *Financial Post*, June 29, 2021.

[690] Canada, Department of Finance, news release "Government of Canada Provides Details on Next Steps for Private Member's Bill C-208," June 30, 2021.

[691] Canada, Department of Finance, "Tax Planning Using Private Corporations," July 18, 2017 (The Honourable Bill Morneau, Minister of Finance). (Disclosure: I participated in preparing the portion of the paper on corporate surplus stripping and the related proposals. The discussion on corporate surplus stripping is in Part D, pp. 55–60.) Lanthier's private-sector panel that presented "Surplus Stripping: Analysis and Discussion with Finance," 2017 Taxation of Private Corporation Tax Policy Conference, consisted of four leading tax professionals: Greg Bell (KPMG), Mark Brender (Osler), Bruce Harris (PWC) and Robert Raizenne (Osler). See PowerPoint Presentation (ctf.ca) and Finance's paper https://www.canada.ca/content/dam/fin/migration/activty/consult/tppc-pfsp-eng.pdf.

These and related rules represent a scheme against corporate surplus stripping dating in one form or another to the 1920s.

One of the main recommendations of the 1966 *Royal Commission on Taxation* (the "Carter Commission") sought to end corporate surplus stripping by fully integrating the corporate and personal income tax systems. While the proposal was two-fold, only the relieving aspect of the proposal was legislated. It gives individual shareholders resident in Canada an enhanced dividend tax credit mechanism that seeks to fully integrate the corporate and personal tax imposed on corporate profits and dividends, although it assumes the corporate tax is paid, which may not be the case. The unlegislated part of the proposal would have taxed the annual increased value of an individual taxpayer's shares.[692] It followed Chairman Kenneth Carter's "a buck is a buck" philosophy. The second aspect of the proposal went nowhere in the uproar that followed.

In the result, the Minister of National Revenue retained his discretionary power to deny corporate surplus-stripping schemes. It was a troublesome holdover from a bygone era in Canadian income taxation. But, by the late 1970s, the "designated surplus" rules avoided in the *Smythe* case were repealed. While the rules had deficiencies, they were backed by ministerial discretion where needed to constrain abuses, including where (1) schemes were concocted to vary from those the Supreme Court denied in *Smythe* and *Craddock*, or (2) surpluses were stripped out of the Canadian economy tax free.

Think for a few minutes on what foreign corporations' and hedge funds' stripping surpluses out of the Canadian economy tax free means for our collective long-term growth in productivity and our long-term influence over investment in the Canadian economy.

[692] *Report of the Royal Commission on Taxation*, Volume I, "Introduction, Acknowledgements and Minority Reports," The Queen's Printer (Ottawa, 1966), pp. 6–9 and 27–30. The minority report opposed full integration, including because there would be no transitional rule to prevent the stripping of surpluses existing on the changeover (see concerns expressed beginning at p. 69).

Allan Lanthier's panel went through the history of corporate surplus stripping in Canada. Among other things, the panel noted that some judges in recent years have indicated in *obiter* that there is no scheme against corporate surplus stripping in the ITA, which seems to ignore history and the rules that have been enacted to counter corporate surplus stripping since the 1920s.

The Progressive Conservative Government headed by Prime Minister Brian Mulroney did end the Minister of National Revenue's discretionary power to constrain corporate surplus stripping in the mid-1980s. It was replaced by a similar anti-avoidance rule with one significant difference—its parameters were subject to judicial rather than ministerial discretion. It, in turn, was repealed, on the enactment of the GAAR, with the related explanatory note indicating that the expectation was the GAAR would apply to abusive transactions. This is like the note concerning the repeal to the old artificial income-reduction rule; how that worked out was detailed earlier in the discussion of the Supreme Court's decision in *Canada Trustco*.

But what was not mentioned earlier is that tax planners got a major win in the Supreme Court's 2011 decision in *Copthorne Holdings* despite the GAAR's application in that case. Copthorne Holdings argued there is no scheme against corporate surplus stripping in the ITA, which some tax planners and lower court decisions suggest. It relied on *Canada Trustco* in which the Court stated: "[C]ourts cannot search for an overriding policy of the Act that is not based on a unified, textual, contextual and purposive interpretation of the specific provisions in issue."[693] Justice Rothstein

[693] *Canada Trustco, supra* note 564, para. 41. Shortly after the *Canada Trustco* decision, Chief Justice Bowman of the Tax Court declined to apply the GAAR to the surplus-stripping transactions in *Evans v. The Queen*, 2005 TCC 684, on the basis that no particular rule had been abused. In doing so, he noted (para. 34) that the Crown's reference to the prior GAAR case *McNichol, supra* note 508 [in which he noted there is a scheme against corporate surplus stripping in the ITA and applied the GAAR], "does not in my view satisfy the onus that the Supreme Court has placed on the Crown." Bowman's decision is at *Evans v. The Queen* - Tax Court of Canada (tcc-cci.gc.ca).

in *Copthorne Holdings* then stated: "What is not permissible is basing a finding of abuse on some broad statement of policy, *such as anti-surplus stripping*, which is not attached to the provisions at issue" [emphasis added].[694]

Rothstein went on to hold in *Copthorne Holdings* that the GAAR applied, based on the doubling of paid-up capital abusing the vertical amalgamation rule in subs. 87(3). But in doing so he left on the table for tax planners and their clients to feast on a judicial finding from the highest court in the land tracing to the Court's 2005 decision in *Canada Trustco* that it simply does not matter whether there is a scheme against corporate surplus stripping in the ITA unless the tax avoidance transaction can be connected to a provision that has been abused. More on that shortly.

Then in late July 2021, a decade after Justice Rothstein's *obiter* on surplus stripping in *Copthorne Holdings*, came the climb-down by Finance Minister Chrystia Freeland on Bill C-208 with a promise not to enact retroactive legislation to constrain the tax avoidance.[695] The promise was couched in terms of allowing *genuine* intergenerational transfers of small business without noting that this is already allowed when transferring shares of a family farm corporation and shares of a family fishing corporation on a tax-deferred basis. Such intergenerational transfers were allowed in the past to other business owners before being ended as too generous. This tells you that something more significant is at stake.

Intergenerational rollovers are not good enough; so-called *small business* owners want to be able to extract the corporate surplus tax free or at tax-preferred rates while their family still owns the corporation. They want to extract the surpluses without paying dividend tax, with a sizable portion of that surplus existing because the corporate tax rate is so low relative to the top marginal rate for personal income: it is 15 percent federally on business income,

---

694 *Copthorne Holdings*, *supra* note 627, para. 118.

695 Canada, Department of Finance, news release "Government of Canada Clarifies Taxation for Intergenerational Transfer of Small Business Shares," July 19, 2021.

which is reduced to 9 percent for a small business corporation on its first $500,000 of active business income annually, shared on an associated corporation basis. One province, Manitoba, does not even bother to impose tax on such corporate income. Premier Greg Selinger's socialist New Democrats enacted the reduction to nil tax in Manitoba effective December 1, 2010, in the lead-up to his government's re-election in 2011. This is one small part of a broader shift to the bottom in domestic corporate income tax, with the added irony of socialist approval.

The general rate of federal corporate income tax on business income is at 15 percent—18 points less than the top bracket of 33 percent applicable to personal income, and at 9 percent for small business income—24 points lower. Individuals who pay the federal 33 percent personal rate tend to earn income from an office or employment; they cannot divert their income into a private corporation like many successful individuals who carry on a business through a small business corporation, which activity ranges across the economy. The corporate-personal income tax rate gap is so large that it often drives tax avoidance plans.[696]

Alan Freeman, a former senior Department of Finance media relations official, wrote about the circus over Bill C-208 for *iPolitics* in his "Forget the Isle of Man. Ottawa Is Our Latest Tax Haven," on July 21, 2021. He described the situation as a "train wreck." He ended his watch over that train wreck by stating: "Special interests are thrilled, tax lawyers and accountants are busy figuring out how to structure the juicy, tax-free transactions, and backbench MPs are jubilant that they stuck it to Freeland and Finance Canada. We get the government we deserve."[697]

---

[696] But it should also be noted that the personal top federal marginal rate of 33 percent appears to be too high by at least three points, as it results in some individuals' having a top marginal tax rate of more than 50 percent of federal-provincial taxes.

[697] Alan Freeman, "Forget the Isle of Man. Ottawa Is Our Latest Tax Haven," *iPolitics*, July 21, 2021.

Freeman missed mentioning something important. *MPs from all parties* stuck the bill on every taxpayer who does not own a corporation with surplus to strip. In his 2021 *Financial Post* article, Lanthier noted there were 1.2 million small and medium-sized businesses in Canada and estimated the cost at $5 billion in federal and provincial tax if 1 percent of those businesses were owned by individuals in the top bracket and implemented a plan he detailed.[698] This was the state of the Canadian income tax system in the summer of 2021 before the federal election in September 2021, which ended with no substantive change in the elected members representing the various political parties.

The overarching theme of *Bench Strength* concerns the Supreme Court's shift in judicial policy terms in the *Charter* era to emphasize the legal form of taxpayer transactions and using the plain-meaning approach when interpreting the statutory income tax law to read down the context and purpose in which that text exists. The Court, through its judges, took the opposite approach in the pre-*Charter* era, in which the judges emphasized the commercial substance of transactions and the context, object and spirit of the text of the statutory income tax law. The judicial results flowed accordingly.

The reasons the Supreme Court has given for its interpretive approach varied after the enactment of the *Charter* in 1982 until the end of the financial crisis in world markets in 2009:

> A transaction may be effectual and not in any sense a sham (as in this case) but may have no business purpose other than the tax purpose. The question then is whether the Minister is entitled to ignore it on that ground alone. If he is, then a massive inroad is made into Lord Tomlin's dictum that "Every man is entitled if he can to order his affairs so as that the tax attaching under the appropriate Acts is less than it otherwise would be": *Inland Revenue Commissioners v.*

[698] Allan Lanthier, "Ottawa's Blunder on Business Transfers Could Cost Billions," *Financial Post*, July 27, 2021.

Duke of Westminster, [1936] A.C. 1, at p. 19: Indeed, it seems to me that the business purpose test is a complete rejection of Lord Tomlin's principle. (*Stubart Investments*,[699] 1984, per Justice Wilson)

Interpretation according to the "object and spirit" of the legislation cannot, in my view, overcome a clear statutory definition. This is not a case in which the Court has a choice of the interpretations it may put upon the language used by the legislature. (*Mattabi Mines*,[700] 1988, per Justice Wilson)

I agree with the sentiment [that the values embodied in the *Charter* must be given preference over an interpretation that is inconsistent with or contrary to *Charter* values] reflected in both of these quotations, but I fail to see their relevance in this case. ... In both *Hills* [[1988] 1 SCR 513] and *Slaight Communications* [[1989] 1 SCR 1038], this Court was confronted with statutory language which was ambiguous. In each case, the values of the *Charter* were consulted to resolve the ambiguity. However, each case recognizes that to consult the *Charter* in the absence of such ambiguity is to deprive the *Charter* of a more powerful purpose, namely, the determination of a statute's constitutional <u>validity</u>. If statutory meanings must be made congruent with the *Charter* even in the absence of ambiguity, then it would never be possible to <u>apply</u>, rather than simply <u>consult</u>, the values of the *Charter*. Furthermore, it would never be possible for the government to justify infringements as reasonable limits under s. 1 of the *Charter*, since the interpretative process would preclude one from finding infringements in the first place [emphasis in original]. (*Symes*,[701] 1993, per Justice Iacobucci)

---

699 *Stubart Investments, supra* note 386, p. 540.
700 *Mattabi Mines, supra* note 442, para. 23.
701 *Symes, supra* note 93, p. 752.

While it is true that the courts must view discrete sections of the *Income Tax Act* in light of the other provisions of the Act and of the purpose of the legislation, and that they must analyze a given transaction in the context of economic and commercial reality, such techniques cannot alter the result where the words of the statute are clear and plain and where the legal and practical effect of the transaction is undisputed: *Mattabi Mines* ... [and] *Symes* ... (*Antosko*,[702] 1994, per Justice Iacobucci)

As Hogg and Magee stated in *Principles of Canadian Income Tax Law, supra*, at p.453: "It would introduce intolerable uncertainty into the *Income Tax Act* if clear language in a detailed provision of the Act were to be qualified by unexpressed exceptions derived from a court's view of the object and purpose of the provision." Therefore, the object and purpose of a provision need only be resorted to when the statutory language admits of some doubt or ambiguity. (*Friesen*,[703] 1995, per Justice Major)

[I]n applying the principles of interpretation to the Act, attention must be paid to the fact the Act is one of the most detailed, complex, and comprehensive statutes in our legislative inventory and courts should be reluctant to embrace unexpressed notions of policy or principle in the guise of statutory interpretation. (*65302 British Columbia*,[704] 1999, per Justice Iacobucci)

[A]bsent a specific provision to the contrary, it is not the courts' role to prevent taxpayers from relying on the sophisticated structure of their transactions, arranged in such a way that the particular provisions of the Act are met, on the basis that it would be inequitable to those taxpayers who

[702] *Antosko, supra* note 471, pp. 326–27.

[703] *Friesen, supra* note 536, paras. 59–60.

[704] *65302 British Columbia, supra* note 458, para. 51.

have not chosen to structure their transactions that way. (*Shell Canada*,[705] 1999, per Justice McLachlin)

[T]axpayers are entitled to arrange their affairs for the sole purpose of achieving a favourable position regarding taxation: see *Stubart*, *supra*, at p. 540, *per* Wilson J., and at p. 577 *per* Estey J.; *Hickman Motors Ltd.* at para. 8, *per* McLachlin J.; *Duha Printers* at para. 88, *per* Iacobucci J.; *Neuman* at para. 63, *per* Iacobucci J.; *Shell Canada*, at para. 46, *per* McLachlin J. (*Ludco Enterprises*,[706] 2001, per Justice Iacobucci)

[C]ourts should avoid judicial innovation and rule-making in tax law. (*Stewart*,[707] 2002, per Justices Iacobucci and Bastarache, 2002)

A proper approach to the wording of the provisions of the *Income Tax Act* together with the relevant factual context of a given case achieve balance between the need to address abusive tax avoidance while preserving certainty, predictability and fairness in tax law so that taxpayers may manage their affairs accordingly. (*Canada Trustco*,[708] 2005, per Chief Justice McLachlin and Justice Major)

In reassessment cases, the role of the court is solely to adjudicate disputes between the Minister and the taxpayer. It is not a protector of government revenue. (*McLarty*,[709] 2008, per Justice Rothstein)

After 2009, the Supreme Court appears to be a bit more circumspect in what is says about its judicial policy when interpreting the ITA. In 2011, in *Copthorne Holdings*, it made no grand statements (setting aside its statement about surplus stripping) and couched its *obiter* in terms of saying it reapplies the TCP interpretative approach in a GAAR context to determine the "object, spirit and

[705] *Shell Canada*, *supra* note 636, para. 45.
[706] *Ludco Enterprises*, *supra* note 504, para. 39.
[707] *Stewart*, *supra* note 518, para. 4.
[708] *Canada Trustco*, *supra* note 564, para. 61.
[709] *McLarty*, *supra* note 597, para. 75.

purpose" of the provision to see whether the first go-round leaves an abuse of the tax law.[710]

In this interpretive merry-go-round, the Supreme Court appears to be tying itself up in interpretive knots, unable to discern the major policy themes in the ITA read as a whole. It is doing so despite a clear statement in para. 245(4)(*b*) of the GAAR that the judiciary is supposed to determine "if it may reasonably be considered that … [the avoidance transaction] would result directly or indirectly in an abuse having regard to those provisions [the list includes those in the Act, its regulations and tax treaties], other than this section, read as a whole."

It is not as if the Supreme Court is incapable of discerning schemes in the ITA read as a whole. Justice Rothstein when a member of the Federal Court of Appeal found a scheme against arm's length corporate loss trading in *OSFC Holdings*,[711] only for the Supreme Court in *Canada Trustco* to hold that there cannot be an abuse of the Act unless it concerns a specific provision.[712] It did so despite agreeing there is such a scheme, asking: "[H]ow one can abuse the Act as a whole without misusing any of its provisions?" This not only undermines the GAAR but also reveals the extent to which the Court is prepared to read out clear statutory language telling it otherwise.

Despite this, some suggest that the Supreme Court's 2011 decision in *Copthorne Holdings* has noticeably improved the Crown's success rate in GAAR cases. But, based on the Court's precedent, the pool of cases going forward presumably does not include cases that can be perceived to be an abuse of the Act read as a whole—be it artificial reductions of income or abusive corporate surplus

---

710 *Copthorne Holdings, supra* note 627, para. 70.

711 *OSFC Holdings Limited v. The Queen*, 2001 FCA 260, 2001 DTC 5471, [2001] 4 CTC 82 (FCA).

712 *Canada Trustco, supra* note 564, paras. 28–29. Marshall Rothstein discusses the Supreme Court's reversing him on this point in "A Judge's Perspective on the General Anti-Avoidance Rule" at pp. 551–72, in Brian J. Arnold (Editor), *The General Anti-Avoidance Rule, supra* note 299.

stripping that, unlike in *Copthorne Holdings*, cannot point to provision such as subs. 87(3). Statistics can be deceiving.

James Wilson notes with his usual clarity that the reason the Supreme Court has not rendered the GAAR meaningless under its current interpretive approach is that the Court relies, in GAAR cases, on the misuse and abuse rule in subs. 245(4) to determine the "purpose, object and spirit" of the provisions in issue. In a footnote, Wilson refers to a 2010 British report that recommended a British GAAR that targets artificial and abusive transactions that survive the TCP interpretive approach. That report rejected the taking of the Canadian "purposive" GAAR approach, which presented the British with the paradox of trying to discern legislative purpose after applying the TCP approach.[713]

But Wilson points out that the British report failed to appreciate that the Canadian judiciary applies an essentially textual approach in non-GAAR cases, not the true TCP approach. This paradox traces to the Supreme Court's 2005 *Canada Trustco* decision to turn the GAAR into a rule of interpretation essentially trying to align the Court with the British House of Lord's 2004 non-GAAR *Barclays Mercantile Finance* decision concerning a similar *sale in, lease out* transaction. The approach resulted in a significant misalignment that many want to gloss over.

In other words, it took Parliament to enact a GAAR to get the Supreme Court to actually apply the true TCP approach in the *Charter* era, and then only in GAAR cases. In Britain, the GAAR is needed to address artificial and abusive tax avoidance transactions that survive an interpretation of the statutory law that is based on the true TCP approach. The Canadian approach could not be more dysfunctional—to the benefit of those undertaking abusive tax avoidance transactions.

---

[713] James R. Wilson, "The Legislative History of the General Anti-Avoidance Rule: From the White Paper Draft GAAR to the GAAR Enacted," pp. 91–128, at pp. 125–28 (Wilson's footnote 112), in Brian J. Arnold (Editor), *The General Anti-Avoidance Rule*, *supra* note 299.

You should feel some sympathy for the Supreme Court as an institution and its judges; they preside as the final judicial arbitrators of interpretive issues arising under an income tax system, the progressivity of which is in a state of collapse at the upper end of the top one percentile. Many wealthy taxpayers can simply hide behind a wall of high-end tax advice and business associations, shift corporate and personal income tax to other taxpayers and arm themselves to the teeth with tax avoidance plans, solicitor-client privilege, favourable precedent, lobbyists, politicians and friendly media.

The direction the Supreme Court takes navigating forward when interpreting the statutory law upon which rests an income tax system in crisis is for it to decide. But it cannot begin to do so unless it starts granting leave on a regular basis in income tax cases. Doing so is of national importance.

Perhaps the Supreme Court can inject interpretive balance back into the income tax system. It could use it. That better balance exists somewhere between the pre-*Charter* and *Charter* approaches. While it will not be easy to build the precedent upon which that better balance can be achieved, it needs to be pursued with vigour case by case, opinion by opinion, built upon the differing facts and law present in each case in issue.

Those watching are not just those who represent sophisticated taxpayers or change their proverbial hats to lobby politicians and government officials for changes that benefit their clients' narrow interests. Canadians are watching. The minimum any citizen should expect from his or her Parliament, institutions and government officials is that they appreciate that the taxes raised and spent are their funds, and that the tax not paid because it is avoided is paid by someone else.

Epilogue

ALTHOUGH *BENCH STRENGTH* INDICATES that the Supreme Court began to shift away from emphasizing a textual approach when interpreting income tax legislation after the financial crisis of 2007–09, any such shift hit a roadblock in late 2021. The Court once again relied on the 1935 British *Duke of Westminster* principle in an income tax avoidance context: (1) to narrowly interpret the GAAR meant to constrain tax avoidance and (2) in a non-GAAR context.

In *Alta Energy Luxembourg,* Justice Suzanne Côté led a 6–3 majority for the taxpayer despite the GAAR; it is an international tax treaty shopping case in which significant amounts of Canadian tax were avoided by an offshore entity that invested in Canada's resource sector. Its details are beyond the space permitted in this epilogue. There is enough space, however, to point out that there is a notable incongruity in Justice Côté's citation of Brian Arnold. The citation is in the following excerpt:

> Like all statutes, tax legislation must be interpreted by conducting a "textual, contextual and purposive analysis to find a meaning that is harmonious with the Act as a whole" (*Canada Trustco*, at para. 10). However, where tax provisions are drafted with "particularity and detail," a largely textual interpretation is appropriate in light of the well-accepted

> *Duke of Westminster* principle that "taxpayers are entitled to arrange their affairs to minimize the amount of tax payable" (*Canada Trustco*, at para. 11, citing *Commissioners of Inland Revenue v. Duke of Westminster*, [1936] A.C. 1 (H.L.)). This principle, derived from the rule of law, has been deemed the "foundation stone of Canadian law on tax avoidance" (Brian J. Arnold, "Reflections on the Relationship Between Statutory Interpretation and Tax Avoidance" (2001), 49 *Can. Tax J.* 1, at p. 3).[714]

My initial reaction to the citation was that it appeared to have been plucked from the tax literature devoid of the context in which Arnold wrote the quoted phrase. That it is a recent example of the previously mentioned criticism that former Chief Justice W.R. Jackett made about the Supreme Court in tax cases, as reported by Richard Pound in the context of their discussion of the Court's 1995 decision in *Friesen*.[715]

Arnold wrote about the citation in his 2021 review of the Supreme Court's decision. He stated:

> This suggests that my view is that the *Duke of Westminster* principle is the foundation stone of Canadian tax avoidance law. In fact, what I wrote in the article was: "the Supreme Court has consistently endorsed the *Duke of Westminster* principle as the foundation stone of Canadian law on tax avoidance." Furthermore, in the same article I concluded: "With respect to tax avoidance, I have shown that the court's analysis never gets beyond the monotonous mantra of the *Duke of Westminster* principle. I have argued that the shift from a strict or literal interpretation to a more

[714] *The Queen v. Alta Energy Luxembourg S.A.R.L.*, 2021 SCC 49, para 29; Justice Côté with Justices Abella, Moldaver, Karakatsanis, Brown and Kasirer, concurring; Chief Justice Wagner and Justices Rowe and Martin, dissenting. *Canada v. Alta Energy Luxembourg S.A.R.L.* – SCC Cases (scc-csc.ca).

[715] Pound, *Chief Justice W.R. Jackett*, *supra* note 541.

> purposive interpretative approach should have resulted in a repudiation (or at least a reconsideration) of the *Duke of Westminster* principle in Canada, just as it did in the United Kingdom."[716]

On further reflection, my reaction to the citation and Arnold's clarification has shifted to a deeper unease about the Supreme Court's post-1983 suggestion that the *Duke of Westminster* principle derives from the rule of law. I question that suggestion, including because it seems to me that the principle allows well-advised persons not to respect the rule of law. But, even if one disagrees with my view, what does the Court's failure to adhere to the principle from 1935 to 1983 in income tax avoidance cases say about the rule of law as the Court and its judges applied it in Canada during that period? And does the United States Supreme Court, which generally follows a business substance over legal form approach, not respect the rule of law? To me, these questions expose something deeply mistaken about Justice Côté's *obiter* on the *Duke of Westminster* principle deriving from the rule of law.

In *Loblaw Financial*, Justice Côté wrote the unanimous 7–0 decision for the taxpayer. It concerns a domestic corporate group placing capital in Barbados to avoid domestic income tax on income earned from that capital, by reliance on an exception for banks in the FAPI rules, which were previously discussed when profiling *Ludco Enterprises*. The case is about whether that exception applied, which was hotly contested by the Crown and the taxpayer.

Côté uses in *Loblaw Financial* the colloquial English expression "where the rubber hits the road" to suggest that the challenge for judges is to determine what relative weight should be given to each component of the unifying textual, contextual and purposive interpretive approach.

---

[716] Brian J. Arnold, *The Arnold Report*, "Supreme Court Decides Alta Energy Luxembourg for the Taxpayer," Posting 219, December 9, 2021, Canadian Tax Foundation. For the article Arnold cited, see Arnold, "Reflections on the Relationship Between Statutory Interpretation and Tax Avoidance," *supra* note 3.

This narrow question of statutory interpretation requires us to draw upon the well-established framework that "statutory interpretation entails discerning legislative intent by examining statutory text in its entire context and in its grammatical and ordinary sense, in harmony with the statute's scheme and objects." … Where the rubber hits the road is in determining the relative weight to be afforded to the text, context and purpose. Where the words of a statute are "precise and unequivocal," their ordinary meaning will play a dominant role (*Canada Trustco Mortgage Co. v. Canada*, …). In the taxation context, a "unified textual, contextual and purposive" approach continues to apply (*Placer Dome Canada Ltd. v. Ontario (Minister of Finance)*, 2006 SCC 20, [2006] 1 S.C.R. 715, at para. 22, quoting *Canada Trustco*, at para. 47).

In applying this unified approach, however, the particularity and detail of many tax provisions along with the *Duke of Westminster* principle (that taxpayers are entitled to arrange their affairs to minimize the amount of tax payable) lead us to focus carefully on the text and context in assessing the broader purpose of the scheme (*Placer Dome*, at para. 21; *Canada Trustco*, at para. 11). This approach is particularly apposite in this case, where the provision at issue is part of the highly detailed and precise FAPI regime. I must emphasize again that this is not a case involving a general anti-avoidance rule. The provision at issue is part of an exception to the definition of "investment business" within the highly intricate, highly defined FAPI regime. If taxpayers are to act with any degree of certainty under such a regime, then full effect should be given to Parliament's precise and unequivocal words.[717]

[717] *The Queen v. Loblaw Financial Holdings Inc.*, 2021 SCC 51, para. 41; Justice Côté with Chief Justice Wagner and Justices Moldaver, Karakatsanis, Brown, Martin and Kasirer, concurring. *Canada v. Loblaw Financial Holdings Inc.* – SCC Cases (scc-csc.ca).

As the full citation above notes, Côté relied on the 1935 British *Duke of Westminster* principle to give no interpretive weight to the purpose of the text or legislation, and little or no weight to its anti-avoidance context.

Appointed to the Supreme Court in 2014 by the Conservative government of Prime Minister Stephen Harper, Justice Côté is from the Gaspé region of Quebec, and she was a leading civil litigator in Montreal at the law firms Stikeman Elliott and later Osler.

On April 7, 2022, Liberal Finance Minister Chrystia Freeland delivered her first post-2021 election Budget on behalf of the Justin Trudeau minority-Liberal government.[718] Four matters stand out in the context of the conclusion to *Bench Strength.*

First, what the government didn't do in 2022. This is written about six years after the government withdrew in 2017 its proposals on constraining abusive corporate surplus-stripping transactions used by high-income Canadians who own private corporations to convert otherwise taxable dividends or salary into tax-exempt or tax-preferred amounts. In 2017, the federal-provincial income tax savings on surplus conversions into taxable capital gains could exceed $20,000 on a $100,000 strip, $200,000 on a $1 million strip, and $20 million on a $100 million strip.[719] Five-years later, the government still hadn't addressed the tax abuse.

---

[718] Canada, Department of Finance, Budget 2022, *A Plan to Grow Our Economy and Make Life More Affordable*, April 7, 2022 (The Honourable Chrystia Freeland, Minister of Finance). The 2022 Budget is at (https://www.budget.canada.ca/2022/home-accueil-en.html).

[719] Canada, Department of Finance, "Tax Planning Using Private Corporations," July 18, 2017, *supra* note 691, Table 12, Part D, p. 56. For example, there was a 20.54 tax point spread in 2017 favouring taxable capital gains over taxable dividends for non-eligible dividends in Manitoba. That spread was 19.97 points in Nova Scotia, 18.54 points in Ontario, 17.19 points in Quebec, 16.76 points in British Columbia. The narrowest spread was 12.19 points in the Northwest Territories.

Second, in a section of Budget 2022 titled "A Fair Tax System," the government announced that it would be reviewing the minimum tax rules, because despite "increasing taxes on the wealthiest one per cent of Canadians … [there remain] some Canadians [who] still pay relatively little in personal income tax (PIT) as a share of their income—28 per cent of filers with gross income above $400,000 pay an average federal PIT rate of 15 per cent or less, which is less than some middle class Canadians pay."[720] The following comes to mind when parsing the sentence in the context of the ITA's underlying history as discussed in *Bench Strength* and tax policy choices:

- Without more, increasing the top marginal rate is often ineffective in raising revenues from very high-income persons because it fails to address their numerous tax preferences and tax avoidance opportunities. The Bennett government learned this lesson after it raised the top marginal tax rate well above 50 percent in 1933, after which it acted in 1935 to constrain certain tax preferences in order to make the rate effective. It was then defeated in the 1935 election, and the incoming King government extended even more valuable tax preferences to its key supporters. Bennett's tax policy mistake was that he never integrated the way in which the top marginal tax rate would become effective, to ensure it was less than 50 percent of federal-provincial income tax for the highest incomes.
- You may think it obvious that a significant policy deficiency may exist if high-income Canadians who own private corporations can avoid up to about 20 percent in taxes otherwise payable, by converting their corporate surpluses into taxable capital gains.

[720] Budget 2022, *supra* note 718, pp. 206–07. For this purpose, gross income includes 100 precent of capital gains (see Table at top of p. 207).

Third, the government increased the limit that applies when determining which *small business* corporations and their associated corporations can benefit from the small business deduction. The limit went up to $50 million of corporate taxable capital from $15 million. As mentioned in the conclusion, the actual value of a corporation and its associated corporations is normally a multiple of taxable capital, which should mean that families and their trusts that control corporate groups worth hundreds of millions of dollars will benefit.

This, in turn, means that significantly more corporate profits will be taxed at 9 percent, which is 24 tax points below the 33 percent top marginal personal rate. Tax planners and their clients should be able to gorge themselves on the results, with the government exacerbating the problem at its estimated cost of $560 million annually (which does not appear to include the cost associated with the beneficiaries converting their additional corporate surpluses into tax-preferred capital gains, or tax-exempt amounts). It makes no commercial, economic or tax fairness sense; but it is prime example of how wealthy taxpayers, their representatives and lobby groups gain, and then extend, valuable tax preferences to themselves.

Fourth, the Trudeau government announced consultations on possible amendments to the GAAR, which consultations began after Finance Canada published a paper on the matter in August 2022. Edward Short and I made a joint submission in late September 2022.

On March 28, 2023, Finance Minister Chrystia Freeland delivered Budget 2023. The out-of-control spending continued with large deficits forecast for the foreseeable future. The new spending included multibillions of dollars for the government's carbon-neutral green agenda in the form of new 30 percent refundable investment tax credits (ITCs) for a host of initiatives.

Freeland also proposed rules that would supposedly limit tax-assisted intergenerational transfers of qualifying shares of a small business corporation to "genuine" transfers.[721] Those rules did not take effect until 2024 in a context where her government and Parliament have failed to counter blatant corporate surplus stripping schemes. This occurred despite multibillions of dollars in forgone tax revenues being in play according to Allan Lanthier's 2021 *Financial Post* article.

By November 2023, KPMG indicated in a study that 70 percent of small business succession plans would be put into effect before the end of 2023.[722] Keep in mind Allan Lanthier's 2021 $5 billion estimate (discussed in the conclusion) of foregone federal-provincial tax revenues if 1 percent of the owners of 1.2 million businesses mentioned were in the top bracket and implemented a plan. For some, perhaps—What are multibillions of dollars in foregone tax revenues when the debt is piling up like derailed freight cars at a national train wreck? Especially when others will have to repay the resulting debt.[723]

---

[721] Canada, Department of Finance, Budget 2023, *A-Made-in-Canada Plan: Strong Middle Class, Affordable Economy, Strong Future*, "Tax Measures: Supplementary Information," March 28, 2023, pp. 16-19. Budget 2023 is at *Government of Canada releases Budget 2023* - https://www.budget.canada.ca/2023/home-accueil-en.html.

[722] Noella Ovid, "Family business owners are rushing to hand over their companies," *Financial Post*, November 24, 2023. On December 6, 2023, the *Globe and Mail* reported that accountants and advisors were under a time limit to assist clients planning to transfer their business to a family member. Why? The article quoted an accountant who stated that new rules taking effect in 2004 have "conditions … [that] will be required to prove a business transfer between family members is *a genuine transaction*" [emphasis added]. Deanne Gage (Globe Advisor Reporter), "How to Prepare for Intergenerational Business Transfers Before Key-Tax-Related Changes Kick, In," *Globe and Mail*, December 6, 2023.

[723] By the end of 2020, more than $2.8 trillion of assets were controlled by owners of small (less than 100 employees) and medium (100 to 499 employees) businesses in Canada. Statistics Canada undertook a special tabulation of its data to make the estimate, which the Canadian Federation of Independent Business (CFIB) cited in its 2023 special report titled "Succession Tsunami." See CFIB release "Over $2 trillion in business assets are at stake as majority of small business owners plan to exit their business over the next decade," January 10, 2023. By the end of 2023, the total value of assets could have been significantly

Minister Freeland also announced in Budget 2023 that the government would be broadening the personal minimum tax, which can be seen as resulting from the government's inability to directly address tax policy failings. The main changes are (1) treating 100 percent of an individual's capital gains and stock option benefits as income for minimum tax purposes (except only 30 percent where the gain is eligible for the approximate $1 million capital gains deduction for qualifying shares of a small business corporation and 30 percent of the gain from donations of publicly listed shares); (2) limiting an individual's deduction of certain amounts to 50 percent of the benefit when computing taxable income and tax payable for minimum tax purposes (e.g., limited partnership and business loss carryovers); and (3) increasing the minimum tax rate to 20.5 percent from 15 percent on income above $173,000 (from above $40,000).[724]

If subject to minimum tax, an individual can carry the tax paid forward for up to seven years and deduct it from their tax payable on income subject to tax at more than 20.5 percent under the regular rules. That is, they can use their minimum tax credits to avoid the 33 percent personal tax rate. This is because the 20.5 percent minimum tax rate is 12.5 points below the 33 percent maximum personal tax rate, which further reveals the extent to which the government virtue signals to its progressive base a too-high 33 percent personal tax rate while preserving the tax treats doled out to high-income Canadians who own corporations, receive stock

---

more than $3 trillion given the high rate of inflation in the intervening years and that the tabulation's reference to "value" appears to be based on corporate accounting and tax data filed with the CRA rather than reflecting true corporate fair market value. Note: I have refrained from making a ballpark estimate of the multibillions of dollars of foregone tax revenues but whatever the figure, it is significant.

[724] Budget 2023, *supra* note 721, pp. 13–15.

option benefits, or earn significant amounts of tax-preferred capital gains and tax-exempt receipts.

The *coup de grâce* for high-income tax avoiders was Minister Freeland's 2023 proposals to amend the GAAR. The proposals failed to address in any substantive way the two main failings in the Supreme Court's interpretive approach to the GAAR. The proposals do not ensure that the Supreme Court gives effect to Parliament's express direction in the GAAR that it applies to an abuse of the tax law that occurs when the ITA is "read as a whole" even though no one provision of that Act is abused. Edward Short and I put it this way in our GAAR submission:

> In other words, unless a specific provision in the ITA is misused, the Supreme Court indicates that the GAAR does not apply to a tax avoidance transaction even if it is an *artificial transaction that is intended to avoid tax, or a transaction that is intended to circumvent a distinct scheme in the ITA*. This can occur even if such transactions would have been subject to reversal under the pre-1988 special anti-avoidance rules replaced by the GAAR. Those repealed rules include the old artificial transactions rule in former s. 245 that denied undue and artificial reductions of income and former s. 247, which imposed tax on corporate surplus stripping transactions, that removed corporate surplus tax free or as tax-preferred capital gains.
>
> Repealed sections 245 and 247 of the ITA concerned the avoidance of separate and distinct schemes in the ITA: (1) the scheme that concerns computing and imposing tax on commercial profits, which defers to "best commercial principles" when computing "profit" and "loss" under s. 9 of the ITA; and (2) the scheme against corporate surplus stripping dating to the 1920s, which scheme is comprised of various rules including those that apply to employee benefits, shareholder benefits, employee loans, shareholder

> loans, appropriations of corporate assets, conversions of corporate surplus into tax preferred capital gains and so on.[725]

As well, while the GAAR proposals include an economic substance test, it is defective for reasons explained below. A simple example involving the government's decision to extend multibillions of dollars of new green tax credits may assist.

On March 31, 2023, Andrew Coyne of the *Globe and Mail* wrote the following in respect of the government's projected multibillions of dollars in new tax credits:

> And it will be greater because the availability of such rich, open-ended subsidies is likely to attract a lot more take-up than the government assumes – not all of it involving the actual manufacture of anything. Tax lawyers and accountants do this kind of thing in their sleep.[726]

Why tax professionals can "manufacture" costs and tax credits "in their sleep," using Coyne's terminology, is a combination of the previously discussed failings in the Supreme Court's approach to the GAAR, including its approach to economic substance. It seems clear that to be effective any new economic substance test must *recharacterize* the legal substance of the transactions to determine their true economic substance, as tax professionals can control the legal substance of a transaction to achieve an artificial result such as occurred in *Canada Trustco*. We proposed an economic substance test like the following:

> For the purpose of subsection (4) *(misuse and abuse)*, an avoidance transaction … undertaken by a taxpayer may

---

[725] Edward Short and Kerry Harnish, "Reviving the Purpose of the General Anti-Avoidance Rule (GAAR)," September 29, 2022, p. 10. The submission is 17-pages long. Finance Canada released it under Access to Information law presumably to tax professionals. To date, it has not posted the submission on its website although we asked that it do so.

[726] Andrew Coyne, "A Subsidy War with the U. S. is Not the Way Out of Our Economic Crisis," *Globe and Mail*, March 31, 2023.

> be recharacterized as an alternative transaction if the economic substance of the taxpayer's rights, property, obligations or capital resulting from the avoidance transaction is materially different from the legal substance of those rights, property, obligations or capital, or if that economic substance is not materially different from the economic substance before the avoidance transaction.[727]

Instead, the 2023 Budget documents state in respect of the proposed economic substance test under the GAAR that:

> *The proposal would not supplant the general approach under Canadian income tax law, which focuses on the legal form of an arrangement.* In particular, it would not require an enquiry into what the economic substance of a transaction actually is (e.g., whether a particular financial instrument is, in substance, debt or equity). Rather, it requires consideration of a lack of economic substance in the determination of abusive tax avoidance [emphasis added].[728]

But if the proposed economic substance test isn't supplanting the legal form of the transaction when determining if there is an abuse, what if anything of substance is it doing? In comparison, and as noted before, the U.S. Supreme Court has applied a business substance over legal form test to constrain abusive tax avoidance since 1935. But no, not in Canada despite the fact the Supreme Court took a commercial substance over legal form approach to constrain tax avoidance until 1984.

On May 26, 2023, Justice Malcolm Rowe led a 7 to 1 majority in the Supreme Court's GAAR decision known as *Deans Knight Income Corp.* (Justice Suzanne Côté dissented.[729]) The dispute concerned

[727] *Supra* note 725, p. 7.

[728] Budget 2023, *supra* note 721, Tax Measures: Supplementary Information, p. 39.

[729] *Deans Knight Income Corp. v. The King*, 2023 SCC 16 (Justice Rowe with Chief Justice Wagner and Justices Karakatsanis, Martin, Kasirer, Jamal and O'Bonsawin concurring; Justice Côté dissenting). Appointed to the Supreme

an insolvent corporation in which new investors acquired a dominant equity interest while avoiding an acquisition of control rule in the ITA that would have denied use of its tax attributes (e.g., loss carryovers). Since the original corporate business that produced the tax attributes had been shut down, the plan relied on voting control not being technically acquired although commercial and legal realities were such the old owners were paid to give up effective control of the company. Assets producing otherwise taxable income were stuffed into Deans Knight Income Corp. to be offset by its loss carryovers. The Crown applied the GAAR, and the Tax Court held for the taxpayer while the Federal Court of Appeal reversed the Tax Court.

Rowe had written the dissent in the Supreme Court's abovementioned 2021 decision in *Alta Energy Luxembourg*. In *Deans Knight*, he found for the majority that the series of transactions was an abuse of the same rule against corporate loss trading that the Court did not apply in Justice Iacobucci's profiled 1998 decision in *Duha Printers*.[730] The key takeaway in this context is that Rowe, relying on the Court's 2005 GAAR decision *Mathew*,[731] found that there is a policy (legislative scheme) in the ITA against transferring losses between taxpayers (with certain exceptions) and that the series of

---

Court by the Liberal government of Prime Minister Justin Trudeau on October 28, 2016, Justice Rowe is from St. John's, Newfoundland and Labrador, and is the first judge appointed to the Court from Canada's newest province. Rowe began his career as a clerk assistant to the House of Assembly, Newfoundland and Labrador, after which he joined the Department of External Affairs as a foreign service officer. He later practiced law with Gowlings in Ottawa but left to work on behalf of the Honourable John Crosbie on the team that negotiated a fisheries boundaries dispute between Canada and France, which resulted in his participation in addressing Canadian fisheries disputes with other counties including Portugal and Spain. Before his appointment to the judiciary, Rowe was the Clerk of the Executive Council and Secretary to the Cabinet of the Government of Newfoundland and Labrador. https://scc-csc.lexum.com/scc-csc/scc-csc/en/item/19939/index.do.

[730] *Duha Printers*, *supra* note 453.

[731] *Mathew*, *supra* note 565.

transactions in issue sought to abuse the object, spirit and purpose of one of its provisions (i.e., ss. 111(5)). In doing so, he reviewed at length the text, context and purpose of the key provisions and the scheme.

Nevertheless, there are at least two significant concerns. First, the Supreme Court's 2023 *Deans Knight* decision continues an interpretive approach under which the Court does not apply the true unifying textual, contextual and purposive approach when interpreting income tax legislation unless it concerns applying the GAAR. Two, the decision highlights the Court's approach of giving relevance in GAAR cases to a legislative scheme in the ITA only if it can be established that there is an abuse of the text of a particular provision(s), despite the fact that the presence of the scheme is the outcome of a series of provisions that delineates a policy theme be it against loss trading among taxpayers, corporate surplus stripping or relying on best commercial practices to compute *commercial* profit (loss).

Next, the Trudeau government released its draft GAAR legislation for consultation in August 2023. In it, the government pleaded that the GAAR "strikes a balance between … [1] the Government of Canada's responsibility to protect the tax base and the fairness of the tax system, and … [2] taxpayers' need for certainty in planning their affairs."[732] Under the then proposal, an avoidance transaction that is "significantly lacking" in economic substance was to be "presumed" to be a misuse or abuse, which could be rebutted.[733]

The above was a prelude to the government caving on its 2023 GAAR proposals. On November 28, 2023, it replaced the proposed presumption that a lack of economic substance is an abuse of the

[732] Canada, "Government consults Canadians on Budget 2023 measures to grow the clean economy, close tax loopholes, and deliver tax relief for Canadians," August 4, 2023 (with update of September 29, 2023). For draft amendment of GAAR, see section 3 of "Legislative Proposals Relating to *Income Tax Act* and *Income Tax Regulations*," at https://fin.canada.ca/drleg-apl/2023/ita-lir-0823-l-2-eng.pdf.

[733] *Ibid.*

ITA with the words it "is an important consideration that tends to indicate that the transaction results in a misuse … or an abuse" under the GAAR.[734] This milquetoast provision was released under the cover of the government's 2023 Fall Economic Statement on November 21, 2023, seven days later.

After referring to the stealth nature of government's tabling of the GAAR amendments, Brian Arnold wrote on December 6, 2023, that the withdrawn presumption test "frightened many tax practitioners, who argued and lobbied strongly against it."[735] He added that "Some of the arguments were extreme, (all tax planning who be potentially abusive) but many commentators, including tax litigators and myself, thought the revised GAAR would have little impact on how GAAR cases were litigated or decided by the courts."[736]

The related explanatory note indicates the change was made to "avoid subsection [245] (4.1) being interpreted simply as a procedural shifting of the onus to demonstrate misuse or abuse from

---

[734] Canada, news release November 28, 2023: "Government of Canada Announces Legislation to Make Life More Affordable, Build More Homes, and Create Good Jobs for Canadians." Attaching Notice of Ways and Means Motion to introduce An Act to implement certain provisions of the fall economic statement tabled in Parliament on November 21, 2023 and certain provisions of the budget tabled in Parliament on March 28, 2023. Motion 66 (see Motion 66(3)). The motion indicates that transactions "significantly" lacking in economic substance "may" include any of the following: where (1) "all or substantially all" of the opportunity for gain or profit and risk of loss "remains unchanged"; (2) "it is reasonable to conclude … that the expected value of the tax benefit exceeded the expected non-tax economic return"; and (3) "it is reasonable to conclude that the entire, or almost entire, purpose for the undertaking or arranging the transaction or series was to obtain the tax benefit." For news release, see https://www.canada.ca/en/department-finance/news/2023/11/government-of-canada-announces-legislation-to-make-life-more-affordable-build-more-homes-and-create-good-jobs-for-canadians.html. For Motion 66, see pp. 225-28 of https://fin.canada.ca/drleg-apl/2023/nwmm-amvm-1123-bil.pdf.

[735] Brian J. Arnold, *The Arnold Report*, "The Final? Version of the New and Improved GAAR," Posting 271, December 6, 2023, Canadian Tax Foundation.

[736] *Ibid.*

the Crown to the taxpayer."[737] Not mentioned is that there is no such onus on the Crown as written in the ITA; rather the Supreme Court via a judicial construct placed the burden on the Crown.[738]

Bench Strength has shown in detail the extent to which the success or failure of a tax avoidance transaction turns on the approach taken by the judiciary. This is the key variable in whether the government's weak legislative response will be effective. Based on the Supreme Court's post-1983 tax avoidance precedent, to use a phrase in the GAAR legislation, it is "reasonable to conclude" at this time that the adverse fiscal consequences of tax avoidance will continue to be substantive for taxpayers who are not part of the small minority who benefit from it.

One detailed example should suffice.

On April 17, 2024, Finance Minister Chrystia Freeland tabled her government's Budget 2024 in the House of Commons under the banner "Fairness for Every Generation."[739] Going into the budget, the government had doubled the national debt since 2015 to over $1.2 trillion. The uncontrolled spending continued with the *caveat* that the government proposed to pay, in part, for its largess by increasing the taxable portion of capital gains to 66.66 percent from 50 percent for corporations, and for individuals to the extent their gains exceed $250,000 in a taxation year.[740] Net new spending would be $5 billion with a projected deficit of $40 billion for fiscal

---

[737] *Supra* note 734. *Explanatory Notes Relating to Income Tax Act and Other Legislation.* See the note to subsection 245(4.1) of the ITA, p. 329 at https://fin.canada.ca/drleg-apl/2023/nwmm-amvm-1123-n-eng.pdf.

[738] *Canada Trustco, supra* note 564.

[739] Canada, Department of Finance, Budget 2024, "Fairness for Every Generation," tabled by the Honourable Chrystia Freeland on April 17, 2024.

[740] *Ibid.*, "Tax Measures: Supplementary Information," April 17, 2024, pp. 7-8. As a carrot, the government increased the capital gains deduction to $1.25 million from $1,016,836, which preference zeros out tax on gains realized from disposing of shares of a qualified small business corporation. Budget 2024 and its supplementary tax information is at https://budget.canada.ca/2024/home-accueil-en.html#pdf. The government's policy justification for the proposals is in Chapter 8.1 of the main budget document, pp. 332-340, which is at the same link.

2024–2025. Interest charges of $54 billion on the national debt now exceed government transfers to the provinces for health care.

The government estimates that it will raise $19.35 billion in revenue from its capital gains proposals over the next five fiscal years, which is represented by $8.805 billion from individuals and $10.55 billion from corporations.[741] It has also faced significant criticism for the changes and has sought to justify them on the basis they are part of advancing intergenerational fairness by asking the most successful to pay only a little more in tax.

The controversy over the changes is not relevant in the context of *Bench Strength* because they are not the direct result of the Supreme Court's approach to income tax and its avoidance. But the changes are relevant in the indirect sense that the government failed to address the judiciary's approach to corporate surplus stripping. This is because the capital gain changes do not end the arbitrage opportunity. The opportunity remains in place for capital gains including those that exceed the $250,000 threshold in cases where the tax-planning alternative is to pay tax on an ineligible dividend (i.e., in general, the dividend tax credit is lower because the distribution is made from after-tax corporate income that was subject to the 9 percent small business tax rate). But the government has also enhanced the tax benefit in certain other cases, which are discussed below after commenting on cases where the tax benefit is reduced; or reversed for individuals residing in two provinces and two territories.

When the $250,000 threshold is exceeded, whether, and the extent to which, the tax benefit has been reduced or reversed

[741] *Ibid.*, Table 1, p. 4. However, the Office of the Parliamentary Budget Officer estimates that the increase in taxes on capital gains will be $17.4 billion instead of $19.35 billion over the initial five-year period. The main difference is that it estimates that additional taxes realized from individuals will be $5.765 billion instead of $8.805 billion. The reason given is that individuals have "more options to mitigate the impact of the changes … over the longer term" by avoiding the annual $250,000 threshold. https://www.pbo-dpb.ca/en/publications/LEG-2425-010-S–increasing-capital-gains-inclusion-rate–augmentation-taux-inclusion-gains-capital.

depends on several factors including an individual's tax circumstances; for example, their province of residence, the portion (if any) of the capital gain that is treated as income for minimum tax purposes, and whether the dividend is an eligible dividend (e.g., eligible for the higher dividend tax credit available where the general corporate tax rate of 15 percent applied). This should result in plans to spread the capital gains out among family members to multiply the $250,000 threshold.

Investment Executive advised its readership on September 9, 2024, that the tax rate that applies to eligible dividends received by residents of two provinces (New Brunswick and Saskatchewan) and two territories (Yukon and Northwest Territories), will be lower as taxable dividends than capital gains if the gains exceed the $250,000 threshold.[742]

The government is also not being clear about who will pay most of the increased personal income taxes on capital gains of $8.805 billion over five fiscal years. While it has said it is asking high-income and wealthy Canadians to pay only a little more in support of intergenerational fairness, we know from its previous budgets that 28 percent of individual filers with gross income exceeding $400,000 pay tax at a federal marginal rate of less than 15 percent. The government has not stated the extent to which individuals with gross income above $400,000 pay tax at less than the minimum tax rate of 20.5 percent, let alone anywhere close to 33 percent.

The Trudeau government also made two changes to its tax proposals that show it is all talk when it comes to ensuring very high-income Canadians pay a marginal tax rate that is at least the minimum tax rate of 20.5 percent, which should be clear to anyone following the debacle related to its GAAR proposals.

First, the government revised its 2023 minimum tax proposals to allow high-income and wealthy persons to claim 80 percent of

---

[742] Rudy Mezzetta, "Capital Gains Hike Results in Tax Inversion for Some Canadians," *Investment Executive*, September 9, 2024.

their charitable tax credits for minimum tax purposes instead of the previously proposed 50 percent. These tax credits often arise in respect of high-profile donations including gifts of shares of a public corporation for which no capital gains tax is payable and only 30 percent of the gain is treated as income for minimum tax purposes.

Second, the Trudeau government further opened the tax avoidance floodgates for those high-income Canadians who own private corporations and want to strip their corporations of millions of dollars of corporate surpluses at tax-preferred capital gains rates. On Monday, August 12, 2024, it announced a significant broadening of a brand-new tax preference to owners of corporate businesses. As originally proposed in the 2024 budget, the preference would *reduce* the capital gains inclusion rate to 33.33 percent, on up to $2 million of capital gains realized by "founders" of eligible corporations on the sale of their shares, with the $2 million benefit phased-in over 10 years.[743]

On Monday August 12, 2024, eligible individuals no longer needed to be so-called *founders* who own at least 10 percent of the corporation for 5 years and be actively involved in it for the five years immediately before sale; now an individual qualifies if they own at least 5 percent of the company's shares for a reduced minimum period of "any continuous 24-month period," and be actively involved in the company for "any combined three-year period."

[743] *Ibid.*, Budget 2024 initially announced a new tax preference for start-up entrepreneurs which would reduce the taxable portion of capital gains to 33 percent from 50 percent if the gain is from disposing of "qualifying shares" of up to $2 million (phased-in at $200,000 a year beginning in 2025). As noted at *supra* note 740, the budget also enhanced the capital gains deduction to $1.25 million from $1,016,836. Note: In Budget 2023, the government extended tax benefits to Employee Ownership Trusts to encourage employee purchases of employer corporations. But, of course, this resulted in the government upping the benefits by extending, in its fall 2023 Economic Statement, a new $10 million capital gains exemption to individuals (other than a trust) who sell their eligible shares to an Employee Ownership Trust.

As well, the phase-in of the $2 million was reduced to five years from 10 years (i.e., a phase-in of $400,000 a year for 5 years instead of $200,000 a year for 10 years).[744]

Further, it does not appear the government has announced what, if any, portion of capital gains realized under its proposed $2 million entrepreneur incentive will be included in income for the purpose of the alternative minimum tax regime. My prediction is the government will align the inclusion to that applicable to capital gains eligible for the $1.25 million Lifetime Capital Gains Exemption, which inclusion is 30 percent of the gain rather than 100 percent. Otherwise, those representing potential beneficiaries will complain that they are not being treated fairly, relative to the $1.25 million exemption, albeit 100 percent of most types of capital gains are included in income for minimum tax purposes.

Those technical details are significant in big-picture tax policy terms. They mean the Trudeau government has enhanced the ability of high-income and wealthy Canadians who own private corporations carrying on certain types of business activity to undertake self-dealing related-person transactions to avoid personal tax. It has done so because it is allowing them to convert *up to an additional $2 million of corporate surpluses into capital gains only 33.33 percent of which are taxable.*

Recall, the tax savings in comparison to dividend taxation are up to 20 percent when the receipts are taxed as a capital gain if

[744] Canada, Department of Finance, "Government Announces Details of New Canadian Entrepreneurs' Incentive," August 12, 2024; and "Government Consults Canadians on Budget 2024 Measures to Deliver Fairness to Every Generation," August 12, 2024. Note, the new tax preference excludes certain types of corporate businesses, including those engaged in professional services such as law, accounting, dentistry and medicine, as well as service providers in other sectors such as real estate, financial, insurance, and hospitality. See (1) https://www.canada.ca/en/department-finance/news/2024/08/government-announces-details-on-new-canadian-entrepreneurs-incentive.html and (2) https://www.canada.ca/en/department-finance/news/2024/08/government-consults-canadians-on-budget-2024-measures-to-deliver-fairness-for-every-generation.html

50 percent of it were taxable. That benefit will increase significantly for gains only 33.33 percent of which are taxable. As this epilogue is being updated on September 20, 2024, private-sector tax professionals across Canada have calculated the extent to which the government has further incented the tax abuses, the cost of which it and Parliament are foisting on every other Canadian taxpayer, the vast majority of whom do not have the knowledge to complain about the abuses they are, or will be, called on to pay for in the form of higher taxes.

Further, it needs to be repeated that the low corporate tax rates of 9 percent and 15 percent are justified on the tax policy basis that they "incent" corporations and their owners to invest in the economy thereby creating jobs, with the expectation that the surpluses would eventually be subject to dividend taxation on distribution. Instead, the government has failed to constrain the abuse, and is instead further incenting owners of private corporations to remove the surpluses at tax-preferred rates. It defies belief. A policy dating decades no longer applies to private corporations earning active business income, in which case the government has turned the integration of the personal and corporate tax systems into a farce.

The government went so far as to brag to the beneficiaries in one of the two press releases it issued on August 12 that the changes will make "eligible business owners better off when selling business shares worth up to $6.25 million."[745] This means it knows millions are involved yet it wants to make millionaires "better off" while making other taxpayers pay for its largess.

This situation harkens back almost 100 years to Prime Minister Mackenzie King and his minority government's cunning 1930 pre-election budget extension of a tax holiday from dividend taxation to wealthy owners of corporations liquidated of their pre-1930 surpluses, which was discussed in the context of profiling Chief

[745] Canada, Department of Finance, "Government Announces Details on New Canadian Entrepreneurs' Incentive," August 12, 2024. https://www.canada.ca/en/department-finance/news/2024/08/government-announces-details-on-new-canadian-entrepreneurs-incentive.html.

Justice Patrick Kerwin's 1942 decision in *Emily Merritt*. That 1930's little-known tax preference was buried in the details of an almost forgotten tax measure that deepened the Great Depression in Canada instead of incenting economic activity. Is history repeating itself?

The bottom line is the Trudeau government does not appear to understand its own capital gains measures in terms of their tax policy, economic, or even political, implications. On August 14, 2024, a *Globe and Mail* headline to a Special written by a person in the accounting, capital raising, and financial sector stated: "Ottawa has softened its capital-gains hike. But it's still not enough." That headline can be interpreted in many ways, and I will leave it you to do so from your perspective.

We do know that corporations are expected to pay $10.550 billion of the $19.35 billion increase in federal capital gains taxes, with a 66.66 percent inclusion rate regardless of the extent of their capital gains and whether they are controlled by high-income Canadians. Two observations are made below.

First, having a higher inclusion rate for corporate capital gains than for individuals confirms the government is in the process of abandoning Canada's long-standing policy of integrating personal and corporate taxes. Since 1972, the corporate capital gains inclusion rate has mirrored the personal rate and has been accompanied by rules that allow for the non-taxable portion of corporate capital gains to be distributed, under an election available to private corporations, as tax-free capital dividends to individual shareholders. But only 33.33 percent of a corporate capital gain will be eligible for capital dividend treatment under the change even though 50 percent of personal capital gains are normally exempt unless they exceed the $250,000 annual threshold. As a result, a significant portion of the anticipated revenues from capital gains concerns abandoning a key aspect of the integration principle.

Second, one outcome of the Covid pandemic is that the percentage of income tax paid by corporations increased by a significant amount. Corporate tax was 29.8 percent of all income taxes in fiscal 2022–23, rather than its 20–24 percent share after fiscal 2017–18. But the 29.8 percent share is projected to decline to

26.3 percent in fiscal 2023–24, which period ends before the changes to the capital gains inclusion rate applies. Accounting for the increased taxes on corporate capital gains, Budget 2024 projects the corporate percentage to be 26.9 percent for fiscal 2024–25 and 25.5 percent for fiscal 2025–26. Without the change, the percentage of corporate taxes would be 25.8 percent for fiscal 2024–25. In other words, while the corporate share of income taxes has resumed its downward trend noted at the start of the conclusion, it is doing so from a higher base because of the government changes to increase certain corporate taxes such as on capital gains.[746]

The above-two observations suggest that the government's search for revenue has caused it to target not only individuals who realize a one-time large capital gain, but also all corporations without adequate consideration of the policy implications for the economy and our collective standard of living. That is not to say that corporations should not pay a higher percentage of income tax than they have been paying since at least fiscal 2017-18, but it does mean that there should not be a piece-meal abandonment of key aspects of long-term tax policies (including constraining surplus stripping and integration) without due consideration being given to the broader economic and tax equity implications. Many of these tax policies have served Canada well in terms of its collective economic advancement.

Here is an apt question: How does the government square its messaging that its capital gain measures are all about intergenerational fairness, when it and Parliament are allowing the wealthiest of families who own Canadian private corporations to strip their corporations of surplus at tax free or tax-preferred capital gains rates including *on intergenerational transfers*?

One can only wonder what political messaging the Trudeau government would dream up if a person in the working class who is in their 20s asked it: "What does extending tax preferences to, and facilitating tax abuses undertaken by, high-income and wealthy

[746] Budget 2024, *supra* note 739. These percentages were calculated based on the information in Table A1.6 of Budget 2024, p. 366 (Annex 1).

Canadians have to do with intergenerational fairness given the tax benefits further widen the gulf between the wealthy and the working class?" They should then ask the Conservatives, New Democrats, Bloc Québécois, and Greens about their involvement and the role they play in these extensions and facilitations.

Next, now that significant amounts of accumulated corporate surpluses have been drawn down out of private corporations at tax-preferred rates, expect academics and think tanks on the right to drum the beat louder that no corporate tax should be imposed on corporate business activity to rebuild corporate surpluses on the tax policy basis doing so would incent productive economic activity. That is, expect that those benefiting from the abuses will want to be rewarded with even more valuable tax benefits, such as paying no corporate tax on corporate profits.

Some readers may think or suggest that I am overreacting to matters discussed above; that I have overstated my concern that our federal income tax system is in crisis. If so, consider together Parliament's tax-preference extensions in the last two years, at the urging of the Trudeau-minority government backed by the New Democrats, as of September 20, 2024:

- Increased the corporate taxable capital limit to $50 million from $15 million, for determining which small business corporations are eligible for the 9 percent tax rate on up to $500,000 of active business income, in circumstances where the fair market value of such corporations is often a significant multiple of taxable capital, which taxable capital and value does not include amounts moved into one or more family trusts (enacted).
- Allowed intergenerational transfers of qualifying shares of a small business corporation, which transfers allow a parent (and family) to convert its accumulated surpluses into tax-preferred capital gains instead of being taxed as taxable dividends (enacted).

- Granted a new $10 million capital gains exemption in respect of dispositions by individuals (other than trusts) of eligible shares to a qualifying Employee Ownership Trust, which gains are not subject to inclusion into income for minimum tax purposes (enacted).
- Allowed for minimum tax purposes, 80 precent of an eligible charitable donation tax credit, instead of 50 percent as announced in Budget 2023, that may be deducted when computing minimum tax payable, which credit arises from gifts made to registered Charities and Public and Private Foundations subject to the amount of gifts not exceeding 75 percent of net income (including in-kind donations of eligible shares of a public corporation to which no capital gains tax applies under the regular income tax regime) (enacted).

These four changes occurred during a period in which the government neutered its original plan to address deficiencies in the GAAR (enacted), while also proposing to extend to high-income and wealthy taxpayers:

- An increase in the Lifetime Capital Gains Exemption to $1.25 million (*indexed* for inflation) for dispositions made by individuals of their qualifying shares of a small business corporation (not enacted, as of September 20).
- A new entrepreneur tax preference that reduces to 33.33 percent the taxable portion of up to $2 million of capital gains arising from disposing eligible shares, further incenting individuals to remove corporate surpluses at tax-preferred rates, with no announcement as of September 20 as to what portion, if any, will be required to be included in income for minimum tax purposes (not enacted, as of September 20).

Meanwhile, the government failed to ensure that Parliament enacted its capital gain tax increases as of September 20, 2024, as Canada teeters towards a federal election. Whether that election occurs before any enactment depends on whether elected New

Democrats, or Bloc Québécois, vote in the House of Commons for or against the continuation of a weak minority-Liberal government, which the New Democrats, lobbyists and lobby groups appear have been exploiting for the maximum benefit of their funders. The Bloc Québécois entered the exploitation fray soon after the New Democrats ended in early September its supply-and-confidence voting agreement to prop up the Liberal-minority government, which agreement resulted in significant deficit spending that is increasing the national debt, and the resulting interest charges.

We know the Opposition Conservatives want an election sooner than later, but we don't know what their views are on the above tax preferences, other than they promise tax reform in a context in which some on the right are advocating for no corporate tax on business profits. This should be no surprise because the Conservatives put forward and passed in 2021 the infamous Bill C-208 (with the support of some, or all, elected members of the other political Parties), which bill opened the tax avoidance floodgates and has resulted in $billions of foregone tax revenues that the working and middle classes, and their children, will be called on to pay for in the form of higher taxes. Is it a mere coincidence that that bill was followed by the above-detailed stream of additional tax preferences from the left of the political spectrum that Parliament has been enacting for the benefit of high-income and wealthy Canadians? It's the working and middle classes that are caught in this tax avoidance, tax benefit, vice.

In political terms, the $10 million capital gains exemption for gains from selling eligible shares to an Employee Ownership Trust announced in 2024 is especially intriguing, including because it is (1) a late addition to the original 2023 proposal; (2) is a so-called *temporary* tax preference, ending December 31, 2026; that (3) provides a 100 percent exemption for the related $10 million of gains from the minimum tax regime. It has been placed at the very top of a valuable hierarchy of exemptions from capital gains taxation, some of which are either exempt from, or subject to only a 30 per-cent, income inclusion under that regime.

This has occurred in a context in which the North American economy appears to have teetered, or is teetering, into a significant recession that would disproportionately harm the working and middle classes. The preferences and especially the $10 million preference also harken back to the Mackenzie King-Thomas Crerar 1936 so-called *temporary* three-year exemption from income tax for profits earned from new mines that they had Parliament enact for the mining sector during the Great Depression, in the wake of their successful 1935 election campaign.

It is worth repeating what former Prime Minister Richard B. Bennett stated in the House of Commons, on May 5, 1936, during the Great Depression soon after he learned of the incoming King government's extension of that tax preference to the mining sector, which lasted 35 years:

> Is it not right and just and fair that, as far as possible, everybody in Canada should stand equal under our taxation laws?

These 2022–24 tax pretences have also occurred in a context in which the Supreme Court of Canada and its judges have used their judicial activism in the *Charter* era to interpret the ITA in a manner that has not only weakened intent and purpose tests that date to 1948 and which are fundamental to maintaining the integrity of Canada's income tax system *for the benefit of all taxpayers*, but also to interpret in a narrow manner the GAAR that is meant to constrain abusive tax avoidance. In comparison, the Court and its judges have used their judicial activism to undertake a broad and liberal interpretation of the rights and freedoms delineated in the *Charter*. Also, in comparison to before 1982, substantive Parliamentary debate on significant issues affecting all Canadians has increasingly withered, as activists advance many of the most contentious public policy issues through litigation in the courts, by-passing Parliament.

Given the above, in a tax context, to what extent will the wealthy be paying a sizable portion of that almost $20 billion tax increase, if it is enacted, in respect of taxable capital gains (not enacted, as of September 20)? Perhaps, we should accept Minister Freeland's claim that the wealthy and high-income individuals will pay only a *little* more in income tax; but what about others? As noted in the conclusion, Brian Arnold wrote in 2021 "that the favourable treatment of the wealthy in our tax system is not a new phenomenon," although the above summary shows the extent to which that phenomenon has quickened pace since he wrote about it in 2021.

The current income tax situation, the government's fast accumulating debt and Canada's faltering industrialization do not bode well for a fairer income tax system nor sustainable economic growth occurring anytime soon. Those in the working class with well-paying jobs and middle-class taxpayers who pay personal income tax at a rate anywhere near the top marginal tax rate should fear what could come next in a context in which the costs associated with the tax abuses and uncontrolled government spending will essentially be extracted from their pay cheques under an economy producing a lower standard of living for most Canadians.

The highest of income taxpayers can rest comfortably full in the knowledge of a dysfunctional income tax system, the Supreme Court of Canada's *Charter* era income tax precedent and a GAAR that is not up to the challenge of constraining certain types of income tax abuses for reasons detailed at length in the conclusion and this epilogue.

But the above gloom is not the end of this story. The future begins anew each day and, while *Bench Strength* has sought to tell the story of where we have been, and are, in terms of our federal income tax system, doing so should put us in a better place to start a new journey tomorrow if I have told this story well. A journey that has as its object the determination of the way in which we better share the burden of income tax in terms of ensuring economic efficiencies and equity amongst taxpayers. Things worth pursuing often take commitment and time and are seldom easy to do.

Annex (List of Tax Avoidance Cases)

THIS ANNEX PROVIDES FOUR tables that identify which cases have been classified as tax avoidance, and they do so for four periods: (1) 1920–49; (2) 1950–59; (3) 1960–April 17, 1982; and (4) April 18, 1982–the end of 2019.[747] Each table

[747] Cases (not disputes which exceed total cases). The classification of cases and disputes as tax avoidance is based on my view of each case (and its issue or issues) supplemented by certain guidelines. Those guidelines treated cases (and issues) as tax avoidance where the Minister (1) applied the associated corporation rules because the Minister invariably reassesses corporations in such disputes to prevent a multiplication of a tax preference normally being the small business deduction; (2) applied the restricted farming loss rules or the matter concerned a tax shelter, including corporate loss trading; (3) applied the adventure in the nature of trade case law to treat a gain as ordinary income (subject to certain exceptions); and (4) sought to tax the gains in respect of discounted mortgages (subject to certain exceptions). But cases and disputes not classified as tax avoidance include those that concern administrative law principles (except the discretion to constrain tax avoidance), collection of tax, criminal law and constitutional law. Neither *Stickle* (1974) for the taxpayer nor *Bronfman Trust* (1987) for the Crown [for reason, see *supra* note 659] were classified as tax avoidance although a case can be made for doing so. Two adventure cases not classified as tax avoidance are *Fabi Estate* (1965) and *Friesen* (1995). *Army & Navy Department Stores et al.* (1953) concerns two separate corporations that appealed and one being successful; the case was classified as two separate tax avoidance cases. Further, *Dworkin Furs et al.* (1967), which concerns the associated corporation rules and the meaning of corporate control, was classified as five tax avoidance cases—all won by the respective taxpayers. Obviously, if that case were classified as one case, the pre-*Charter* statistics would be even more favourable for the Crown. Classifying it as five cases also

indicates whether the Supreme Court decided the case for the taxpayer or for the Crown.

Taxpayer successes 1920–49	**Crown successes 1920–49**
1. *M.D. Donald Ltd.* (1933)	1. *David June Waterous* (1933)
2. *Executors of the Estate of Kenneth Molson* (1933)	2. *Pioneer Laundry & Dry Cleaners Limited* (1938)
3. *Clarence E. Snyder* (1939)	3. *Executors of the Estate of Walter E.H. Massey* (1939)
4. *Wrights' Canadian Ropes Limited* (1946)	4. *Emily Merritt* (1942)
	5. *C. Kerr v. Superintendent of Income Tax and the Attorney-General for Alberta* (1942)
	6. *British Columbia Electric Ry. Co. Ltd.* (1946)
	7. *Percy Walker Thomson* (1946)
	8. *Carden S. Bagg* (1949)
	9. *Fraser D.R. & Co.* (1947)
	10. *T.E. McCool Limited* (1949)

Taxpayer successes 1950–59	**Crown successes 1950–59**
1. *Army & Navy Department Stores (Western) Ltd.* (1954)	1. *Robson* (1952)
2. *Sheldon's Engineering* (1955)	2. *Manning Timber* (1952)
	3. *Thomas Campbell* (1952)
	4. *Henry Goldman* (1953)
	5. *Edith Noak* (1953)
	6. *Army & Navy Department Stores Ltd.* (1954)
	7. *Byron Kennedy* (1953)
	8. *Gairdner Securities Ltd.* (1954)
	9. *Miron & frères* (1955)
	10. *International Fruit Distributers Ltd.* (1955)
	11. *Minerals Limited* (1958)
	12. *Ronald McIntosh* (1958)
	13. *Granite Bay Timber Co. Ltd.* (1959)
	14. *Ronald Curran* (1959)
	15. *Caine Lumber* (1959)
	16. *General Construction Co.* (1959)

increased the percentages of decisions decided for taxpayers by the members of the panel, which included Justices Abbott and Judson. The objective of this layered approach is to provide a database that identifies tax avoidance cases for statistical analysis, the results of which do not vary materially despite possible differences of opinions about whether particular cases and issues concern tax avoidance.

The above tables for 1920 to 1959 show something very interesting. Before 1960, the Crown was more successful in tax avoidance cases *after* the *British Duke of Westminster* decision in 1935 than before it. The next table shows that the Crown's success continued under the modern ITA through the 1960s.

Taxpayer successes 1960–69	**Crown successes 1960–69**
1. *Irrigation Industries* (1962)	1. *Regal Heights* (1960)
2. *Dworkin Furs et al.* (1967) [five cases]	2. *Abe Barron* (1960)
a. Dworkin Furs (Pembroke)	3. *Eric Cerny* (1961)
b. Allied Business Solutions	4. *Frank Sura* (1961))
c. Alpine Drywall and Decorating	5. *Isaac Shulman* (1962)
d. M.F. Esson & Sons	6. *Dr. John MacLean* (1962)
e. Aaron's Ladies Apparel	7. *Harvey Graves Curlett (#1)* (1962)
3. *Foreign Power Securities* (1967)	8. *Louis Jarry* (1963)
	9. *West York Coach Line Limited (*1963)
	10. *William MacInnis* (1963)
	11. *Osler, Hammond and Nanton Ltd.* (1963)
	12. *Ronald Fraser* (1964)
	13. *Robwaral Ltd.* (1964)
	14. *Samual Fabi* (1965)
	15. *Claude Belle-Isle* (1966)
	16. *Alphée Gagnon* (1966)
	17. *Highway Sawmills* (1966)
	18. *Roger Vincent* (1966)
	19. *Louis Harris* (1966)
	20. *Barkman Developments Limited et al.* (1967)
	21. *Harvey Graves Curlett #2* (1967)
	22. *Norman R. Whittall* (1967)
	23. *H. Richard Whittall* (1967)
	24. *Harry C. Walker et al. (*1967)
	25. *Norman Stuart Robertson* (1967)
	26. *Philip Morris* (1967)
	27. *Vineland Quarries and Crushed Stone Limited* (1967)
	28. *J. Émile Groulx* (1967)
	29. *C.I. Burland Properties Limited* (1968)
	30. *Vina-Rug Canada* Ltd. (1968)
	31. *Balstone Farms* (1968)
	32. *James N. Sissons* (1969)
	33. *Edgeley Farms Ltd. (*1969)
	34. *Charles-Édouard Saint-Germain* (1969)
	35. *Smythe et al.* (1969)
	36. *Craddock et al.* (1969)

But the table for 1970 to April 1982 below shows the Crown's success rate oscillated by the end of the 1970s when the Supreme Court decided 4 of the 5 tax avoidance cases it resolved for taxpayers during the period.

Taxpayer successes 1970–April 17, 1982	**Crown successes 1970–April 17, 1982**
1. *James Cameron* (1972)	1. *Lea-Don Canada Limited* (1970)
2. *Alberta & Southern Gas Co.* (1978)	2. *First Torland Investments et al.* (1970)
3. *Maloney's Studio* (1979)	3. *Avril Holdings* (1970)
4. *Shofar Investments* (1979)	4. *Normac Investments Ltd.* (1970)
5. *Dr. H. Hoyle Campbell* (1980)	5. *Oakfield Developments* (1971)
	6. *Donald Applicators Ltd.* (1971)
	7. *Inland Industries* (1971)
	8. *Consolidated Holding Co.* (1971)
	9. *Western Electric Company Inc.* (1971)
	10. *Richardson Terminals Ltd.* (1972)
	11. *Stewart & Morrison Limited* (1972)
	12. *Swiss Bank* (1972)
	13. *International Iron* (1972)
	14. *The Deltona Corporation* (1973)
	15. *Jack Appleby* (1974)
	16. *Rapistan Canada Ltd.* (1976)
	17. *Geophysical Engineering* (1976)
	18. *Estate of John Stewart Tory* (1976)
	19. *Gustavson Drilling (1964) Limited* (1977)
	20. *Cam Guard Supply Ltd.* (1977)
	21. *William Moldowan* (1977)
	22. *John Christopher Doyle* (1977)
	23. *John C. Doyle* (1978)
	24. *Compagnie Immobillière BCN Limitée* (1979)
	25. *Julius Lipson* (1979)
	26. *Lawrence H. Mandel* (1980)

The next and final table shows that a clear judicial trend toward allowing taxpayers to succeed in tax avoidance cases crystalized after the Supreme Court's 1984 decision in *Stubart Investments*; especially after Justice Willard "Bud" Estey and Chief Justice Brian Dickson retired in 1988 and 1990, respectively.

Taxpayer successes April 18, 1982–2019	**Crown successes April 18, 1982–2019**
1. *Stubart Investments* (1984)	1. *Imperial General Properties Ltd.* (1985)
2. *George Golden et al.* (1986)	2. *Crown Forest* (1995)
3. *McClurg* (1990)	3. *Backman* (2001)
4. *Friedberg* (1993)	4. *Mathew* (2005)
5. *Antosko* (1994)	5. *Earl Lipson* (2009)
6. *Mara Properties* (1996)	6. *Copthorne Holdings* (2011)
7. *Hickman Motors* (1997)	7. *Fundy Settlement* (2012)
8. *Neuman* (1998)	8. *Envision Credit Union* (2013)
9. *Duha Printers* (1998)	
10. *Continental Bank Leasing* (1998)	
11. *Continental Bank of Canada* (1998)	
12. *Shell Canada* (1999)	
13. *Singleton* (2001)	
14. *Spire Freezers* (2001)	
15. *Ludco Enterprises* (2001)	
16. *Stewart* (2002)	
17. *Walls* (2002)	
18. *Canada Trustco* (2005)	
19. *McLarty* (2008)	
20. *GlaxoSmithKline* (2012)	
21. *Craig* (2012)	

Acknowledgments

I WANT TO THANK SEVERAL people for their assistance and encouragement over the many years of my researching and writing this book.

The place to start is to thank the two people whose comments propelled me forward—the late Davine Roach and Daryl Boychuk. Without them, there is no book. It, in turn, rests on the shoulders of the many people cited—historians, academics, tax professionals, journalists, politicians, non-fiction authors and especially the judges. I can only aspire to come close to their style and clarity.

Over the years, various librarians assisted me, and I thank you all.

I thank Chantal Carbonneau (Registrar) and Kelly Armstrong (Communications and Outreach Services) of the Supreme Court of Canada for their assistance. I extend a special thank you to Mario Laurier (retired Supervisor, Records Division).

Thank you, Michael Lawlor for your assistance. Likewise, for the two Michaels, Arabelle, and Colleen.

Robert—Merci, mon ami!

Len Farber, thank you for your assistance. Likewise for Michael O'Connor—a leading tax practitioner in the private sector whom I worked with all too briefly at the CRA.

Edward Short, I cannot thank you enough for the time you took and for your insights on matters—especially the GAAR.

Thaddeus Hwong, thank you for assisting me. Any mistakes in the statistics are mine, not his.

Brian Arnold, what can I say about your agreeing to read the draft and also to write a foreword? That is more than I could have hoped for. You remind of my hockey coach and teacher at St. Andrews, John J. Cruikshank, Jr. Thank you for your support.

I also want to thank Colwyn Griffith for his photography and his friend Simon Cooper, a leading graphic artist based in Toronto. Colwyn is a Quebec based artist who has exhibited his artwork nationally and internationally.

Thank you, John MacIntire.

I extend special thanks to Neil Seeman, Sheila Penton and Sydney Druckman at Sutherland House Experts.

I would be remiss if I did not thank four others. Professor Philip Girard referred me to Brock Martland in Vancouver. Brock Martland, in turn, referred me to David Judson in Toronto. Each took time from their busy law practice to comment on their grandfather, which comments have been included at the end of each respective part on Justices Martland and Judson. The fourth person is Stephen McKenna who resides in Ottawa. He took the time to clarify certain matters about Chief Justice Kerwin. Any reader wanting to know more about the life of Patrick Kerwin should read McKenna's biography of his grandfather. I thank each of you.

Dorothy, I owe you more than I can say adequately for your patience and understanding. Thank you.

To you all, including those whom I may have missed, I have tried my best to ensure that this book does not disappoint you. Each mistake I have made, missed or failed to correct falls on me and not you.

Bibliography

Anderson (Ellen), *Judging Bertha Wilson: Law as Large as Life* (Toronto: University of Toronto Press published for The Osgoode Society for Canadian Legal History, 2001).

Armstrong (Christopher), *Moose Pastures and Mergers: The Ontario Securities Commission and the Regulation of Share Markets in Canada, 1940–1980* (Toronto: University of Toronto Press, 2001).

Arnold (Brian J., Editor), *The General Anti-Avoidance Rule: Past, Present, and Future* (Toronto: Canadian Tax Foundation, 2021).

Balcome (Randall P.H.), McBride (Edward J.), and Russell (Dawn A.), *Supreme Court of Canada Decision-Making: The Benchmarks of Rand, Kerwin, and Martland* (Toronto: Carswell, 1990).

Bloom (Murray Teigh), *Rogues to Riches: The Trouble with Wall Street* (New York: G.P. Putman's Sons, 1971).

Bothwell (Robert), Drummond (Ian), and English (John), *Canada 1900–1945* (Toronto: University of Toronto Press, 1987).

Boyko (John), *Bennett: The Rebel Who Challenged and Changed a Nation* (Toronto: Key Porter Books, 2010).

Bushnell (Ian), *The Captive Court: A Study of the Supreme Court of Canada* (Montreal-Kingston: McGill-Queen's University Press, 1992).

Bushnell (Ian), *The Federal Court of Canada: A History, 1875–1992* (Toronto: Published for the Osgoode Society for Canadian Legal History by the University of Toronto Press, 1997).

Bryce (Robert B.), *Maturing in Hard Times: Canada's Department of Finance through the Great Depression* (Kingston-Montreal: The Institute of Public Administration of Canada, McGill-Queen's University Press, 1986).

Cameron (Stevie), *Blue Trust* (Toronto: MacFarlane, Walter and Ross, 1998).

Crosbie (John) with Geoffrey Stevens, *No Holds Barred: My Life in Politics* (Toronto: McClelland & Stewart Inc., 1997).

Girard (Philip), *Bora Laskin: Bringing Law to Life* (Toronto: University of Toronto Press published for The Osgoode Society for Legal History, 2005).

Gordon (Walter), *A Political Memoir* (Toronto: McClelland & Stewart Ltd., 1977).

Gray (Charlotte), *Murdered Midas: A Millionaire, His Gold Mine, and a Strange Death on an Island Paradise* (Toronto: HarperCollins Publishers Ltd., 2019).

Greene (Ian) and McCormick (Peter), *Beverley McLachlin: The Legacy of a Supreme Court Chief Justice* (Toronto: James Lorimar & Company, 2019).

How (Douglas) and Costello (Ralph), *K.C.: The Biography of K.C. Irving* (Toronto: Key Porter Books Limited, 1993).

Kaplan (William), *Canadian Maverick: The Life and Times of Ivan C. Rand* (Toronto: University of Toronto Press for The Osgoode Society for Legal History, 2009).

Leach (Campbell W.), *Coopers & Lybrand in Canada: A Chronicle of the McDonald, Currie Years 1910–1973* (Coopers & Lybrand, 1976).

LeBourdais (D.M.), *Metals and Men* (Toronto: McClelland & Stewart Limited, 1957).

Lund (Anthon H.) of the U.S. Securities and Exchange Commission, *The Canadian Problem: Illegal Securities Offerings, 1933–1955*, "Draft" Confidential [SEC] Staff Report, March 30, 1955. The study is posted at www.sechistorical.org.

MacKenzie (David), *The Clarkson Gordon Story: In Celebration of 125 Years* (Toronto: Clarkson Gordon, 1989).

McCormick (Peter), *Supreme at Last: The Evolution of the Supreme Court of Canada* (Toronto: James Lorimer & Company Ltd., 2000).

McIntosh (Dave), *The Collectors: A History of Canadian Customs and Excise* (Ottawa: NC Press Limited with Revenue Canada, Customs and Excise and the Canadian Government Publishing Centre, Supply and Services Canada, 1984).

McKenna (Stephen G.), *Grace and Wisdom: Patrick G. Kerwin 1889–1963* (Ottawa: Petra Books, 2017).

McMechan (Robert) and Bourgard (Gordon), *Tax Court Practice* (Toronto: Carswell, 1993).

McParland (Kelly), *The Lives of Conn Smythe* (Toronto: Fenn/McClelland & Stewart Ltd., 2011).

Miner (Richard B.), *Associated Corporations* (Toronto: The Carswell Company Limited, 1983).

Newman (Peter), *Bronfman Dynasty*, (Toronto: McClelland & Stewart, 1978).

Newman (Peter), *The Canadian Establishment* (Toronto: McClelland & Stewart, 1973).

Newman (Peter), *The Establishment Man* (Toronto: McClelland & Stewart Limited, 1982, Seal ed., 1983).

Perry (J. Harvey), *Taxes, Tariffs, and Subsidies: A History of Canadian Fiscal Development*, Volumes I and II (Toronto: University of Toronto Press, 1955).

Plamondon (Bob), *Blue Thunder: The Truth about Conservatives from MacDonald to Harper* (Toronto: Key Porter Books, 2009).

Pound (Richard), *Chief Justice W.R. Jackett: By the Law of the Land* (Montreal-Kingston: McGill-Queen's University Press, 1999).

Pound (Richard), *Stikeman Elliott: The First Fifty Years* (Montreal-Kingston: McGill-Queen's University Press, 2002).

Rae (James Edgar), *T.A. Crerar: A Political Life* (Montreal-Kingston: McGill-Queen's University Press, 1997).

Reynolds (Terry S.) and Dawson (Virginia), *Iron Will: Cleveland Cliffs and the Mining of Iron Ore*, (Detroit: Wayne State University Press, 2011).

Royal Commission on Customs and Excise, *Interim Reports (No. 1 to 10)* (Ottawa: King's Printer, 1927).

Sharpe (Robert J.) and Roach (Kent), *Brian Dickson: A Judge's Journey* (Toronto: University of Toronto Press for The Osgoode Society for Legal History, 2003).

Slayton (Philip), *Mighty Judgment: How the Supreme Court of Canada Runs Your Life* (Toronto: Penguin Canada, 2011).

Smith (Philip), *Brinco: The Story of Churchill Falls* (Toronto: McClelland and Stewart Ltd., 1975).

Snell (James G.) and Vaughan (Frederick), *The Supreme Court of Canada: History of the Institution* (Toronto: University of Toronto Press for The Osgoode Society for Legal History, 1985).

Vaughan (Frederick), *Aggressive in Pursuit: The Life of Justice Emmett Hall* (Toronto: University of Toronto Press published for The Osgoode Society for Legal History, 2004).

Waite (Peter B.), *In Search of R.B. Bennett* (Montreal-Kingston, McGill-Queen's University Press, 2012).

White (Sir Thomas), *The Story of Canada's War Finance* (Montreal: Bank of Commerce, 1921).

Index

65302 British Columbia decision (Supreme Court, 1999), 252, 411

A

A.G. of British Columbia v. Canada Trust Co. et al. (Supreme Court, 1980), 135
Abbott (Douglas), 12, 16, 50, 58–60, 62–70, 76, 77, 82–84, 86–90, 92, 95, 105, 108, 119, 120, 124, 139, 147, 152, 154, 155, 167, 168, 176, 178, 186, 187, 229, 240–243, 261, 266, 271, 299–300, 327, 334, 352, 372, 374, 375, 388–389, 391, 403, 445
Abbott decision (Supreme Court, 1908), 46n62
Abella (Rosalie), 297, 340, 341, 345, 355, 357, 380, 392
Aikens MacAulay (law firm), 180
Alberta & Southern Gas Co. decision (Supreme Court, 1978), 119–128
Alberta Law Review, xviii
Ablerta (Treasury Branches) decision (Supreme Court, 1996), 369
Alta Energy Luxembourg decision (Supreme Court, 2021), 416–418, 428
Anderson (David), 338
Anderson (Ellen), 7, 210, 211, 247, 251
Angle (Ethel Annabelle) decision (Supreme Court, 1974), 181–189, 223
Angle (Richard), 181–183, 189
Antosko decision (Supreme Court, 1994), 252, 258, 263–266, 271, 286, 299, 368, 369, 411
Appleby (Jack) decision (Supreme Court, 1974), 158–163, 389
Arbour (Louise), 285, 291, 293, 305, 318
Army & Navy Department Store (Western) Ltd. decision (Supreme Court, 1953), 383
Army & Navy Department Stores Ltd. / Army & Navy Department Store (Western) Ltd. decisions (Supreme Court, 1953), 150n273
Arnold (Brian J.), 6, 346, 359, 378–379, 401–403, 416–418, 430, 443, 450
Arthur Anderson LLP (accounting firm), 332–333
Atlantic Sugar Refineries decision (Supreme Court, 1947), 44–46, 172
Avril Holdings decision (Supreme Court, 1970), 166n301

B

Backman (Philip Douglas) decision (Supreme Court, 2001), 252n459
Ballard (Harold), 143
Bannerman (William) decision (Supreme Court, 1959), 48–50, 66
Barclays Mercantile Finance decision (House of Lords, 2004), 393, 394, 414
Baron decision (Supreme Court, 1993), 258
Bastarache (Michel), 252–253, 274, 285, 291–294, 304, 306, 318, 340, 341, 368, 369, 412
Bastien Estate decision (Supreme Court, 2011), 347–351
Beatty (Perrin), 230, 232
Beetz (Jean), 92, 116, 126, 130, 195, 200, 203, 212, 221, 225, 231, 235, 245
Bennett (Prime Minister R.B.), 17, 28, 29, 34, 35, 70–74, 77–82, 401, 403, 421, 442
Bennett Jones (law firm), 298
Benson (E.J.), 142, 403
Bernstein (Jack), 279
Binnie (Ian), 274, 285, 291, 293, 304, 305, 318, 340, 345–346, 348, 368, 380
Bloc Québécois, 439, 441
Bloom (Murray Teigh), 113, 181–182
Boidman (Nathan), 279
Borden (Prime Minister Sir Robert), 17, 30–31, 72
Bothwell (Robert), 25
Bowater's Pulp & Paper Mills (Reference) decision (Supreme Court, 1950), 15, 16
Boychuk (Daryl), xiv
Boylen (Jim), 98–99
Breadner (Robert), 29
British Columbia Electric Railway Co. decision (Supreme Court, 1958), 60–70, 124, 240–242, 327
Bronfman family, 27, 199
Bronfman Trust decision (Supreme Court, 1987), 199–201, 267, 269, 270, 287, 305, 306, 343, 358, 368–370, 391
Brown (Russell), 362, 417n714, 419n717
Bureau (Jacques), 28
Bushnell (Ian), 33, 185, 254–256, 258, 296, 390

C

C.I. Burland decision (Supreme Court, 1968), 109n191
Cameron (James A.) decision (Supreme Court, 1972), 106–109, 107n189, 111, 216–218, 295, 383
Cameron (Stevie), 279
Campbell (Thomas) decision (Supreme Court, 1952), 47
Canada Safeway decision (Supreme Court, 1957), 262n475
Canada Trustco #2 decision (Supreme Court, 2011), 379
Canada Trustco decision (Supreme Court, 2005), xii, xvi, 298, 319–335, 353, 357, 364, 379, 380, 392, 394, 406, 407, 412–414, 416, 417, 419, 426
Canadian Bank of Commerce decision (Supreme Court, 1962), 228, 231
Canadian Javelin Ltd., 76, 114–117
Canfor Ltd. decision (Supreme Court, 1977), 109n191
Caron (J.E., Minister) decision (Supreme Court, 1922), 46n62
Cartwright (John), xii, 12, 16, 48, 65, 66, 69, 77, 84, 88, 95, 98, 100–101, 106, 147, 164–178, 183, 228, 229, 307, 334, 352, 371, 375–376
Charron (Louise), 297, 340, 345, 348

Charter of Rights and Freedoms, xii, xix, 2, 7, 136
Charter, xii, 3, 5, 6, 8–12, 179, 205–208, 227, 230, 245–249, 253, 254, 258–260, 263, 266, 300, 301, 308, 311, 312, 314, 316–318, 351, 367, 373–377, 380–385, 390, 391, 399, 409, 410, 414, 415, 442, 443
Charter values, xix, 249, 254, 258–261, 263, 390, 410
Chouinard (Julien), 130, 195, 231, 235, 236
Chretien (Prime Minister Jean), 336, 363
Ciglen (Samuel) decision (Supreme Court, 1970), 101–106, 126, 182, 308
Clarie (T. Emmet), 112
Clarkson Gordon (accounting firm), 138
Commercial reality, 3, 215, 265, 271, 332, 377, 411
Commercial substance, 2–4, 30, 34, 36, 37, 56, 122, 138, 146, 149, 164, 165, 200, 212, 219n405, 236–238, 253, 259, 268, 270, 305, 319, 358, 378, 382, 389, 391, 392, 395, 398, 409, 427
Consolidated Holding decision (Supreme Court, 1971), 153–156, 271, 274
Continental Bank Leasing decision (Supreme Court, 1998), 369
Copthorne Holdings decision (Supreme Court, 2011), 342, 351–353, 395, 403, 406–407, 412–414
Corp. Notre Dame de Bon-Secours decision (Supreme Court, 1994), 266n479
Cory (Peter), 12, 201, 257–259, 261, 268, 366, 369
Côté (Suzanne), 416, 418, 420, 427
Covert (Frank), 128–136
Covert (Jodrey Estate) decision (Supreme Court, 1980), 127–129, 132, 134, 135, 147
Coyne (Andrew), 426
Craddock (Wilbour Lee) decision (Supreme Court, 1969), 138, 143, 276, 306, 389, 403, 405
Craig (John H.) decision (Supreme Court, 2012), 353–356
Crerar (Thomas), 32, 72–73, 239, 442
Crocket (Oswald), 20, 57
Cromwell (Thomas), 348, 350, 355, 358, 362, 380
Crosbie (John), 75, 114, 207, 428n729
Crown Forest decision (Supreme Court, 1995), 253
Cullity (Maurice), 227
Curlett #1 decision (Supreme Court, 1962), 91
Curlett #2 decision (Supreme Court, 1967), 91
Curran (Robert) decision (Supreme Court, 1959), 50–57, 199
Customs scandal of 1926, 27, 28

D

Davis (Henry), 20, 41
Day (Clarence "Hap"), 143–145, 147
de Grandpré (Louis-Philippe), 92, 160
Deans Knight Income Corp. decision (Supreme Court, 2023), 427–429
Deltona Corporation decision (Supreme Court, 1973, Exchequer Court, 1971), 108–111, 223
Denning (Lord), 127–128, 131
Deschamps (Marie), 340, 346, 349, 350, 355, 357, 380
Dickson (Brian), xii, 12, 116, 126–128, 131–135, 157, 180–204, 225, 235, 245, 269, 276, 277, 282,

286, 287, 289, 291, 305–307, 343, 351, 353–356, 358, 368–370, 375–378, 391, 447
Diefenbaker (Prime Minister John), 93, 101, 112, 113, 119, 137
Diplock (Lord Justice), 123
Dominion Taxicab decision (Supreme Court, 1954), 164–166
Dominion Telegraph Securities decision (Supreme Court, 1946), 222n410
Doré decision (Supreme Court, 1974), 185–187
Doyle (John Christopher), 75–76, 111
Doyle (John Christopher) decisions (Supreme Court, 1977, 1978), 111–118
Driedger (E.A.), 219, 285–286, 299, 389
Drummond (Ian), 25
Dubé decision (Supreme Court, 2011), 347, 349–351
Duff (David), 219, 397
Duff (Sir Lyman), 20
Duha Printers decision (Supreme Court, 1998), 252, 270–276, 286, 412, 428
Duke of Westminster (decision, principle), xii, 5, 6, 19, 21, 22, 36, 53, 55–57, 104, 110, 127, 133–135, 147, 172, 174, 176, 218–225, 227, 236, 237, 253, 258, 259, 286, 344, 352, 366, 367, 377, 383, 387, 399, 410, 416–420
Dunning (Charles), 24
Duplessis (Maurice), 75, 177
Dworkin Furs et al. decision (Supreme Court, 1967), 87, 152, 383

E

Eisenhower (President Dwight), 75
Elliott (Fraser), 139
English (John), 25
Enron scandal, 330–332, 392
  United States Congressional Joint Committee on Taxation (2003 Report), 330
  United States Senate Permanent Subcommittee on Investigations, 332
Envision Credit Union decision (Supreme Court, 2013), 360–362
Ernst & Young (accounting firm), 139
Estey (James), 39, 43, 150n273, 163, 176
Estey (Willard), 12, 163, 195, 203, 208, 212, 215, 220–223, 225–227, 231, 234–236, 239, 240, 243–245, 259, 271, 277, 286, 287, 299, 307, 377, 391, 412, 447
Evans (Gladys) decision (Supreme Court, 1960), 66–68
Evans decision (Tax Court, 2005), 406n693

F

Farmers Mutual Petroleums decision (Supreme Court, 1967), 64, 69, 95–97, 242
Fauteux (Gérald), 48, 50, 65, 67, 77, 87, 92, 93, 99, 105, 154, 165, 175, 178, 186–187, 229
Ferguson (John), 230
Fielding (William), 33
Financial crisis of 2007–09, 206, 395, 409, 416
Fish (Morris), 340, 345, 348, 380
Flaherty (James F.), 356, 361
Fleming (Donald), 149–150, 313
Forbes [also, Worthington] decision (Supreme Court, 1936), 46n62
For the purpose of gaining or producing income test, 48, 50, 60, 62–65, 224, 225, 241, 242,

261, 280, 283, 320, 323, 327, 343, 365, 377, 388, 391
Foreign Power Securities decision (Supreme Court, 1967, Exchequer Court, 1965), 168–178, 226, 307
Fraser (D.R.) & Co. decision (Supreme Court, 1947), 19, 42–43
Fraser (Ronald) decision (Supreme Court, 1964), 148–149
Freeland (Chrystia), 407, 408, 420, 422, 424, 425, 431, 443
Freeman (Alan), 408, 409
Friedberg decision (Supreme Court, 1993), 252
Fries (Wally) decision (Supreme Court, 1990), 109n191
Friesen (Jake) decision (Supreme Court, 1995), 299–301, 306, 368, 369, 411, 417
Furness, Withy & Company decision (Supreme Court, 1968), 87, 88

G

Gairdner Securities decision (Supreme Court, 1954), 100n78
Gauthier (Andre), 279
General Anti-Avoidance Rule (GAAR), xiv, 9, 125, 221, 234, 237–238, 287, 298, 304, 318–320, 326–330, 333, 335–337, 342–347, 351–353, 357, 358, 364, 370, 379, 392–399, 404, 406, 407, 412–414, 416, 419, 422, 425–431, 433, 440, 443, 450
Gibson (Dale), 168
GlaxoSmithKline decision (Supreme Court, 2012), 356–360
Golden (George) decision (Supreme Court, 1986), 234, 235, 376
Golombek (Jamie), 344
Gonthier (Charles), 201, 257, 259, 261, 265, 268, 274, 285, 291, 293, 300, 304, 305, 318, 348, 368
Gordon (Walter), 138–139, 141–142, 403
Gray (Charlotte), 70, 78, 79, 81, 82
Great Depression, 25, 26, 34, 81, 169, 180, 206, 389, 396, 437, 442
1930 election, 24, 34, 71, 436
1935 election, 71, 72, 421, 442
Great Sweet Grass stock scandal, 101–103
Greene (Ian), 363
Gregory decision (U.S. Supreme Court, 1935), 36, 37, 399
Guindon decision (Supreme Court, 2015), 336
Gunnar Mining decision (Supreme Court, 1968), 77n133
Guthrie & Kerwin (law firm), 212
Guthrie (Hugh), 17–18, 29, 31, 33

H

Hall (Emmett), 68, 69, 87, 92, 106, 148, 154, 178, 180, 241–242
Harlan (John), 112
Harper (Prime Minister Stephen), 336, 420
Harris (Dr. Louis) decision (Supreme Court, 1966), 334, 335, 394
Hickman (Albert Edger), 364
Hickman Motors decision (Supreme Court, 1997), 286, 363–367, 412
Highway Sawmills decision (Supreme Court, 1966), 166–169
Hills decision (Supreme Court, 1988), 410
Hershfield (Joe), 275
Home Oil Controversy, 119–120
Home Oil decision (Supreme Court, 1955), 59, 60, 119, 120

Hudson (Albert), 20, 36, 39, 57
Hughes (Frank), 17
Humphrey (George), 75
Hwong (Thaddeus), xv

I

Iacobucci (Frank), xii, 208, 251–301, 304, 305, 315, 318, 358, 365, 366, 368, 369, 374, 377, 378, 390, 391, 410–412, 428
Ilsley (J.L.), 13, 23, 388
Imperial General Properties decision (Supreme Court, 1985), 234–237, 271–274
Income tax Bill in return for Conscription Bill (1917), 31, 32
  Borden (PM Sir Robert) makes deal with Conscription Liberals, 31
  Maclean becomes acting Finance Minister in Union Government, 31
  Maclean, Guthrie and other Conscription Liberals join Union Government, 31
Interpretive approach
  context and object, 235
  context, object and spirit, 4, 409
  literal, xii, 2, 3, 212, 219, 235, 253, 254, 397, 417–418
  object, xvii, 329
  object and purpose, 133–135, 237, 299, 411
  object and spirit, 2, 4, 125, 126, 212, 223, 238, 244, 265, 353, 367–369, 382, 391, 398, 410
  object, spirit and purpose, 326, 328, 344, 345, 352, 398, 412–414, 429
  plain meaning, xii, xviii, xix, 3, 212, 236, 245, 250, 251, 253–255, 258, 259, 263, 265, 266, 270, 278, 286, 288, 291, 296–299, 301, 303, 304, 306, 352, 358, 368, 377, 381, 383, 390–392, 395, 397, 398, 409
  purposive, 253, 254, 393, 418
  spirit, 35, 142, 211, 332, 387
  strict (strictly), 2, 3, 5–6, 36, 56, 93, 110, 134, 138, 142, 147, 176, 209, 221, 251, 286, 352, 377, 383, 390, 397, 417
  teleological approach, 266n479
  text, context and object, 219n495, 221, 286, 328, 389
  textual, contextual and purposive, xii, 167, 221, 259, 263, 265, 299, 326, 327, 352, 353, 355, 392, 397, 399, 406, 416, 419, 429
  words-in-total context, 285n509, 306
Irrigation Industries decision (Supreme Court, 1962), 98–101, 147, 148, 174, 389
Investment Executive, 433
Irving (K.C.), 98, 99, 282
Irwin (Joseph) decision (Supreme Court, 1964), 82–84, 299

J

Jackett (W.R.), 6, 53, 124, 126, 300, 417
James Richardson & Sons decision (Supreme Court, 1984), 229–234, 245, 249, 250, 384, 390
Jarvis (Warren) decision (Supreme Court, 2002), 298, 308–312, 314, 315, 317, 318, 370
Jodrey (Roy A.), 128–130, 132–135
John Colford Contracting Co. decision (Supreme Court, 1962), 372n658
Johnston (Donald), 76

Judges decision (Privy Council, 1937), 46n62
Judicial Committee of the Privy Council, 5, 15, 22, 40–43, 46, 55, 136, 387, 388, 399
Judson (David), 162
Judson (Wilfred), xii, 16, 50, 55, 56, 67, 84, 87–89, 92, 95, 98–99, 100–101, 105, 111, 137–164, 167, 168, 172, 173, 178, 186, 187, 193, 229, 235, 271, 273, 274, 276, 305–306, 334, 347, 352, 375, 389, 391, 403, 445

K

Karakatsanis (Andromache), 355, 357, 358, 362
Kasirer (Nicholas), 417n714, 419n717
Kellock (Roy), 39, 45, 48, 137
Kellogg decision (Supreme Court, 1943), 68n109
Kennedy (Byron B) decision (Supreme Court, 1953), 47, 48
Kennedy (Robert), 113
Kerwin (Patrick), xii, 12, 16–20, 22–24, 29, 34–37, 39, 41–50, 53, 55–58, 65, 66, 97, 101, 146, 165, 172, 173, 176, 211, 212, 229, 352, 375, 387, 388, 399, 403, 437
Kienapple decision (Supreme Court, 1974), 185–187
King (Prime Minister William Lyon Mackenzie), 18, 22, 24–27, 32–36, 71–74, 77, 81, 82, 401, 403, 436, 442

L

La Forest (Gérard), 200, 201, 203, 235, 245–248, 257–260, 265, 268, 276, 348, 366
Lamer (Antonio), 195, 199, 200, 231, 235, 236, 246, 248, 259, 260
Lanthier (Allan), 404, 406, 409, 423
Laskin (Bora), 89, 93, 108, 111, 132, 178, 181, 186–188, 203, 205
Laurier (Prime Minister Sir Wilfrid), 33
Le Dain (Gerald), 239, 245
Leach (Campbell), 26
LeBel (Louis), 285, 291, 293, 306, 318, 340, 343–346, 355, 362, 379
Legal form, xii, 2–5, 34, 36, 37, 56, 77, 128, 132, 135, 138, 146, 149, 200, 212, 236, 250, 253, 267, 268, 270, 278, 296, 298, 305, 322, 335, 358, 368, 381, 389, 392, 397, 398, 409, 418, 427
Lévesque (Anne-Marie), 304
Lévesque (René), 118
Lewis decision (Supreme Court, 1979), 294n532
L'Heureux-Dubé (Claire), 201, 245–248, 258, 260–263, 265, 274, 291, 293, 299, 304, 318, 365, 366, 368
Likhovski (Assaf), 399
Ling (Dr. Chee) decision (Supreme Court, 2002), 298, 308, 312–314, 318, 370
Lipson (Earl) decision (Supreme Court, 2009), 342–347, 351, 370, 394, 395
Lipson (Julius) decision (Supreme Court, 1979), 223, 224, 226, 283, 289, 291, 296
Lloyd Estate decision (Supreme Court, 1965), 91
Loblaw Financial Holdings decision (Supreme Court, 2021), 418–419
Locke (Brian), 98, 99
Locke (Charles), 12, 44, 48, 55, 56, 65, 165, 176, 229

Lougheed (Peter), 118
Ludco Enterprises decision (Supreme Court, 2001), 252, 253, 278–289, 291, 292, 305, 344–345, 364, 370, 412, 418
Lyon (Frank) decision (U.S. Supreme Court, 1978), 295n533

M

M.D. Donald Ltd. decision (Supreme Court, 1933), 21n25, 399n681
MacGibbon (RCMP Staff Sargent Richard), 113
MacInnes decision (Supreme Court, 1963), 91
Maclean (A.K.), 30–37, 146
Magladry (Ray), 142
Major (John), 208, 257, 259, 261, 265, 268, 274, 285, 291, 293, 298–336, 343, 358, 364–367, 373, 376, 378, 390, 391, 411, 412
Mandel (Lawrence H.) decision (Supreme Court, 1980), 339–341, 394
Manning (Preston), 206–207
Mara Properties decision (Supreme Court, 1996), 109n191
Marshall (John), 45
Martin (Prime Minister Paul), 234, 338
Martin (Robert), 378–379
Martin (Sheilah), 371, 417n714, 419n717
Martland (Brock), 136
Martland (Ronald), xii, 16, 55–56, 68, 69, 77, 84, 89, 93–136, 147, 148, 152, 161, 163, 175, 176, 178, 180, 186–187, 193, 203, 209, 218, 229, 240, 242, 243, 352, 372, 375, 389, 391
Mathew decision (Supreme Court, 2005), 298, 319, 333, 364, 379, 392, 428
Mattabi Mines decision (Supreme Court, 1988), 238–245, 250, 259, 260, 265, 266, 368, 390, 410
McClurg decision (Supreme Court, 1990), 201–204, 276–277, 376
McCormick (Peter), 363
McCreath et al. decision (Supreme Court, 1976), 131–132, 134–135
McDonald, Currie (accounting firm), 26
McGregor (Gwyneth), xvi, 56, 101, 142, 148, 229
McIntosh (Ronald) decision (Supreme Court, 1958), 46–48, 97, 101
McIntyre (William), 12, 134, 195, 199, 200, 209, 212, 221, 231, 235, 245, 363
McKinlay Transport decision (Supreme Court, 1990), 245–251, 314, 315
McLachlin (Beverley), xii, 208, 258, 260, 263, 268, 274, 286, 291, 293, 298, 304, 318, 326, 340, 348, 354, 357, 362–371, 375–380, 391, 392, 396, 412
McLarty (Allan) decision (Supreme Court, 2008), 337–342, 394–395, 412
McLaughlin (Roy), 190
McLeod (James B.) decision (Supreme Court, 1926), 194n355
Meghji (Al), 357
Meighen (Prime Minister Arthur), 32
Merritt (Emily) decision (Supreme Court, 1942, Exchequer Court, 1941), xvii, 19, 23–37, 36, 146, 403, 437
Mezzetta (Rudy), 433n742
Miner (Richard), 153
Minerals Limited decision (Supreme Court, 1958), 95–99
Mitchell (Sir Harold), 116
Moldaver (Michael), 355, 357, 358, 362

Moldowan (William) decision (Supreme Court, 1977), 189–193, 296, 353–354, 356, 365, 391
Moloney decision (Federal Court of Appeal, 1992), 292–293
Molson (Hartland deM.), 26
Molson family, 26, 27
Mulroney (Prime Minister Brian), 75, 206, 207, 233–234, 252, 298, 363, 406

N

Natarelli decision (Supreme Court, 1967), 183n335
Natural Gas Scandal, 177
Neuman (Melville) decision (Supreme Court, 1998), 252, 275–278, 286
Newman (Peter), 51, 128, 129, 177
Noak (Edith) decision (Supreme Court, 1953), 47
Nolan (Henry), 12, 93
Nowegijick (Gene) decision (Supreme Court, 1983), 193–196, 198, 351

O

Oakes (Sir Harry), 70, 71, 77–81
Oakfield Developments decision (Supreme Court, 1971), 149–153, 235, 271, 273, 274
Olan et al. decision (Supreme Court, 1978), 202–204, 277, 307
OSFC Holdings decision (Federal Court of Appeal, 2001), 413
Osler (law firm), 142, 209, 210, 212, 357, 390, 420

P

Pearson (Prime Minister Lester), 112–113, 141
Peck (Sydney), 94–95
Pigeon (Louis-Philippe), 88, 90–92, 105, 108, 116, 126, 130, 147, 152, 157, 161, 193, 203, 224–225, 289, 389
Pioneer Laundry decision (Privy Council, 1939), 22, 23, 39, 42, 43, 55, 57, 172, 387, 399
Pioneer Laundry decision (Supreme Court, 1938), xvii, 19–23, 41, 128, 134, 360, 387
Pipe Line Debate, 170, 171
Pound (Richard), 7, 60, 138, 140, 417
Pratte (Yves), 116, 126, 203, 225
Premium Iron Ores decision (Supreme Court, 1966), 64, 67, 240–243

R

Ralston (Colonel J.L.), 22–23
Redeemer Foundation decision (Supreme Court, 2008), 379
Regal Heights decision (Supreme Court, 1960), 99, 101, 172
Regan (President Ronald), 206
Reguly (Eric), 386
Reiche (Robert), 279
Resolution to amend the Constitution (Reference) decision (Supreme Court, 1981), 94n165
Ritchie (Roland), 12, 67–69, 77, 89, 92, 100, 105, 108, 111, 116, 134, 147, 148, 152, 157, 160, 163, 168, 178, 195, 199, 203, 212, 218, 229, 242
Roach (Davine), xiv, xv
Roach (Kent), 180, 204
Robert (Bobby) Brown Jr., 51–52, 54–55, 57
Robinette (John J.), 145
Roosevelt (President Franklin D.), 71
Rothstein (Marshall), xii, 208, 276, 277, 291, 335–362, 376, 378,

380, 395, 403, 406–407, 412, 413
Rowe (Malcolm), 427–428
Royal Trust decision (Exchequer Court, 1957), 240, 241, 243
Ruby (Clayton), 230
Russell (Bruce), 304

S

Salomon decision (House of Lords, 1896), 128, 160, 161, 172, 383
Savage (Elizabeth) decision (Supreme Court, 1983), 196–199
Scott decision (Supreme Court, 1963), 92
Selinger (Greg), 408
Sham, xv, xvi, 107–110, 122–124, 134, 135, 142, 161, 173, 185, 188, 189, 204, 214–218, 221–223, 225–226, 274, 287, 288, 293–295, 306–307, 343, 368–369, 409
Sharpe (Robert), 180, 204
Shell Canada decision (Supreme Court, 1999), 345, 354, 364, 367–370, 412
Sheppard (Lee), 393
Short (Edward), xvii, 422, 425–426
Sie-Mac Pipelines decision (Supreme Court, 1993), 256–259
Singleton (John R.) decision (Supreme Court, 2001), 285, 305–308, 342–347, 357–359, 370, 395
Slaight Communications decision (Supreme Court, 1989), 410
Slattery (Trustee) decision (Supreme Court, 1993), 258–260
Slayton (Philip), 137, 164, 296
Smallwood (Joey), 75, 76, 112–114
Smythe (C. Stafford), 111, 138, 142–145, 147, 305, 306, 389, 403, 405
Smythe (Conn), 138, 143–145
Smythe (Conn) decision (Supreme Court, 1969), 111, 138–147, 276, 305, 306, 347, 403, 405
Snell (James), 178
Sopinka (John), 201, 246–248, 258, 260, 268, 299, 366
Spence (Wishart Flett), 57, 68, 69, 84, 87, 105, 111, 116, 132, 137, 148, 152, 155, 157, 167, 168, 175, 181, 186–188, 193, 203, 334
Spire Freezers decision (Supreme Court, 2001), 252
St. Laurent (Prime Minister Louis), 15, 26, 58, 164, 169
Statistics, 3, 363, 371–378, 380–382, 414
Stelco decision (Supreme Court, 1990), 246n452
Stevens (Harry), 28
Stevenson (William), 204, 298
Stewart (Brian) decision (Supreme Court, 2002), 252, 289–291, 293, 353–355, 364, 412
Stickel (Ernest) decision (Supreme Court, 1974), 156–158
Stikeman (Heward), 53, 76, 138–140, 145, 241
Stikeman Elliott (law firm), 76, 138, 420
Stubart Investments decision (Supreme Court, 1984), 211–229, 232–234, 236, 237, 239, 243, 250, 258, 259, 271–272, 277, 298, 299, 307, 340, 366, 377, 384, 390, 391, 410, 412, 447
Succession Quebec (Reference) decision (Supreme Court, 1998), 396, 397
Symes decision (Supreme Court, 1993), 61, 253, 258, 260–263, 265, 266, 410, 411

T

Tara Exploration decision (Supreme Court, 1972), 87–89
Taschereau (Robert), 36, 43, 44, 50, 56, 67, 92, 99, 175, 176, 229
Taylor (E.P.), 190
Tennant (John) decision (Supreme Court, 1996), 252, 266–270, 358, 368, 369
Thatcher (Prime Minister Margaret), 205
The rule of law, 363, 396, 417, 418
Thibaudeau decision (Supreme Court, 1995), 261n474
Thom (Stuart), 142, 210
Thomson Newspapers decision (Supreme Court, 1990), 245n452
Thorsteinsson (Paterson (Pat)), 76
Thorsteinssons (law firm), 76
Timmins family (Noah, Henry and Jules), 70, 71, 73–76, 82
Tomlin (Lord), 104, 147, 176, 218, 220, 222, 409–410
Trudeau (Prime Minister Justin), 420, 422, 428n729, 429
Trudeau (Prime Minister Pierre), 93–94, 118, 180, 209
Truman (President Harry), 181
Turner (Prime Minister John), 241

V

Vaughan (Frederick), 178
Verchère & Gauthier (law firm), 279–281
Verchère (Bruce), 145, 279
Vina-Rug (Canada) decision (Supreme Court, 1968), 84–87, 271
Volpe (Paul), 183

W

Wagner (Richard), 362
Waite (Peter), 28
Walls (Jack) decision (Supreme Court, 2002), 252, 289–295, 353, 364
Ward (David), 227
Wells (Paul), xvii, xviii
White (Sir Thomas), 30, 31
Williams (Glen) decision (Supreme Court, 1992), 348
Will-Kare Paving decision (Supreme Court, 2000), 301–305
Wilson (Bertha), xii, 7, 136, 199–201, 205–253, 258–260, 265, 270–272, 274, 286, 287, 307, 314, 340, 366, 368, 376–378, 383, 390, 410, 412, 414
Wilson (James), 346, 414
Wilson (Michael), 234, 302
Wood (J. Harold) decision (Supreme Court, 1969), 89, 92
Wood (J. Harold) decision (Supreme Court, Leave to Appeal, 1968), 90, 91
Worthington [also Forbes] decision (Supreme Court, 1936), 46n62
Wrights' Canadian Ropes decision (Privy Council, 1946), 37, 39–42
Wrights' Canadian Ropes decision (Supreme Court, 1946), 37–39, 42

Z

Zlatic decision (Supreme Court, 1993), 202n373